Sukhoi

INTERCEPTORS

Sukhoi
INTERCEPTORS
THE SU-9, SU-11, AND SU-15 UNSUNG SOVIET COLD WAR HEROES

Yefim Gordon
Dmitriy Komissarov

SCHIFFER MILITARY

4880 Lower Valley Road   Atglen, PA 19310

Designed by Polygon Press Ltd., Moscow
Cover Designed by Justin Watkinson
Type set in Times New Roman/Titan Text/Tasse/Optima Lt Std/Square 721 BT

ISBN: 978-0-7643-5868-5
Printed in China

Published by Schiffer Publishing, Ltd.
4880 Lower Valley Road
Atglen, PA 19310
Phone: (610) 593-1777; Fax: (610) 593-2002
E-mail: Info@schifferbooks.com
www.schifferbooks.com

For our complete selection of fine books on this and related subjects, please visit our website at www.schifferbooks.com. You may also write for a free catalog.

Schiffer Publishing's titles are available at special discounts for bulk purchases for sales promotions or premiums. Special editions, including personalized covers, corporate imprints, and excerpts, can be created in large quantities for special needs. For more information, contact the publisher.

We are always looking for people to write books on new and related subjects. If you have an idea for a book, please contact us at proposals@schifferbooks.com.

Contents

Acknowledgments

This book is illustrated with photos by Yefim Gordon, V. Chepiga, Viktor Drushlyakov, Dmitriy Komissarov, Viktor Kudryavtsev, Vasiliy Kunyayev, Anton Pavlov, Dmitriy Pichugin, Sergey Popsuyevich, Sergey Skrynnikov, Boris Vdovenko, Vyacheslav Yegorov, and Danijel Vuković, as well as from the archives of the Sukhoi OKB, the M. M. Gromov Flight Research Institute (LII), the ITAR-TASS News Agency, Novosti Press Agency, the Royal Swedish Air Force, the Russian Aviation Research Trust (RART), the Polish Military Photo Agency (WAF), and the personal archive of Yefim Gordon.

The authors have also used the following web sources: www.testpilot.ru, www.cqham.ru, www.trud.ru, www.topwar.ru, www.airwar.ru, www.themess.net, www.bvvaul.ru, www.militaryrussia.ru, www.secretprojects.co.uk, www.russianplanes.net, www.airforce.ru, www.aveaprom.ru, www.umpro.ru, www.patronen.su, www.i-f-s.nl, www.forums.eagle.ru, and www.flygtorget.se.

Line drawings by Viktor Mil'yachenko, Vyacheslav Zenkin, and Nikolay Gordyukov.

Colour artwork by Aleksandr Rusinov, Sergey Ignatyev, and Andrey Yurgenson.

A crew chief places a boarding ladder against the side of a late-production Novosibirsk-built Su-9 (c/n 1415343) as the pilot prepares to climb in. The aircraft is loaded with a full complement of four RS-2-US missiles and PTB-600 drop tanks.

Introduction

For years, the Soviet Union's political and military leaders could remain confident that the nation's northern and eastern borders were safe. They were guarded by Mother Nature herself; the vast expanses of water and ice made them inaccessible for any foes. Things changed dramatically in the late 1940s, when the former Second World War allies became adversaries in the First Cold War and began fielding strategic bombers with intercontinental range capable of striking at the Soviet Union even across the North Pole. The Boeing B-50 Superfortress (one might say 'Super-Superfortress') entered US Air Force service in 1948, followed by the Convair B-36 Peacemaker in 1949 and the Boeing B-47 Stratojet in 1951. The Boeing B-52 Stratofortress first flew in 1952, eventually entering service in 1955. Quite apart from this, there was the threat posed by high-flying reconnaissance aircraft such as the Lockheed U-2, whose development had just begun.

Considering that the Soviet Union found itself at odds with nations possessing strategic aerial strike assets that were capable of wiping out nearly all key industrial and military targets of the USSR and its allies within a very short time, the creation of a highly effective national air defence system protecting the country from any attack became a top-priority task.

Now, what was the situation in the Soviet Union at the time from this standpoint? In the early 1950s the Moscow-based OKB-155, headed by General Designer Artyom I. Mikoyan, had become the principal 'fighter maker' in the Soviet Union. (OKB = *opytno-konstrooktorskoye byuro*: experimental design bureau; the number is a code allocated for security reasons.) Fighters bearing the MiG brand (derived from the surnames of Mikoyan and his closest aide, Mikhail I. Gurevich) were making up the backbone of both the Soviet Air Force (VVS: *Voyenno-vozdooshnyye seely*) and the organisationally separate Air Defence Force (PVO: *Protivovozdooshnaya oborona*). The world-famous MiG-15 (NATO reporting name 'Fagot') was produced by eight (!) aircraft factories in the Soviet Union alone, not to mention foreign production, becoming the main (or unified, in the terminology of the time) jet fighter of the two services; it was soon augmented and eventually superseded by its more refined derivative, the MiG-17 Fresco.

OKB-115, headed by General Designer Aleksandr S. Yakovlev, the wartime 'king of the hill' in Soviet fighter design, was losing ground, especially after Yakovlev had lost his position in the government as vice people's commissar (that is, vice minister) of aircraft industry. Its postwar jet fighters were being produced in negligible numbers; on the other hand, the Yakovlev OKB had

created one of the first purpose-built interceptors for the PVO—the twin-turbojet, two-seat Yak-25 Flashlight-A all-weather interceptor. OKB-301, headed by General Designer Semyon A. Lavochkin, another 'fighter maker' of wartime fame, was being gradually reoriented from aircraft to missile design by the powers that be. Other fighter design bureaus—Semyon M. Alekseyev's OKB-21 in Gor'kiy and Pavel O. Sukhoi's OKB-134 in Moscow—fared even worse, having been closed down.

By the mid-1950s, however, the subsonic MiGs armed with cannons could no longer cope with high-flying and fast targets. Nor could the subsonic Yak-25, having a service ceiling of some 15,000 m (49,200 ft.) and armed with only a pair of 37 mm (1.45 calibre) cannons. The first Soviet surface-to-air missile (SAM) systems—the S-25 *Tunguska* and S-75 *Volkhov* (named after Russian rivers and known to the Western world as the SA-1 Guild and the SA-2 Guideline, respectively)—had limited range and a kill altitude not exceeding 20 km (65,620 ft.). Thus, they could be used only for point defence of major cities and military bases. SAMs alone were not enough to protect the vast country that the Soviet Union was. By then the Western powers were developing supersonic strategic bombers, such as the Mach 2–capable Convair B-58 Hustler, having a range of 5,000 km (3,105 miles), and cruise missiles capable of carrying 1-megaton nuclear warheads. This put the Soviet Union in a situation where highly effective countermeasures had to be developed pronto.

At that time the Soviet 'fighter makers' began developing supersonic designs. Starting in 1952, the Mikoyan OKB brought out a series of experimental fighters culminating in the SM-9—the prototype of the MiG-19 Farmer, the Soviet Union's first production supersonic fighter. The Yakovlev OKB, too, had a number of fighter projects in the making but appeared unable to challenge the positions of Artyom I. Mikoyan.

Also, in the 1950s cannons alone were no longer adequate as a fighter weapon; it was time to switch to air-to-air missiles (AAMs). Two approaches were pursued; the first was to equip a production tactical fighter with an airborne intercept (AI) radar and AAMs, while the other option was to design a dedicated interceptor from scratch, tailoring it to the PVO's needs. At first, Mikoyan and Yakovlev tried the first approach with the MiG-17PFU Fresco-E and the Yak-25K; both aircraft were armed with RS-1-U (NATO AA-1 Alkali) beam-riding radar-guided missiles.

The adoption of the aerial-intercept weapons system concept by the Soviet military in the mid-1950s was of prime importance for the Air Defence Force. The interceptor was now regarded as part of an integrated system comprising the aircraft as a missile platform, AAMs, AI/fire control radars, and ground-based guidance systems. Incidentally, the first Soviet aerial-intercept weapons systems to enter squadron service were the ones based on the MiG-17PFU and the Yak-25K. Yet, the two types were subsonic aircraft and were built (or, in the case of the MiG-17PFU, converted) in very limited numbers, which meant they could not satisfy the PVO's needs. Thus, the obvious solution was to create a 'clean sheet of paper' missile-armed supersonic interceptor. Such interceptors could destroy approaching enemy aircraft and incoming standoff missiles while these were still a long way from the Soviet borders. Manned interceptors were an effective solution for covering the huge expanses of Siberia and the Soviet Far East, where building a lot of SAM sites was virtually impossible because the areas in question were almost uninhabited. Thus the task of providing uninterrupted air defence (AD) radar coverage of the frontiers and fielding new interceptors that could patrol the borders for an extended time received the highest priority.

The situation changed dramatically in 1953—not only because the worshipped and feared Soviet leader Iosif V. Stalin died in March 1953, ending a whole era in the nation's history. That year major changes took place in the Soviet defence industry as a whole and the aircraft industry in particular. Among other things, the design bureau of Pavel O. Sukhoi was reestablished—and it was just as well that it was, because it went on to create outstanding examples of Soviet/Russian aviation technology that won international acclaim.

As mentioned earlier, Pavel Osipovich Sukhoi had been chief designer of OKB-134. Having started off with piston-engined aircraft during the Great Patriotic War of 1941–45 (of which only the Su-2 tactical bomber saw service in limited numbers), the design bureau ventured into jet aircraft development after the war. Within four years, OKB-134 created a string of twin-turbojet prototypes—the Su-9 (manufacturer's designation *izdeliye* K) fighter-bomber of 1946 (which bore a certain resemblance to the Messerschmitt Me 262 but was no copy), the closely related Su-11 (*izdeliye* LK) fighter-bomber of 1947, and the Su-15 (*izdeliye* P) all-weather interceptor of 1949, which had a curious layout with the two jet engines in tandem, one exhausting under the centre fuselage and the other at the end of the fuselage. (*Izdeliye* [product] such and such is a code for Soviet/Russian military hardware items commonly used in paperwork to confuse outsiders.) All of them were the first aircraft to bear these (provisional) service designations. On 14 November 1949, however, the design bureau was liquidated; the official pretext was the crash of the first prototype Su-15 on 3 June, though other reasons of a more personal character were also involved. The last two aircraft developed by OKB-134— the Su-17 fighter (again the first to be thus designated, *izdeliye* R) and the Su-10 four-turbojet medium bomber (*izdeliye* E)—never had a chance to prove their worth because the prototypes were scrapped without ever being flown.

In the spring of 1953 the Korean War was still raging. This conflict had many implications for the Soviet military and the Soviet aircraft industry; for example, it showed that five years after the Second World War the good old dogfight tactics still held good, despite the fact that propeller-driven fighters had been replaced by transonic jets (and they would still hold good ten years later, as the Vietnam War would show!). In the course of the war the Soviet Union had succeeded in obtaining and studying a largely intact example of the North American F-86A Sabre, the most advanced fighter used by the Western coalition in Korea. For a while the People's Commissariat of Aircraft Industry (NKAP: *Narodnyy komissariaht aviatsionnoy promyshlennosti*) even toyed with the idea of reverse-engineering the Sabre, which had been floated by OKB-1 under Chief Designer V. V. Kondrat'yev.

That said, Sukhoi's appointment as the new head of OKB-1 in May 1953 was a rather unexpected move. Nobody in the nation's aircraft industry took this seriously: the general opinion was that the bosses of NKAP were simply pursuing their own ends by unseating one chief designer who had fallen from favour and replacing him with another man who was temporarily back in from the cold. They were utterly wrong.

Pavel O. Sukhoi was absolutely dissatisfied with the F-86A reverse-engineering project inherited from Kondrat'yev, since this was obviously a dead-end approach. Hence, winning support from what had by then become the Ministry of Aircraft Industry (MAP: *Ministerstvo aviatsionnoy promyshlennosti*), he managed to get permission to develop aircraft of his own again. A draft Council of Ministers (that is, government) directive titled 'On the Development of New High-Speed Tactical Fighters with Swept and Delta Wings' said, among other things: '*2. The Ministry of Defence Industry (D[mitriy]. F. Ustinov) and Chief Designer P. O. Sukhoi are hereby authorised to design and build a single-seat experimental fighter with delta wings and a turbojet engine designed by A[rkhip]. M. Lyul'ka for the purpose of further enhancing the performance* [of fighters] *and mastering the new layout of fighters.*' After the basic performance parameters had been set at a meeting of the MAP Board, on 5 August 1953 the Council of Ministers issued directive no. 2072-839 ordering the development of these two aircraft.

In November 1953 the reborn Sukhoi OKB finally received its own premises—a section of the Mikoyan OKB located on the south side of Moscow's now-defunct Central Airfield, named after Mikhail V. Frunze (better known as Moscow-Khodynka), a mere 6 km (3.7 miles) from the Kremlin. Before the war the premises had been occupied by OKB-51, led by the famous 'fighter king' Nikolay N. Polikarpov; after his death the place had been home to a missile systems design bureau under Vladimir N. Chelomey from 1944 to 1952. Now, Chelomey moved out and Sukhoi moved in.

On 15 January 1954 Pavel O. Sukhoi's OKB-1 and its prototype construction facility were renumbered, inheriting the number of the Polikarpov OKB. Now they were officially designated the State Experimental Factory No. 51; hereinafter it will be called OKB-51, since this designation was used in numerous official documents. Yevgeniy S. Fel'sner was appointed deputy chief designer (Pavel O. Sukhoi's closest aide); he was later joined by Nikolay G. Zyrin and V. A. Alybin. They were responsible for the power plant, airframe, and systems/equipment, respectively. The reborn Sukhoi OKB could now embark on the development of supersonic fighters—the kind of aircraft the nation needed urgently.

Chapter 1

Second-Generation Sukhois: The Beginning

S-3 Interceptor (Project)

After its resurrection in 1953 the 'new' Sukhoi design bureau started work in two main areas, developing a tactical fighter for the VVS and a dedicated interceptor for the PVO. As mentioned earlier, Council of Ministers directive no. 2072-839, dated 5 August 1953, ordered the OKB to develop a fighter and an interceptor— each in two different versions (with swept wings and with delta wings). Shortly afterward the Air Force presented a common general operational requirement (GOR) for the two aircraft. The interceptor version was to have a maximum speed of 1,900–1,950 km/h (1,180–1,210 mph) and a service ceiling of 19,000–20,000 m (62,335–65,620 ft.), climbing to 15,000 m (49,210 ft.) in two minutes flat. Effective range at 10,000 m (32,800 ft.) was to be 1,400 km (870 miles) in 'clean' configuration (that is, without external stores) and 2,250 km (1,397 miles) with two drop tanks. The interceptor was to be armed with two 30 mm (1.18 calibre) cannons.

In the early 1950s the use of delta wings utilising a thin airfoil and a high wing loading was accepted as the key to achieving high speeds. Yet, such wings incurred a marked deterioration of the fighter's manoeuvrability and field performance; as a result, close-in dogfighting was gradually replaced by missile attacks at long range as the main tactic. Later, high-agility and built-in cannons made a comeback. For now, however, the wing design was the greatest problem area in the development of many advanced combat aircraft. A heated argument broke out at the Soviet Union's top authority on aircraft design—the Central Aero- & Hydrodynamics Institute, named after Nikolay Ye. Zhukovskiy (TsAGI: *Tsentrahl'nyy aero- i ghidrodinamicheskiy institoot*)—as to which wing planform was best for aircraft designed for high supersonic speeds. Sometimes even the researchers disbelieved their own findings. Former OKB-1 employee Yevgeniy G. Adler, who joined OKB-51, helped resolve the issue, cutting away the trailing edge of the rhomboid wings proposed by TsAGI and obtaining delta wings. As a matter of fact, OKB-1 had placed its bets on delta wings back when Kondrat'yev was the boss.

Only practice could determine if swept wings or delta wings were best, so OKB-51 worked in both directions at once. Its first product was a tactical fighter that bore the manufacturer's designation S-1 (in keeping with a new practice at the Sukhoi OKB, the S prefix denoted *strelovidnoye krylo*: swept wings). This was a single-seat aircraft with a circular-section monocoque fuselage, midset wings featuring 60° sweepback at quarter chord (the maximum value recommended by TsAGI), a thickness/chord ratio of 7% and 3° anhedral, conventional tail surfaces swept back 55° at quarter chord (initially with variable-incidence tailplanes and inset elevators), and a tricycle undercarriage. The wings, with an

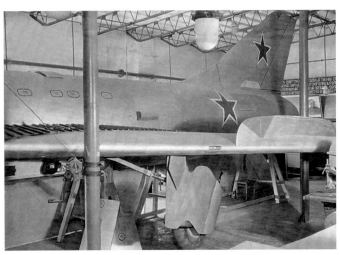

Two views of the full-size wooden mockup of the S-3 swept-wing fighter at MMZ No. 51. Note the conical radome of the Almaz-3 radar's search antenna, the cannons in the wing roots (with blast plates ahead of them), and the large boundary layer fences.

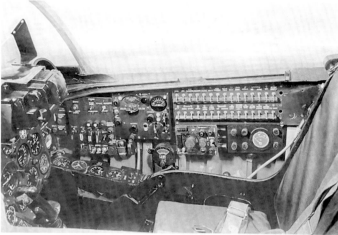

area of 34 m² (365.59 sq. ft.), were of single-spar construction and had ailerons and extension flaps but no leading-edge devices. They were provided with two boundary layer fences to limit span-wise airflow, delaying the onset of tip stall. The pressurised cock-pit, equipped with an ejection seat, was placed well forward and enclosed by a bubble canopy. The power plant was a single AL-7F axial-flow afterburning turbojet developed by OKB-165 under Chief Designer Arkhip M. Lyul'ka, with an advertised thrust of 7,500 kgp (16,530 lbst) dry and 10,000 kgp (22,045 lbst) reheat.

The engine was accommodated in the centre fuselage and fitted with an extension jet pipe, breathing through an axisymmetrical nose air intake with rounded lips and a fixed conical centre body (shock cone); the latter was mounted on an air intake splitter, which housed an avionics bay accessible via a dorsal cover. The no. 1 bag-type fuel tank (fuel cell) was accommodated between the cockpit and the engine in the space between the inlet ducts; the no. 2 integral tank, split into port and starboard halves, was located in the wing root portions. A fuselage break point allowed the rear fuselage to be detached for engine maintenance/removal; the rear fuselage incorporated four rectangular airbrakes positioned in two perpendicular planes at 45° to the vertical. The landing gear was initially patterned on that of the unflown Su-17, all three units retracting forward into the fuselage so that the large single main-wheels stowed obliquely; as a result, the wheel track was narrow. The armament consisted of three 30 mm (1.18 calibre) NR-30 can-nons designed by Aleksandr E. Nudel'man and Aron A. Rikhter. They were accommodated in the wing roots (one to port and two to starboard), with 65 rounds per gun; the ammunition belts curved around the centre fuselage.

Several major changes to the project were made before the S-1 prototype was built. In particular, the inefficient elevators were replaced with all-movable stabilisers (stabilators); the main gear units were completely redesigned to give a much-wider track,

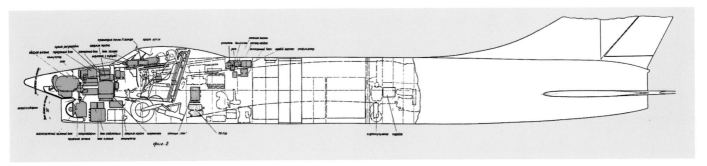

Left: The starboard cockpit console of the S-3 mockup, featuring the radio control panel, systems circuit breakers, and some of the instruments

Below left: The port cockpit console of the S-3 mockup

Far left: The main instrument panel of the S-3 mockup, showing the collimator gunsight and the radar display

Far left, below: This view of the mockup shows how the S-3's ejection seat was to take the canopy with it during ejection, protecting the pilot against the slipstream.

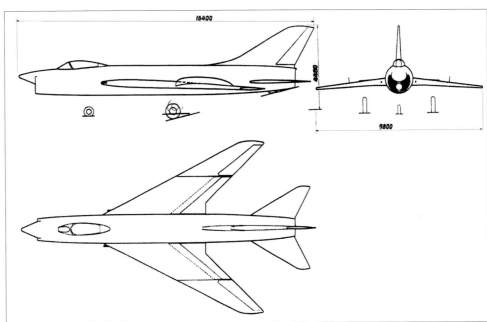

This page, *top*: A cutaway drawing of the S-3 from the ADP documents, showing the twin-antenna radar

Above right: A three-view drawing of the S-3 from the ADP documents, showing the sharply swept wings. Note that the two cannons in the wing roots are slightly staggered due to the location of the ammunition sleeves in the fuselage.

Right: An exploded view of the S-3 from the ADP documents. The four panels on the detachable rear fuselage are the airbrakes.

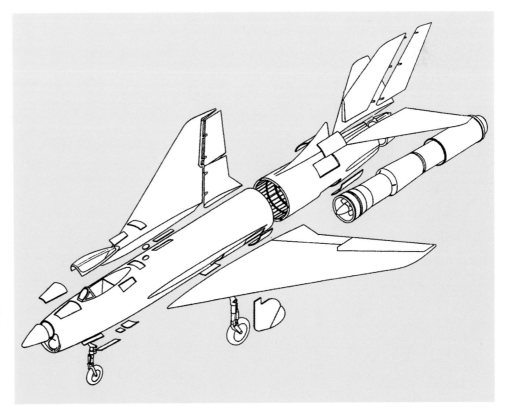

Left: An artist's impression of the T-1 delta-wing fighter with an axisymmetrical air intake. Note the asymmetrically located cannons in the wing roots (one to port and two to starboard).

Right: A three-view drawing of the T-3 interceptor from the ADP documents, showing the side-by-side drop tanks under the fuselage, the two cannons, and the unguided rocket pods under the wings. Note how the ailerons extend all the way to the wingtips. Unusually, the boundary layer fences are mounted on the underside of the wings in line with the flap/aileron joints.

retracting inward so that the wheels stowed in the wing roots. A movable intake shock cone was introduced, and the forward-hinged canopy was replaced by an aft-sliding one with a fixed windshield. The S-1, which first flew on 7 September 1955, was the first step toward the successful Su-7 Fitter-A fighter-bomber, which lies outside the scope of this book.

Now why do we mention all this? In parallel, the Sukhoi OKB designed an interceptor that received the in-house designation S-3. It was identical to the S-1 except for the extreme nose section of the fuselage, where an indigenous *Almaz-3* (Diamond-3) aerial-intercept radar was to be installed. The radar was developed by OKB-15, a branch of MAP's NII-17 headed by Chief Designer Viktor V. Tikhomirov. (The latter establishment became the Instrument Engineering Research Institute, named after Viktor V. Tikhomirov [NIIP: *Naoochno-issledovatel'skiy insti**toot** priboro-stroyeniya*], a renowned radar design house, in 1967.) The Almaz was a twin-antenna radar; this necessitated the use of a fixed-area air intake, the search antenna being located in a fairly large conical

radome of elliptical cross section on the upper lip and the tracking antenna in a smaller hemispherical radome on the air intake splitter. The aerodynamics of supersonic flight were not yet properly studied in the Soviet Union at the time; hence, little effort was made to maximise inlet efficiency.

By mid-1954 the OKB had prepared the advanced development project (ADP) of the S-3 and built a full-size mockup of the swept-wing interceptor. The aircraft was 16.4 m (53 ft., 9⁴³⁄₆₄ in.) long and 4.4 m (14 ft., 5¹⁵⁄₆₄ in.) high, with a wing span of 9.8 m (32 ft., 1⁵³⁄₆₄ in.) and a stabilator span of 4.88 m (16 ft., ⅛ in.). In the summer of 1954 the project was assessed and approved by the so-called mockup review commission (*maketnaya komissiya*), an expert panel composed of industry and air force representatives. This stage (similar to the so-called 'gates' of today) was an obligatory procedure ensuring that any obvious errors were detected and corrected before the first metal was cut, thereby avoiding waste of time and resources. However, further work in this direction was deemed inexpedient by MAP, and the S-3 was abandoned.

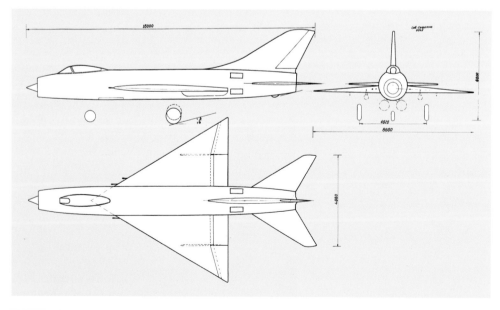

A provisional three-view drawing of the T-1 fighter from the ADP (marked *sover**shen**no sek**ret**no*: top secret). Note the extremely short nose ahead of the cockpit, causing the air intake shock cone to protrude considerably. Again, there are provisions for two unguided rocket pods to complement the three cannons.

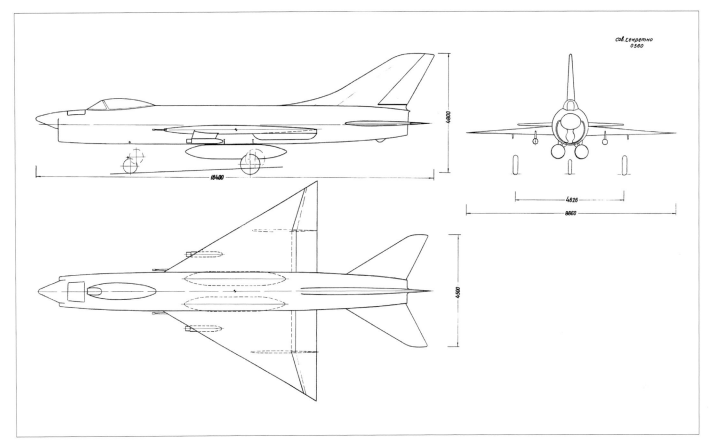

T-1 Tactical Fighter and T-3 Interceptor (Project Stage)

By the autumn of 1954 OKB-51 had completed a joint ADP for the delta-wing T-1 tactical fighter and T-3 interceptor (in similar manner, the *T* prefix stood for *treugol'noye krylo*: delta wings). The project passed the internal-review stage and then the mockup review commission with flying colours in October–November, whereupon both types were cleared for prototype construction. Interestingly, originally the T-1 was allocated higher priority, the T-3 being on the back burner.

To speed up development, the T-1 had considerable commonality with the swept-wing S-1, which was by then at a more advanced development stage. The fuselage structure and tail unit were much the same, and the power plant was again a single AL-7 turbojet. The main difference lay in the delta wings having 60° leading-edge sweep and 2° anhedral, with boundary layer fences on the underside. The trailing edge was occupied by constant-chord flaps and tapered ailerons, the latter extending all the way to the wingtips.

A special research team headed by Pyotr P Krasil'shchikov was formed at TsAGI to explore the aerodynamics of Sukhoi's future fighters. The team recommended that the delta wings of the T-1 and T-3 should utilise a TsAGI S9-series symmetrical airfoil with a thickness/chord ratio of about 6% and a rounded leading edge. Another suggestion was that all-movable tailplanes be used; similar recommendations were made to the Mikoyan OKB with regard to the SM-9 (MiG-19), the swept-wing Ye-2, and delta-wing Ye-4 experimental fighters.

The cockpit of the T-1/T-3 was enclosed by a two-piece bubble canopy. A curious feature of the projected aircraft was that in the event of ejection, a pair of clamps on the ejection seat headrest engaged a pair of lugs on the sliding-canopy portion so that the canopy stayed with the seat, protecting the pilot against the slipstream. (The same principle was used by the Mikoyan OKB for the closely related Ye-2, Ye-4, and Ye-6 fighter prototypes, the latter of which evolved into the production MiG-21F Fishbed-A; however, these aircraft had a one-piece forward-hinged canopy.)

The aircraft had fully powered flight controls, with irreversible hydraulic actuators in all three control circuits. The fuel system included two fuel cells in the forward fuselage and two integral tanks in the wing torsion box (aft of the mainwheel wells), holding a total of 3,130 litres (688.6 Imp gal.); the fuel load was 2,570 kg (5,665 lbs.).

The T-1 and T-3 were related in the same way as the S-1 and S-3, differing mainly in forward fuselage design. Like the S-1, the T-1 fighter had an axisymmetrical air intake with a two-position shock cone housing an SRD-3 Grad (Hail; pronounced *grahd*) gun-ranging radar, a reverse-engineered version of the Sperry Gyroscope Co. AN/APG-30 fitted to the F-86A (SRD = *samolyotnyy* **rahd***iodal'nomer*: aircraft-mounted radio rangefinder). Conversely, the T-3 interceptor was to feature the same Almaz-3 radar as the S-3; as a result, the aircraft was 40 cm (1 ft, $3^3/_4$ in.) longer than the T-1, with an overall length of 16.4 m. Otherwise, the two were dimensionally identical, with a wing span of 8.86 m (29 ft, $^{13}/_{16}$ in.), a height of 4.8 m (15 ft, $8^{31}/_{32}$ in.), and a wheel track of 4.626 m (15 ft, $2^1/_8$ in.).

The other avionics were identical for the two aircraft. They included the ASP-5N computing gunsight (*avtomaticheskiy strelkovyy pritsel*: automatic gunsight), an RSIU-4 Doob-4 (Oak) command radio (RSIU = *rahdiostahntsiya samolyota-istrebitelya ool'trakorotkovolnovaya*: VHF radio for fighters), an *Oozel* (Knot) identification friend-or-foe (IFF) interrogator, an MRP-48P *Dyatel* (Woodpecker) marker beacon receiver (*markernyy rahdio-priyomnik*), a Sirena-2 radar-warning receiver (RWR), a new GIK-1 gyro-flux gate compass (*gheeroinduktsionnyy kompas*), and an AGI-1 nontoppling artificial horizon (*aviagorizont istre-bitelya*: artificial horizon optimised for fighters).

The two aircraft also differed in armament fit: the T-1 was to have three NR-30 cannons in the wing roots (one to port and two to starboard), whereas the T-3 had only one cannon on each side. The ammunition supply in both cases was 65 rpg. Both types had provisions for carrying ORO-57K eight-tube launcher pods with 57 mm (2.24 in.) ARS-57 *Skvorets* (Starling) folding-fin aircraft rockets (FFARs) on underwing pylons. The ORO-57K (*odnozary-adnoye reaktivnoye oroodiye*: literally, 'single-round jet gun', by analogy with recoilless guns; also called 8-ORO-57 to reflect the number of launch tubes) had originally been developed by the Mikoyan OKB for the MiG-19 but found use on other aircraft as well. The ARS-57 (*aviatsionnyy reaktivnyy snaryad*: aircraft rocket) was codeveloped by the Moscow-based OKB-16 weapons design bureau (a subdivision of the Ministry of Armament) and the Moscow-based NII-1 (a subdivision of the Ministry of Agricul-tural Machinery, which developed munitions, among other things!). It was included into the inventory as the S-5 in March 1955 and was also intended as an air-to-air weapon.

Detail design of the T-1 was completed in December 1954; meanwhile, construction of the prototype and a static-test air-frame began at the OKB's experimental production facility, MMZ No. 51 (*Moskovskiy mashinostroitel'nyy zavod*: Moscow Machin-ery Plant No. 51), in November. The work on the T-3 took rather longer, the detail design stage being completed in May 1955 and prototype construction beginning in April. At the detail design stage the T-3 underwent a major change, switching from a mono-coque fuselage structure to a semimonocoque fuselage with lon-gerons. Another important change was the provision of a third fuel tank in the detachable rear fuselage beneath the engine's jet pipe to provide the required range in the event that T-2 jet fuel, with a specific gravity of 0.766 g/cm³, was used (which was lighter than the T-1 aviation kerosene considered initially, with a specific grav-ity of 0.83 g/cm³); this tank increased total fuel capacity to 3,180 litres (699.6 Imp gal.) and the fuel load to 2,600 kg (5,730 lbs.). Additionally, two 500-litre (110 Imp gal.) cigar-shaped drop tanks could be carried side by side on pylons under the centre fuselage, giving an extra 820 kg (1,810 lbs.) of fuel.

Another important change concerned the armament. On 30 December 1954 the Council of Ministers issued directive no. 2543-1224, concerning a whole range of aircraft and their weap-ons. Among other things, this document amended the specific operational requirement (SOR) for the T-3, stating that the inter-ceptor was to be armed with air-to-air missiles—specifically, the K-7L medium-range AAM, developed by OKB-134 under Chief Designer Ivan I. Toropov (K = *kompleks* [*vo'oruzheniya*]: weapons system). The K-7L, whose development had been initiated by the same directive, was a beam-riding AAM; hence, the

L suffix denoting *oopravleniye po luchoo rahdiolokahtora* (radar beam guidance) to discern it from the K-7S homing version (*samo-navedeniye*: literally, 'self-guidance'). The missile, which was also intended for such fighters as the Yak-25K and the Mikoyan/Gurevich I-75, had cruciform cropped-delta wings and aft-mounted cruciform trapezoidal rudders. The PRD-21 solid-fuel rocket motor (*porokhovoy raketnyy dvigatel'*) was located amid-ships and featured a bifurcated nozzle because the tailcone housed the guidance system and carried the aft-pointing guidance aerial. The high-explosive/fragmentation warhead was detonated by a radar proximity fuse. The missile was 3.57 m (11 ft., 8³⁵⁄₆₄ in.) long, with a wing span of 0.81 m (2 ft., 7⁵⁷⁄₆₄ in,), and a body diameter of 220 mm (8²¹⁄₃₂ in.); the launch weight was 150 kg (330 lbs.), and 'kill' range was 6–9 km (3.73–5.59 miles).

In those days each Soviet aircraft design bureau developed its own ejection seats for its combat aircraft. Thus OKB-51 created the KS-1 seat for the S-1/S-3 and T-1/T-3 (KS = [*katapool'tnoye*] *kreslo Sukhovo*: Sukhoi [ejection] seat); the design effort was led by V. M. Zas'ko. Starting in April 1955, the seat underwent trials on one of the three UTI-MiG-15 Midget trainers converted into ST-10 ejection-seat test beds by the Flight Research Institute, named after Mikhail M. Gromov (LII: *Lyotno-issledovatel'skiy institoot*); the aircraft in question was most probably serialled '401ᵁ Blue' (401ʸ in Cyrillic characters; construction number 10401). The experimental KS-1 seat was installed in the rear cock-pit, which had the standard sliding-canopy section replaced by a longer canopy designed for the Sukhoi jets. However, the first ejections with dummies showed that the arrangement with the canopy doubling as a slipstream shield incurred major technical problems that proved difficult to overcome. Hence the designers soon opted for a more traditional arrangement where the canopy was jettisoned prior to ejection. This was duly tested on the ST-10 and a suitably modified Yak-25 interceptor known as the Yak-25L, another LII test bed, in 1956, allowing the S-1 and T-3 prototypes to be equipped with prototype KS-1 seats in a timely manner.

T-3 Interceptor Prototype (*izdeliye* 81)

By May 1955, MAP had shifted its priorities from the T-1 tactical fighter to the T-3 interceptor; a similar situation existed at the Mikoyan OKB, which was instructed by MAP to concentrate on interceptors. By the end of the year the T-1 programme had been cancelled altogether, leaving only the S-1 in the running in this area at the Sukhoi OKB. However, as already mentioned, con-struction of the T-1 prototype had begun in November 1954, and by the end of 1955 the work was well advanced. This is where the commonality between the T-1 and T-3 came in handy. Not wishing to let the effort be wasted, the Sukhoi OKB decided to convert the airframe into the flying prototype of the T-3 (known in-house as *izdeliye* 81). The conversion involved replacing the fuselage nose up to and including the cockpit section, as well as changes to the forward bays of the wings. The upper radome was tipped with an air data boom carrying yaw transducers.

By the end of 1955 the static-test article of the T-3 had been completed; so had all major airframe subassemblies of the flying prototype except the wings, and overall programme readiness for the first flight had reached 95%. Due to the later delivery of some

The T-3 prototype in its initial form. Note the metal upper 'radome' tipped by an air data boom and the gun blast plates ahead of the wing roots (no cannons are fitted). The K-7L missiles are carried for aerodynamic testing only, since no radar is fitted.

equipment items, the prototype lacked the Almaz-3 radar, the PVU-67 computing sight (*pritsel'no-vychislitel'noye oostroystvo*: targeting/computing device), designed for aiming the K-7L AAMs, and the SRZO-2 identification friend-or-foe interrogator/transponder (*samolyotnyy rahdiolokatsionnyy zaproschik-otvetchik* aircraft-mounted radar [IFF] interrogator/responder). Instead, the avionics bay in the fuselage nose accommodated test equipment and ballast to maintain the correct centre of gravity (CG) position. Nor were the cannons fitted at this stage, although the oval gun blast plates ahead of the wing roots were there. This was no great problem—after all, nobody expects a first prototype to be fully combat capable. Much the worse for wear, engine development was running behind schedule, since OKB-165 had run into problems with the AL-7F turbojet and could not complete the bench tests in time; also, it transpired that the engine was rather heavier than anticipated.

The Sukhoi OKB's experimental production facility completed the airframe of the first prototype T-3 (c/n 01?) in March 1956, and

a flight-cleared prototype engine was delivered to MMZ No. 51 in early April for installation in this aircraft. The actual aircraft differed somewhat from the ADP drawings, having a longer, tapered nose, clipped wingtips, and no wing fences. It wore Soviet air force star insignia but no tactical code. (Note: Unlike Western military aircraft, which have serial numbers allowing positive identification, since 1955 Soviet/CIS military aircraft have had two-digit tactical codes, which are usually simply the number of the aircraft in its unit. Three-digit codes are usually allocated to aircraft operated by flying colleges or to development aircraft; in the latter case they are based on the construction number, fuselage number [f/n or line number], or the manufacturer's designation. Some Soviet/Russian air force transports had three-digit codes, which were the last three digits of their former quasi-civil registration.)

On the night of 23 April the T-3 was trucked to LII's airfield in the town of Zhukovskiy, south of Moscow, where OKB-51 had its flight test facility, like nearly all other Soviet aircraft design bureaus. At the time the Sukhoi OKB had no test pilots of its own

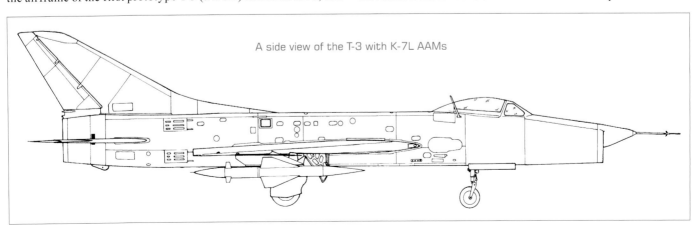

A side view of the T-3 with K-7L AAMs

Left: This view illustrates the T-3's distinctive intake design, making the aircraft appear to be grinning from ear to ear. The conical upper radome is for the search antenna, and the hemispherical lower one for the missile guidance antenna.

Below: A side view of the T-3 with the missile pylons removed. As compared to the project configuration, the actual aircraft had a longer nose and no wing fences. Note the tail bumper and the dielectric fin cap housing the radio antenna.

Left: A three-quarter rear view of the T-3. The dark patch on the centre fuselage is an air outlet in the engine bay. Note the perforations on the airbrakes immediately aft of the wings.

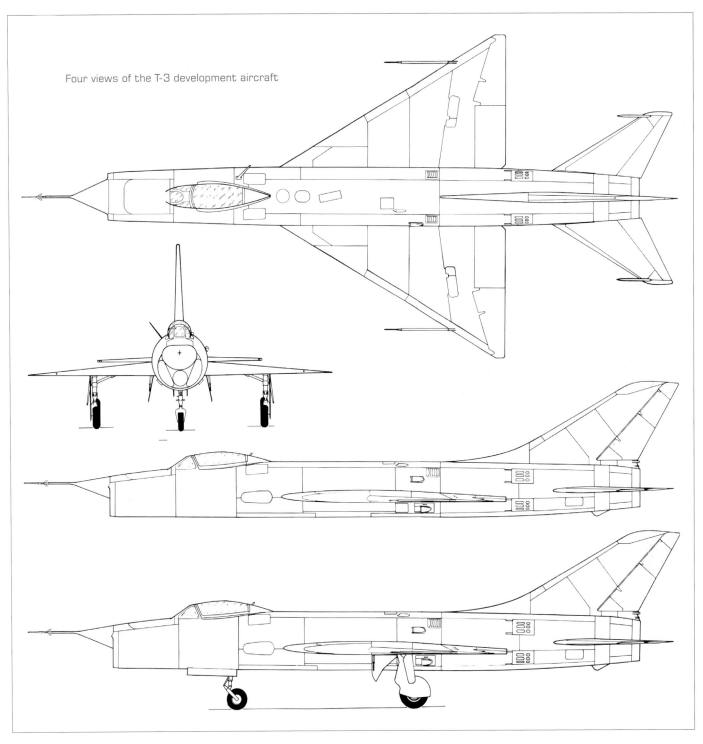

Four views of the T-3 development aircraft

yet, so Vladimir N. Makhalin, a pilot from the Soviet Air Force State Research Institute, named after Valeriy P. Chkalov (GK NII VVS: *Gosudarstvennyy Krasnoznamyonnyy naoochno-issledovatel'skiy institoot Voyenno-vozdooshnykh seel*), had been seconded to OKB-51 a short while earlier. He was appointed the T-3's project test pilot by a special MAP order, with M. I. Zooyev as engineer in charge of the flight tests.

For the next 30 days the aircraft underwent ground systems checks and taxiing tests. Finally, on 26 May 1956, after a lengthy delay caused by a malfunctioning communications radio that took

some time to fix, the T-3 prototype took to the air with Vladimir N. Makhalin at the controls. Less than a month later, on 24 June, the aircraft made its public debut, participating in the annual Aviation Day flypast at Moscow's Tushino airfield together with another brand-new Sukhoi aircraft, the S-1 fighter prototype. Needless to say, their designations were not stated, being classified; both aircraft were announced merely as 'new jet fighters'. The T-3 and S-1 exhibited certain 'family traits' that were to become Sukhoi hallmarks for the next 20 years, including characteristically shaped tails topped by dielectric fairings. After the

Above: Vladimir N. Makhalin, Hero of the Soviet Union, the project test pilot of the T-3
Above right: The T-3 pictured in an early test flight from Zhukovskiy. The radomes are now dielectric, and the revised rudder has a dielectric upper end.

T-3's Tushino debut, the NATO's Air Standards Coordinating Committee (ASCC) allocated the reporting name 'Fishpot' to the new interceptor; this was subsequently amended to Fishpot-A when the production versions became known to the West.

The manufacturer's flight tests proceeded in several stages, the aircraft being grounded from time to time by the need to make various modifications and engine changes. Stage A lasted until 28 September and was concerned with exploring the T-3's flight envelope; it included 31 flights, 27 of which were test flights. At this stage the interceptor's performance with K-7L missiles was determined (the missiles were carried on short swept pylons outboard of the main gear units), stability and handling at high angles of attack were checked, and even spin trials were performed. In the course of the latter, Vladimir N. Makhalin found himself in a tight spot. On 1 September, when he initiated a spin at 10,000 m (32,800 ft.), a compressor stall occurred and the engine flamed out. Recovering from the spin, the pilot put the aircraft into a shallow dive and set about restarting the engine. This proved reluctant to relight; Makhalin managed it on the fifth try, making a safe landing.

By late October the original engine had run out of service life and the T-3 was sent back to MMZ No. 51 for a refit. The aircraft was in layup until early March 1957; apart from the engine change, it underwent a number of modifications. The intended Almaz-3 radar and PVU-67 computing sight were installed, as was a missile launch control system for the K-7L AAMs and the SRZO-2 IFF. A new RSIU-4V *Mindal'* (Almond, a.k.a. R-801V) command radio was fitted instead of the original RSIU-4 Doob-4 (a.k.a. R-801), ensuring radio contact at higher altitudes (hence the *V* for *vysotnaya*: high-altitude); finally, a revised sliding-canopy portion was fitted and the brake parachute container was enlarged.

Stage B of the manufacturer's flight tests began on 8 March 1957, considerably behind schedule due to the late delivery of the replacement engine. At this stage, LII test pilots Vladimir M. Pro-

nyakin and Vladimir S. Ilyushin (the latter was subsequently transferred to the Sukhoi OKB and eventually became its chief test pilot) started flying the T-3. In the summer of 1957 the aircraft was ferried to the Ministry of Defence's 6th Test Range at Vladimirovka AB, near the town of Akhtoobinsk (Saratov Region), located in the estuary of the Volga River; this base would soon become the main facility of GK NII VVS. Between 1 June and 23 August the K-7L missile system was tested in accordance with a joint MAP / air force decision; this included live missile launches, checks of the antisurge system, and verification of the engine inflight-restarting procedure, among other things. Vladimir S. Ilyushin flew the aircraft at this stage.

On 28 August the T-3 returned to Zhukovskiy. After nearly a month's lull, the tests resumed on 20 September and were completed on 16 October 1957; the vibration characteristics of the K-7L missile/pylon combination and the missile-armed aircraft as a whole were determined at the closing stage. Apart from the pilots already mentioned, test pilots Leonid G. Kobishchan, Anatoliy A. Koznov (both Sukhoi OKB), and Mikhail L. Petushkov (LII) also flew the T-3 for familiarisation purposes.

All in all, in the course of 18 months the T-3 made nearly 80 flights totalling 38 hours, 21 minutes; the results obtained in these flights confirmed that the chosen layout was sound and the basic design features worked. The aircraft showed quite decent performance, even though range and endurance fell short of the expectations, while the unstick speed and landing speed were higher than anticipated. This was because the gross weight was well above the design figure, while the engine performance figures advertised by the Lyul'ka OKB proved decidedly optimistic. As a result, range and endurance fell short of the expectations, while the unstick and landing speed were higher than expected.

The following is an excerpt from the manufacturer's flight test report of 'the T-3 experimental interceptor no. 01' [*sic*; that is, c/n 01?].

Above: The T-3 makes its public debut at Moscow-Tushino during the Aviation Day display on 24 June 1956.

Right: This view of the T-3 shows the wing planform and various details of the fighter's underside and the 'grinning' air intake. Note the varying shades of skin on the wings and the landing light on the port wing. The small dark rectangles adjacent to the fuselage were probably associated with the planned cannon installation.

Below, *below right*, and *bottom right*: Three more views of the T-3 during the Tushino flypast. Note the additional pitots on the wings and the faired antiflutter weight on the stabilators.

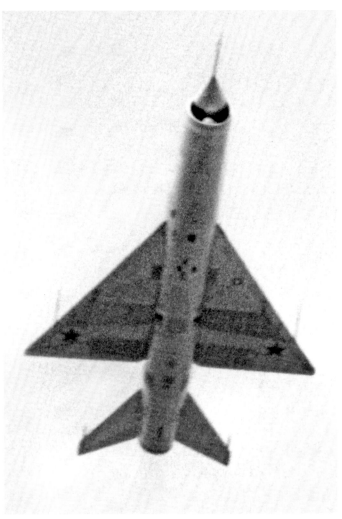

'The first prototype (no. 01) underwent tests at the LII airfield from 23 April 1956 to 28 September 1956, from March 1957 to 28 May 1957, and from 20 September 1957 to 16 October 1957. In addition to flight performance testing, special tests were held at the LII airfield to determine the vibration characteristics of the K-7 missiles carried by the aircraft and test the performance of the AL-7F engine involving the use of the KS system. [KS stands for **kla**pan **sbro**sa: bypass valve, referring to the abovementioned antisurge system developed in 1956 by MAP's NII-2 and the Central Aero-Engine Institute (TsIAM: *Tsentrahl'nyy insti**toot** aviatsion**novo** motorostroyeniya*). This system featured a valve on the engine's fuel control unit that opened automatically when the cannons were fired or rockets launched, throttling back the engine and thereby

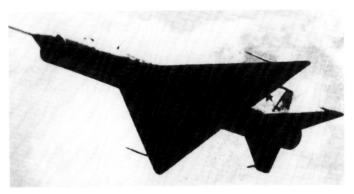

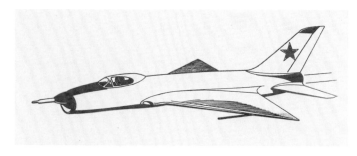

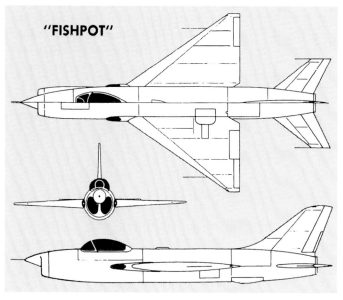

"FISHPOT"

The first provisional drawings of the T-3 that appeared in the Western aviation press after the 1956 Tushino flypast.

preventing engine surge.] . . . *The T-3 no. 01 has made a total of 80 flights with a total time of 38 hrs, 21 min. . . .*

1. The manufacturer's flight tests revealed that the aircraft has the following performance:

a) maximum speed in level flight in full afterburner at 12,000 m [39,370 ft.], *2,100 km/h* [1,304 mph]

b) climb time from 1,000 m to 10,000 m [from 3,280 ft. to 32,800 ft.] *from the start of stable climb at full military power, 2.3 minutes*

c) service ceiling in afterburner mode, 18,000 m [59,055 ft.]

d) technical range at 12,000 m on internal fuel, 1,440 km [894 miles]; *ditto with drop tanks, 1,840 km* [1,140 miles]

e) endurance at 12,000 m on internal fuel, 1 hour, 39 minutes; ditto with drop tanks, 2 hours, 10 minutes

2. The K-7L [missile] *carriage and launch system operates faultlessly throughout the explored range of speeds (Mach numbers) and altitudes.*

K-7L missiles were fired at altitudes of 5,100-18,300 m [16,730–60,040 ft.]. *The missile launch does not affect engine operation and does not require the use of a fuel check valve* [throttling back the engine automatically to prevent surge caused by missile exhaust gas ingestion].

The aircraft's handling and manoeuvrability ensure normal flight operation.

In order to facilitate piloting during future operation of the T-3, it is necessary:

1. to replace the control cables in the aileron and tailplane control circuits with rigid linkages

2. to install an ARZ-1 artificial-feel unit to adjust the stick forces, depending on the flight mode

3. to install an AP-106 [yaw] *damper in the directional control circuit.* [*sic*; the designation is more similar to that of an autopilot]

The landing gear, hydraulics, power plant, and other systems of the aircraft have been brought up to an adequate reliability level in the course of manufacturer's flight tests and permit safe operation of the aircraft.'

It may be added that the takeoff run was 1,050–1,150 m (3,445–3,770 ft.), and the landing run without the use of a brake parachute was 1,780–1,840 m (5,840–6,040 ft.).

The greatest problems encountered during the T-3's tests were caused by the AL-7F engine, which was still suffering from teething troubles and was extremely capricious. Suffice it to say that in the course of the 38-hour flight test programme, the aircraft had to undergo four engine changes! The AL-7F ran at a high temperature, necessitating the provision of additional engine-cooling air scoops on the centre fuselage and replacement of wiring bundles in the engine bay with heat-resistant ones.

Building on experience gained with the S-1, which was powered by the same engine, the T-3's never-exceed speed was limited to Mach 1.83 for the duration of the manufacturer's flight tests in order to avoid engine surge. Another remedy was to incorporate so-called bleed bands (that is, bleed valves) at the AL-7F's fourth and fifth compressor stages. The downside of this feature was that the valves markedly reduced available thrust at speeds in excess of Mach 1.6; instead of 7,500 kgp (16,530 lbst) at full military power and 10,000 kgp (22,045 lbst) in full afterburner, the modified engine delivered only 6,850 kgp (15,100 lbst) and 8,950 kgp (19,730 lbst), respectively. Hence, when powered by an AL-7F incorporating bleed valves, the T-3 could not accelerate beyond 1,830 km/h (1,136 mph) and climb above 18,000 m (59,055 ft.); the 2,100 km/h top speed quoted above in the manufacturer's flight test report applied to a configuration with an engine lacking bleed valves.

Test pilots noted an excessively sharp reaction to aileron inputs; this led to the recommendation to incorporate push-pull rods in the pitch and roll control circuits and provide an artificial-feel unit and a yaw damper. Originally the T-3 featured perforated airbrakes for maximum braking efficiency; however, the pilots reported that the airbrakes produced an infernal racket when deployed, and the perforated airbrakes were replaced with 'solid' ones. Also, it became clear that the aircraft would be unable to reach the specified maximum speed and altitude with a fixed-area air intake and the existing radome arrangement; by then, however, OKB-51 was working on more-efficient intake designs.

The following is a brief structural description of the T-3.

Type: Single-engined, single-seat supersonic interceptor designed for day and night operation in visual meteorological conditions (VMC) and instrument meteorological conditions (IMC).

The airframe is of all-metal construction. Length overall 17.07 m (56 ft., 0 in.), wingspan 8.54 m (28 ft., ¼ in.), height on ground 4.82 m (15 ft., 9¾ in.), wing area 34.0 m² (365.5 sq. ft.), tailplane area 5.58 m² (60.0 sq. ft.).

Fuselage: Semimonocoque, riveted, stressed-skin structure of circular cross section. Structurally the fuselage consists of two sections: forward (section F-1) and rear (section F-2), the latter being detachable for engine maintenance or removal.

The *forward fuselage* incorporates a fixed-area nose air intake divided by a vertical splitter into two air ducts passing along the fuselage sides, flanking the cockpit. A conical radome is provided at the upper intake lip/splitter junction, plus a hemispherical radome low on the intake splitter; they house the search and tracking antennas of the radar, respectively.

The cockpit is enclosed by a bubble canopy comprising a fixed windshield (having an optically flat windscreen and triangular curved sidelight) and an aft-sliding rear portion. The latter parts company with the airframe together with the ejection seat in the event of an ejection, serving as a shield for the pilot. The windscreen is made of triplex glass; all other transparencies are Perspex.

Two fuel tanks are located aft of the cockpit between the inlet ducts. The centre portion of the fuselage incorporates wing attachment fittings; the centre fuselage underside features two side-by-side hardpoints for drop tanks.

The *rear fuselage* is a one-piece structure accommodating the engine with its extension jet pipe and afterburner. The rear fuselage incorporates the no. 3 fuel tank, four airbrakes arranged in cruciform fashion on the upper/lower fuselage sides, and a ventrally located brake parachute bay, with a tail bumper aft of it.

Wings: Cantilever midwing monoplane with delta wings. Leading-edge sweep 60°, anhedral 2° from roots, incidence 0°, no camber; aspect ratio 2.148, taper 27.7. The mean aerodynamic chord (MAC) is 5,122.7 mm (16 ft., 9¹¹/₁₆ in.).

The wings are one-piece structures utilising a TsAGI S-9S symmetrical airfoil. The root portions incorporate the mainwheel wells ahead of the main spar. The trailing edge is occupied by hydraulically actuated one-piece Fowler flaps, with one-piece ailerons outboard of them. The flaps have an area of 3.515 m² (37.79 sq. ft.) and a maximum deflection of 20°; the aerodynamically balanced ailerons, carried on three hinges, have an area of 1.73 m² (18.6 sq. ft.) each, which equals 10.33% of the overall wing area, and a travel limit of ±15°. Each wing has a single hardpoint for a pylon with a missile launch rail.

Tail unit: Conventional tail surfaces; sweepback at quarter chord 55°. The *vertical tail* comprises a one-piece fin and an inset rudder carried on three hinges.

The cantilever *horizontal tail* consists of slab stabilisers (stabilators) rotating on axles set at 48°30' to the fuselage axis; dihedral 0°, aspect ratio 1.01. The stabilator travel limits are 5° up and 17° down. The stabilators use a TsAGI S-11S-6 symmetrical airfoil.

Landing gear: Hydraulically retractable tricycle type, with single wheel on each unit; the nose unit retracts forward, the main units inward into the wing roots. Wheel track 4.698 m (15 ft., 4³¹/₃₂ in.), wheelbase 4.88 m (16 ft., ⅛ in.) in no-load condition and 5.055 m (16 ft., 7¹/₆₄ in.) under static load. All three landing-gear struts have oleo-pneumatic shock absorbers; the nose unit is equipped with a shimmy damper.

The semilevered suspension nose unit is equipped with a 570 × 140 mm (22.4 × 5.5 in.) K-283 nonbraking wheel and a shimmy damper. The nosewheel is castoring; steering on the ground is by differential braking. The levered suspension main units have 800 × 200 mm (31.5 × 7.87 in.) KT-50/2 mainwheels (*koleso tormoznoye*: brake-equipped wheel) with pneumatically operated disc brakes. The nosewheel well is closed by twin lateral doors, the mainwheel wells by triple doors (one segment is hinged to the front spar, one to the root rib, and a third segment attached to the oleo leg). All doors remain open when the gear is down.

Power plant: One Lyul'ka AL-7F axial-flow afterburning turbojet with a specified thrust of 7,500 kgp (16,530 lbst) at full military power and 10,000 kgp (22,045 lbst) in full afterburner; the actual thrust with bleed valves was 6,850 kgp (15,100 lbst) and 8,950 kgp (19,730 lbst), respectively. A detailed description of this engine is found in the description of the Su-9 (see chapter 3).

Control system: Conventional powered controls with irreversible actuators. Control inputs are transmitted to the stabilator actuators by rigid linkages (push-pull rods, control cranks and levers); the ailerons are controlled by means of cables, and a combined control linkage with both rods and cables is used in the rudder control circuit.

Fuel system: Internal fuel is carried in two fuel cells in the forward fuselage and two integral tanks in the wings (aft of the mainwheel wells), holding a total of 3,130 litres (688.6 Imp gal.); the fuel load is 2,570 kg (5,665 lbs.). There are provisions for carrying two 500-litre (110 Imp gal.) drop tanks on pylons under the centre fuselage, holding an extra 820 kg (1,810 lbs.) of fuel.

Avionics and equipment: The avionics suite includes an Almaz-3 fire control radar, an RSIU-4 Doob two-way VHF communications radio (later replaced by a Mindal' radio but then changed back to the previous model), an MRP-48P marker beacon receiver, an ARK-5 automatic direction finder (*avtomaticheskiy rahdiokompas*) with a buried loop aerial aft of the cockpit and a directional aerial glued to the canopy transparency, a Sirena-2 radar-warning receiver, a GIK-1 gyro-flux gate compass, an AGI-1 fighter-type nontoppling artificial horizon, a PVU-67 computing sight, and an SRZO-2M Kremniy-2M IFF interrogator/transponder.

Armament: Two K-7L beam-riding air-to-air missiles carried on pylon-mounted launch rails under the wings. Provisions were made for installing two 30 mm Nudelman/Rikhter NR-30 cannons with 65 rpg in the wing roots, but these were never fitted.

Crew rescue system: Sukhoi KS-1 ejection seat, permitting safe ejection at speeds up to 850 km/h (528 mph) and altitudes of 150–15,000 m (490–49,210 ft.).

Close-up of the PT-7 mockup's air intake assembly and the twin radomes of the Almaz-7 radar

PT-7 Experimental Interceptor

In 1955–56, OKB-51 continued work on adapting the T-3 interceptor for carrying K-7L medium-range AAMs or K-6V short-range AAMs. The K-6V (*vysotnaya*: high altitude) was developed by OKB-2 under Chief Designer Pavel D. Grooshin pursuant to a Council of Ministers directive dated 23 August 1956, in response to the Lockheed U-2 spyplane's first intrusions into Soviet airspace in the summer of 1956. The K-6V, which was intended for the Sukhoi T-3, was a more potent version of the original K-6 developed for the Mikoyan I-3P (I-440) experimental fighter; the maximum 'kill' altitude was increased from the previous version's 16,000 m (52,490 ft.) to 22,000–25,000 m (72,180–82,020 ft.). Like Grooshin's earlier K-5 missile (known in service as the RS-1-U), the K-6/K-6V was a beam-riding missile. Other shared features were the solid-fuel rocket motor located amidships (with canted lateral nozzles) and the guidance system bay in the tailcone, with an aft-pointing aerial receiving signals from the radar.

Unlike the predecessor, however, the K-6 had a conventional layout with cruciform cropped-delta wings located amidships and cruciform trapezoidal rudders aft of them. The K-6V version was 3.5 m (11 ft., 5⁵¹⁄₆₄ in.) long, with a wing span of 0.786 m (2 ft., 6¹⁵⁄₁₆ in.) and a body diameter of 220 mm (8²¹⁄₃₂ in.); the launch weight was 150 kg (330 lbs.), including the 23 kg (50.7 lbs.) high-explosive/fragmentation warhead, which was detonated by a radar proximity fuse. 'Kill' range was 2–6 km (1.24–3.72 miles), and the missile was designed to destroy targets flying at up to 2,000 km/h (1,242 mph).

However, we are jumping ahead of the story. The second prototype T-3, known as the *dooblyor* (literally, 'understudy'; this was the Soviet term for second prototypes used until the late 1960s), received a separate designation, PT-7 (PT probably stood for *perekhvatchik s treugol'nym krylom*: delta-wing interceptor). The PT-7 was designed to be armed with missiles from the start and was to be equipped with an improved Almaz-7 fire control radar and a PVU-67 computing sight instead of an ASP-5N optical sight. The installation of the new radar required changes to the forward fuselage—the tracking antenna was moved down to the air intake's lower lip and enclosed by a new conical radome angled slightly downward; again, the upper radome carried an air data boom. The effect was rather bizarre, the aircraft looking like a misshapen elephant with two tusks. The air intake leading edge was no longer vertical but angled 16° forward.

The missiles were carried on underwing pylons, one under each wing; no cannons were fitted. In this guise the aircraft was intended to enter mass production.

Detail design was completed in December 1955, prototype construction commencing at the end of the year. The changes were not limited to the new radar and attendant 'nose job'; the wing design was altered in accordance with TsAGI's recommendations. This, together with the late delivery of the engine, caused the PT-7 to be completed much later than intended. At the time, the testing of the T-3 and S-1 prototypes was in progress; as already mentioned, they were powered by the AL-7F engine (manufacturer's designation *izdeliye* 45)—the first afterburning version rated at

An artist's impression of the PT-7, 'the horror borne on the wings of the night'. The twin pointed radomes and the raked air intake leading edge gave the aircraft a positively hair-raising look.

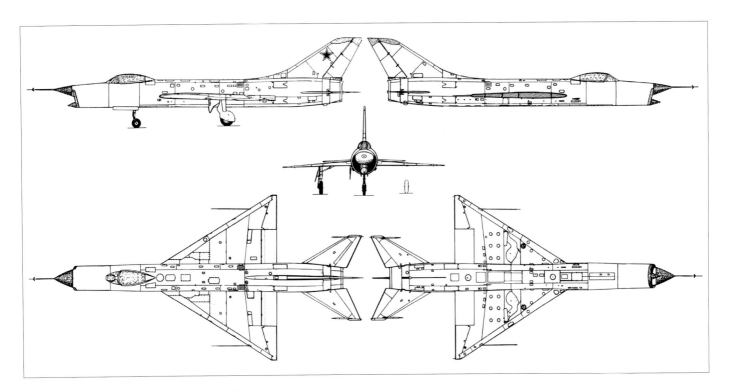

Five views of the PT-7 development aircraft

6,850 kgp (15,100 lbst) dry and 8,800 kgp (19,400 lbst) reheat. Soon, however, the Lyul'ka OKB offered an uprated version designated AL-7F-1 (*izdeliye* 45-1), which delivered 9,200 kgp (20,280 lbst) in full afterburner; try as it would, OKB-165 still could not get the engine to deliver the required 10,000 kgp (22,045 lbst). The idea was supported, and on 25 August 1956 the Council of Ministers issued a directive requiring the Sukhoi OKB to install the AL-7F-1 on the T-3 and S-1 with a view to ensuring a service ceiling of at least 21,000 m (68,900 ft.).

Once again the Sukhoi OKB had to make changes to the manufacturing drawings. The AL-7F-1 had a slightly larger casing diameter and was too big to fit inside the existing detachable rear fuselage, which had to be widened somewhat. Apparently at the same time, the airbrakes were revised—the perforations were eliminated and a V-shaped dent was added in the middle of the trailing edge. These changes concerned both the interceptor and the S-1. This meant further delays while MMZ No. 51 manufactured a new rear fuselage section, and the PT-7 was not delivered to Zhukovskiy until early June 1957. Eduard V. Yelian was appointed project test pilot, with K. N. Strekalov as engineer in charge of the test programme.

The maiden flight took place at the end of June 1957. The manufacturer's flight tests involved 24 flights to check the aircraft's performance and handling and verify the principal systems; after that, on 23 September, the PT-7 was ferried to the GK NII VVS facility at Vladimirovka AB. Since the T-3's state acceptance trials schedule had gone to the dogs because of development problems, on 13 September the Council of Ministers issued a new directive setting a new deadline for the commencement of the trials (December 1957). The Sukhoi OKB did its utmost to complete the manufacturer's tests of the K-7L weapons system, including

live launches, before the aircraft was handed over to the military. However, these plans were shattered. After making only two flights under this programme, the aircraft was grounded for yet another engine change; a replacement engine was not delivered until November, which meant a mere six flights could be made until the end of the year. The work continued in 1958, with another 18 flights following by the end of June, in which only six missile launches were made; the PT-7 was flown by OKB-51 test pilots Leonid G. Kobishchan and Anatoliy A. Koznov.

PT-8 Interceptor (*izdeliye* 27)

Since the T-3 interceptor was expected to enter production in its PT-7 configuration, MAP issued an order to the effect that MAP aircraft factory no. 153, named after Valeriy P. Chkalov, in Novosibirsk, should manufacture three preproduction aircraft in 1956, delivering them to OKB-51 in order to broaden the scope of development work and expedite the trials. (Here it should be noted that, unlike Western aircraft manufacturers, the Soviet aircraft design bureaus had no aircraft factories of their own, apart from prototype manufacturing facilities; the latter could build anything, but only in a handful of copies, being unsuited for mass production. The major aircraft factories were all controlled by MAP and built what the ministry told them to. On the other hand, most of these factories historically had strong ties with a particular OKB and built predominantly aircraft of the same make; this made sense because aircraft from the same OKB often had considerable technological commonality, meaning no complete change of the manufacturing process was required when a new type entered production. Factory No. 153 had specialised in fighters since 1936; now the assignment to build the T-3 started a close association with the Sukhoi OKB, which has lasted to this day.)

An artist's impression of the envisaged production configuration of the first Su-9s as per OKB drawings (designated as the T-3 but featuring a PT-7-style nose). The aircraft was to be armed with two cannons in the wing roots, two revolver-type FFAR launchers outboard of them, and two K-5M AAMs under the outer wings; only the missile rails are shown here, not the missiles proper.

The envisaged production version of the PT-7 was allocated a new designation, PT-8; hence the three preproduction machines mentioned above were known in-house as the PT8-1, PT8-2, and PT8-3. It was standard operational procedure at the Sukhoi OKB to designate development aircraft in this fashion (with a hyphen after the digits in the model designation rather than before them, as when referring to the type in general). At that time, plant No. 153 was mass-producing the MiG-19S Farmer-C tactical fighter, which had the internal product code *izdeliye* 26; since these codes were sequential, the PT-8 (which was next in line) was allocated the code *izdeliye* 27.

As originally envisaged, the production T-3 (PT-8) had pure delta wings with an unbroken leading edge. The aircraft was to have a mixed armament fit. Two NR-30 cannons were housed in the wing roots, their ammunition sleeves being accommodated in the fuselage. Just outboard of these were two automatic rocket launchers looking like outsized revolvers, with a long barrel protruding beyond the wing leading edge and a drum holding FFARs. These could be ARO-57-6 Vikhr' (Whirlwind, a.k.a. *izdeliye* 3P-6-III) six-round launchers (*avtomaticheskoye reaktivnoye oroodiye*: literally, 'automatic jet gun'), designed to fire ARS-57 FFARs, or, equally possibly, ARO-70 eight-round launchers, designed to fire 70 mm (2.75 in.) ARS-70 *Lastochka* (Swallow) FFARs. Finally, two horizontal pylons with launch rails for K-5M beam-riding AAMs were mounted on the wing leading edge in line with the flap/aileron joints; more will be said about these missiles in chapter 2.

The time schedule proved to be a little too optimistic, considering that the plant was mastering a completely new aircraft coming from an OKB with whose products it had no prior experience. The first preproduction aircraft (PT8-1) was completed in February 1957, bearing the construction number 0015301, which followed the traditional c/n system in use at the Novosibirsk factory (that is, Batch 00, plant no. 153, 01st aircraft in the batch; often quoted simply as 0001). The PT8-2 and PT8-3 (c/ns 0015302 and 0015303) followed in the spring of that year. All three aircraft were dismantled straight away and delivered by rail to OKB-51 in Moscow, where they were to be tested. However, only one of the three ever flew in as-built configuration in the hands of LII test pilot Vladimir

M. Pronyakin, the other two being extensively modified as the PT-95 (see chapter 2) and the T-39, respectively. The aircraft in question was flown by, and in time to be able to participate in that year's Aviation Day flypast at Tushino, but the event was cancelled at the last moment.

The three aircraft listed above were not the only PT-8s; according to some sources, 20 initial-production interceptors in batches 1 and 2 were also built in this configuration (even though 30 had been ordered initially). Unlike the three Batch 00 aircraft, they had the outer wing chord extended forward to create a prominent leading-edge dogtooth approximately at half span; at high angles of attack this dogtooth (introduced on the recommendations of TsAGI) was to generate a vortex that limited spanwise airflow, delaying the onset of tip stall and increasing wing lift. Another change resulted from the early flight test results obtained with the T-3 prototype—aileron area was reduced. Ten of them were immediately converted to T-47 configuration as part of the Su-11's development effort (see chapter 2).

In April 1958 the Council of Ministers issued a new directive specifying the performance targets for the T-3 interceptor. Importantly, the new SOR envisaged that a new armament system was to be integrated in the course of further work.

T-39 Development Aircraft

Striving to increase the T-3's service ceiling, in 1958 the Sukhoi OKB began exploring the possibility of increasing engine thrust by injecting water (more probably, a water/methanol mixture) into the afterburner. Hence the third preproduction T-3—that is, the PT8-3 (c/n 0015303)—was earmarked for conversion into a development aircraft designated T-39. The conversion involved replacing the no. 3 fuel tank in the rear fuselage with a 700-litre (154 Imp gal.) water tank for the water injection system; to compensate for this, an extra fuel tank was provided in the fuselage nose.

The aircraft was never tested in this configuration because the water injection system programme was transferred to TsIAM for further research, using ground test rigs. The unflown T-39 was further converted to become the T-49 development aircraft described later in this book.

Chapter 2

The 'Delta' Matures: The Su-9

T-43 (T43-1) Development Aircraft

Starting in the mid-1950s, American high-altitude reconnaissance aircraft began intruding ever more frequently into Soviet airspace. This led the Soviet Union to accelerate development of not only SAMs but manned interceptor aircraft as well. The Central Committee of the Soviet Union's Communist Party held a session attended both by top-ranking Ministry of Defence officials and by representatives of most defence industry branches. On 25 August 1956 the Council of Ministers let loose with a huge directive requiring all Soviet fighter design bureaus to increase the service ceiling of their new fighters within an extremely brief period. In particular, Pavel O. Sukhoi was ordered to increase the service ceiling of the S-1 fighter and the T-3 interceptor (both of which were then

under development) to 21,000 m (68,900 ft.). To this end, both aircraft were to be powered by the uprated AL-7F-1 engine, and the OKB was authorised to delete some systems of secondary importance for the purpose of cutting the interceptor's empty weight.

Following up on the said directive, MAP issued a series of orders requiring each of the Soviet 'fighter makers' to perform research-and-development work with the purpose of increasing the fighters' service ceiling. This accounts for the sudden revival of interest in rocket boosters displayed by the Soviet aircraft industry in the late 1950s. Specifically, the Sukhoi OKB was instructed to equip the basic T-3 interceptor with two alternative liquid-propellant rocket boosters. One was the disposable U-19 (U = *ooskoritel'*: booster), which was built around an SZ-20M rocket motor devel-

The T43-1 prototype seen during manufacturer's tests, with four K-5M missiles on the pylons. Note the bulged rear fuselage to accommodate the AL-7F-1 engine and the differently shaped gun blast plates, for which, again, there are no guns.

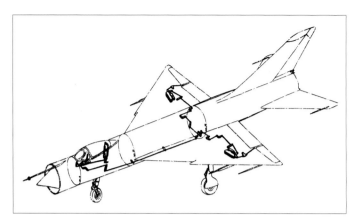

A schematic drawing of the first Su-9s with a wing dogtooth and only two missile rails. The ailerons have rigid linkages instead of the earlier cable runs. Note the large diameter of the air intake (not matching the real thing), probably depicted like this because the PT-8 was already in existence.

oped by OKB-3 under Chief Designer Dominik D. Sevrook at the Ministry of Defence Industry's NII-88 (although Aleksey M. Isayev also had a hand in the design). The SZ-20M had two operating modes—minimum thrust (1,300 kgp/2,865 lbst) and full thrust (3,000 kgp/6,613 lbst or, according to some documents, 3,200 kgp/7,100 lbst). These were selected by a fuel feed valve, and the booster could go from full thrust to minimum thrust but not vice versa; when fully fuelled the U-19 had an operation time of 3.5–4

minutes at minimum thrust or two minutes at full thrust. The other was the reusable U-19D, which was based on the 4,000 kgp (8,820 lbst) RU-013 rocket motor (*raketnyy ooskoritel'*: rocket booster) designed by Leonid S. Dooshkin (hence the *D*). In both cases the booster was totally self-contained, being housed in a jettisonable conformal pod occupying most of the fuselage underside. It ran on TG-02 (***toplivo ghipergolicheskoye***: hypergolic or self-igniting fuel), a 50/50 mixture of xylidine and triethylamine that self-combusted when combined with AK-20F oxidiser. (AK = *azotnaya kislota*: nitric acid; '20' means 20% nitrogen tetroxide, added to give a 5% power boost; F = ***fosfornaya kislota***: phosphoric acid added as a corrosion inhibitor.) Water injection into the afterburner as a means of increasing thrust was also considered.

The Sukhoi OKB decided to fit the rocket booster concurrently with the AL-7F-1 turbojet, for which the aircraft would act as a test bed. The mixed-power derivative of the T-3 received the manufacturer's designation T-43 (the first thus designated).

In addition to the power plant, the T-43 featured a new air intake design. The high speeds specified by the said C of M directive could not be attained with the T-3's fixed-area subsonic intake, having rounded lips, since this design incurred considerable pressure losses. Hence, teaming up with TsAGI, the Sukhoi OKB had been working on a more efficient intake design since 1955. The engineers decided to use a variable air intake utilising a series of sloping shock waves to provide gradual deceleration of the airflow with minimum pressure losses. However, the need to accommodate the bulky fire control radar was still there.

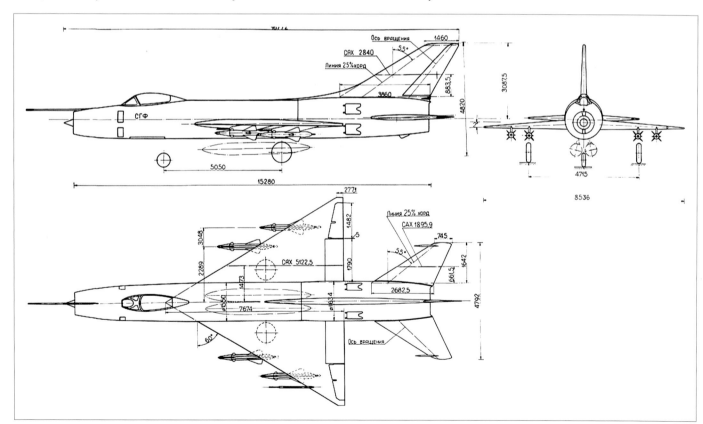

A three-view drawing of the Su-9 in the principal production configuration, with an unbroken wing leading edge (no dogtooth) and four missile rails. Note that the ailerons now terminate short of the wingtips.

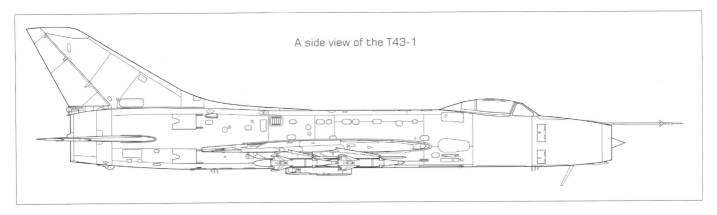

A side view of the T43-1

The most obvious solution was to use an axisymmetrical circular air intake with a conical centre body (shock cone) as used on the S-1 fighter, with a compound shape creating two shock waves—a so-called two-shock cone. Unlike the S-1 at the preliminary development project stage, the axisymmetrical air intake featured sharp lips. The centre body was movable, featuring two positions; when the aircraft accelerated to Mach 1.35, an automatic control system triggered by an airspeed sensor moved the shock cone fully forward, retracting it into full aft position at lower speeds. The OKB decided to test this new intake design on the T-43 as well.

The T-43 had a bulged rear fuselage to accommodate the AL-7F-1 engine (which, as noted earlier, had a slightly larger casing diameter), and altered wings with a leading-edge dogtooth and smaller ailerons. Also, the cable runs in the aileron control circuit were replaced by rigid linkages, and an ARZ-1 stick force limiter (*avtomaht reguleerovaniya zagroozki*) was added for the ailerons.

Design work on the altered airframe components was completed in December 1956; the manufacturing drawings for these were issued both to MMZ No. 51 and to aircraft factory no. 153 in Novosibirsk so that appropriate changes could be incorporated on production T-3s (PT-8s). (By then the decision to launch full-scale production had already been taken, and MAP's production plan for 1957 included thirty PT-8s.) As a 'belt-and-braces policy', MAP had agreed with the customer (the Ministry of Defence) that provisions would be made for equipping the initial-production interceptors with the old AL-7F engine and NR-30 cannons in case the envisaged AL-7F-1 engine and the K-7 air-to-air missile were not available on schedule.

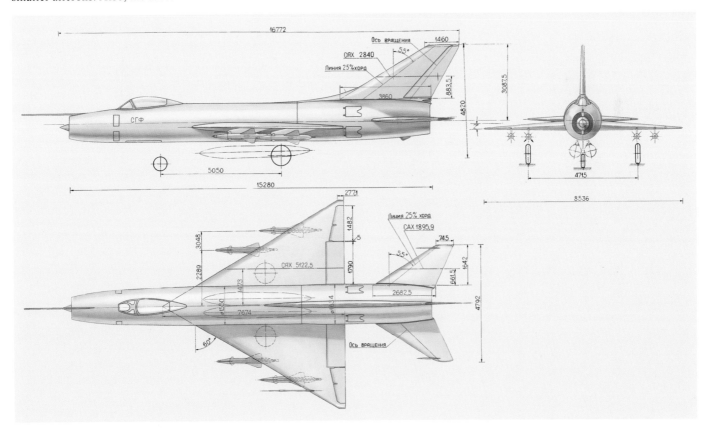

A colour version of the same three-view drawing of the Su-9 from the ADP documents, featuring all the basic dimensions. With the new intake design, the air data boom was relocated to the intake's upper lip; note that only one (port side) backup pitot is fitted.

Since the T-43 was purely an experimental aircraft, no provisions were made for armament or mission avionics. The avionics bay and the space inside the air-intake centre body were occupied by test equipment and ballast to maintain the correct CG position.

The OKB's experimental shop manufactured three sets of rocket booster fairings for the T-43; however, development of the U-19/U-19D boosters proper was running behind schedule, and OKB-51 chose to begin initial flight tests in as-is condition (sans booster). Vladimir S. Ilyushin was appointed project test pilot, while M. I. Zooyev was engineer in charge. The T-43's airframe was completed in the late summer of 1957 but remained at MMZ No. 51 for another month pending delivery of a flight-cleared AL-7F-1. At the end of September the still-engineless aircraft was trucked to Zhukovskiy; on 1 October, OKB-165 finally delivered the engine, which was promptly installed, and on 10 October the T-43 successfully performed its maiden flight.

In its third flight, on 20 October, the T-43 confirmed the promise it held by climbing to 21,500 m (70,540 ft.)—higher than the government directive required—on the power of the main engine alone (no booster was fitted). Three days later the aircraft excelled again, clocking a speed of 2,200 km/h (1,366 mph), which was equivalent to Mach 2.06. This success came at exactly the right moment—the MAP bosses needed something to show the Soviet head of state Nikita S. Khrushchov, who was becoming increasingly and notoriously biased toward missile systems, to the detriment of military aviation, that manned combat aircraft were still a force to be reckoned with. The ministry issued a special order commending Vladimir S. Ilyushin for this performance; meanwhile, the Sukhoi OKB was instructed to install a fire control radar in an interceptor featuring the new air intake design. Nobody mentioned rocket boosters or water injection anymore.

In the course of later trials the original T-43 (subsequently redesignated **T43-1** because other examples appeared) was retrofitted with an ESUV-1 electrohydraulic air intake control system (*elektroghidravlicheskaya sistema oopravleniya vozdukhoz-abornikom*) designed to prevent engine surge; the system provided continuous control of the shock cone throughout the flight envelope. In subsonic flight the shock cone was in the fully aft position

but then moved forward gradually as the aircraft accelerated past Mach 1, ensuring the optimum position of the shock waves. This system later found use on other aircraft in the T-3 series featuring axisymmetrical air intakes.

T-5 Experimental Interceptor (*izdeliye 81-1*)

To meet an air force requirement, the Sukhoi OKB developed a much-modified version of the T-3 designated T-5 or *izdeliye* 81-1. The aircraft was powered by two R11F-300 axial-flow afterburning turbojets (*izdeliye* 37F) developed by Sergey K. Tumanskiy's OKB-300, with a takeoff thrust of 4,200 kgp (9,260 lbst) dry and 6,120 kgp (13,490 lbst) reheat, and was effectively a propulsion test bed designed to verify this twin-engine power plant.

The R11-300 was the first Soviet two-spool turbojet. Being lighter and more compact than the AL-7F-1, the new engines were installed side by side in a completely redesigned and much-wider rear fuselage; the result was a pronounced 'waist' at the wing trailing edge. The fuselage break point was moved aft from frame 28 to frame 34. The section between frames 28 and 34 was a sort of adapter between the existing forward fuselage structure and the new rear fuselage, incorporating a bifurcated inlet duct for the two engines; it also housed an enlarged no. 3 fuselage tank, increasing the total internal fuel capacity from the T-3's 3,180 litres (699.6 Imp gal.) to 3,480 litres (765.6 Imp gal.). (In reality, however, not more than 3,330 litres (732.6 Imp gal.) was filled during trials, so as not to exceed the maximum takeoff weight, the missing 150 litres (33 Imp gal.) being distributed between the wing tanks.)

Other structural changes included a new fuselage nose with an axisymmetrical air intake identical to the one tested on the T43-1. The inboard ends of the flaps were slightly cropped to match the increased width of the rear fuselage. Unlike the AL-7, which was started by a so-called turbostarter (a small gas turbine engine), the smaller and lighter R11-300 had electric starting; hence, the single 12-kilowatt GS-12T generator was replaced by two 9-kilowatt GSR-ST-9000A starter-generators. Finally, the existing BU-30 and BU-34 hydraulic control surface actuators were replaced with identical BU-49 actuators in all three control circuits, and the control cables in the rear fuselage were replaced by push-pull rods.

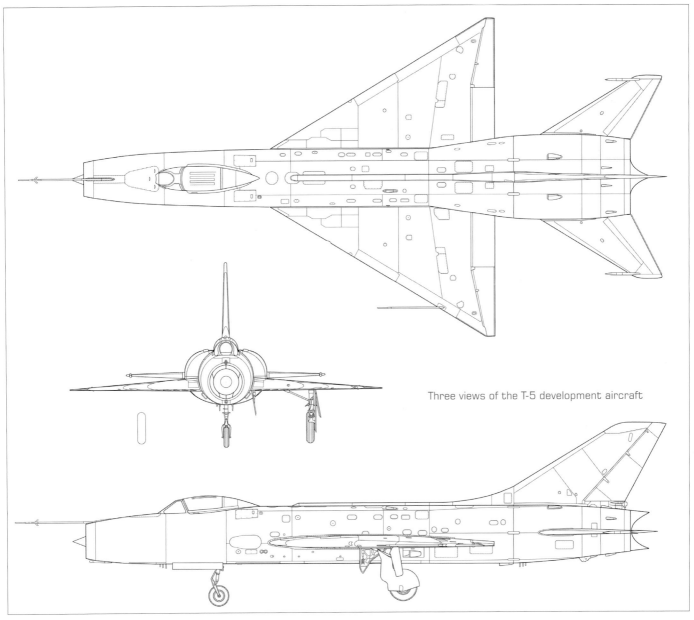

Three views of the T-5 development aircraft

This view of the T-5 shows well the 'hips' of the substantially widened rear fuselage. Note the engine bay cooling air scoops and the forward avionics bay cover ahead of the windshield.

This rear view of the T-5 illustrates the new rear fuselage housing two Tumanskiy R11F-300 engines side by side. The flaps are partially lowered.

The T-5 was converted from the T-3 prototype (c/n 01) at MMZ No. 51. Due to the extent of the changes, the conversion job took eight months (from October 1957 to June 1958). In early July the aircraft was delivered to the flight test facility in Zhukovskiy to commence ground checks, with M. I. Zooyev as engineer in charge of the tests. On 18 July the T-5 made its first flight in the hands of Vladimir S. Ilyushin. The manufacturer's flight test programme, involving 26 flights, showed that with the engines in afterburner mode, the aircraft was overpowered and, in spite of the decidedly higher drag (primarily due to the wider rear fuselage), could reach much-higher speeds than the T-3. In fact, the engines' structural strength was the limiting factor, since the R11F-300 was not designed to withstand speeds above Mach 2.

On the downside, the R11F-300's automatic fuel control unit still had a few bugs to be eliminated; as a result, the engines ran unstably, the afterburners often shutting down spontaneously during climb. Engine starting proved problematic as well, since both engines used a common air intake and, figuratively speaking, were short of breath. (It was much the same story with the MiG-19, where the two engines breathed through a single air intake divided by a splitter into individual inlet ducts; the downwind engine had to be started first, otherwise the upwind engine would literally take all the air away from it!) Furthermore, the T-5's longitudinal stability proved to be unacceptably low (to be precise, the aircraft had virtually zero stability due to the CG being positioned well aft). In May 1959 the aircraft's chief project engineer, Yevgeniy G. Fel'sner, called a halt to the test programme.

PT-95 Test Bed

The second preproduction T-3—that is, the PT8-2 (c/n 0015302)—never flew as such but was immediately converted into a propulsion test bed designated PT-95. Receiving a specially instrumented engine with test equipment sensors and a new forward fuselage patterned on the T43-1, the aircraft was delivered to its new owner, LII, in 1958. In 1958–59 the PT-95 served as a test bed for the new AL-7F-1, helping the engine's teething troubles to be overcome, and was used to explore the interaction between the air intake and the engine. The programme was performed by LII test pilot Valentin P. Vasin; on one occasion he had to make a dead-stick landing in the PT-95.

T-3-51 Aerial-Intercept Weapons System
T43-2, T43-3, T43-4, T43-5, T43-6, T43-11, and T43-12 Interceptor Prototypes

After the success of the T43-1 development aircraft the Sukhoi OKB concentrated on two main areas of work—attempts to achieve a satisfactory radar installation within the small shock cone used on the T43-1, and studies on accommodating the Almaz radar in a new and larger shock cone. The latter effort culminated in a new project designated T-47, which is described in chapter 2.

In the mid-1950s the NII-17 research institute was the Soviet Union's sole maker of aircraft radars. Only two principal airborne intercept radar types developed by NII-17—the RP-1 *Izumrood-1* (Emerald-1) twin-antenna radar (plus its refined version designated RP-5 Izumrood-5; both versions had the NATO code name 'Scan Odd') and the RP-6 **Sokol** (Falcon; NATO code name 'Scan Three')

single-antenna radar—had entered production by 1957. (RP = **rahdiopritsel**, 'radio sight', the Soviet term for fire control radars.) The Izumrood-series radars were fitted to the Yak-25 Flashlight-A, MiG-17P Fresco-B, MiG-17PF Fresco-D, MiG-17PFU Fresco-E, MiG-19P Farmer-B, and MiG-19PM Farmer-D interceptors, while the more powerful Sokol equipped the Yak-25M, Yak-25K Flashlight-A, and Yak-27 Flashlight-C interceptors. However, neither of these radars were suitable for an advanced supersonic interceptor; the RP-1/RP-5 had inadequate performance, while the more capable RP-6 was too bulky to fit inside the shock cone of an adjustable supersonic air intake. True, NII-17 had a couple of aces up its sleeve—the new and advanced Uragan (Hurricane, pronounced *ooragahn*) and *Pantera* (Panther) fire control radars, but their development was making painfully slow progress.

Just then, a competitor popped up like a jack-in-the-box; OKB-1, a division of the Ministry of Defence Industry (MOP: *Ministerstvo oboronnoy promyshlennosti*), suddenly emerged as a new airborne radar design house. Putting the know-how gained in the development of air-to-surface missile guidance systems to good use, an OKB-1 design team headed by project chief A. A. Kolosov had quietly developed the TsD-30 fire control radar. This was an X-band radar with a 100-kikowatt transmitter and a pulse rate frequency (PRF) of 825–950 pulses per second (pps) in search mode or 1,750–1,850 pps in target-tracking mode. The TsD-30 was optimised for guiding the K-5 (*izdeliye* ShM) air-to-air missile, created by Pavel D. Grooshin's OKB-2—and, importantly, it was compact enough to fit inside the T-43's movable shock cone without any trouble. Another major point in favour of this radar was that the K-5, known in service as the RS-1-U (*raketnyy snaryad, oopravlyayemyy*: missile, type 1, guided; NATO code name AA-1 Alkali), was the only AAM officially on the Soviet Air Force's inventory by 1957, arming the subsonic MiG-17PFU. It was a very basic beam-riding AAM—that is, it followed the beam of the interceptor's fire control radar. Having detected a target with the radar operating in search mode, the pilot got the target into the 'crosshairs' in the centre of the radar display by manoeuvring the aircraft, selected target lock-on mode, and, after closing in to the required range, fired the missiles. After that, the pilot was to keep the target in the 'crosshairs' until the missile detonated; the missile was controlled by a guidance system monitoring the position of the radar's directional pattern axis.

The K-5 missile had a tail-first layout with cruciform wings and cruciform rudders for pitch/yaw control; both of these had a cropped-delta planform and were set at 45° to the vertical. The wings, with a leading-edge sweep of 65°, had inset ailerons for roll control, helping to stabilise the missile along the longitudinal axis, and carried tracer flares at the tips allowing the pilot to track the missile's trajectory at night. The body, with a diameter of 200 mm (7⅞ in.), was divided into five sections, the foremost of which accommodated the 9.2 kg (20.3 lb.) high-explosive/fragmentation warhead, the skin serving as the fragmentation liner. It was tipped with an AR-10 radar proximity fuse with a maximum detection radius of 10 m (32 ft., 9 in.). Aft of the warhead were the rudder servo bay and the solid-fuel rocket motor, having a bifurcated jet pipe with nozzles angled outward 15°. This placement of the rocket motor amidships was dictated by two reasons: the need to avoid a

A test of the Su-9's canopy jettison system in TsAGI's T-109 subsonic wind tunnel, using a forward fuselage mockup

drastic shift of the CG as the propellant burned out (which might adversely affect the missile's control characteristics) and the need to accommodate the control system components, including an aft-pointing aerial receiving guidance signals from the radar, in the tailcone. The missile was 2.356 m (7 ft., 8¾ in.) long, with a wing span of 0.549 m (1 ft., 9³⁹⁄₆₄ in.) and a launch weight of 74.2 kg (163.5 lbs.). 'Kill' range was a mere 2–3 km (1.24–1.86 miles), and the launch altitude envelope was 5,000–10,000 m (16,400–32,810 ft.). The missile could manoeuvre with a load factor of up to 9 g.

For the supersonic MiG-19PM, however, OKB-2 developed a growth version of the missile designated K-5M (*modifitseerovannyy*: modified). Known in-house as *izdeliye* I (the capital letter *I*), it retained the K-5's basic layout and guidance method but featured a longer-burn PRD-45 rocket motor to increase the 'kill' range, a 13 kg (28.66 lb.) directional HE/fragmentation warhead having a 50% greater lethal radius, a reshaped nose with a new AR-45 radar proximity fuse whose detection radius was likewise increased 50% (to 15 m / 49 ft.), and other changes. The missile was larger and heavier—while the body diameter remained unchanged, overall length increased to 2.494 m (8 ft., 2³⁄₁₆ in.), the wing span to 0.65 m (≈ 2 ft., 1¹⁹⁄₃₂ in.), and the launch weight to 82.2 kg (181.2 lbs.). The 'kill' range envelope was expanded to 1.95–5.2 km (1.21–3.23 miles), and the launch altitude envelope to 2,500–16,500 m (8,200–54,130 ft.). The missile's g limit was doubled to 18 g, increasing the chances of a 'kill' against a target making evasive manoeuvres; terminal velocity was more than doubled, being 1,620 m/sec (5,832 km/h, or 3,622 mph). As with the K-5, the missiles could be fired singly, in pairs, or all together, with a couple of seconds in between.

In October 1957 the K-5M missile successfully passed check trials on the Mikoyan SM-7M interceptor, equipped with the RP-2-U Izumrood-2 radar—the prototype of the MiG-19PM. The proper conclusions were drawn in high places, and on 28 November the Council of Ministers issued a directive requiring OKB-51 to integrate the TsD-30 radar and K-5M missiles on the T-3 interceptor with the AL-7F-1 engine.

A further C of M directive that appeared on 16 April 1958, in effect, ordered the development of the T-3's production version,

formulating the requirements for the interceptor's definitive form. The aircraft was no longer regarded merely as a stand-alone interceptor—it was to be part of an integrated aerial-intercept weapons system comprising the aircraft proper and the *Vozdukh-1* (Air-1) ground-controlled intercept (GCI) system. The directive envisaged two versions of the interceptor; one was equipped with the TsD-30 radar and armed with four K-5M AAMs, while the other featured an *Oryol* (Eagle) radar and two K-8M AAMs. The weapons systems built around these two versions of the aircraft were designated T-3-51 and T-3-8M, respectively (the latter is described in chapter 3). OKB-51, the main organisation responsible for the development of both weapons systems, was also tasked with creating a combat-capable trainer version of the aircraft. All further work on the K-6V missile was terminated; the K-7L (and the K-7 missile programme in general) was similarly cancelled by a Council of Ministers directive on 4 June 1958.

The directive set a fairly tight development schedule—the aircraft were to be submitted for state acceptance trials in the third quarter of 1958. For the first time in Soviet practice, due to the high priority allocated to the programme, the OKB was required to submit no fewer than six flying prototypes instead of the usual two. (It may well be said now that this directive ultimately allowed the two weapons systems to be progressively put into production and fielded, the T-3-51 system first. In practice, however, test and development work on the two versions in 1958–60 proceeded in parallel.)

OKB-51 allocated the existing T-43 product code to the T-3-51 weapons system. In addition to the existing T-43 development aircraft (which now became the T43-1), a further five initial-production T-3s (PT-8s) were to be converted to the new standard. In order to speed up the process, it was decided to convert two of the aircraft in Moscow (at MMZ No. 51), while the others would be modified in situ at the Novosibirsk aircraft factory. The interceptors were to be equipped with Sukhoi KS-2 ejection seats; the new model, which had successfully completed manufacturer's tests in March 1958, featured more-effective arm restraints, allowing ejection to take place at indicated airspeeds up to 1,000 km/h (620 mph) instead of 850 km/h (528 mph) for the KS-1. Also, the aircraft were to be fitted with the ARL-S *Lazoor'* (Prussian Blue) data link receiver (*apparatoora rahdiolinii*: 'radio line equipment') working with the Vozdukh-1 GCI system.

Meanwhile, OKB-2 adapted the K-5M missile (*izdeliye* IS, service designation RS-2-U, NATO code name AA-1 Mod 1 or AA-1A Alkali Mod 1A) to the T-43; the resulting version was designated K-5MS, the *S* standing for Sukhoi. The 'Sukhoified' version was optimised for working with the TsD-30 radar instead of the RP-2-U. Also, the MiG-19PM had identical APU-4 launch rails (*aviatsionnoye pooskovoye oostroystvo*: aircraft-mounted launcher device) on all four pylons, whereas the Sukhoi interceptor had specially developed APU-19 inboard wing pylons, and APU-20 outboard wing pylons. The pylons were almost horizontal; the inboard pair was located in line with the main landing-gear fulcrums, and the outer pair halfway between these and the wingtips. Together with the TsD-30 radar and the launch control equipment the K-5MS missiles formed the K-51 (S-2-US) armament system; the '51' was again a hint at Sukhoi (OKB-51).

The two prototypes converted in Moscow received the designations T43-2 and T43-6, the three examples modified in Novosibirsk being designated T43-3 through T43-5. The **T43-2** had started life as the third production PT-8 (c/n 0115303), which was delivered to MMZ No. 51 in early February 1958. By the end of May that year, LII test pilot Vladimir N. Ilyin had made the first three flights of the manufacturer's test programme in this aircraft. The first Novosibirsk-built example, the **T43-3**, was converted almost concurrently from the fifth production PT-8 (c/n 0115305), LII test pilot Vladimir M. Pronyakin arriving from Moscow to perform this aircraft's maiden flight; factory test pilot T. T. Lysenko also made a familiarisation flight in the T43-3 in the course of predelivery tests. In June Pronyakin ferried the aircraft to Zhukovskiy. Concerned about the development schedule being maintained, the MAP top brass kept a close watch on the programme, harassing the OKB; between May and August 1958 alone the T-43 programme came under close scrutiny four times!

A major problem that had been plaguing the T-3 family was eliminated in the summer of 1958: the aerodynamicists at OKB-51 suggested installing auxiliary blow-in doors controlled by the ESUV-1 intake control system aft of the air intake to admit additional air and prevent engine surge. The feature was tested on the T43-1 and proved so effective that MAP immediately prescribed such blow-in doors to be added on the Su-7B fighter-bomber and the MiG-21F fighter, both of which had just entered production.

The **T43-6** joined the test programme in July 1958, followed by the **T43-4** and **T43-5** in August; thus all six aircraft envisaged by the C of M directive were available and flying at the end of the manufacturer's test programme. On 30 August 1958 Pyotr V. Dement'yev, chairman of the State Committee for Aviation Hardware (GKAT: *Gosudarstvennyy komitet po aviatsionnoy tekhnike*), wrote an official letter to the Soviet air force commander in chief Air Marshal Konstantin A. Vershinin, submitting the T-43 for state acceptance trials. (Note: In December 1957 MAP was 'demoted' to a state committee along with several other ministries due to changing government policies during the Khrushchov era. In 1965, however, their names and status were restored after Nikita S. Khruschchov had been unseated and replaced by Leonid I. Brezhnev as the Soviet leader in 1964.)

A state commission chaired by the PVO's deputy commander in chief Col.-Gen. Fyodor A. Agal'tsov was formed for conducting the state acceptance trials. However, these could not begin for another three months because the Sukhoi and Lyul'ka design bureaus were forced to eliminate the numerous defects unearthed in the course of the aircraft's formal acceptance for the trials.

Stage A of the T-3-51 weapons system's state acceptance trials began on 3 December 1958, continuing until May 1959; this was the so-called General Designer's stage; that is, the flights were performed by OKB personnel. Stage B, held jointly by the OKB and the air force, lasted from June 1959 to April 1960. The T-43 prototypes were flown by OKB-51 test pilots Vladimir S. Ilyushin, Anatoliy A. Koznov, Leonid G. Kobishchan, Yevgeniy S. Solov'yov, and N. M. Krylov, as well as GK NII VVS pilots Gheorghiy T. Beregovoy, Nikolay I. Korovushkin, Leonid N. Fadeyev, Boris M. Adrianov, Vladimir G. Plyushkin, and Stepan A. Mikoyan (the Mikoyan OKB founder's nephew).

Above: A military test pilot climbs into a Su-9 coded '01 Blue' during trials at GNIKI VVS.

Below: Su-9 '02 Blue' takes off for a test flight at GNIKI VVS with inert K-5M AAMs and PTB-600 drop tanks.

The trials proceeded with a fair share of problems due to the newness of the aircraft as a whole and the inevitable teething troubles of its systems, including the power plant and the air intake control system, which surfaced at this stage. The engine often surged when throttled back at speeds equivalent to Mach 1.8 and higher, or at speeds above Mach 1.5 at altitudes in excess of 15,000 m (49,210 ft.). To cure the problem, all six prototypes had the intake centre body travel increased from 21.5 to 23 cm (from $8^{15}/_{32}$ to 9 in.), and the ESUV-1 air intake control system installed in January 1959 after these measures had been tried successfully on the T43-1. No more cases of engine surge were recorded during the state acceptance trials.

At a conference held in February 1959 to check up on progress, V. P. Belodedenko, who was assigned to the T-43 programme as GK NII VVS's project engineer, said that *the* [T-3-51 weapons] *system is very good. We need it desperately. We believe in this*

Left: Head-on view of a Novosibirsk-built production Su-9 coded '78 Blue' with two drop tanks and four live RS-2-US missiles.

Right: Three-quarters front view of the same aircraft. The production-standard canopy had a reduced glazing area (compare this to the T43-1 on page 25).

Below right: This view shows the shape of the production Su-9's airbrakes. The chin-mounted aerials are for the instrument landing system (probe aerial) and the ARL-S Lazoor' data link (blade aerial).

Bottom right: Three-quarters rear view of the same aircraft, showing the transponder aerials below the rudder.

system, and we believe it holds great promise and can be brought up to operational level easily, but delays in this process can discredit everything.' Even before the T-43 entered the decisive phase of the state acceptance trials, the engine makers at OKB-165 promised to increase the AL-7F-1's maximum speed to 8,500 rpm (until then the engine had been incapable of doing more than 8,350 rpm) and install the upgraded engine on production aircraft from the third quarter of 1959 onward. Speaking at the same conference, test pilot Vladimir S. Ilyushin assured the air force representatives in attendance that in a few days the T43-2, equipped with auxiliary blow-in doors aft of the main air intake, would demonstrate stable engine operation when intercepting a simulated target at 20,000 m (65,620 ft.), with no tendency to flame out when four K-5MS AAMs were fired.

On 20 July 1959 the T43-6 crashed during a postmodification check flight from Chkalovskaya AB (a GK NII VVS facility east of Moscow), killing test pilot Leonid G. Kobishchan. When the pilot stopped responding to radio transmissions from the tower, a search-and-rescue operation was mounted. Presently the SAR team found a deep crater on the outskirts of Serkovo village 4 km (2.5 miles) northwest of the airbase; the aircraft had hit the ground in a near-vertical dive with tremendous force, burying itself deep in the soft soil. Extracting the wreckage proved impossible because the crater was in the middle of a quicksand and kept filling with water and liquid mud; only a few fragments were recovered. The cause of the crash was thus never ascertained; however, eyewitnesses reported that the aircraft had started disintegrating in mid-air. This may indicate that the pilot had passed out for some reason and the uncontrollable aircraft had entered a dive in full afterburner, accelerating past its never-exceed speed (V_{NE}). A monument was later erected to mark the T43-6's and Kobishchan's place of eternal rest.

To make up for the loss of the T43-6 the air force transferred another production PT-8 to the Sukhoi OKB; upon conversion this aircraft was redesignated **T43-11**, joining the state acceptance tri-

als programme in August 1959. Stage B was concerned mostly with determining the aerial-intercept weapons system's efficiency and performance. Since no high-altitude target drones were available, live missile launches were made at medium altitudes only—mostly against MiG-15M radio-controlled target drones (a.k.a. M-15, for *mishen'*: practice target or, in this case, target drone). The OKB wasted no time making the necessary changes to the aircraft when deficiencies were discovered. Thus the DC battery was placed in a pressurised, thermally stabilised container to ensure stable performance at high altitudes, and the radar display was provided with a rubber sunblind to facilitate sighting in bright sunlight.

To meet the air force's demand that the interception range be increased, a very early-production T-43 manufactured in 1959 (c/n 0415317) was modified by replacing the no. 1 fuselage fuel cell with an integral tank and incorporating additional integral tanks in the wings. As a result, total internal fuel capacity was increased from 3,060 to 3,780 litres (673.2–831.6 Imp gal.). Designated **T43-12**, the modified aircraft first flew in January 1960. Tests gave good results, and this modification was incorporated on late-production aircraft.

Earlier it was mentioned that the T-3 prototype was able to carry drop tanks; so was the T-43. Three versions of these tanks were tested during the trials—one model limited to subsonic speeds and two models capable of supersonic speeds. 'Supersonic' tanks designated PTB-600 (*podvesnoy toplivnyy bahk*: suspended, that is, external fuel tank), with a capacity of 600 litres (132 Imp gal.), were selected for production as a result.

The state acceptance trials, which included a total of 407 flights, were concluded on 9 April 1960 when the state commission signed the final protocol. The commission pointed out that virtually all of the performance targets stipulated by the Council of Ministers directive had been met. In particular, the aircraft was capable of destroying targets flying at speeds of 800–1,600 km/h (495–990 mph) and altitudes of 5,000–20,000 m (16,400–65,620 ft.), with a 'kill' probability of 70%–90%; the maximum

Su-9s in the final assembly shop of the Novosibirsk aircraft factory

radius of action (interception range) was 430 km (267 miles) instead of the specified 400 km (248 miles).

Su-9 Production Interceptor (T-43, *izdeliye* 27, *izdeliye* 34; *izdeliye* 10)

In the autumn of 1960 the T-43 successfully underwent evaluation at the PVO's Aircraft Test Centre in Krasnovodsk, Turkmenia, whereupon on 15 October 1960 the Council of Ministers issued a directive clearing the T-3-51 aerial-intercept weapons system for service entry. All of the system's components received new names in so doing. The T-43 interceptor armed with four K-5MS AAMs received the official (classified) service designation Su-9, the missile itself was redesignated RS-2-US, the TsD-30 radar became the RP-9U (NATO code name 'Spin Scan'), and the T-3-51 system as a whole was renamed Su-9-51.

Series production of the Su-9 was initially organised at the Novosibirsk aircraft factory no. 153 in accordance with a Council of Ministers directive issued back in September 1958 (that is, immediately after the completion of the PT-8 LRIP batch). Interestingly, initially the production Su-9 retained the product code of the original T-3 (*izdeliye* 27); in paperwork sent to the factory from the Sukhoi OKB, the aircraft was referred to as the T-43—or even as the T-3 (!).

In 1958 plant no. 153 built 40 T-3-series aircraft in various configurations, including the T-43; some of them were used for various test and development work. The first aircraft manufactured to full Su-9 standard—the so-called *etalon* ('standard measure'; that is, pattern aircraft)—was c/n 0215310. (According to some sources, the Su-9's batch numeration continued that of the PT-8, which was not normally the case at plant no. 153—usually the sequence was started anew when a fresh version entered production. The size of the batches grew from batch 3 onward, with as many as 100 aircraft per batch. On the actual aircraft the c/n was stencilled on the landing gear doors in an abbreviated four-digit format, the factory number being omitted and replaced with a hyphen—in this case, 02-10.)

In the autumn of 1958, factory test pilots T. T. Lysenko, Boris Z. Popkov, V. V. Proshchevayev, and others commenced predelivery tests of production Su-9s. Since the runway at Novosibirsk-

Yel'tsovka was more of a 'ruinway' (it was in extremely poor condition and in need of resurfacing), the fighters made a short hop to the nearby Tolmachovo AB (now Novosibirsk-Tolmachovo airport) on their first flight to undergo the rest of the predelivery tests there.

The factory test pilots' job was no easier than that of an OKB test pilot, and losses occurred too. Five accidents and incidents occurred in the course of predelivery tests in 1959. On two occasions the pilots (Vladislav A. Bogdanov and Yuriy N. Kharchenko) managed a safe landing at the airfield of origin after experiencing an engine failure. Factory test pilot Aleksandr D. Dvoryanchikov was less lucky; on 19 November 1959 he attempted a dead-stick landing after an engine failure but crashed, losing his life. That same year V. P. Krooglov, a test pilot of the air force's quality control and acceptance team at plant no. 153, attempted an emergency landing when the port main gear strut refused to extend. Another brand-new Su-9 was lost during predelivery tests in 1960, test pilot Vladimir T. Vylomov ejecting safely.

Su-9 production in Novosibirsk continued until 1962. Additionally, the interceptor was built in small numbers at MMZ No. 30 '***Znamya Trooda***' ('Banner of Labour'), a production factory located at the east end of Moscow-Khodynka airfield, next door to the Sukhoi OKB's premises. This plant received a full set of manufacturing documents and several shipsets of airframe/systems components from Novosibirsk in 1959, assembling the first two preproduction (batch 000) aircraft in midyear; full-scale production commenced in 1960, continuing until 1961. The Su-9's in-house product code at MMZ No. 30 was *izdeliye* 10. Moscow-built Su-9s had nine-digit c/ns, following the then-current system in use at the plant. For example, c/n 109000103 means *izdeliye* 10, year of production 1959, MMZ No. 30 (the first digit is omitted), batch 001, and 3rd (03) aircraft in the batch (usually with ten aircraft per batch). The c/n was stencilled on both sides of the fin at the root.

Between them the two production plants completed 1,058 Su-9s. The Novosibirsk factory built a total of 888 T-3 series aircraft in various guises in 1957–62, while Moscow production totalled 126 single-seaters and 50 Su-9U dual-control trainers (this version is described later in this chapter).

The production interceptor was publicly unveiled on 9 July 1961, when a formation of Su-9s took part in the traditional Aviation Day flypast at Moscow-Tushino. The aircraft were flown by instructor pilots from the PVO's 148th TsBP i PLS (*Tsentr boyevoy podgotovki i pereoochivaniya lyotnovo sostahva*: Combat Training & Aircrew Conversion Centre), located at Savasleyka AB near Gor'kiy (now renamed back to Nizhniy Novgorod). Immediately afterward the Western press published the first pictures of the Su-9, intelligence experts unerringly identified it as a Sukhoi aircraft, and the Su-9 received the NATO reporting name Fishpot-B.

In early 1961 LII held a full-scale test programme with the Su-9 to explore its spinning characteristics and evolve spin recovery procedures. The aircraft in question, a very early Novosibirsk-built machine (c/n 0415314), was owned by LII and coded '14 Blue' (in keeping with the institute's practice, the tactical code was derived from the last two digits of the c/n). The aircraft was flown by LII test pilots Sergey N. Anokhin (project test pilot) and Aleksandr A. Shcherbakov; the latter specialised in spin trials and had

Above: '75 Blue', an early-production Su-9 (note the nonfunctional gun blast plates), taxies out for a practice sortie without missiles.

Below and *bottom right*: '14 Blue' (c/n 0415314), a Su-9 used for spin tests at LII. Note the T-shaped photo calibration markings and the PPR-900 spin recovery rockets attached to the outer pair of wing pylons.

Bottom: The cockpit of the same aircraft with a test equipment oscillograph (upper centre) and spin recovery rocket controls.

Above: Despite wearing the same code '14 Blue' and being operated by LII, this is a different Su-9—a Moscow-built machine (c/n 101000914). Note the nonstandard position of the GCI data link aerial aft of the nose gear unit.

considerable expertise in this field. V. M. Zamyatin was the engineer in charge.

'14 Blue' was flown without missiles or drop tanks; instead, two PPR-900 rockets (*porokhovaya* **protivoshtopornaya** *raketa*: solid-fuel spin recovery rocket) able to fire both forward and rearward were mounted on the APU-20 outer wing pylons. Test equipment sensors and oscillographs were fitted to record the flight speed, altitude, g-loads, angle velocities, control inputs, engine rpm, and engine compressor pressure, as was a data link system transmitting the parameters to the tower in real time. The aircraft

wore T-shaped photo calibration markings on both sides of the nose and the rear fuselage.

Spins were initiated at 12,000 m (39,370 ft.) in both straight and level flight and in spiral turns at Mach 0.85 with growing g-loads; the all-up weight was 9,400–10,300 kg (20,720–22,710 lbs.) and the CG at 35%–36% MAC. The engine was found to be prone to surging at the moment of spin entry; therefore the pilots usually shut the engine down in advance to minimise the risk of damage, restarting it after spin recovery at indicated airspeeds not less than 500 km/h (310 mph). The aircraft would lose about 100 m (330 ft.) of altitude

Su-9 '14 Blue' (c/n 0415314), used for spin tests at LII

Above: The same aircraft with a differently styled tactical code and PPR-900 spin recovery rockets

Right and *far right*: A different Su-9 (c/n 0409) used by LII in a test programme, with a 'coordinate measurement device' on the port side of the engine nozzle.

per second in a spin, and between 2,500 and 3,500 m (8,200–11,480 ft.) of altitude between spin entry and recovery. Right-hand spins were found to be more intensive than left-hand spins. In some flights, aileron inputs were used to check their influence on spin recovery; in other cases the ailerons stayed neutral.

GK NII VVS pilots joined in the spin trials programme awhile later. On 30 March 1961, when air force test pilot Col. Leonid N. Fadeyev was flying Su-9 '14 Blue', the engine surged and flamed out, refusing to relight after spin recovery. Fadeyev attempted a forced landing on LII's unpaved runway (probably purpose-built for rough-field tests, since the LII airfield in Zhukovskiy had a concrete runway by then!), but the aircraft turned turtle after hitting a pothole during the landing run, the pilot sustaining serious spinal injuries.

According to the pilots' reports, the Su-9 could enter a spin only due to a grave piloting error—or if the spin was intentional. The spin itself was unstable, the aircraft falling like a maple leaf, with angles of attack around 45°–50° and yaw/roll rates up to 1.7 radian per second. Hence the number of turns from entry to recovery was disregarded; what mattered was the time from entry to recovery. If the angle of attack (AoA) remained beyond critical after initiation of spin recovery, the pilots recommended applying full opposite rudder while keeping the ailerons and stabilators neutral.

Later, in 1962, LII used a different Su-9 coded '14 Blue'—a Moscow-built aircraft (c/n 101000914)—in a different test programme, with the purpose of exploring the aircraft's handling when aileron inputs were made at transonic and supersonic speeds. Again, the aircraft was flown by LII test pilots Sergey N. Anokhin,

Su-9 '14 Blue' (c/n 101000914), operated by LII

Right: A sequence of stills from a documentary showing a Su-9 launching a live RS-2-US from the no. 1 (port inboard) pylon. Note the distinctive twin smoke trail left by the missile as it departs.

Below: A further still from the same movie, showing a second RS-2-US being fired from the no. 2 pylon. The missiles could be fired singly, in pairs, or in a ripple of four.

Aleksandr A. Shcherbakov, and Leonid D. Rybikov; Viktor V. Vasyanin was the engineer in charge.

The aircraft was flown either in 'clean' configuration or with PPR-900 rockets. Subsonic measurements were made at speeds of Mach 0.9–0.95 and altitudes of 10,000–14,000 m (32,810–45,930 ft.), and supersonic measurements were made at Mach 1.9–2.0 and 17,000–19,000 m (55,770–62,340 ft.), with the aircraft pulling –1 to +3 g in both cases. The pilots checked the influence of the momentary g-load on the aircraft's subsequent travel, the roll rate, and the vertical/lateral g-forces in a sideslip. The verdict was that there was little danger of departure from controlled flight due to the combination of vertical/lateral g-forces during such a manoeuvre; the risk occurred only if large aileron inputs were used while the aircraft was pulling negative g. Stability was restored immediately by setting the stick neutral.

Despite persistent efforts by the OKB and the manufacturing plants to improve reliability, incidents and accidents (including fatal ones) involving production Su-9s were all too frequent. According to the air force's attrition statistics, in 1961 alone there were 34 accidents of varying seriousness with the type, including 18 caused by design flaws and manufacturing defects. The mean time between accidents was 677 hours overall and 1,278 hours for those caused by manufacturing defects. By comparison, the Su-7 enjoyed a much-better safety record, with only five accidents in 1961 (albeit four out of five were again due to defective workmanship); the mean time between accidents was 1,561 and 1,952 hours, respectively. Perhaps the answer lies in the fact that the Su-9, as already mentioned, was built in Novosibirsk and Moscow, whereas the Su-7 and its derivatives were manufactured solely by aircraft factory no. 126 in Komsomol'sk-on-Amur in the Soviet Far East, where quality control was probably better.

By 1965 the situation had improved, since the Su-9's main bugs had been cured in the course of production; the mean time between accidents rose to a palatable 14,274 hours. Despite the fact that the most-critical design changes aimed at improving reliability were promptly introduced on the production lines, a few early-production aircraft did find their way to service units in as-was condition. As early as August 1961, however, they were either withdrawn from use or upgraded on site in accordance with OKB bulletins.

The OKB and the factories immediately started refining the interceptor. The principal changes introduced into the design of the Su-9 in the course of production are as follows:

• The first production Su-9s (up to and including c/n 0315310) had the aforementioned wing dogtooth and, in spite of the C of M directive dated 16 April 1958, were armed with only two K-5MS AAMs; the missile pylons were at the outboard locations (in line with the flap/aileron joints). However, tests had shown the dogtooth to be ineffective, and as early as c/n 0315311 onward the Su-9 reverted to a simple unbroken wing leading edge and the inboard pair of missile pylons was added where the dogtooth used to be.

• Four auxiliary blow-in doors arranged in vertical pairs were added on the sides of the nose a short way aft of the air intake leading edge; like the air intake shock cone, they were controlled by the ESUV-1 system. This feature was introduced on the Novosibirsk production line at an early stage (all Moscow-built aircraft

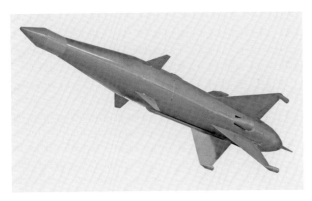

Above: A dummy RS-2-US AAM; note the cap over the radio proximity fuse, the wingtip tracers, and the aft-mounted guidance aerial.

Above right: An R-55 AAM, showing the reshaped wings, the IR seeker, and the windows of the optical proximity fuse

had it from the start); again, aircraft built previously were either updated accordingly or struck off charge.

• From c/n 0715302 onward the no. 1 bag-type fuel tank in the forward fuselage was replaced by an integral tank patterned on that of the T43-12 development aircraft, and extra integral fuel tanks were provided in the wing roots. As already mentioned, this increased internal fuel capacity from 3,060 to 3,780 litres (673.2 –831.6 Imp gal.). The Novosibirsk-built Su-9 with the integral no. 1 tank received a new product code, *izdeliye* 34.

• The cannon bays in the wings and the ammunition sleeves in the fuselage were retained as far as c/n 1015350, even though no cannons were fitted. Moreover, aircraft up to the middle of batch 2 even had the cannon barrel fairings; in the PVO unit at Tolmachovo AB, where such aircraft ended up, they were dubbed *kabahn* (wild boar) because the fairings resembled a boar's protruding teeth! From c/n 1015351 onward the unnecessary cannon bays were finally eliminated and the integral fuel tanks in the wings were reshaped; concurrently the sloping fuselage frames nos. 17–19, adjacent to this tank (which were originally intended to serve as guides for the cannons' ammunition belts), were replaced by ordinary ones set at right angles to the fuselage waterline.

• The gun blast plates ahead of the wing roots were deleted.

• All surviving Su-9s were retrofitted with SARPP-12 flight data recorders (*sistema avtomaticheskoy reghistrahtsii parahmetrov polyota*: automatic flight parameter recording system).

• The radar was modified to improve target tracking reliability.

• The PVD-5 pitot (*preeyomnik vozdooshnovo davleniya*) was replaced on the entire fleet, with the standardised PVD-18 ensuring more accurate altitude determination.

• An AP-28Zh-1B autopilot and red cockpit lighting were introduced.

• The AL-7F-1 engine was replaced by the improved AL-7F1-100, offering marginally higher thrust and a longer (100 hour) service life.

• The K-283 nonbraking nosewheel was replaced with a KT-51 brake-equipped wheel, and the KT-50U mainwheels by KT-89 mainwheels, all having identical dimensions to the earlier models.

• Late-production Su-9s were built with APU-19D launch rails on the inboard wing pylons, and APU-20D launch rails on the

outboard ones (the *D* stood for *dorabotannoye*: modified). The new models had a new OR-4 umbilical connector (*otryvnoy razyom*) for the missile, replacing the earlier OSh-56, and had an electric distribution box deleted.

• The KS-1 ejection seat was replaced first with the KS-2 and then, on the final batches, with the KS-2A. Later all surviving Su-9s were retrofitted with more-refined KS-3 ejection seats.

The interceptor's armament received much attention. Back in the mid-1950s it was deemed advisable that fighters should carry a mix of radar-guided and IR-homing AAMs for maximum efficiency, and for a while the military considered complementing the Su-9's RS-2-US beam-riding missiles with IR-homing short-range AAMs for close-in engagements. The then-new K-13 missile was contemplated at first; this weapon was tested both on Mikoyan fighters and on Sukhoi aircraft (see below). Eventually, however, operational Su-9s were up-armed with an IR-homing derivative of the RS-2-US. Originally known as the K-55, this missile was redesignated R-55 (AA-1B Alkali Mod 1B) in service; again, this will be discussed later. The R-55 necessitated the use of new APU-68UM launch rails and a modified radar designated RP-9UK that was compatible with the new missile.

In 1966–67, two production Su-9s underwent a two-stage trials programme with a view to using the Su-9 as a strike aircraft armed

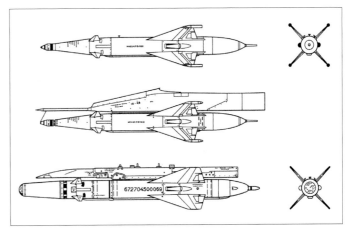

Top and *centre*: The RS-2-US separately and on an APU-20 pylon
Bottom: The R-55 on an APU-68UM launch rail

Sukhoi OKB test pilot Anatoliy A. Koznov

Sukhoi OKB test pilot Vladimir S. Ilyushin

Sukhoi OKB test pilot Yevgeniy S. Solov'yov

GK NII VVS test pilot Stepan A. Mikoyan

GK NII VVS test pilot Nikolay I. Korovushkin

GK NII VVS test pilot Gheorgiy T. Beregovoy. He went on to become an astronaut.

Sukhoi OKB test pilot Leonid G. Kobishchan. He was killed on 20 July 1959 in the crash of the T43-6.

Sukhoi OKB test pilot Eduard V. Yelian

LII test pilot Aleksandr A. Shcherbakov, who performed spin tests on the Su-9

with bombs (!); at that time the general view was that all fighters had to be strike capable—just in case. The ordnance load recommended for service in strike configuration comprised a combination of two 250 kg (550 lb.) FAB-250 high-explosive bombs (*foogahsnaya aviabomba*) and two RS-2US AAMs.

As already mentioned, the cannons had been eliminated from the T-3 when AAMs were integrated; however, Vietnam War experience showed that omitting the cannons was a bad idea after all. Hence the UPK-23-250 pod (*oonifitseerovannyy pushechnyy konteyner*: standardised gun pod), containing a 23 mm (.90 calibre) Gryazev/Shipunov GSh-23 twin-barrel cannon with 250 rounds, was tested on the Su-9 in the late 1960s and early 1970s. The pod was carried on one of the fuselage hardpoints; no drop tanks were carried in this case because it was impossible to carry a 'lopsided' combination of one drop tank and one cannon pod. The trials programme performed by GK NII VVS test pilots Stal' A. Lavrent'yev, Valeriy V. Migunov, and Vladimir K. Ryabiy included gunnery attacks against paradropped targets, Lavochkin La-17 target drones, and ground targets. Yet, even though the cannon pod was undoubtedly an asset for close-range air combat, the impossibility to carry drop tanks impaired range unacceptably, and the UPK-23-250 did not gain wide use on the Su-9.

In 1963, two Su-9s were involved in an effort to explore the possibility of operating the type from unpaved tactical strips. Building on the results of this test programme, IA PVO units received appropriate recommendations concerning such operations.

Above: LII technicians inspect the air intake of a Su-9 equipped with a DUA-3 pitch sensor on the side of the nose, a nonstandard feature.

Below: A fine picture of a production Su-9 in colour. The wing pylons have black antiglare strips, and the spikes are painted red for conspicuity to prevent injuries to ground personnel.

Above: A Su-9 (T-43) armed with four K-55 prototype AAMs at GNIKI VVS during state acceptance trials. The missiles have nose-mounted probe aerials (probably for data link) and no optical proximity fuse windows. Note the partially open airbrakes.
Right: IA PVO Commander Air Marshal Yevgeniy Ya. Savitskiy, who was the motive power behind the introduction of the Su-9
Below: A Su-9 fitted experimentally with an ATG-2 ram air turbine instead of the brake parachute

Until the late 1960s, when the Soviet air force started taking delivery of the new MiG-25P interceptor, the Su-9 was the Soviet Union's fastest and highest-flying combat aircraft.

***

From the start of the Su-9's series production, a number of aircraft were used in assorted research and development programmes held by MAP, the air force, and other agencies. Refining the T-3-51 weapons system alone involved about 20 T-43 development aircraft. Other aircraft were used as 'dogships' for verifying structural changes, systems and avionics test beds, weapons test beds, and control-configured vehicles (CCVs). Some of these are listed below.

T43-3, T43-4, and T43-8 Development Aircraft

Upon completion of the T-3-51 weapons system's state acceptance trials, the T43-3, T43-4, and T43-8 served as weapons test beds for IR-homing air-to-air missiles. in 1958, when the Soviet defence

industry began its effort to reverse engineer the Naval Weapons Center (NWC) AIM-9B Sidewinder short-range AAM as the K-13 (see next page), someone suggested fitting the IR seeker developed for the K-13 to the existing K-5M missile instead of the radio command guidance system. Designated K-55 (*izdeliye* TsM-6), the missile was developed by OKB-455, headed by Nikolay T. Pikot—the design office of GKAT's production plant no. 455 in Kaliningrad (Moscow Region), manufacturing the RS-1-U and RS-2-U, not by Pavel D. Grooshin's OKB-2. (Note: The *town* of Kaliningrad, immediately northeast of Moscow, was later renamed Korolyov to honour Sergey P. Korolyov, the famous Soviet space rocket designer. It should not be confused with the *city* of Kaliningrad, in Russia's westernmost region, which still bears the name.)

The task of turning the Alkali into a 'fire and forget' weapon was not so simple after all. Far from being a straightforward adaptation of the RS-2-U, the K-55 ended up as a separate design, despite sharing the same tail-first/midengine layout; in fact, the only thing the two missiles had in common was the PRD-45 rocket motor. The IR seeker occupying the K-55's nose (section 1) was rather bulky; hence a new HE/fragmentation warhead was developed for the K-55 by the Moscow-based GSKB-47 (*Gosudarstvennoye soyooznoye konstrooktorskoye byuro*: State All-Union Design Bureau; the 'All-Union' bit means the establishment had national importance). The warhead was divided into two modules located fore and aft of the rocket motor; a special mechanism located in a ventral fairing ensured simultaneous detonation. Despite the 25% lower warhead weight as compared to the RS-2-US, the new missile was much more lethal because the fragments spread out in all directions. Apart from the warhead's forward module, section 2 of the missile's body carried the rudders with electropneumatic actuators and housed the fuse—originally the *Lastochka* (Swallow) radio proximity fuse; section 4, which was longer than that of the

RS-2-US, housed the rear module of the warhead and the safety/detonator mechanism, which initiated self-destruction 32–38 seconds after launch if no hit had been scored. The wings were similar to those of the RS-2-US but had a trapezoidal planform, shorter span, and greater area.

The project was completed in 1960; in the same year the control system and the warhead were tested on ground rigs. The first prototype missiles were test-fired in 1961, using a modified MiG-19; they were built in TsM-6P configuration with no seeker head, the *P* standing for *programmnaya* ('programmed'—that is, controlled by a programmed autopilot). Also in 1961, a homing version of the K-55 was tested on the Sukhoi T43-5, converted into a weapons test bed. The missile featured an IGS-59 seeker (*infrakrasnaya golovka samonavedeniya*: infrared seeker head) developed by NII-10. This was originally intended for the K-13 AAM but had lost out to the competing TGS-13 (*teplovaya golovka samonavedeniya*: 'thermal seeker head'), developed by MOP's TsKB-589; now the IGS-59 got a second chance. Between 4 February and 25 March 1961 the T43-3 launched an instrumented test round in this configuration and a further six TsM-6P 'headless' rounds.

Also, the T43-4 was used (apparently at a different date) to test a so-called preemptive starting system that precluded engine flameout caused by missile exhaust gas ingestion when missiles were fired.

T43-7 and T43-10 Development Aircraft

In 1960–61 the T43-7 and T43-10 development aircraft served as avionics test beds for the AP-28Zh-1 electric autopilot. The latter aircraft, manufactured in 1960, was eventually damaged beyond repair in an accident, so a further aircraft (an unidentified produc-

tion Su-9) was fitted with the autopilot in order to continue the trials. Like the preemptive starting system mentioned above, the autopilot later became a standard fit on production Su-9s.

T43-5 and T43-12 Weapons Test Beds

In accordance with an air force requirement, the Sukhoi OKB modified two initial production Su-9s—the aforementioned T43-5 and T43-12 (no code, c/n 0415317)—as weapons test beds for the aforementioned K-13 IR-homing short-range AAM. This was a Soviet derivative of the AIM-9B Sidewinder, a largely intact example of which had been captured during the Second Taiwan Strait Crisis and supplied to the Soviet Union for study after the missile had scored a direct hit on a Chinese fighter without exploding, lodging in its fuselage and being retrieved. The AIM-9B was reverse engineered by OKB-134 (now called GMKB *Vympel*, *Gosudarstvennoye mashinostroitel'noye konstrooktorskoye byuro*: 'Pennant' State Machinery Design Bureau, named after Ivan I. Toropov), except for the rocket motor and the IR seeker,

Top and *above*: The uncoded T43-12 development aircraft— the first Su-9 to have an integral no. 1 fuel tank—was fitted with a large teardrop-shaped pod low on the starboard side of the nose, apparently housing a camera for recording missile launches. Note the '43-12' tail titles and the red-painted inert RS-2-US missiles.

The T43-12 development aircraft

which were indigenous. (There were no US originals to copy these from—the Sidewinder's rocket motor was spent and the seeker was destroyed by the impact.) The K-13 entered production and service in 1960 as the R-3S (*izdeliye* 310); the *S* stood for *sereey-naya*: production, used attributively. The missile had a launch weight of 75.3 kg (166 lbs.) and a 'kill' range of 1–3.6 km (0.62–2.23 miles). Its NATO code name was AA-2 Atoll.

For testing the K-13, in early 1961 the T43-5 and T43-12 had their wingtips cropped in line with the ailerons' outer ends to permit installation of tip-mounted APU-13 launch rails for K-13 AAMs. (A while earlier the T43-12 had a large, teardrop-shaped camera pod offset to starboard fitted under the nose to record missile launches.) The new arrangement was not introduced on production aircraft, since it was deemed easier to develop an IR-homing derivative of the K-5MS (RS-2-US) missile—the K-55.

Top and *above*: The T43-15 prototype with a full load of external stores—four K-5MS missiles and two 600-litre (132 Imp gal.) drop tanks. Note the two cine cameras under the nose to record missile launches.

The T43-15 development aircraft

In 1962 the T43-5 and T43-12 began a new round of trials with the objective of further testing the K-55 AAM. Three versions of the missile were used—the K-55TG and K-55SV instrumented test rounds (for verifying the IR seeker and the fuse, respectively) and the K-55TS live version. Nine launches against flare bombs and target drones were made that year. As a result, the IGS-59 IR seeker was revised to feature a cooling system, while the original Lastochka radio proximity fuse was replaced first by the *Ogonyok* (Little light, or Little flame) radio proximity fuse and then by the NOV-55 **Roza** (Rose) optical proximity fuse (*nekontaktnyy opticheskiy vzryvahtel'*: 'nonimpact optical fuse for the K-55'), developed by TsKB-589. The NOV-55 was a passive fuse featuring a row of 'viewing ports' for two independent optical channels working at different angles to the missile's axis; it was triggered by the heat emitted by the target within a certain radius.

The definitive version of the missile had a body diameter of 200 mm (7⅞ in.), an overall length of 2.76 m (9 ft., 0⅝ in.), a wingspan of 0.53 m (1 ft., 8⁵⁵⁄₆₄ in.) and a launch weight of 91.1 kg (200.8 lbs.), the warhead weight being variously reported as 8.6 kg (18.96 lbs.), 9.1 kg (20.06 lbs.), or even 12 kg (26.46 lbs.). The IR seeker head allowed the missile to be used against targets flying at 200–22,000 m (660–72,180 ft.); maximum 'kill' range was 1.2–2.8 km (0.75–1.74 miles), depending on the target's size and heat signature. The heavier missile necessitated the use of new APU-68UM launch rails.

Manufacturer's tests of the missile continued throughout 1963 on the T43-12 alone and were successfully concluded in May 1964, the aircraft shooting down IL-28M and MiG-15M target drones with K-55 missiles. Next, the missile was submitted for state acceptance trials. The latter began in the second quarter of 1965 in keeping with ruling no. 228 issued by of the Council of Ministers Presidium's Commission on Defence Industry Matters (VPK: *Voyenno-promyshlennaya komissiya*), a policymaking organ, on 9 September 1964. Due to development problems with the missile and to periods when the fighters were grounded for heavy maintenance, the trials dragged on for a long time, finally being completed in 1967. Eventually, on 21 January 1969, the missile was officially included into the Soviet air force inventory as the R-55 (*izdeliye* 67), and the IGS-59 seeker was redesignated S-59. As already mentioned, the R-55 was used on the Su-9 along with the RS-2-US.

T43-2 and T43-15 Avionics Test Beds

In 1960–61 the T43-2 and T43-15 served as test beds for the modified TsD-30TP fire control radar. This version did not enter production, and operational Su-9s were still equipped with the standard TsD-30. The uncoded T43-15 (sometimes reported as Novosibirsk-built Su-9 c/n 1115310 but actually Moscow-built Su-9 c/n 109000103) had two camera pods mounted side by side under the nose for recording missile test launches.

T43-17 Avionics Test Bed

Another aircraft bearing the in-house designation T43-17 was used to test a new avionics suite subsequently fitted to the Su-11 interceptor. No details are known.

Su-9 Cockpit Lighting Test Bed

In 1961 a Moscow-built Su-9 built in 1960 (c/n 100000308) was used for testing a new red cockpit lighting system making the aircraft less observable to enemy aircraft at night.

Su-9 Development Aircraft with Ram-Air Turbines

In 1963–64, two Su-9s were fitted experimentally with an ATG-2 ram-air turbine (*avareeynyy toorbogenerahtor*: emergency turbine-driven generator or RAT), providing electric power in an emergency. The RAT was located ventrally in the former brake parachute bay, and the parachute was relocated to a Su-7BKL-style fairing with clamshell doors at the base of the rudder. This feature was not incorporated on production aircraft.

Su-9 Automatic Flight Control System Test Bed

Acting on instructions from GKAT, in 1961 OKB-51 converted a Moscow-built Su-9 (c/n 100000603) into a test bed for the *Polyot-1* (Flight-1) automatic navigation/approach/instrument landing system developed for new advanced fighters. The aircraft was equipped with the SAU-1I automatic flight control system (*sistema avtomaticheskovo oopravleniya*). LII and GK NII VVS pilots tested the system in various flight modes, including automatic landing approach and low-level flight, until 1964 (some sources say 1968).

Su-9 Target Simulation Aircraft

During the trials of the Su-15T, a single Su-9 was used to determine the efficiency of the new interceptor's *Taifoon* (Typhoon)

Left and *far left*: The T43-1 coded '22 Red' was used for establishing four world records as the T-431.

Below left: Wearing a pressure suit and pressure helmet, Vladimir S. Ilyushin is depicted in the cockpit of the T-431 before a record-breaking flight.

Bottom left: Ilyushin closes the canopy of the T-431 prior to engine starting.

Below: The T-431 begins its takeoff run.

fire control radar. To this end an angle reflector was installed on the rear fuselage to increase the aircraft's radar cross section (RCS) for the purpose of emulating a larger aircraft.

T-431 Record-Breaking Aircraft

At a very early stage it became apparent that the future Su-9's high performance made an attempt on the existing speed and altitude records possible—the estimated sustained service ceiling and maximum speed were 20,000 m (65,620 ft.) and Mach 2.1, respectively. In the spring of 1958 the Lockheed F-104A Starfighter had established a string of world speed, altitude, and time-to-height records at Edwards AFB (Palmdale, California)—on 7 May, USAF pilot Maj. Howard C. 'Scrappy' Johnson reached 27,811 m (91,243 ft.) in a preproduction YF-104A serialled 55-2957, while on 16 May, Capt. Walt Wayne Irwin set three records in YF-104A 55-2969, climbing to 3,000 m (9,842 ft.) in 41.8 seconds, climbing to 25,000 m (82,021 ft.) in 4 minutes, 26.03 seconds, and clocking a speed of 2,259.538 km/h (1,404.012 mph) over a 15 km / 25 km (9.3/15.5 mile) straight course. The records were officially recognised by the International Aeronautics Federation (FAI: Fédération Aéronautique Internationale).

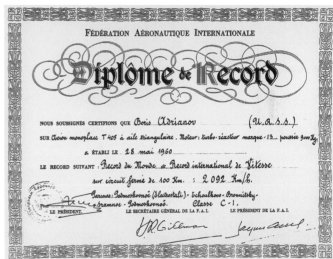

The FAI diplomas for the world records set (*left to right, top to bottom*) by Anatoliy Koznov on 25 September 1962, Vladimir Ilyushin on 14 July 1959, Vladimir Ilyushin on 4 September 1962 (all in the T-431), and Boris Adrianov on 28 May 1960 in the T-405

The Sukhoi OKB decided to have a go at beating these records, and the T43-1 prototype (by then coded '22 Red') was assigned to the mission. Vladimir S. Ilyushin was the project test pilot, with M. I. Zooyev as engineer in charge of the record-setting programme. Ilyushin began practicing in the autumn of 1958 to see how high the aircraft could go in a zoom climb, but the practice sessions were cut short when the cockpit canopy shattered at 24,000 m (78,740 ft.) on one of the flights; the pressure suit and pressure helmet saved the pilot's life. Investigation of the incident showed that the canopy transparency had had vents drilled in it when the T43-1 was used in a dynamic-strength-test programme. Subsequently the vents had been filled up, but still they compromised the canopy's integrity, acting as stress concentrators which eventually caused the canopy to crack and explode.

When the canopy had been replaced, the training flights resumed. Finally, on 14 July 1959 Ilyushin established an absolute world altitude record, reaching 28,852 m (94,658 ft.) in a zoom climb; this record was later recognised by the FAI. Now, to have the records officially registered, the aircraft type and engine type had to be duly entered in the documents submitted to the FAI. Using the true designations was out of the question because they were classified; hence the Soviet Union entered the aircraft under a fictitious designation, T-431 (which was very close to the truth). The engine was enigmatically referred to as 'type 31'—which was also perfectly true, since the AL-7F-1's product code at the manufacturing plant (not OKB-165) was *izdeliye* 31.

Further record attempts had to be put on hold because of the need to test and refine the TsD-30 radar. The programme resumed in 1962, by which time the T43-1 had undergone major changes. A more powerful AL-7F-2 engine was installed, some equipment items (notably in the weapons control system) were removed to save weight, and most of the cooling-air scoops on the rear fuselage were likewise deleted to cut drag. On 4 September that year, Vladimir S. Ilyushin attained 21,170 m (69,455 ft.) in sustained level flight over a 15 km / 25 km straight course. A third world record followed on 25 September, when OKB test pilot Anatoliy A. Koznov averaged 2,337 km/h (1,451.5 mph) in level flight over a 500 km (310.5 mile) closed circuit.

Above: Su-9 '61 Blue' (c/n 100000610) was converted into the 100L aerodynamics research aircraft for testing possible wing designs for the T-4 missile strike aircraft. This is the first configuration (designated 100L1) with delta wings of increased area.

Above right and *right*: The same aircraft as the 100L2 with double-delta wings. The starboard wing has wool tufts and a painted grid for airflow visualisation, which is filmed by a faired cine camera aft of the cockpit. Note the L-shaped back-up pitot on the nose.

Far right: The same aircraft in even later configuration as the 100L-2M, with mildly ogival wings
Below: The aircraft's evolution (*left to right*) from standard Su-9 to 100L1 to 100L2 to 100L2M

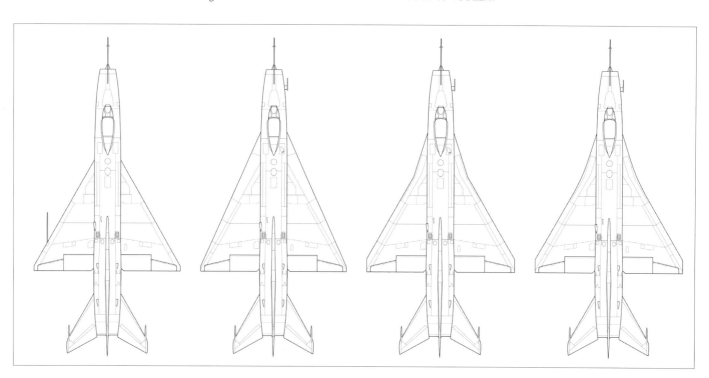

T-405 Record-Breaking Aircraft

A further Su-9—this time a production aircraft (c/n 0415305)—was modified in 1960 for the purpose of setting new world records. On 28 May 1960, GK NII VVS test pilot Boris M. Adrianov established a world speed record on a 100 km (62 mile) closed circuit, attaining 2,092 km/h (1,299.3 mph). The official documents submitted to the FAI referred to the aircraft by the fictitious designation T-405, derived from the construction number, while the engine was euphemistically called 'type 13'.

'100L' Aerodynamics Research Aircraft ('100L1' through '100L8')

In 1966–67 a Moscow-built Su-9 coded '61 Blue' (c/n 100000610) was extensively modified for aerodynamics research as part of the programme to create the T-4 Mach 3 strategic missile strike aircraft. Since the latter had the product code *izdeliye* 100, the research aircraft was designated '100L', the letter standing for [*letayushchaya*] *laboratoriya*: literally, 'flying laboratory'. (In Russian the term *letayushchaya laboratoriya* is used indiscriminately to denote any kind of flying test bed or research/survey aircraft.)

The '100L' was intended for exploring the aerodynamics of low-aspect-ratio wings with a thin, sharply swept leading edge over a wide range of AoAs and at speeds ranging from Mach 0.3 to Mach 2.0. It was, in effect, a subscale demonstrator helping the designers to choose the optimum planform for the T-4's wings. The thin wings, with a sharp leading edge selected for one of the T-4's project versions, were to combine a high lift/drag ratio in supersonic cruise with acceptable field performance.

The conversion involved rewinging the Su-9—well, not exactly rewinging: the greater part of the structure remained unchanged. The leading-edge portion of each wing ahead of the main spar was replaced with a new one featuring greater chord and a sharper airfoil; as a result, leading-edge sweep was increased from 60° to 65° and wing area increased accordingly. In so doing, the straight backup pitot on the port wing was replaced with an L-shaped pitot on the starboard side of the nose.

This was not the only change. The '100L' had nearly 1,000 kg (2,200 lbs.) of ballast installed in the forward fuselage to shift the CG forward; hence the nose landing-gear unit had to be reinforced by fitting a larger, stronger nosewheel. The wing tanks were ren-

dered inoperative and converted into test equipment bays, reducing the fuel supply by more than 600 litres (132 Imp gal.); more test equipment was housed in the avionics bays fore and aft of the cockpit. To visualise the airflow over the modified wings, the aircraft was equipped with a smoke generator, the smoke exiting via perforations in the wing leading edge; a cine camera on the starboard side recorded the pattern. The modifications increased the aircraft's empty weight by 1,300 kg (2,865 lbs.) and the maximum takeoff weight by 750 kg (1,650 lbs.) as compared to a stock Su-9.

The '100L' first flew in July 1966, the research programme continuing until 1972; LII test pilot Eduard I. Knyaginichev did most of the flying. The aircraft had eight different configurations, each with a sequence number as a suffix to the designation—from '100L1' (the one with 65° wing sweep) to '100L8'. The '100L2' reverted to 60° wing sweep but had small leading-edge root extensions and switched from a smoke generator to wool tufts for airflow visualisation, while the '100L2M' had mildly ogival wings. Three versions with a sharp wing leading edge and one with a rounded leading edge were tested, as were modified tailplanes with a sharp leading edge. Tests revealed that top speed remained unchanged, but the landing speed was reduced by a sizeable 40 km/h (25 mph).

Left and *above left*: Su-9 '93 Blue' in standard configuration prior to being modified as the L.02-10 CCV

Below left: A model of the L.02-10 in one of TsAGI's wind tunnels.
Below: The L.02-10 in the course of conversion; note that the air intake shock cone has been removed to facilitate access.

Right and *below right*: The L.02-10 in early configuration with two all-movable 'foretails' and a standard fin

A second Su-9 (c/n 1301; the full c/n was probably 1315301) was also converted into a similar research aircraft likewise designated '100L'. The test results gave a wealth of valuable data that allowed the OKB to select the most efficient wing design (double-delta wings) for the T-4.

Later, when development of the T-4 had been completed, the '100L' aerodynamics research aircraft found further use in the development of the Su-27 Flanker fourth-generation fighter. Flight tests of the first prototype Su-27 in the original T-10 Flanker-A configuration quickly revealed unacceptably intense vibration at AoAs in excess of 8°. Prior wind tunnel tests had given no hint of this problem; a new and more precise method of predicting vibration levels was needed. To this end the Sukhoi OKB teamed up with LII and the Siberian Aviation Research Institute, named after Sergey A. Chaplygin (SibNIA: *Sibeerskiy naoochno-issledovatel'skiy institoot aviahtsiï*), in Novosibirsk to hold a joint research programme, measuring pressure distribution over the wings. This was done both in SibNIA's T-203 wind tunnel, using scale models of the T-10, and in actual flight on the '100L' test bed rigged with pressure sensors. The results obtained on the 100L corroborated the results of the wind tunnel tests.

L.02-10 CCV

Between 1968 and 1975, LII undertook a massive test and development effort with a Su-9 coded '93 Blue' (c/n 1215393), which had been converted to a control-configured vehicle. Canard foreplanes are a familiar thing, but have you ever heard of a canard *foretail*? Well, Su-9 c/n 1215393 featured two all-movable vertical control surfaces installed above and below the fuselage, ahead of the cockpit. The upper 'foretail' sitting on top of the avionics bay cover was of cropped-delta planform, while the lower one was trapezoidal, considerably shorter and with broader chord; both 'foretails' were provided with antiflutter weights. A special word—*dekil'* (literally 'de-fin')—was coined for these surfaces by analogy with canard foreplanes, which are called *destabili-zahtor* (destabiliser) in Russian. Before the actual conversion was

undertaken, a metal model was built and tested in one of TsAGI's wind tunnels. Originally the aircraft flew with both 'foretails' in place, but the upper 'foretail' was found to impair cockpit visibility unacceptably and was soon removed, although the axle remained, protruding like a primitive gunsight on a World War I fighter. Shortly after the beginning of the tests, the dielectric fin cap was replaced by a cylindrical metal fairing housing a forward-looking cine camera filming the upper 'foretail'.

Originally '93 Blue' was used to investigate the flight dynamics and stability of a directionally unstable aircraft and test an automatic directional stability augmentation system. Between 1975 and 1978 the aircraft underwent more modifications performed jointly by LII and OKB-51, receiving a direct side-force control (DSFC) system and the designation L.02-10 (the *L* stood for [*letayushchaya*] *laboratoriya*). In this guise the aircraft was tested at Zhukovskiy between 1979 and 1984. This designation is rather misleading because it appears to suggest that '93 Blue' was involved in the Su-27's development, fitting nicely into the 'L. xx-10' designation pattern of other test beds used in the pro-

Left: The L.02-10 sits on a rain-drenched hardstand at Zhukovskiy, showing the differently sized 'fore-tails' ahead of the cockpit equipped with antiflutter weights.

Below left: Here the aircraft is shown taxiing for takeoff.

Below: A rare view of the L.02-10 CCV in flight with both 'foretails'.

Right: The L.02-10 in later guise; the upper 'foretail' has been removed, its axle protruding ahead of the cockpit. Note the faired forward-looking camera at the top of the fin, and the non-standard rod aerial for the radio aft of the cockpit, replacing the usual fin cap antenna.

The L.02-10 hangared for maintenance or modifications at LII. The winged emblem on the nose is based on the badge of the Komsomol (Young Communist League), the letters reading KME (*Komso**mol's**ko-molo**dyozh**nyy eki**pazh***: Young Communist League crew).

Su-9 '93 Blue' (c/n 1215393) prior to modifications

The same aircraft as the L.02-10 in early form with two 'foretails'

The L.02-10 in late configuration

The L.02-10 uses its airbrakes to keep formation with the slow camera ship. The two 'foretails' are barely visible in this head-on view.

gramme (the '-10' refers to the in-house designation T-10). Compare L.01-10 (a fly-by-wire control system test bed based on a Su-7U *Moujik* trainer), L.03-10 (a Tu-16LL engine test bed fitted with the Su-27's Lyul'ka AL-31F afterburning turbofan), L.05-10 (a flight/navigation suite test bed based on a Su-24 Fencer-A 'swing-wing' tactical bomber), etc. Also, a wind tunnel model built for exploring the T-10's spin characteristics in TsAGI's specialised T-105 vertical wind tunnel featured a similar *dekil'* mounted dorsally aft of the cockpit. However, this was in the mid-1970s, and nothing of the sort was present in any of the actual T-10 project configurations. (One source, however, states the test dates of the L.02-10 as 1966–69 and says the results were used in the development of the Su-27.)

U-43 Combat Trainer Prototypes

The aforementioned C of M directive of 16 April 1958 concerning the T-3-51 weapons system also ordered the development of a two-seat combat-capable conversion trainer variant of the T-3. That year, however, OKB-51 was physically unable to commence work on the trainer, being much too busy getting the single-seater up to scratch. Hence on 18 March 1959 the Council of Ministers issued another directive, this time dealing specifically with a trainer version of the T-3 [*sic*]. The use of the T-3 designation in this document is rather surprising, since the T-43 interceptor was already undergoing state acceptance trials at the time.

At OKB-51 the aircraft was known as the U-43 (U = *oochebnyy* [*samolyot*]: trainer), implying that it was a trainer derivative of the T-43. To accommodate a second cockpit for the instructor pilot, a 600 mm (1 ft., 11⅝ in.) 'plug' was inserted aft of the existing cockpit to avoid encroaching on the fuselage fuel tanks; thus the fuel capacity of the single-seat and two-seat versions was identical. As is usually the case, the trainee sat in the front cockpit, with the instructor behind him. The tandem cockpits were enclosed by a common canopy having individual aft-hinged portions with a glazed intercanopy frame in between; the trainee's canopy section was rather longer than the instructor's and was provided with a

blind flying hood. The fixed windshield was longer and wider than the single-seater's, featuring an ordinary glass windscreen instead of a bulletproof one; the hinged portions were actuated pneumatically. The canopy terminated in a parabolic metal fairing; there was no fuselage spine running from this to the base of the fin to house piping runs and wiring bundles for the aircraft's systems, as would be the case on the later Su-7U (U-22) trainer of 1964.

Both cockpits had full controls and instrumentation; the instructor was able to override the trainee's actions in case of need. The U-43 retained the single-seater's avionics suite, including the radar and the ARL-S Lazoor' GCI data link receiver; radar displays were installed in both cockpits. The ordnance load, however, was reduced to two RS-2-US AAMs, to which the air force agreed; thus the APU-19 inboard wing pylons were deleted, leaving only the outer pair of APU-20 pylons. In flight the crew members communicated by means of an SPU-2 intercom (*samolyotnoye peregovornoye oostroystvo*). The structural changes increased the empty weight by 630 kg (1,390 lbs.).

Detail design of the U-43 was completed in the spring of 1960. One of the OKB's development aircraft, a Moscow-built Su-9 known as the T43-14, was selected for conversion into the trainer prototype, the conversion job continuing until late September 1960. The prototype featured slightly reduced internal fuel capacity (3,430 litres / 7554.6 Imp gal.) because the wing roots were occupied by test equipment.

On 23 November, after a series of vibration tests to determine the airframe's resonance frequencies, the uncoded U-43 was delivered to Zhukovskiy; K. N. Strekalov was appointed engineer in charge of the flight test programme. Beastly weather delayed the maiden flight by two months, with only taxiing trials and high-speed runs being possible in the meantime. On 25 January 1961 the trainer finally took to the air, with OKB-51 test pilot Yevgeniy K. Kukushev at the controls. The manufacturer's flight tests proceeded rapidly, poor visibility from the instructor's cockpit being the only major deficiency noted in the course of the five-month programme.

In early May the U-43 was officially submitted for state acceptance trials; however, on 14 July an engine failure occurred when the aircraft was due to be ferried to Vladimirovka AB, and the prototype was grounded for an engine change, which delayed the beginning of the trials by another six weeks. It was not until 1 September that GK NII VVS test pilots Viktor M. Andreyev and Igor' I. Lesnikov started flying the *sparka*. (This slang appellation for a trainer is derived from *sparennoye opravleniye*—dual controls—and translates loosely as 'Two Sticks'.) B. M. Korshunov was assigned to the U-43 as engineer in charge of the trials, with Ye. N. Boobnov as his assistant.

The trials programme was completed on 23 December, involving a total of 83 flights. With two K-5M (RS-2-US) AAMs, the trainer's acceleration parameters and service ceiling were almost identical to those of the single-seat Su-9, armed with four missiles. At 12,800 m (42,000 ft.) the trainer attained its V_{NE} of 2,230 km/h (1,385 mph) or Mach 2.1 in full afterburner. At an all-up weight of 9,700 kg (21,380 lbs.) with missiles and drop tanks, the service ceiling in level flight was 17,500 m (57,415 ft.); range with full external stores at 11,000 m (36,090 ft.) was 1,370 km

Top: The U-43 (or possibly U43-1)—the prototype of the Su-9U trainer—with two RS-2-US missiles and two drop tanks. Note the vertical canopy frame member on the trainee's canopy section, a characteristic feature of the prototype, and the wider windscreen.

Above: This side view illustrates the trainer's longer forward fuselage and wheelbase.

Right: Three-quarters rear view of the U-43 (U43-1) prototype

The first prototype Su-9U (U43-1)

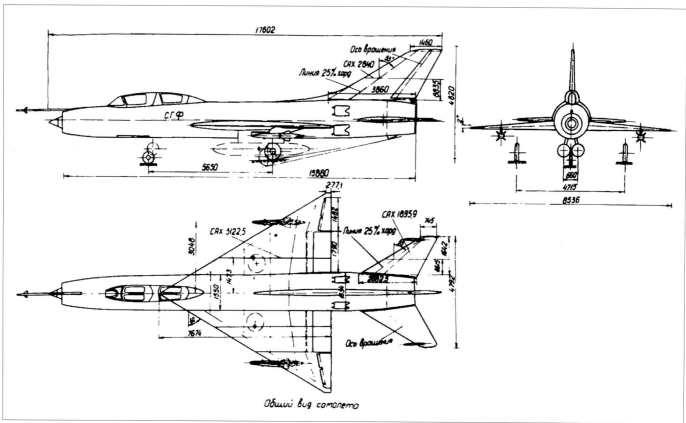

Presumably the second prototype (U43-2)

(850 miles). The aircraft possessed all-weather, day/night capability, making it possible to perform conversion training and train pilots in intercepting targets flying at speeds of 800–1,600 km/h (495–990 mph) and altitudes up to 20,000 m (65,620 ft.); the interception range determined by available fuel was 105–130 km (65–80 miles).

The state acceptance trials protocol said that the two-seater met all of the customer's requirements, except for the inadequate visibility from the rear cockpit. The state commission recommended the U-43 for production and service, providing that this and a few other shortcomings were eliminated. Hence the prototype was flown back to Moscow for modification work, which continued until February 1962. The headrest of the trainee's ejection seat was cropped at the sides, and the glazing area of the forward canopy section was increased for better visibility; in the rear cockpit, a section of the instrument panel was moved to the right, and the

glass pane separating the two cockpits was widened. On 23 March, Yevgeniy K. Kukushev reflew the upgraded prototype; a brief check test programme at GK NII VVS followed between 11 and 26 April, and the field of view was deemed satisfactory.

(Note: Some sources claim that *two* trainer prototypes were built and that the changes described above were incorporated on the second prototype designated **U43-2**, whereas the first aircraft [**U43-1**] remained unmodified. There are reasons to believe them—see L-43 ejection-seat test bed, *below*.)

Su-9U Combat Trainer (*izdeliye* 11)

Back in 1961, having received a set of manufacturing documents from the Sukhoi OKB, MMZ No. 30 at Moscow-Khodynka began low-rate initial production of the U-43 trainer. The aircraft received the service designation Su-9U (*oochebnyy*); the factory product code was *izdeliye* 11 because it followed the single-seater version,

Above left: The same aircraft with red-painted inert AAMs

Left: A three-view drawing of the Su-9U from the ADP documents

Right: This totally unmarked aircraft may be the second prototype (U43-2).

Below: Probably the same aircraft with insignia applied. Note the revised forward canopy adopted for the production version.

Below left: Su-9U '49 Red' was used by GK NII VVS in Akhtoobinsk for trials involving missile launches.

Left and *far left*: Red-painted inert RS-2-US missiles on Su-9U '49 Red'. The protective cap, which is connected to the pylon by a cable and whisked away at the moment of launch, encloses the proximity fuse and the generator driven by a ram-air turbine.

Unlike the single-seater, the Su-9U featured the AP-28Zh-1 autopilot, a D-3K-110 three-channel (pitch/roll/yaw) damper and red cockpit lighting from the outset. Production Su-9Us had longer range than the prototype thanks to the functional wing tanks. Late-production aircraft were powered by an AL-7F-1-100U engine.

Su-9U – LII development aircraft

A late-production Su-9U coded '18 Blue' (c/n 112001118) was used by LII and GK NII VVS to test the canopy jettison system in keeping with the GK NII VVS Director's order No.0606 dated 21st July 1962 and an appropriate GKAT decision. The aircraft was flown by LII test pilot Aleksandr A. Shcherbakov and GK NII VVS test pilot Col. Viktor M. Andreyev, the engineers in charge being Yu. A. Nagayev (LII), Maj. A. I. Pavlenko (GK NII VVS) and V. A. Skvortsov (MMZ No.30). Photo calibration markings were applied to the cockpit area, the rear fuselage and the fin.

The objective was to check the canopies for safe separation in the most unfavourable conditions, check the possibility of flying the aircraft with the canopy gone (for example, in the event of unintentional jettisoning) and measure the loads applied to the front canopy with a revised fixed windshield. The tests included jettisoning the front canopy at 3,240 m (10,630 ft) and 450 km/h (279 mph) IAS and jettisoning the rear canopy at 2,900 m (9,510 ft) and 700 km/h (435 mph) IAS. In both cases the departing canopy cleared the vertical tail safely.

which, as the reader remembers, was coded *izdeliye* 10 at MMZ No. 30. The trainer received the NATO reporting name 'Maiden' in the 'M-for-miscellaneous' category, as was normal practice for conversion trainer variants of fighters at the time.

The Su-9U was built in Moscow only, and for reasons unknown production was terminated in 1962 after a mere 50 examples had been completed, which was definitely not enough. The c/ns followed the same nine-digit system as on Moscow-built Su-9s; for example, the highest known c/n 112001301 means *izdeliye* 11, year of manufacture 1962, MMZ No. 30, batch 013, 1st (01) aircraft in the batch. Knowing the overall number built, it appears that most batches were extremely small (literally one or two aircraft each!), but batch 11 had at least 18 aircraft for some reason.

A while later the same Su-9U was used by LII and GK NII VVS in a joint test programme to explore its high-alpha and spinning characteristics. This was necessary because the trainer's weight and inertia forces were substantially different due to the longer fuselage and the two wing hardpoints instead of four. The

This uncoded Su-9 has a cigar-shaped fairing enclosing equipment of some sort (possibly a cine camera) instead of the starboard wing pylon. Note also the absence of the GCI command link aerial under the nose.

aircraft was flown by Aleksandr A. Shcherbakov and GK NII VVS test pilot Gheorgiy T. Beregovoy; this time the engineers in charge were V. M. Zamyatin (LII) and V. P. Toolyakov (GK NII VVS). In the course of the tests the Su-9U flew both in 'clean' configuration and with external stores (drop tanks and RS-2-US AAMs or PPR-900 spin recovery rockets); the rockets and the test equipment recorders were controlled from the front cockpit.

Between 19th December 1962 and 8th April 1963 '18 Blue' made 21 test flights from Zhukovskiy, performing 41 spins. The all-up weight was 9,500-11,250 kg (20,940-24,800 lb) and the CG position at 29-31% MAC. The programme included normal and inverted spins initiated at subsonic (200-470 km/h; 124-292 mph IAS) and supersonic speeds (Mach 1.2) at altitudes of 12,000-22,000 m (39,370-72,180 ft). When recovery was initiated, the rotation ceased at 16,000-9,000 m (52,490-29,530 ft) and the lowest altitude of recovery to straight and level flight was 6,000 m (19,685 ft). Engine behaviour during the spin was not studied because the engine was invariably shut down prior to spin entry.

Apart from exploring the trainer's behaviour in subsonic and supersonic spins and evolving recommendations on recovery techniques, the objective was to study the effect of the D-3K-110 damper's operation on the spin and the extent to which piloting errors complicated spin recovery. Left-hand and right-hand spins were performed; inverted spins were initiated by pushing the stick forward and applying a bootful of rudder in inverted flight. Again, because of the aircraft's peculiar handling in a spin is was the time to recovery that mattered, not the number of turns; as a rule, recovery was possible within 25-35 seconds. Normal spins with external stores (missiles only, drop tanks only, or both) were performed in the closing part of the programme. In 'clean' configuration and

Su-9U '18 Blue' (c/n 112001118) was used by LII in several test programmes. The photos on this page show the aircraft in stock configuration with red-painted inert missiles and drop tanks.

with missiles only (TOW 10,390 kg/22,910 lb) the following restrictions applied: speed 1,200 km/h (745 mph) IAS or Mach 2.1, load factor +7/–3.5 Gs. During deceleration to below 400 km/h (248 mph) IAS the Su-9U was adequately stable, but the presence of drop tanks reduced the available stabilator travel for pitch trim.

Aleksandr Shcherbakov wrote in his report that *'the aircraft glides stably when flown "clean" [...] at 400 km/h or less; only when the speed decays to below 220 km/h [136 mph] IAS it slowly drops*

a wing or drops the nose, pancaking and rocking from side to side at an increasing rate. In a spiral turn the aircraft is stable. When the vertical G limit is reached it reluctantly stops the turn and rolls out in the opposite direction, resuming a normal glide after a small forward stick input. External stores have no noticeable effect on the handling during deceleration in straight and level flight or in a spiral turn. [...] The Su-9U's low-speed longitudinal stability is broadly similar to that of the combat version' (single-seater – Auth.).

Left: Here, Su-9U '18 Blue' is equipped with PPR-900 spin recovery rockets.

Below left: The same aircraft a short while later, with photo calibration markings added.

Bottom left: The front cockpit of '18 Blue' with a control panel for the spin recovery rockets (1) and circuit breakers for the test equipment recorders (2).

Bottom, far left: Close-up of the port PPR-900 spin recovery rocket showing the twin nozzles allowing the rocket to fire in either direction as selected by the pilot.

Right: This sequence filmed from a chase plane shows '18 Blue' jettisoning the front canopy at 3,240 m and 450 km/h IAS. The canopy passes well clear of the tail.

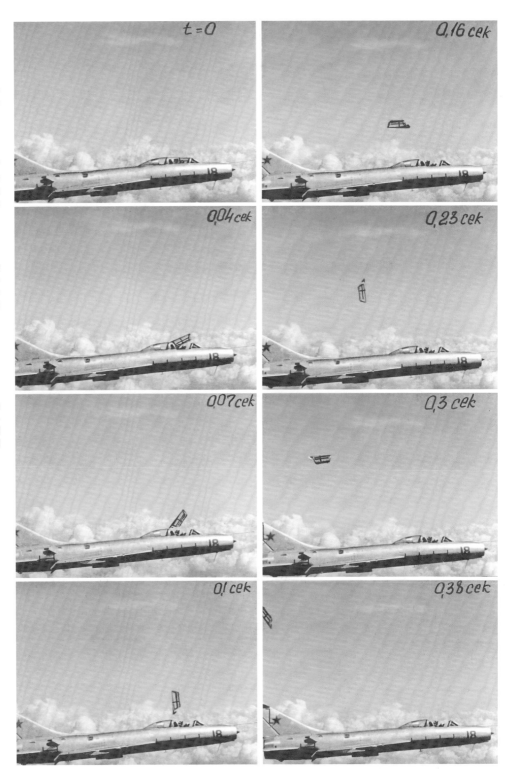

Shcherbakov noted that at 12,000-14,000 m (39,370-45,930 ft) the Su-9U was reluctant to enter a left-hand spin at 220 km/h IAS, falling like a leaf. At 270 km/h (167 mph) IAS the aircraft did spin but the spin was unstable, with spontaneous changes of direction; a stable left spin was impossible. Right-hand spins could be both stable and unstable; at high speed and with the ailerons deflected 'the wrong way' (against the spin) the spin was vigorous, with AoAs up to 40°. Even in a stable right spin the autorotation was easily stopped by setting the controls neutral. Aileron inputs against the spin made it more stable, while aileron inputs in the direction of the spin had no noticeable effect. At high altitude (20,000-22,000 m; 65,620-72,180 ft) and 350 km/h (217 mph) IAS the spin was unstable and very steep, the aircraft pulling negative G from time to time; as Shcherbakov put it, *'the aircraft seems to be alternating between a normal spin and an inverted spin'*. As the aircraft descended it accelerated, transitioning to a dive at

400 km/h IAS and rocking the wings vigorously, losing more than 6,000 m (19,685 ft) of altitude during recovery; similar behaviour had been seen on the single-seat Su-9.

At Mach 1.2 and 470 km/h (292 mph) IAS the Su-9U performed a left-hand spin much more stably than at subsonic speeds. It was particularly willing to enter an inverted spin; this was more stable than a normal one and it was harder to determine the aircraft's attitude. Left-hand and right-hand inverted spins were rather different; also, in an inverted spin the aircraft was pulling negative G all the time, which complicated flying. On the other hand, recovery from such a spin with a −60° attitude and −1.5 Gs was relatively easy and the pilot sensed the moment of recovery clearly. It was harder with a −45-50° attitude and −2-3 Gs because recovery was delayed.

Shcherbakov also noted that at low speeds the rudder was much more effective than the ailerons. In these conditions even small rudder inputs caused the aircraft to roll in the same direction; if the speed was below 300 km/h (186 mph) IAS there was not enough aileron authority to counter the roll, with potential loss of control as a result.

L-43 ejection seat testbed (Su-9U-LL, U43L-1, U43L-2; *izdeliye* 94)

Upon completion of the state acceptance trials the U-43 prototype – according to some sources, the first prototype (U43-1) retaining the initial design of the forward canopy section – was converted into an ejection seat testbed for verifying new ejection seats devel-

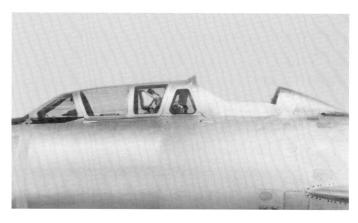

Above: The U43-1 after conversion as the L-43 ejection-seat test bed with a modified canopy. The intercanopy frame features a fixed deflector to reduce turbulence in the open rear cockpit. Note the old design of the forward canopy with a characteristic vertical frame member.

Below: The L-43 wearing photo calibration markings on the fuselage and tail but no tactical code yet. Note the cigar-shaped fairings replacing the wing pylons; these house high-speed cine cameras to capture the ejection sequence.

Right: A K-15 ejection seat with a dummy is fired from the still-uncoded L-43 test bed at 180 km/h (111 mph) IAS.

oped by the Sukhoi OKB. The modified aircraft received the designation L-43 (*izdeliye* 94), the L denoting [*letayushchaya*] *laboratoriya*. The tests confirmed that the latest seats in the KS series permitted safe ejection at speeds up to Mach 1.8 and altitudes between 150 and 15,000 m (490-49,210 ft). The aircraft was anonymous at first but was later coded '10 Blue'.

According to some sources, in 1962 the first two production Su-9Us (c/ns 1110000101 and 111000102?) were converted for testing new ejection seats and high-altitude pilot gear, the modified rear cockpits permitting installation of seats developed by various manufacturers; these testbeds have been referred to as the **U43L-1** and **U43L-2**. One aircraft was delivered to LII, operating from Zhukovskiy, while the other belonged to GK NII VVS and was home-based at Vladimirovka AB.

The conversion involved installing a pressure bulkhead aft of the front cockpit, making sure that the latter remained pressurised and the pilot was able to fly the aircraft in comfort. The flight controls, engine instruments, and pressurisation/air conditioning system components were deleted from the rear cockpit; the barest minimum of flight instruments and the oxygen equipment were retained to enable ejections with live testers. The rear canopy could be fitted for ferry flights but was removed for test flights and replaced by a special open-top fairing. A detachable duralumin plate was mounted on the cockpit's rear bulkhead, with fittings for installing different seats with different ejection guns; seats weighing up to 250 kg (551 lb) and creating G loads up to 20 Gs could be used. The rear cockpit was lined with steel sheet to protect the fuselage structure from the flames of the ejection seat. The testbed was equipped with three high-speed cine cameras to

developed by OKB-918, now called NPP Zvezda (*naoochno-proizvodstvennoye predpriyatiye* – 'Star' Scientific & Production Enterprise). The first round of tests revealed that with the original powder charge delivering an impulse of 540-560 kg/sec (1,190-1,234 lb/sec), ejection at true airspeeds in excess of 1,000 km/h (621 mph) subjected the ejectee to vertical loads of 25 Gs, which could cause injuries. Also, in then-current form the seats and their ejection guns would require major changes to the fuselage and cockpits of the Yakovlev Yak-28 *Brewer* tactical bomber for which they were intended, and the tests were suspended. To reduce the G load, the OKB and NII-6 (an establishment of the former Ministry of Agricultural Machinery specialising in ordnance development) designed a lower-powered powder charge for the ejection gun delivering an impulse of 420-450 kg/sec (925-992 lb/sec). New versions of the K-15 and K-17 seats featuring this charge and a revised parachute system were put through their paces with instrumented test dummies on the Su-9U testbed. The K-15 seat was fired on 19th December 1963 at 1,010 km/h (627 mph) IAS and Mach 0.96 at an altitude of 2,130 m (6,990 ft); the vertical G load was reduced to 21 Gs. The K-17 seat was fired on 3rd January 1964 at 1,150 km/h (714 mph) IAS and Mach 1.9 at an altitude of 12,000 m (39,370 ft). In this case the vertical G load was still an unacceptable 24-25 Gs. As a result, measures aimed at improving the seats further were suggested.

Confusingly, there are reports that in 1967-75 LII used 'Su-9U c/n 1018' (*sic*) as an ejection seat testbed for state acceptance trials of the KS-1, KM-1 (*[katapool'tnoye] kreslo Mikoyana* – Mikoyan [ejection] seat) and KYa-1 (*[katapool'tnoye] kreslo Yakovleva* – Yakovlev [ejection] seat), as well as the Czechoslovak VS-1BRI seat developed for the Aero L-39 Albatros advanced trainer (VS = *vystřelovačí sedačka* – ejection seat) and the later VS-2 model.

Maximum indicated airspeed was 1,230 km/h (764 mph) with the rear canopy in place or 1,165 km/h (723 mph) with the rear cockpit open; the service ceiling at Mach 1.825 with a 9,000-kg (19,840-lb) all-up weight was 20,650 m (67,750 ft). Ejections were performed during high-speed taxi runs, at high altitude and at supersonic speeds. Initially test dummies were used, of course, but these were later joined by live testers. Later the Su-9U ejection seat testbeds were used for testing the Zvezda K-36 zero-zero ejection seat which became standard on all Soviet/Russian combat aircraft developed from the late 1970s onwards.

Su-9U control system testbed

In 1962-64 LII used a modified Su-9U (identity unknown) to test an automatic stability augmentation system.

L.07-10 aerodynamics research aircraft

In 1975-76 the Sukhoi OKB extensively modified a Su-9U (c/n 112001301) as part of the Su-27 (T-10) fighter's development effort. Known in-house as the L.07-10 (that is, 'flying laboratory' No.7 under the T-10 programme), this aircraft served for exploring the T-10's wing aerodynamics; it featured ogival wings with a sharp leading edge having compound curvature.

The L.07-10 entered flight tests at Zhukovskiy in 1977. Tragically, it crashed on 18th August 1982 after suffering a birdstrike

capture the ejection sequence – two in fairings on the wings and one in the cockpit. Performance and handling were almost identical to those of the standard trainer.

In keeping with GKAT order No.145 dated 13th April 1963, in May-October 1963 LII's L-43 (referred to in the document as the Su-9U-LL for *letayushchaya laboratoriya*) was used for testing the K-15 and K-17 ejection seats. These were presumably

Opposite page: Here the L-43 is seen wearing the code '10 Blue'. A Zvezda K-36 seat is fired from the rear cockpit, its distinctive telescopic stabilising booms tipped with drogue parachutes deploying as soon as the seat exits the aircraft.

Right: The L-43 flies a test mission with '64 Red', a MiG-21U prototype, flying chase.

on take-off which knocked out the engine. Simce the aircraft was too low for an attempted return to Zhukovskiy or even a safe ejection, LII test pilot Yuriy V. Nikulin (incidentally, a complete namesake of a famous Soviet circus clown and movie actor) attempted an off-field forced landing. Unfortunately the aircraft hit a hot water pipeline which wiped out the cockpit, killing the pilot instantly.

***

To conclude this chapter the authors would like to give some data on the production of T-3 series aircraft at plant No.153 in

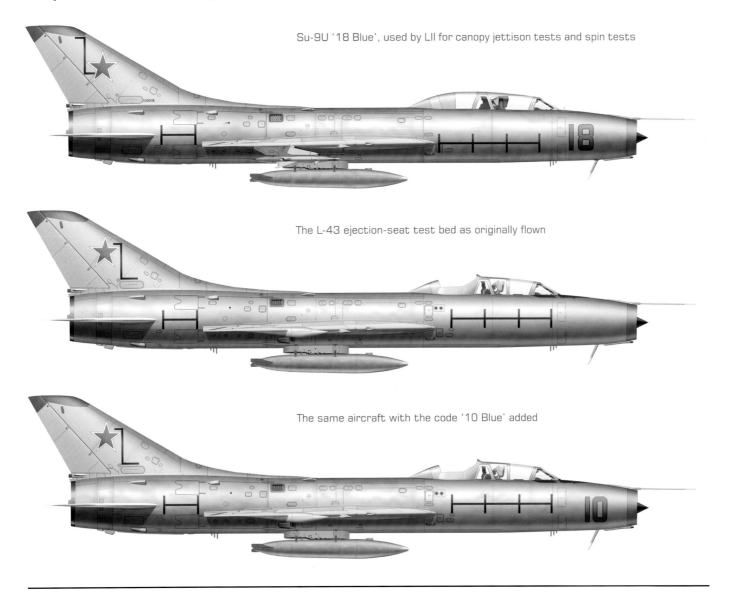

Su-9U '18 Blue', used by LII for canopy jettison tests and spin tests

The L-43 ejection-seat test bed as originally flown

The same aircraft with the code '10 Blue' added

Above: Another view of the L-43 firing a K-36 ejection seat, as seen from a chase plane

Below: Here a test ejection from the L-43 is filmed from the ground via a cine theodolite (hence the crosshairs).

Bottom and *bottom right*: The L.07-10 test bed at the scene of its fatal crash near Zhukovskiy on 18 August 1982.

Novosibirsk. (Interestingly, the T-3 designation persisted for a long time, appearing in the manufacturing documents long after the pure T-3 had vanished.) It should be noted that in the case of this aircraft family the phrase 'production aircraft' need not always be taken literally because, even though some machines were built by the series production factory, to all intents and purposes they were prototypes. (Indeed, at the initial stage of production almost all 'production' aircraft were in fact prototypes of some sort!) Also, remember that the OKB and the factory sometimes used different in-house codes for the same aircraft.

As already mentioned, the full construction numbers included the factory number placed between the batch number and the number of the aircraft within the batch (for example, 0315304); however, on the actual aircraft the c/n was stencilled all over the place in abbreviated form and with a hyphen (03-04). Furthermore, the factory had a confusing habit of putting the letter T (for *treugol'noye krylo* – delta wings) before the batch number in internal paperwork and omitting the zero in batches 01 through 09. Thus, 'T1-07' does not mean the seventh prototype T-1 (no such aircraft existed) but denotes T-3 c/n 0115307. Similarly, 'T10-51' is Su-11 c/n 1015351, not a Su-27 (T-10S) development aircraft – the in-house designations of Su-27s used for test and development work by the OKB stopped at T10-42.

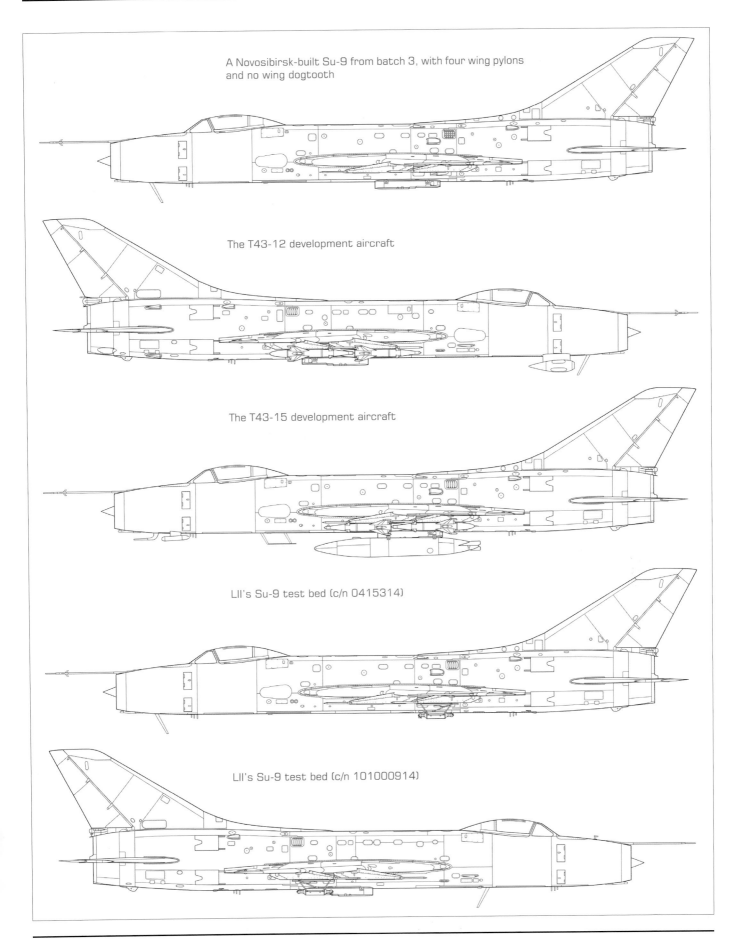

A Novosibirsk-built Su-9 from batch 3, with four wing pylons
and no wing dogtooth

The T43-12 development aircraft

The T43-15 development aircraft

LII's Su-9 test bed (c/n 0415314)

LII's Su-9 test bed (c/n 101000914)

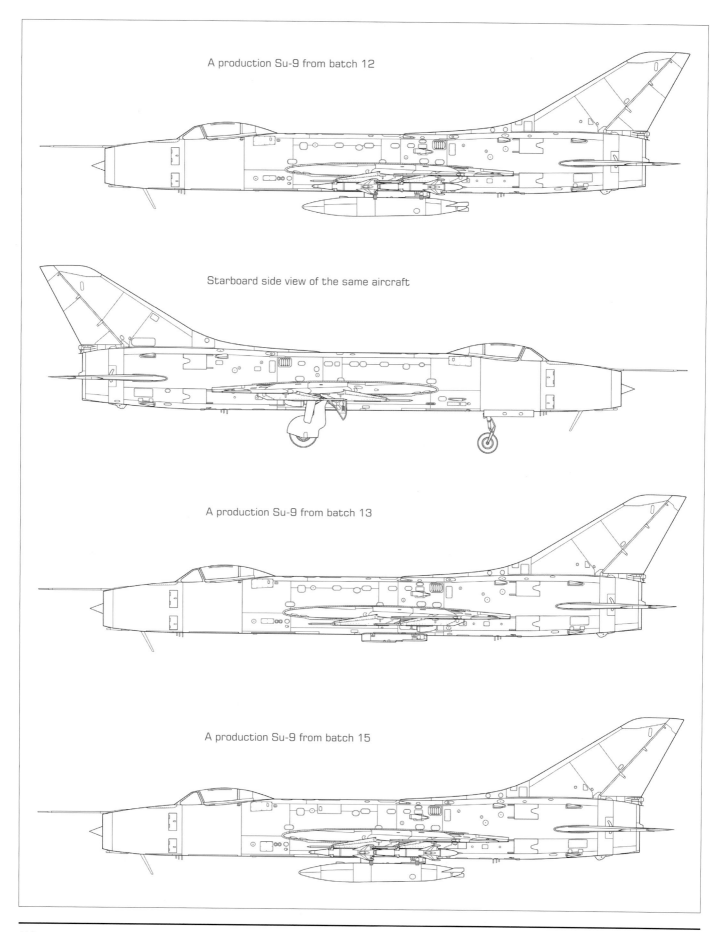

A production Su-9 from batch 12

Starboard side view of the same aircraft

A production Su-9 from batch 13

A production Su-9 from batch 15

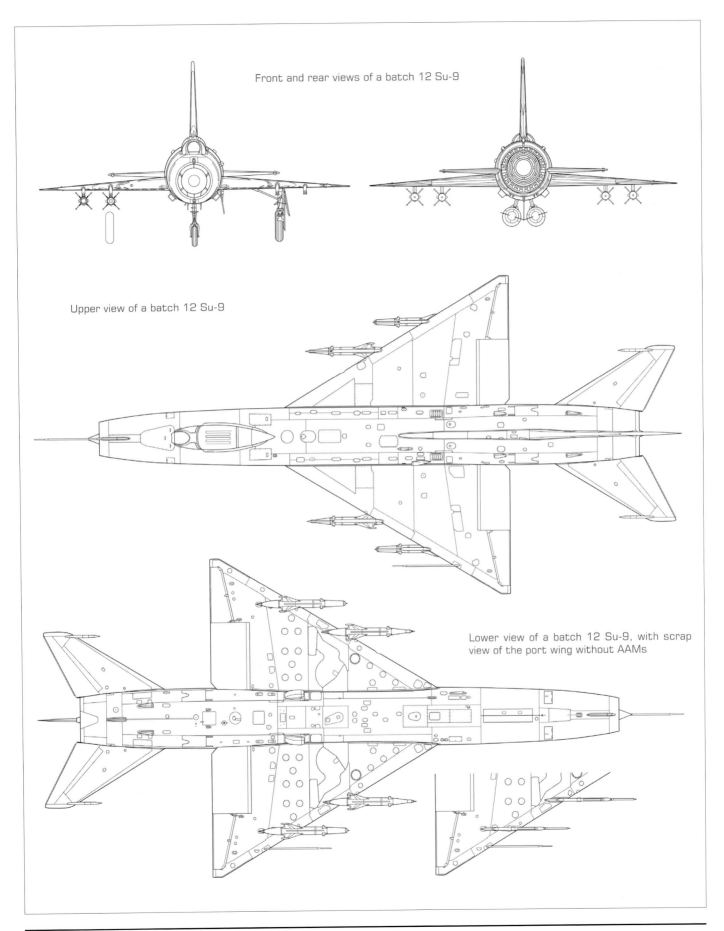

Front and rear views of a batch 12 Su-9

Upper view of a batch 12 Su-9

Lower view of a batch 12 Su-9, with scrap view of the port wing without AAMs

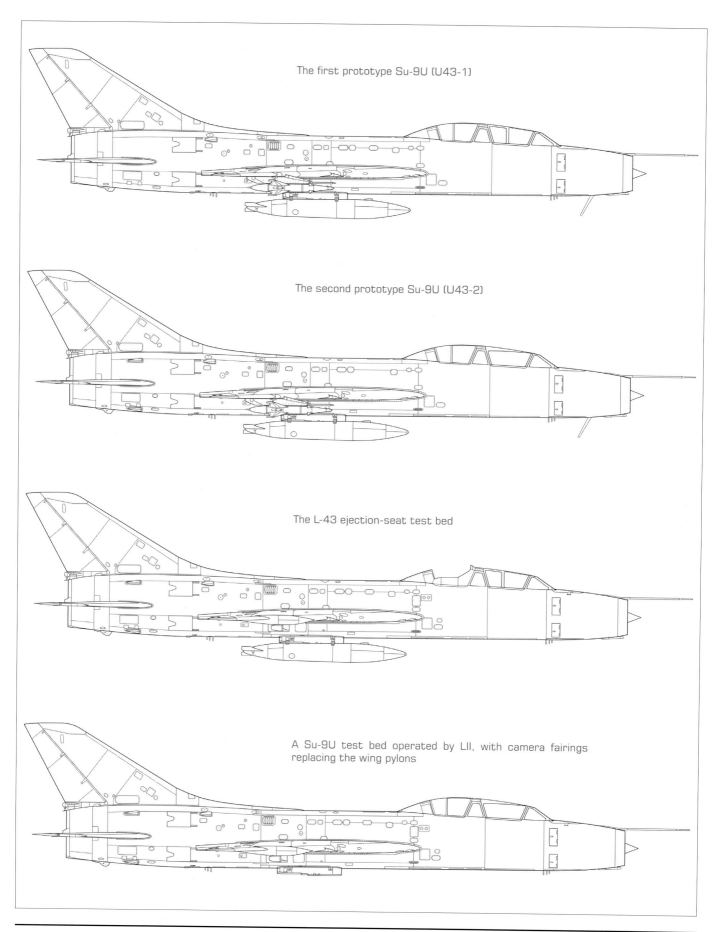

The first prototype Su-9U (U43-1)

The second prototype Su-9U (U43-2)

The L-43 ejection-seat test bed

A Su-9U test bed operated by LII, with camera fairings replacing the wing pylons

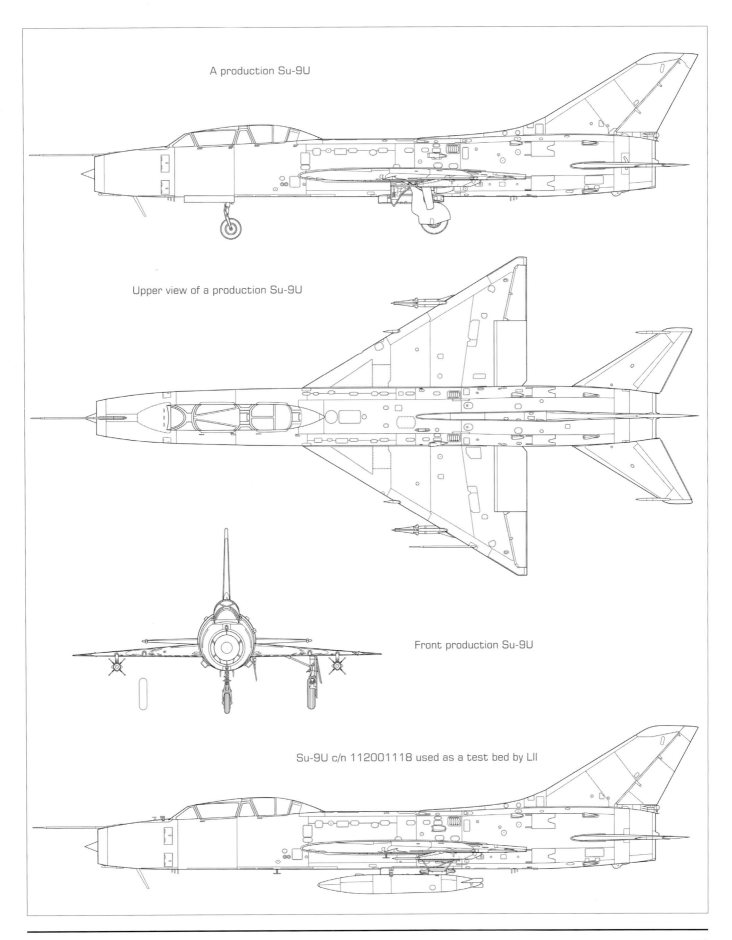

A production Su-9U

Upper view of a production Su-9U

Front production Su-9U

Su-9U c/n 112001118 used as a test bed by LII

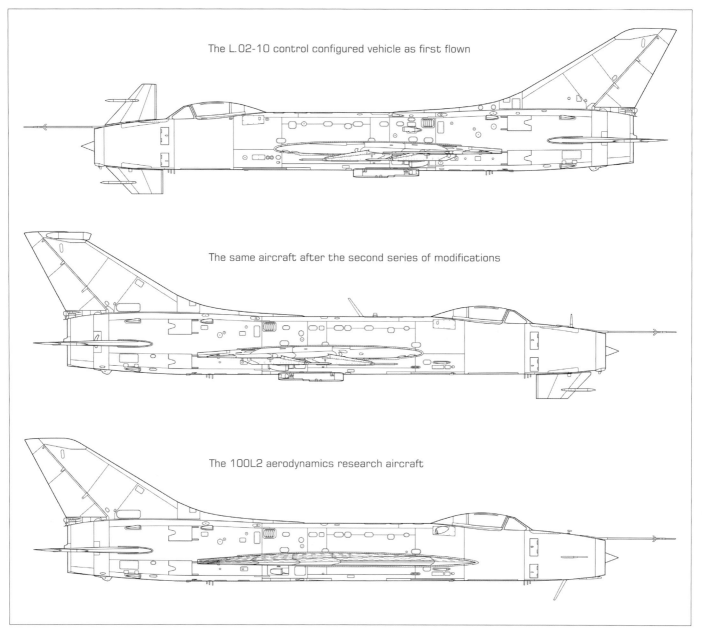

The L.02-10 control configured vehicle as first flown

The same aircraft after the second series of modifications

The 100L2 aerodynamics research aircraft

	T-3-Series Aircraft Production at Plant No. 153		
OKB designation	**Product code**	**C/n (factory listing)**	**Notes**
PT-7	*Izdeliye* 27	0115301 through 0115307 ('T1-01' through 'T1-07')	Wing dogtooth
PT-7	*Izdeliye* 27	0115308 through 0215309 ('T1-08' through 'T2-09')	Wing dogtooth; some aircraft between c/ns T2-02 and T2-09 converted to PT-8s
PT-8	*Izdeliye* 27	0215302 through 0215310 ('T2-02' through 'T2-10')	Wing dogtooth
T-43 [1]	*Izdeliye* 27	0215310 through 0315310 ('T2-10' through 'T3-10')	Wing dogtooth
T-43 [1]	*Izdeliye* 27	0315311 through 06153 . . . ('T2-10' to end of batch 6)	No wing dogtooth
T-43 [2]	*Izdeliye* 34	0715301 through 1515350 ('T7-01' through 'T15-50')	No wing dogtooth
T-47 [3]	*Izdeliye* 36	1015351 through 1515350? ('T10-51' through 'T15-50'?)	No wing dogtooth

Notes:

1. The Su-9 (T-43/*izdeliye* 27) had a bag-type no. 1 fuel tank, while the Su-9 (T-43/*izdeliye* 34) had an integral no. 1 fuel tank.

2. Su-9s with c/ns 0715301 through 1015351 ('T7-01' through 'T10-51') had sloping fuselage frames nos. 17–19 and provisions for installing NR-30 cannons in the wing roots.

3. The T-47 is described in chapter 3.

Chapter 3

The 'Flying Tubes'

T-47 Experimental Interceptor (T47-1 Prototype)
When the Sukhoi OKB started work on equipping the T-3 interceptor with the Almaz fire control radar in a radically redesigned installation, the resulting aircraft received the manufacturer's designation T-47. As mentioned earlier, the Almaz radar had separate search and tracking antennas; these were housed in separate radomes on the T-3 and the PT-7, which had a fixed-area air intake. On the T-47, however, the airframers managed to reach a compromise with the radar makers and reconcile good aerodynamics with acceptable radar performance by placing both antennas inside a large conical centre body within an axisymmetrical adjustable air intake. To accomplish this the forward fuselage diameter was significantly increased, with no taper at the front; the centre body was larger than the T-43's and had a simple conical shape. Moreover, two large rectangular dielectric panels were incorporated high on the sides of the nose to ensure an acceptable directional pattern for the radar's search antenna.

Of course, intake performance and cockpit visibility deteriorated somewhat as a result of this redesign. Still, this was considered an acceptable trade-off because the nation urgently needed a high-altitude interceptor to neutralise the threat posed by high-flying NATO spyplanes. The situation called for an immediate decision on what armament the future interceptor was to carry. In addition to AAMs, the installation of cannons and FFAR pods was still considered at this stage.

On 18 December 1957 the newly reorganised GKAT (formerly MAP) and the Soviet air force issued a joint ruling requiring the Novosibirsk aircraft factory no. 153 to manufacture an initial batch of ten T-47 interceptors in 1958. The aircraft were to be equipped with the Almaz radar in a revised installation with the search and tracking antennas in a common radome (the movable intake shock cone), as described above, and be armed with NR-30 cannons; no missiles were envisaged in the first batch.

Construction of the first prototype T-47 (known as the **T47-1**) proceeded in accordance with a MAP order issued on 6 August 1957. To this end the second production PT-8 (c/n 0115302) was delivered to OKB-51's prototype construction shop in Moscow in the form of separate subassemblies. The wings were modified to feature a leading-edge dogtooth and smaller ailerons terminating short of the wingtips. After appropriate modifications to the fuselage nose, the aircraft was fitted with the Almaz radar, two NR-30

cannons were installed in the wing roots (with quasi-oval steel blast plates ahead of them to protect the duralumin skin), and provisions were made for carrying two ORO-57 rocket pods with ARS-57 FFARs under the wings. On 10 December 1957 the aircraft was trucked to the OKB's flight test facility in Zhukovskiy, V. I. Mosolov being appointed engineer in charge of the tests.

On 6 January 1958 the T47-1 performed its maiden flight. Soon, however, the manufacturer's flight tests had to be suspended because another development aircraft, the PT8-4 (see below) was due to enter flight test imminently; AL-7F-1 engines were still in short supply then, so the engine was simply removed from the T47-1 and installed in the PT8-4. Hence by early June 1958 the T47-1 had made a mere 15 flights—and that was it. On 4 June 1958 the Council of Ministers issued directive no. 608-293, cancelling all work on the K-7 weapons system and the cannon-armed T-47. The K-7 missile did not meet the demands of the Soviet military because the beam-riding guidance system had an inherent shortcoming—guidance accuracy decreased dramatically as the launch range increased. Also, OKB-4, under Chief Designer Matus R. Bisnovat, was working on the K-8 homing AAM, which appeared to hold greater promise (as will be seen later).

Actually this was not yet the end of the T47-1's flying career. In September 1958 the aircraft was transferred from the Sukhoi OKB to LII, which used it until 1963 as a propulsion test bed for refining the AL-7F-1 engine.

PT8-4 Experimental Interceptor
The work on arming the prospective high-altitude interceptor featuring the Almaz radar with air-to-air missiles enjoyed priority over the cannon/rocket-armed T-47, which had entered low-rate initial production (LRIP) by then. Hence, in keeping with MAP order no. 718 of 19 November 1957, in the autumn of 1957 OKB-51 commenced conversion of the first production PT-8 (c/n 0115301) delivered to MMZ No. 51 from Novosibirsk. Since this was the fourth Novosibirsk-built example, being preceded by the three preproduction machines in batch 00 (the PT8-1 through PT8-3), the aircraft picked for conversion into the missile-armed variant was designated PT8-4.

For starters, the PT8-4 was modified to feature a dogtooth wing leading edge and reduced-area ailerons in similar manner to the T47-1 prototype, while the fuselage initially remained unal-

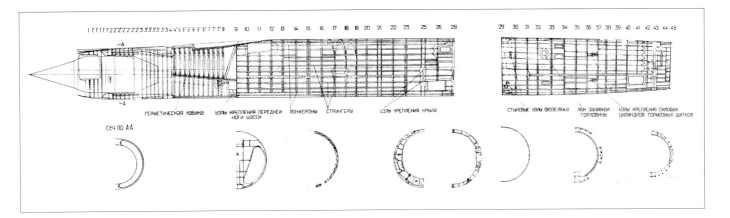

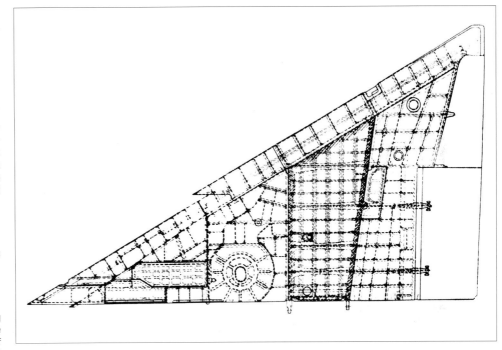

Left: The PT8-4 shows off its thicker nose with an enlarged intake shock cone/radome and lateral dielectric inserts aft of the intake lip. Note the T-3-style canopy with a large glazing area. No pylons are fitted.

Above: A drawing of the PT8-4's fuselage structure. Note the many auxiliary frames between frames 1–8, with duplicate numbers suffixed in Cyrillic alphabetical order (A-B-V-G-D-E); the lateral dielectric inserts are located between frames 0 and 1V.

Left: This view shows well the PT8-4's cannons housed in the wing roots.

Right: A drawing of the PT8-4's wing structure, showing the leading-edge dogtooth, the cannon bay ahead of the mainwheel well, and the integral fuel tank aft of it, as well as the flap tracks

Left: The PT8-4's wing dogtooth is plainly visible in this three-quarters rear view.

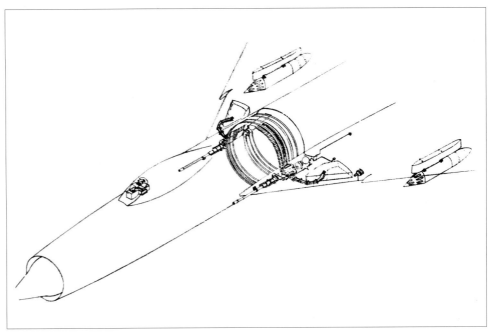

Right: A drawing showing the PT8-4's envisaged armament with cannons and ORO-57K 16-tube FFAR pods under the wings. The ammunition belts are routed around the fuselage in sleeves between frames 17–18 for the port cannon and frames 18–19 for the starboard cannon.

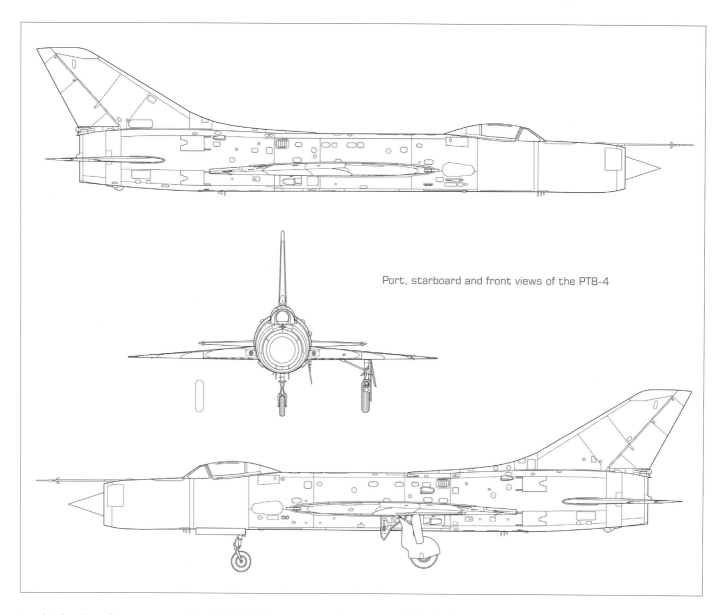

Port, starboard and front views of the PT8-4

tered. The aircraft was prepared for initial flight testing in this configuration with standard PT-8-style separate radomes for the search and tracking antennas, a narrow rear fuselage, and an AL-7F (*izdeliye* 45) engine. K. K. Solov'yov was appointed engineer in charge of the test programme.

However, drawing on the first results of the T43-1 prototype's tests, in late October 1957 the OKB decided that the PT8-4 should have the same fuselage mods as the T-47. The second conversion involved replacing the fuselage nose ahead of the cockpit with a new structure featuring a larger axisymmetrical air intake and shock cone to take the Almaz-3 radar, and manufacturing a new, wider detachable rear fuselage to accommodate the AL-7F-1 (*izdeliye* 45-1) engine. Detachable wing pylons and appropriate launch controls were installed for carrying K-7L or K-6V AAMs, and a pair of NR-30 cannons were also installed in the wing roots, with appropriate blast plates. Thus the T-47 and the PT8-4 were the only aircraft of the T-3 family to feature cannon armament.

Despite the fatter rear fuselage, the PT8-4 was originally powered by an AL-7F engine because the intended AL-7F-1 was still

unavailable. Following completion in January 1958 the aircraft was trucked to Zhukovskiy in the closing days of the month to begin ground checks. On 21 February it became airborne for the first time, flown by Sukhoi OKB test pilot Vladimir S. Ilyushin.

Initiated by GKAT order no. 49 of 15 February 1958, the manufacturer's flight tests of the PT8-4 proceeded in accordance with the so-called Programme 1 (approved on 14 February), which involved checking the aircraft's aerodynamics and performance/ handling characteristics with the redesigned forward fuselage and wing dogtooth. The first five flights under Programme 1 showed that a special test programme was necessary to explore certain peculiarities of the aircraft. Such a programme (the so-called Programme 2) was duly drawn up and completed, whereupon Programme 1 resumed. By the end of June 1958 the PT8-4 had made a total of 33 flights, including eight under Programme 2; by this time, four versions of the air-intake centre body were tried out and the AL-7F-1 engine (sourced from the T47-1) was finally installed. Thus the T-47 configuration of the T-3 interceptor was, in effect, put through its paces on the PT8-4.

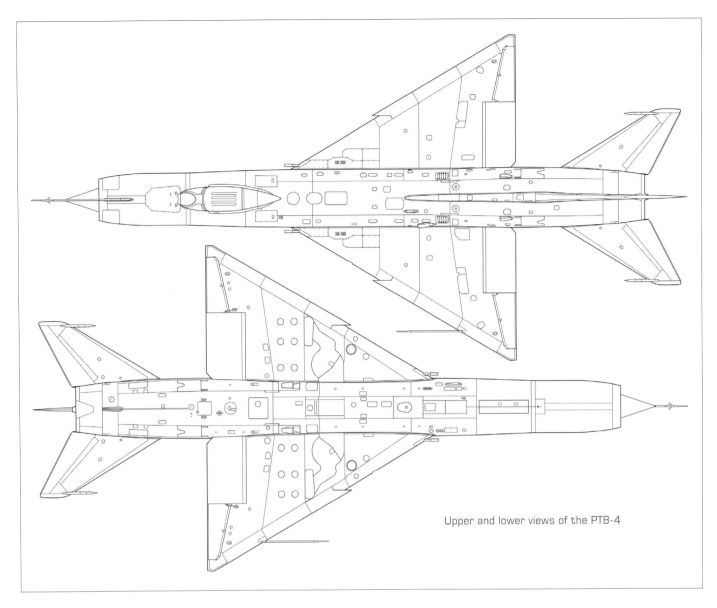

Upper and lower views of the PT8-4

When giving their recommendations concerning the wing design, TsAGI's aerodynamicists were, in effect, staging a large-scale flight experiment to see which way of preventing tip stall (boundary layer fences, as used on Mikoyan fighters, or a leading-edge dogtooth) was more effective. The dogtooth showed disappointing performance on the T47-1 and the PT8-4, and later aircraft of the T-3 family reverted to an unbroken wing leading edge.

According to the manufacturer's flight test report, which called it 'the T-3 experimental supersonic interceptor (factory product code PT8-4)', the modified aircraft displayed the following performance. The takeoff weight was 8,960 kg (19,750 lbs.) without external stores and 9,330 kg (20,570 lbs.) with two K-7 missiles; the maximum permitted landing weight was 8,305 kg (18,310 lbs.).

Top speed at 13,000 m (42,650 ft.) in full afterburner was 2,260 km/h (1,403 mph) in 'clean' configuration (without missiles), decreasing to 2,180 km/h (1,354 mph) with two AAMs. At altitudes up to 8,000 m (26,250 ft.) the maximum indicated airspeed was restricted to 1,250 km/h (776 mph) by a dynamic pressure limit of 7,500 kg/m² (1,537 lbs. / sq. ft.); between 8,000 m and 10,000 m

(32,810 ft.) it was 1,200 km/h (745 mph), restricted by a dynamic pressure limit of 7,000 kg/m² (2,135 lbs. / sq. ft.). The Mach limit at 11,000 m (36,090 ft.) and higher was 2.1; in 'clean' configuration the aircraft could reach 1,250 km/h IAS but was not to exceed Mach 2.25 due to structural integrity and flutter considerations. With two missiles the indicated airspeed limit was still 1,250 km/h, but the maximum permissible Mach number was only 1.19.

At full military power the PT8-4 was able to reach 15,000 m (49,210 ft.). The service ceiling in full afterburner was never established due to the premature termination of the test programme. The aircraft did, however, reach a maximum altitude of 19,000 m (62,335 ft.) with the ultimate (no. 4) air-intake centre body in the fully aft position, climbing at Mach 1.6. The PT8-4's maximum permitted landing weight was 8,305 kg (18,310 lbs.), and the g-limit was set at +7 g.

Apart from Vladimir S. Ilyushin, the aircraft was flown by OKB test pilot Anatoliy A. Koznov and LII test pilot Vladimir N. Ilyin, as well as by the Novosibirsk aircraft factory's checkout pilots. The PT8-4's flying career was not altogether accident free.

One of the first T-47 prototypes (with PT8-4-style dielectric panels) at Akhtoobinsk during state acceptance trials, with K-8M AAMs on the wing pylons and the 'wet' fuselage pylons in place. Note the addition of auxiliary blow-in doors ahead of the cockpit, the lack of cannons, the ventral data link aerial just ahead of the wings, and the two cine cameras under nose recording missile launches.

Ilyushin unwittingly got the distinction of being the first Sukhoi test pilot to make a dead-stick landing in a supersonic jet fighter —especially a delta-wing aircraft. On 5 April 1958, when the PT8-4 was making its second flight with the AL-7F-1, the engine surged and quit at 19,500 m (63,980 ft.). At the time the aircraft was 110 km (68.35 miles) from Zhukovskiy. After several fruitless attempts to relight the engine, Ilyushin, in a remarkable display of airmanship, glided the PT8-4 back to base and performed a perfect landing; the aircraft was saved.

As already mentioned, the Council of Ministers directive of 4 June 1958, which killed off the cannon-armed T-47, also terminated the K-7 missile in favour of new weapons systems. The K-6V AAM, which was due for testing on the PT8-4, not only was compromised by the same design drawbacks as the K-7 but had shorter range into the bargain. Also, the Grooshin OKB was heavily burdened with high-priority design work on SAMs; persisting with the K-6V would have stretched its resources too far. Hence, on 16 April 1958, the Council of Ministers issued a directive, pulling the plug on the K-6 weapons system.

Shortly afterward, in early August 1958, the PT8-4's career came to an abrupt end. An electrics failure during one of the test flights put the artificial-feel mechanism in the tailplane control circuit out of action, and pitch control became sluggish, forcing test pilot Eduard V. Yelian to make a landing at excessively high speed. It never rains but it pours: the brake parachute failed to deploy and the aircraft overran, suffering such grave damage that it was declared a write-off—for the time being, as it turned out.

Later the PT8-4 was extensively rebuilt, emerging as the T47-3 interceptor prototype—but that's another story (see below).

T-3-8M Aerial-Intercept Weapons System T47-2, T47-3, T47-4, T47-5, T47-7, and T47-8 Interceptor Prototypes

Several other interceptors bearing the T-47 designation but equipped with different fire control radars were evolved from the T-3 at OKB-51. The aforementioned Oryol (Eagle; NATO code name 'Skip Spin') X-band radar developed by MAP's Moscow-based OKB-339 under Chief Designer Ghedaliy M. Koonyavskiy had greater appeal than the other contenders—first and foremost because it featured a single antenna for target tracking and missile guidance. This radar was a refined derivative of the production RP-6 Sokol radar fitted to the Yak-25M interceptor. It had a 100 kW transmitter, a detection range of 40 km (24.85 miles), an operating frequency of 8.69–8.995 GHz, and a very high PRF of 2,700–3,000 pps. (OKB-339 later became NPO Phazotron (*naoochno-proizvodstvennoye obyedineniye*: research and production association), an MRP subdivision where virtually all Soviet aircraft radar design work was concentrated in the mid-1960s.

The Oryol radar, originally known as the Sokol-2K, had been developed for the Yak-27K Flashlight-C two-seat transonic interceptor of 1956, where it worked with the K-8 AAM. This advanced missile developed by OKB-4 under Chief Designer Matus R. Bisnovat had much-greater range than the K-7L and, importantly, came in semi-active radar homing (SARH) and infrared homing

The PT8-4 prototype

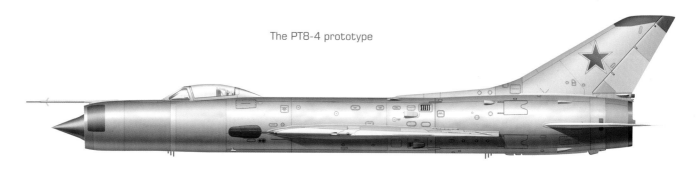

Right and *below right*: The T47-4 development aircraft as originally built, with dummy K-8MR AAMs. Again, it is uncoded and is almost identical to the aircraft on the preceding page, but the undernose cameras are different!

Bottom right: A rare shot of the T47-4 in flight. Small pods are attached to the wing pylons.

versions. The SARH version required continuous target illumination by the interceptor's radar from launch to detonation; conversely, the IR-homing version was a 'fire and forget' missile, which simplified the attack procedure. (OKB-4 is now known as NPO *Molniya* [Lightning].)

When the Yakovlev OKB ran into development problems with the Yak-27K, which eventually proved insurmountable, GKAT proposed adapting the aircraft's armament and radar to the supersonic Sukhoi T-3 (or rather the T-47). As already mentioned in the previous chapter, a Council of Ministers directive to this effect appeared on 16 April 1958, the new aerial-intercept weapons system being accordingly designated T-3-8M. OKB-4 was tasked with developing a 'Sukhoi version' of the missile designated K-8-2 (alias K-8M for *modifitseerovannyy*: modified), while OKB-339 was instructed to reduce the diameter of the Oryol radar's huge antenna dish to a size small enough to fit inside the air intake

The T47-4 development aircraft as first flown

Above: Wearing appropriate tail titles, the T47-4 is depicted here as a ground instructional airframe at the Solntsevo ShMAS (Junior Aviation Tech Staff School); the code '35 Red' was applied locally. Note that the aircraft was modified in the course of the trials—the dielectric panels on the nose have been deleted, a Su-9-style canopy with a reduced glazing area has been fitted, and wiring conduits have been added to the centre fuselage.

Left: A cadet of the Solntsevo ShMAS gives the 'shut down engine' sign to the serviceman in the cockpit of the T47-4. However, the engine is obviously not being ground run—there is no jet blast deflector behind the aircraft, and not even any wheel chocks.

Left: Another view of the T47-4 at Solntsevo; the wing dogtooth is clearly visible here.

Right and *far right*: The T47-8 loaded with AAMs and drop tanks flies over Moscow-Tushino on 9 July 1961.

The T47-4 as an instructional airframe at the Solntsevo ShMAS

shock cone used by the Almaz radar on the PT8-4. (On the original RP-6 radar and its Sokol-2/Sokol-2K derivatives, this was not a problem because the Yakovlev twinjet interceptors had wing-mounted engines, the radome occupying the entire nose ahead of the cockpit.) In so doing, the lateral dielectric panels on the fighter's nose (as seen on the PT8-4) were rendered unnecessary.

The K-8M missile (*izdeliye* 24M) was designed for attacking all kinds of aerial targets in pursuit mode. It had a tail-first layout with cruciform wings and canard rudders set at 45° to the vertical plane. The missile's body was built in four sections. Section 1 housed the seeker head; the SARH version's PARG-1 (*poluaktivnaya rahdi-olokatsionnaya golovka* [*samonavedeniya*]: semi-active radar seeker head), enclosed by a dielectric fairing, was developed by NII-648 (now called NIITP, *Naoochno-issledovatel'skiy institoot tochnykh priborov*: Precision Instrument Design Research Institute), while the S-1 IR seeker head was a product of TsKB-589 (*tsentrahl'noye konstrooktorskoye byuro*: Central Design Bureau), a subdivision of the Ministry of Defence Industry (MOP: *Minister-stvo oboronnoy promyshlennosti*), which is now known as TsKB *Gheofizika*: 'Geophysics' Central Design Bureau). Section 2 carried the rudders, accommodating the control actuators, the APS-8 autopilot, the *Snegir'* (Bullfinch) radar proximity fuse, and the HE/fragmentation warhead. Section 3 housed the PRD-141 solid-fuel rocket motor, with an extra-long nozzle, and carried the trapezoidal wings, having 60° leading-edge sweep and 11° reverse sweep on the trailing edges (which incorporated ailerons), while section 4 was simply a jet pipe fairing mounting a tracer flare to enable visual tracking at night. The missile had a length of 4.266 m (13 ft.,

11⁶¹⁄₆₄ in.) in the SARH version or 4.02 m (13 ft., 2¹⁷⁄₆₄ in.) in the IR-homing version, a wingspan of 1.223 m (4 ft., ⁵⁄₃₂ in.), and a body diameter of 275 mm (10⁵³⁄₆₄ in.). Launch weight was 290 kg (639 lbs.), including the 40 kg (88 lb.) warhead; minimum 'kill' range was 2–3 km (1.24–1.86 miles), and maximum 'kill' range was 20 km (12.4 miles) for the SARH version or 15 km (9.3 miles) for the IR-homing version. Target altitude was anywhere from 8,000 m to 23,000 m (26,250–75,460 ft); estimated 'kill' probability in a two-missile salvo was 80%–90%.

The K-8M was larger and heavier than the K-5MS (RS-2-US), which meant only two missiles could be carried instead of four; they were suspended on larger PU-1-8 pylons (the designation denoted 'single-round launcher for the K-8') located well outboard. Unlike the initial K-8 developed for the Yak-27K, which featured interchangeable IR seeker heads with different sensitivity for day and night use, the 'Sukhoified' K-8M had a single 'round-the-clock' IR seeker. Thus, even though an attack was still possible only in pursuit mode and the Oryol radar lacked 'look-down/shoot-down' capability (the missiles had to be launched from below the target's flight level to avoid ground clutter), the new radar and armament gave the aircraft a considerably higher potential as compared to the T-43, then undergoing trials.

Detail design of the interceptor featuring the Oryol radar and armed with K-8M missiles began in the second half of 1958. All aircraft made available by the termination of the K-7 weapons system—the PT-7 prototype, the wrecked PT8-4, and six of the ten T-47s converted from low-rate initial-production T-3s by plant no. 153 in 1958–59—were earmarked for conversion to this configu-

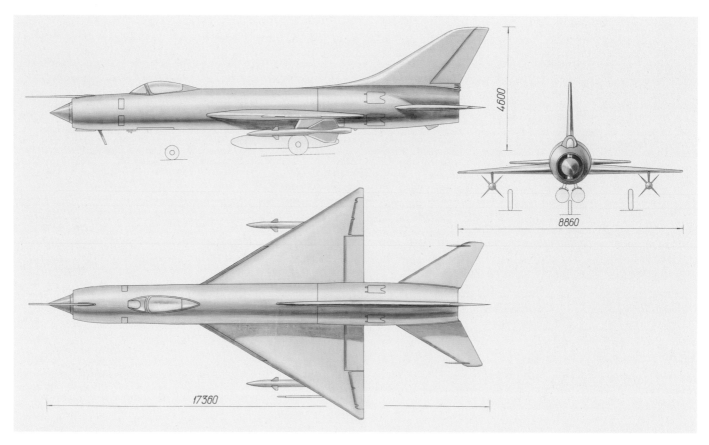

4600

8860

17360

A three-view drawing of the Su-11 from the ADP documents

ration; a total of six aircraft (in-house designations T47-2 through T47-5, T47-7, and T47-8) were to be tested. The first of these to enter flight test was the **T47-2**; however, it was virtually unmodified and no radar was fitted, since the aircraft was purely an aerodynamics test vehicle. Shortly afterward the T47-2 was lost in a crash, the pilot ejecting safely.

The SARH version of the K-8 AAM on a test bench during trials at GNIKI VVS

Thus, the first example to be actually converted under the T-3-8M programme (that is, armed with K-8M missiles) was the PT-7. In the summer of 1958 the aircraft was flown to Moscow and underwent extensive modifications at MMZ No. 51, receiving a T-47-style nose and a new designation, **T47-3**. The prototype Oryol radar was still unavailable and hence the air intake shock cone was of all-metal construction, not dielectric; nevertheless, during the initial stage of the trials the OKB intended to use the T47-3 not only for aerodynamic testing but for verifying the missile launch system as well (apparently the IR-homing version of the missile was used).

On the night of 26 November 1958 the T47-3 was trucked to the Sukhoi OKB's flight test facility in Zhukovskiy. Manufacturer's flight tests began on 25 December, with Roman G. Yarmarkov as engineer in charge. Initially the aircraft was used to verify the intake design and evolve the optimum intake adjustment algorithm; the shock cone and auxiliary blow-in doors were adjusted manually for the time being, since the new ESUV-2 automatic intake control system for the redesigned intake had yet to be developed. The data obtained at this stage allowed the parameters of the ESUV-2 system to be determined. The early test results obtained with the T47-3 confirmed that the redesigned forward fuselage adversely affected flight performance, causing a deterioration of the acceleration parameters and a reduction of the service ceiling, top speed, and range.

On 20 November 1958 the first fatal crash of a T-3 series aircraft occurred at Novosibirsk-Yel'tsovka, the factory airfield of plant no. 153. When factory test pilot V. V. Proshchevayev was

Two views of the T47-5 with dummy K-8T AAMs in 1959. The aircraft had no radar at the time (note the metal shock cone).

making a check flight in a production T-47 (c/n 0215306), the dielectric radome suddenly broke free from its mounting and disintegrated, the fragments blocking the inlet ducts and causing the engine to flame out. After several unsuccessful attempts to restart the engine, realising he was too low to eject safely, the pilot attempted an off-field forced landing but sustained fatal injuries in so doing. As a result of the accident investigation, the design of

the radome was revised to prevent a repetition of the structural failure.

Two more aircraft converted from Novosibirsk-built LRIP T-47s joined the test programme in the spring of 1959. The **T47-4** was converted in Moscow from T-47 c/n 0115309 and delivered to the OKB's flight test facility in Zhukovskiy in April, with V. Vasil'yev as engineer in charge of the tests. In May it was joined

The T47-5 development aircraft with five test mission markers

Left: A display of new PVO hardware at GNIKI VVS for the MoD top brass and high-ranking government officials. A production Su-11 ('53 Red') is seen in company with a Su-9U, a Su-15, a Yak-18P, and a Tu-128.

Below left: A different perspective of the same Su-11. The production version lacked the lateral dielectric inserts.

Below: Close-up of a red-painted inert K-8MR AAM under the wing of this aircraft, showing the conical radome of the PARG-1 radar seeker

Above right: The tenth production Su-11, '10 Blue' (c/n 0115310), with live R-8MT AAMs. The IR-homing version had a reshaped nose with an optical sensor window.

Right and *below right*: Two more aspects of the same aircraft.

by the **T47-5**, converted from T-47 c/n 0215302, with V. Balooyev as engineer in charge. These two aircraft were earmarked for armament/weapons control system trials—specifically, for testing the IR-homing version of the K-8M. Only the T47-4 featured a full avionics fit from the outset, while the T47-5 initially had no radar (which was retrofitted in the course of modifications in January 1960) and thus had a metal shock cone. Interestingly, the T47-4 initially featured the same dielectric panels on the sides of the extreme nose as the PT8-4, but these were later deleted and the apertures were closed with metal skin. The T47-5 introduced a revised Su-9-style cockpit canopy with a reduced glazing area.

In August 1959, having passed predelivery check tests, both fighters were flown to the GK NII VVS facility at Vladimirovka AB in Akhtoobinsk to commence manufacturer's tests of the radar and the K-8M missile. These were performed by OKB-51 test pilots Vladimir S. Ilyushin, Yevgeniy S. Solov'yov, Yevgeniy K. Kukushev, and Anatoliy A. Koznov, who made ten missile launches in

ballistic (unguided) mode and about 40 flights to check the radar's operation during intercepts of real targets. By mid-September the greater part of the test programme had been completed, and on 17 September 1959 the T-3-8M aerial-intercept weapons system was officially submitted for state acceptance trials.

Stage A of the trials lasted from November 1959 to April 1960, involving trials of the aircraft with the IR-homing version of the missile according to an abbreviated programme agreed upon with the air force. Three of the prototypes (the T47-3, T47-4, and T47-5) participated in this stage; they were flown by GK NII VVS test pilots Col. Nikolay P. Zakharov, Col. Pyotr F. Kabrelyov, Lt.-Col. Boris M. Adrianov, Lt.-Col. Eduard I. Knyazev, and Lt.-Col. Viktor M. Andreyev, as well as virtually all Sukhoi OKB test pilots. By the time stage A was completed, two more prototypes—the **T47-7** (c/n 0215304) and the **T47-8** (c/n 0215307)—were ready to join the action. These two aircraft were earmarked for testing the SARH version of the K-8M.

An in-service Su-11 coded '69 Blue' seen after landing. Note the deployed airbrakes and the open brake parachute bay doors.

The T47-8 incorporated major changes made at the request of the military, being powered by an AL-7F-2 engine uprated to 10,100 kgp (22,270 lbst) in full afterburner. An extra fuel tank was provided in the rear fuselage, and the existing bag-type no. 1 fuselage fuel tank was replaced by an integral tank; also, the dry bays between the wings' main spar and no. 1 auxiliary spar were transformed into integral tanks. The combined effect of these changes increased the internal fuel capacity to 4,195 litres (922.9 Imp gal.) and the fuel load to 3,440 kg (7,580 lbs.). Finally, the AL-7F-2 engine was 'hotter' and the wiring bundles in the centre fuselage were in danger of melting; to prevent this, they were relocated to two detachable external conduits on the upper centre fuselage sides, which gave the bonus of easier mainte-nance access to them.

On 26 April 1960 all five aircraft commenced stage B of the trials, which was concerned mostly with the verification/debug-ging of the Oryol radar and development of operational tactics; the latter part involved live missile launches. Additionally, the shape of the radome/shock cone was finalised and the ESUV-2 automatic air intake control system was put through its paces. By the middle of the year the T47-3, T47-4, T47-5, and T47-7 had been upgraded to match the standard of the T47-8; trials showed that the extra fuel increased the range to an acceptable figure.

The trials were completed on 25 May 1961; on 8 June the state commission signed the final protocol. In the course of the state acceptance trials, the five aircraft involved made 475 flights between them; together with the manufacturer's flight tests the total number of flights exceeded 700. (Incidentally, there are indi-cations that the remaining four T-47s converted from LRIP T-3s by plant no. 153 also found use in the trials of the T-3.)

On 9 July 1961 the new interceptor had its public debut when the T47-8 flown by OKB test pilot Yevgeniy S. Solov'yov partici-pated in the traditional Aviation Day flypast at Moscow-Tushino.

The T47-4 eventually became a ground instructional airframe at a PVO junior aviation specialists' school (ShMAS: *Shkola mlahdshikh aviatsionnykh spetsialistov*) located in Solntsevo, a short way southwest of the Moscow city limits, together with two other Su-11s. At the school it received the tactical code '35 Red'. Another Su-11 at the Solntsevo ShMAS ('36 Red') was the first production aircraft (c/n 0115301), of which we shall hear more later; the third aircraft ('37 Red') remains unidentified.

T47-4 Avionics Test Bed
Later, when the state acceptance trials of the T-3-8M aerial-inter-cept weapons system had been completed, the T47-4 was fitted with an AP-28E-1 autopilot, serving as a test bed for it.

T47-5 Weapons Test Bed
During the same period, the T47-5 was used as a weapons test bed for the IR-homing version of the K-8M air-to-air missile.

T47-6 Experimental Interceptor

The reader has probably noticed that one of the aircraft in the above sequence is 'missing'. This aircraft, the T47-6, was set aside for conversion under a different programme. Again, the aircraft was converted from a standard LRIP T-47 (c/n 0215303).

Initially the T47-6 acted as an aerodynamics research aircraft, being fitted with canard foreplanes ahead of the cockpit and a modified air intake featuring a fixed shock cone. In this guise the aircraft entered flight test in January 1960—originally with an AL-7F engine that was later substituted with an AL-7F-1. Tests of the fixed-geometry air intake continued into 1962; several versions were tried, the final one yielding unique results with absolutely stall-free operation. By then, however, the T-47 interceptor equipped with the Oryol radar and armed with K-8M missiles had entered full-scale production, and it was considered inexpedient to make major design changes.

Later the T47-6 found use as an avionics test bed in the development of the T-3A-9 aerial-intercept weapons system based on the ill-starred Sukhoi T-37 heavy interceptor (the latter aircraft is described in chapter 5). The T47-6 was retrofitted with the TsP-1 fire control radar and the launch control system for the Sukhoi

K-9-51 (R-38) SARH air-to-air missiles, both of which had been tailor made for the T-37. Again, the aircraft had a fixed-geometry air intake, featuring the T-37's multishock intake centre body / radome and PR-38 missile pylons under the wings, replacing the standard PU-1-8 pylons.

Eventually, when the T-37 programme had been cancelled, the T47-6 was used in the trials of the T-3-8M aerial-intercept weapons system alongside the other prototypes in the series.

Su-11-8M Aerial-Intercept Weapons System
Su-11 Production Interceptor (*izdeliye* 36)

The T-47 was ordered into production at plant no. 153 in Novosibirsk by a Council of Ministers directive issued on 27 November 1961. According to this document the new aircraft was to supersede the Su-9 completely on the production line by mid-1962, and the plant was required to manufacture 40 aircraft by the end of that year. Moreover, the economic plans for 1961 called for the production of 30 such interceptors by the end of the year—an obviously unrealistic demand.

On 5 February 1962 the Council of Ministers issued a directive officially including the T-3-8M weapons system into the Soviet

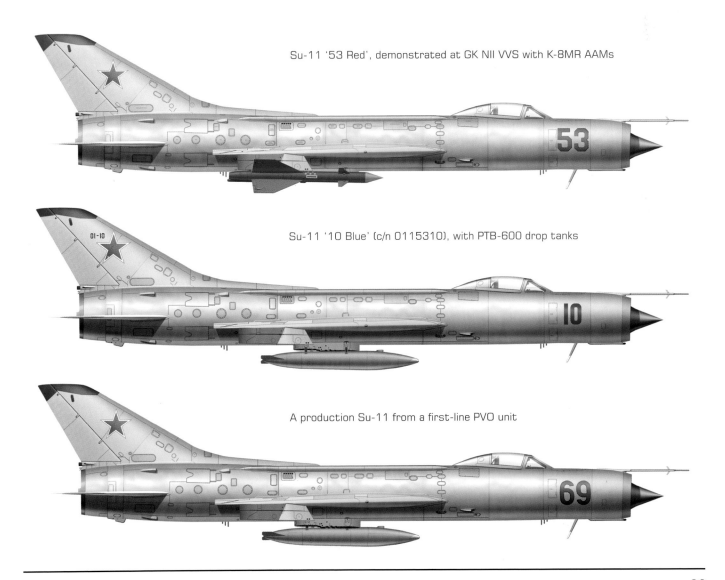

Su-11 '53 Red', demonstrated at GK NII VVS with K-8MR AAMs

Su-11 '10 Blue' (c/n 0115310), with PTB-600 drop tanks

A production Su-11 from a first-line PVO unit

PVO's inventory. In so doing, the T-47 interceptor received the service designation Su-11. The Oryol radar was officially designated RP-11 to match the aircraft type, the K-8M AAM was redesignated R-8M (*R* for *raketa*—in this case, missile; NATO code name AA-3 Anab), and the system as a whole was redesignated Su-11-8M.

No major difficulties were encountered in mastering Su-11 production, since the aircraft had considerable structural and systems commonality with the Su-9. The 'nose job' associated with the new radar resulted in a fuselage of almost constant diameter, which gave rise to the nickname *letayushchaya trooba* (flying tube). The Su-11 received the in-house product code *izdeliye* 36.

Production Su-11s featured an upgraded avionics and equipment suite. This included an RSIU-5V Doob-5 two-way VHF communications radio, a new ARK-10 automatic direction finder (*avtomaticheskiy rahdiokompas*: ADF), an ARL-S Lazoor' data link receiver working with the Vozdukh-1 GCI system, an MRP-56P marker beacon receiver, an SOD-57M decimetre-waveband air traffic control transponder (*samolyotnyy otvetchik detsimetrovyy*), an SRZO-2M Khrom-Nikel' (chromium-nickel; NATO code name Odd Rods) IFF interrogator/transponder (*samolyotnyy rahdiolokatsionnyy zaproschik-otvetchik*), a Sirena-2 RWR, an AGD-1 artificial horizon, and a KSI fighter-type compass system (*koorsovaya sistema istrebitelya*). The aircraft featured many systems components not found on the Su-9 (albeit some of them were later retrofitted to the latter type); namely, an RV-UM low-range radio altimeter (*rahdiovysotomer*), a D-3K-110 yaw/pitch/roll damper, an AP-28Zh-1B autopilot, red cockpit lighting (making the aircraft less observable to the enemy at night), and a new KS-3 ejection seat, permitting safe ejection over a much-wider range of speeds and altitudes.

The production Su-11 differed from the prototypes in having reinforced main gear struts with new mainwheels to absorb the higher weight. This necessitated changes to the wing structure (specifically, the mainwheel wells), and the main gear doors were reshaped accordingly. Early Su-11s featured a 570 × 140 mm KT-100 nosewheel, but this was soon replaced by a 600 × 155 mm (23.6 × 6.1 in.) KT-104 wheel.

The first production aircraft (c/n 0115301) took to the air in July 1962. Again, the construction number system was the same as on the Su-9, and the hyphenated short version of the c/n was stencilled at the same locations.

Production was gaining momentum, and everything seemed to be going nicely when suddenly disaster struck. On 31 October 1962 the engine of Su-11 c/n 0115301 quit during one of the test flights. The aircraft was passing over Novosibirsk at the time, and GK NII VVS test pilot Viktor M. Andreyev chose not to eject, fearing that the uncontrollable aircraft would drop in a residential area, with massive destruction and many fatalities as a result. He attempted a dead-stick landing on the outskirts of the city's old disused airfield and did reach it, but the aircraft touched down so hard that the pilot was killed instantly. After this accident the aircraft was relegated to the ShMAS in Solntsevo.

This tragic crash dealt a crippling blow to the Su-11. Air Marshal Yevgeniy Ya. Savitskiy, who commanded the fighter arm of the Air Defence Force (IA PVO: *Istrebitel'naya aviahtsiya* **Pro**-

tivovozdooshnoy oborony), was extremely unhappy about the Su-9's high accident rate as it was, and the accident played into the hands of the Su-11's opponents. At the time, OKB-115 general designer Aleksandr S. Yakovlev, a man with considerable influence in the aircraft industry, was actively promoting his new Yak-28P Firebar twinjet supersonic interceptor, citing its alleged advantages over the single-engined Sukhoi deltas. He soon succeeded in convincing the powers that be that future interceptors should have two engines powering separate electric and hydraulic systems for greater reliability and operational safety.

As a result, the Novosibirsk aircraft factory's production plan for 1962 came to include 40 Su-11s and 15 Yak-28P two-seat interceptors in addition to the final 120 Su-9s. All subsequent wrangling with the Ministry of Defence, which demanded that the Su-11's operational reliability be improved by the provision of automated systems-monitoring equipment (which, at first glance, was perfectly reasonable), was in reality but a pretext to cut production plans for the Su-11, which had fallen from favour at the top level. In 1963 the plant was reoriented toward Yak-28P production. By then, however, a considerable stockpile of Su-11 components had been built up; on consideration it was decided not to throw them away but to assemble the fighters as long as the stock lasted, delivering them to the IA PVO after the required modifications had been made. Yet, the upgrading process turned out to be a protracted affair, the customer being extremely demanding (or rather biased) after the abovementioned accident, and the completed Su-11s remained at the factory for weeks. Even when plant no. 153 was cranking out and delivering Yak-28Ps (known in-house as *izdeliye* 40) at a steady rate, the apron at Novosibirsk-Yel'tsovka was still crammed with row upon row of undelivered Su-11s sitting under wraps because the PVO top brass could not find the nerve to order them to be delivered to operational units. At length, Aleksandr S. Yakovlev gave vent to his displeasure during one of his visits to Novosibirsk; pointing to the stored Su-11s, he loudly and wryly enquired from the accompanying factory staff: *'How much longer is this junk going to stay here?'*

In early 1963 the VVS transferred several production Su-11s to OKB-51 in order to have the reliability improvement measures incorporated. Throughout 1963 and 1964 these aircraft underwent extensive testing and modifications. The effort paid off—in mid-1964 the Su-11 finally achieved initial operational capability (IOC) with the PVO's 393rd GvIAP (*Gvardeyskiy istrebitel'nyy aviapolk*: Guards fighter regiment), based near Astrakhan', which had previously operated the Su-9. (The Guards units were the elite of the Soviet armed forces, since this title was accorded to a unit for special gallantry in combat.) By then the Sukhoi OKB was commencing trials of the new T-58D twinjet interceptor (see chapter 7); this aircraft fitted the new concept ideally, and the OKB placed its bets on the T-58D.

Su-11 production continued until early 1965, but only 108 aircraft were completed—ten times fewer than the Su-9. The remainder of the production run was enough to equip two more units of the Moscow PVO District—the 790th IAP at Khotilovo AB and the 191st IAP in Yefremov—in the first six months of 1965. The Su-11's NATO reporting name was Fishpot-C.

The Su-11 soldiered on alongside the Su-9 until the early 1980s, when the last ones were retired as time-expired. In the late 1960s

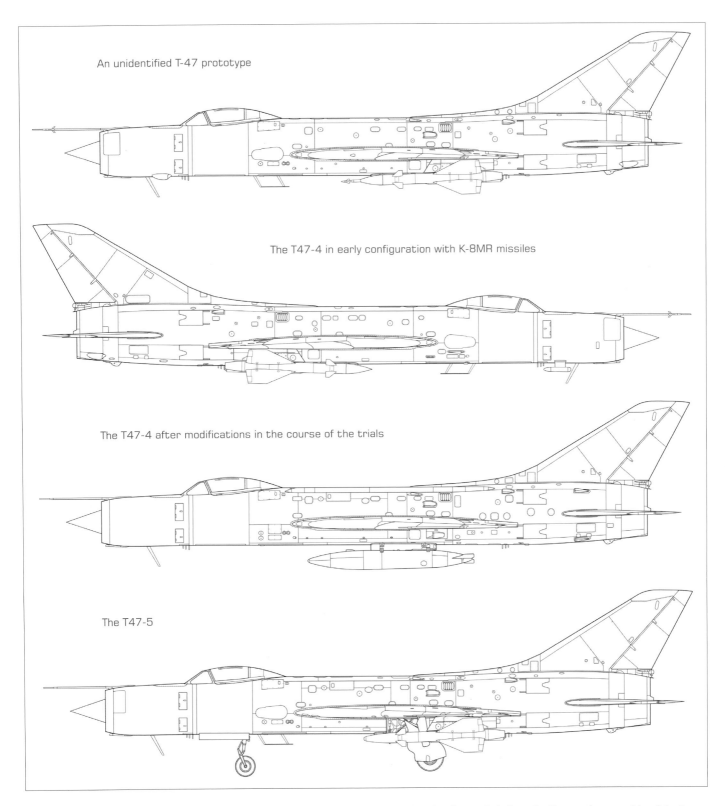

An unidentified T-47 prototype

The T47-4 in early configuration with K-8MR missiles

The T47-4 after modifications in the course of the trials

The T47-5

the surviving Su-11s were upgraded by the addition of SARPP-12 flight data recorders, just as was the case with the Su-9.

Su-11 Test Bed

A Su-11 coded '32 Blue' (the code was probably derived from the c/n) was used by LII as a test bed—probably for a pneumatic foreign-object damage (FOD) prevention system, which used engine bleed air. The air was fed via a pipeline on the port side of the lower fuselage to twin ejector nozzles under the intake lip to create increased pressure, thus preventing ingestion of loose objects from the runway. Outwardly the aircraft differed from a stock Fishpot-C in having a short piping conduit low on the port side of the nose, and a bulged fairing under the rear fuselage housing a nonstandard RA-56V control servo (*roolevoy agregaht*).

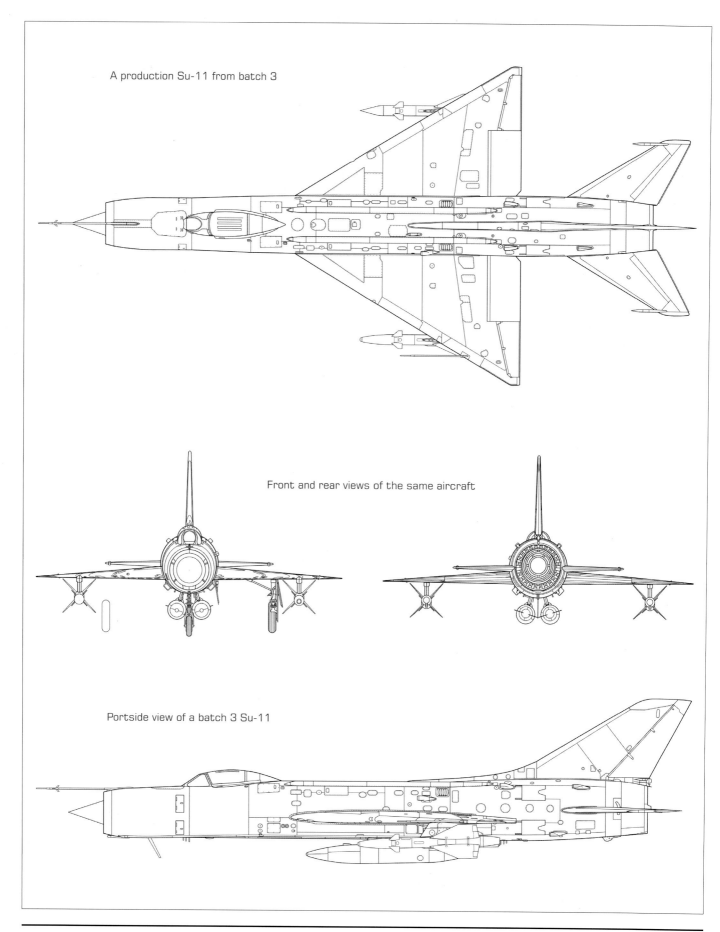

A production Su-11 from batch 3

Front and rear views of the same aircraft

Portside view of a batch 3 Su-11

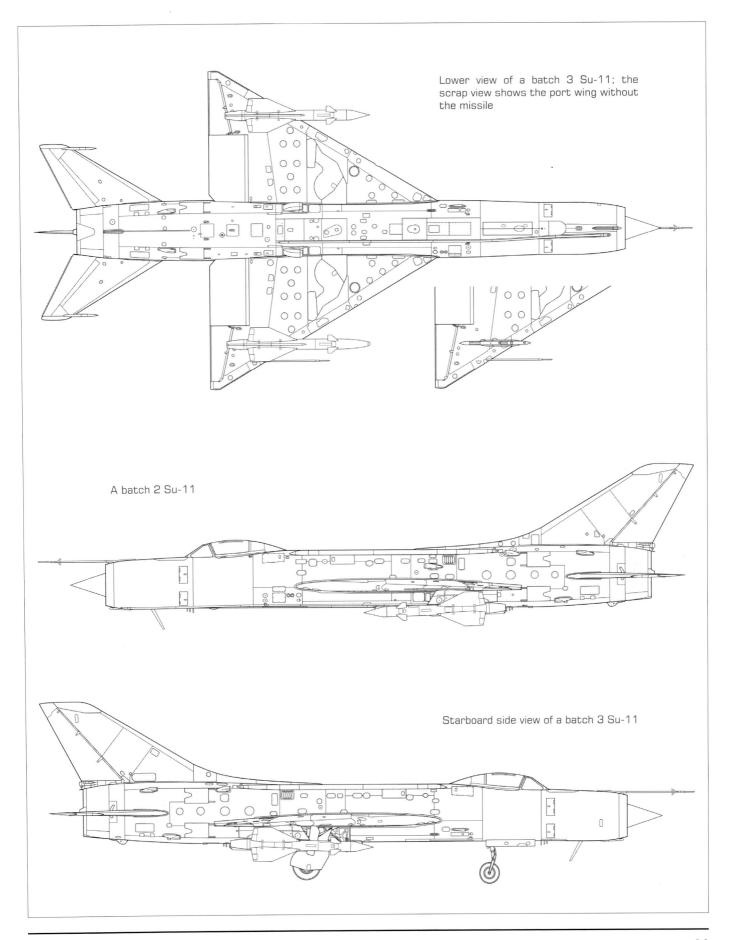

Lower view of a batch 3 Su-11; the scrap view shows the port wing without the missile

A batch 2 Su-11

Starboard side view of a batch 3 Su-11

Su-11 '32 Blue' was a test bed operated by LII. Note the conduit of the FOD protection system's air pipeline under the nose.

This view of '32 Blue' shows the fairing under the rear fuselage housing an RA-56V servo. Note the absence of all four pylons.

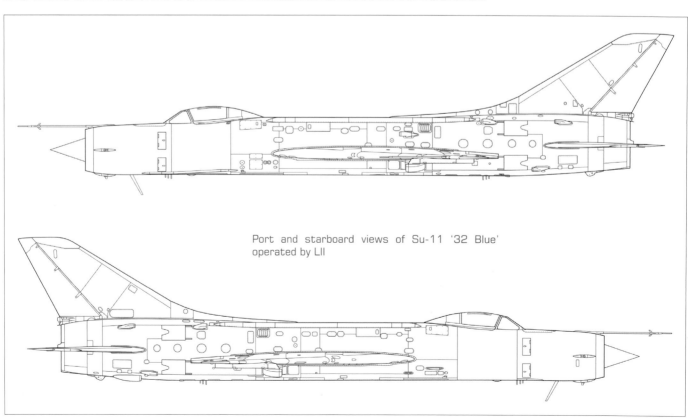

Port and starboard views of Su-11 '32 Blue' operated by LII

Chapter 4

The Su-9 and Su-11 in Detail

The following brief structural description applies to the standard Su-9. The differing design features of the Su-9U and Su-11 are indicated as appropriate.

Type: Single-engined, single-seat, supersonic interceptor designed for day and night operation in VMC and IMC. The airframe is of all-metal construction, the primary structural materials being D16-series duralumin and D19 and V95 aluminium alloys; some highly stressed structural components, such as the landing-gear struts, wing/fuselage attachment fittings, and stabilator axles, are made of 30KhGSA- and 30KhGSNA-grade high-strength steel. OT4 titanium alloy (*ognestoykiy titahn*: fireproof titanium) is used in some areas around the engine. Dielectric fairings are made of glass-fibre-reinforced plastic (GRP).

Fuselage: Semimonocoque, riveted, stressed-skin structure of circular cross section with 61 frames (normal frames 1–45 plus auxiliary frames having duplicated numbers with suffix letters up

Two views of a production Moscow-built Su-9

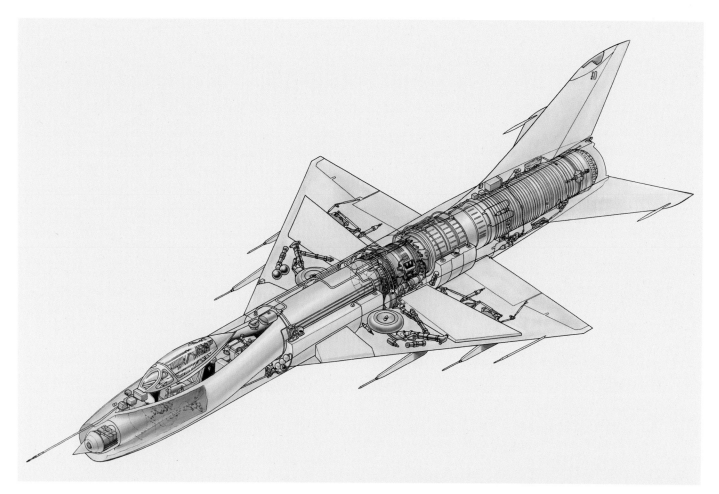

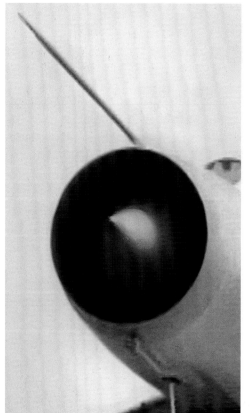

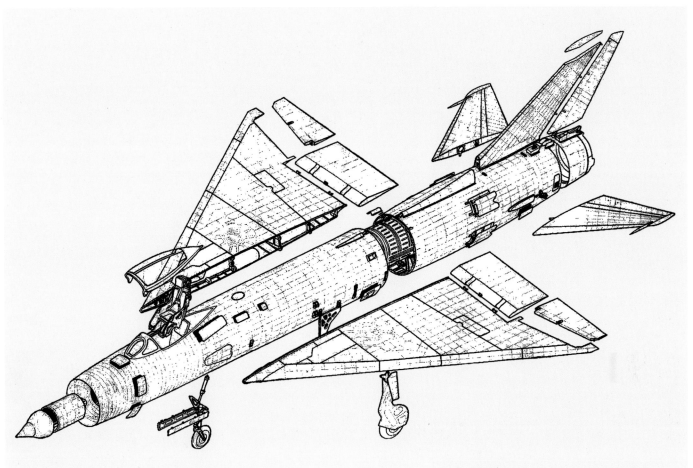

Opposite page, top: A 3-D drawing of the Su-9 from the ADP documents

Opposite page, left and *right*: The Su-9's air intake with the centrebody/radome in the aft position. Note the complex shape of the centrebody.

Opposite page, below right: The PVD-7 main pitot

This page, above: An exploded view of the Su-9

Left: This view shows the closely spaced auxiliary fuselage frames in the Su-9's extreme nose. The undernose aerials are for the ILS and the GCI data link system.

Right: Upper view of the nose, showing the access hatch of the no. 1 avionics bay

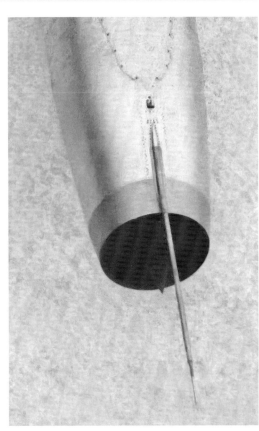

to frame 8), five longerons, and 25 stringers. The fuselage diameter is 1.55 m (5 ft., 1 in.) between frames 15 and 28, increasing to a maximum of 1.634 m (5 ft., $4^{3}/_{8}$ in.) in the rear fuselage. Cutouts in the skin where maintenance hatches are located have reinforcing flanges incorporated into the load-bearing structure.

Structurally the fuselage consists of two sections, with a break point that allows the rear fuselage to be detached for engine maintenance or removal. The two sections are held together by bolts, with pairs of fittings at the rear ends of the said longerons.

The *forward fuselage* (Section F-1, frames 0–28) is built in three portions, with manufacturing breaks at frames 4 and 9. The forward portion incorporates an axisymmetrical, circular air intake with a movable two-shock centre body (shock cone) attached to a vertical splitter. The latter divides the intake into two air ducts that flank the no. 1 avionics bay, the cockpit, and the fuel tank bay, merging ahead of the engine bay; their cross section changes from semicircular at the front to elliptical in the cockpit area and aft of it. The front end of the shock cone is a GRP radome; the splitter accommodates the no. 1 avionics bay ahead of the cockpit, housing the radar set, which is accessible via a trapezoidal dorsal cover between frames 2 and 3A, secured by screw-type fasteners. Four rectangular auxiliary blow-in doors are arranged in vertical pairs on the forward fuselage sides ahead of the cockpit, opening as required to prevent engine surge at high rpm; the shock cone and the doors are controlled by the ESUV-1 electrohydraulic air intake control system. An air data boom tipped with the PVD-7 (early aircraft) or PVD-18 main pitot is positioned on the fuselage centreline above the air intake.

The pressurised cockpit is located between frames 4 and 9, with the nosewheel well located underneath; it is flanked by the

Top left: The cockpit canopy of a very early Su-9 with a large transparency

Above left: The fully open canopy. The streaks on the windshield sidelights and windscreen are associated with the deicing system.

Left: Early Su-9s featured gun blast plates, even though no cannons were fitted! Note the cooling-air scoop underneath.

Below: The centre/rear fuselage featured numerous cooling-air scoops and an air outlet grille on each side.

inlet ducts, which merge again aft of the cockpit at frame 23. The forward and centre portions of Section F-1 (up to frame 9) have no stringers. The cockpit is contained by the inlet duct walls, the sloping pressure floor, and the flat pressure bulkheads; the sloping rear bulkhead (frames 8–9) carries ejection-seat guide rails. The cockpit is enclosed by a two-piece bubble canopy. The fixed windshield features two curved triangular Perspex sidelights and an elliptical, optically flat windscreen of bulletproof silicate glass; the aft-sliding canopy, with blown Perspex glazing, moves on guide rails and can be jettisoned in an emergency. The canopy frame is made of cast ML5-T4 magnesium alloy.

The no. 2 avionics/equipment bay, accessed from below, is located immediately aft of the cockpit, followed by the nos. 1 and 2 fuel tanks. The latter were bag-type tanks (fuel cells) on early Su-9 production batches (*izdeliye* 27 in Novosibirsk aircraft factory nomenclature); from c/n 0715302 onward, the no. 1 fuel cell was replaced by an integral tank (on the *izdeliye* 34 in Novosibirsk aircraft factory nomenclature). Concurrently with this change, the sloping fuselage frames 17–19, meant to serve as guides for the wing cannons' ammunition belts, were replaced by ordinary ones set at right angles to the fuselage waterline. The engine bay starts at frame 23, continuing aft to the fuselage break point. This part of the fuselage features numerous removable access panels and cooling-air scoops.

Fuselage mainframes 15, 21, 25, and 28 incorporate wing attachment fittings. Two 'wet' hardpoints are located side by side under the centre fuselage.

The *rear fuselage* (Section F-2, frames 29–45) is a one-piece structure; the greater part of its internal volume is occupied by the engine's extension jet pipe. A titanium firewall is provided at frame 31. The rear fuselage incorporates the ventrally located no. 3 fuel cell and the brake parachute bay aft of it (frames 34–35). Each of the four airbrakes, with an area of 0.33 m² (3.54 sq. ft.), is incorporated in a cruciform arrangement ahead of the tail unit; the airbrakes are electrohydraulically actuated and have a maximum deflection of 50°. Fuselage mainframes 38, 42, and 43 serve as attachment points for the fin and the stabilator axles.

Wings: Cantilever midwing monoplane with delta wings. Leading-edge sweep 60°, anhedral 2° from roots, incidence 0°. Root chord 7.674 m (25 ft., 2⅛ in.), tip chord 0.277 m (10²⁹⁄₃₂ in.), MAC 5.122 m (16 ft., 9⁴³⁄₆₄ in.).

The wings are of two-spar, riveted, stressed-skin construction; they are one-piece structures attached to the fuselage at frames 15, 21, 25, and 28. Each wing has 14 ribs, 25 rib caps, and three transverse beams (auxiliary spars), which, together with the front and rear spars, form five bays: the leading edge, forward bay, mainwheel well, rear bay, and trailing edge. The first few production Su-9s had a wing dogtooth approximately at half span (between rib caps 9 and 10), which was replaced by an unbroken wing leading edge from c/n 0315311 onward.

Early-production Su-9s had provisions for installing cannons in the forward bays; from c/n 1015351 onward, these bays were transformed into integral fuel tanks. The mainwheel wells are contained by the nos. 1 and 2 auxiliary spars. The space between the nos. 2 and 3 auxiliary spars is occupied by the integral wing

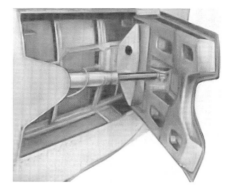

Above and *above right*: Retouched pictures of the airbrakes from the Su-9's structural manual

Below: The partially open airbrakes of a Su-9

tanks, whose skin panels are stamped integrally with the ribs and stringers; ordinary sheet-metal skins are used elsewhere. The port wing carries the auxiliary pitot close to the tip.

The wings have one-piece Fowler flaps terminating outboard of half span, with ailerons outboard of these. The constant-chord flaps are hydraulically actuated, moving on two tracks each; late-production aircraft feature a pneumatic emergency flap extension system. The strongly tapered ailerons, carried on three brackets each, are both aerodynamically balanced and mass balanced. There are two permanently installed pylons equipped with missile launch rails under each wing (see 'Armament'); the inboard pylons are located 2.289 m (7 ft., 6⁵⁄₃₂ in.) from the centreline and the outboard ones 3.046 m (10 ft., ⁵⁄₆₄ in.) from the centreline.

Tail unit: Conventional swept-cantilever tail surfaces of riveted, stressed-skin construction utlising symmetrical airfoils. The *vertical tail* comprises a one-piece fin and an inset rudder. Root chord 3.86 m (12 ft., 7³¹⁄₃₂ in.), tip chord 1.46 m (4 ft., 9³¹⁄₆₄ in.), MAC 2.84 m (9 ft., 3¹³⁄₁₆ in.). The fin is a single-spar structure with a rear auxiliary spar (internal brace), stringers, and 16 ribs; it features a curved root fillet that is built integrally with the fuselage and consists of two portions divided by the fuselage break point at frame

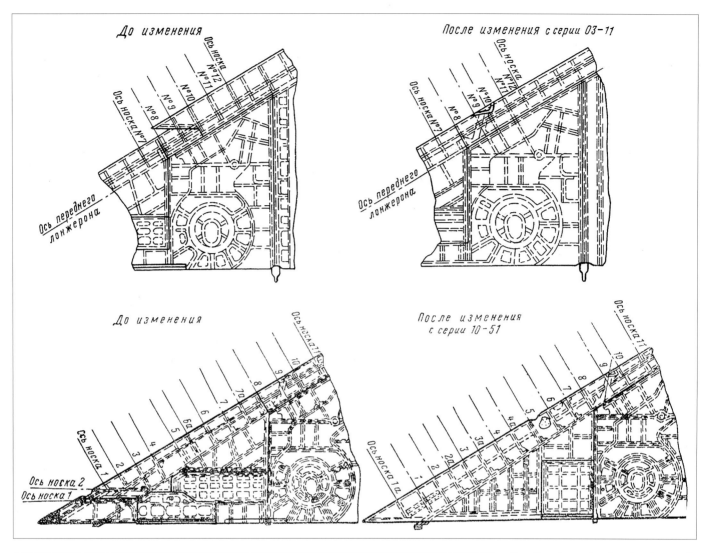

Top: Drawings showing the changes in the wing structure when the dog-tooth was eliminated from c/n 0315311 onward

Above: Drawings showing further changes in the wing structure when the cannon bays were eliminated from c/n 1015351 onward

Opposite page, top: Close-up of the port flap. The stencil reads *Ne stanovitsa* (No step).

Left: The starboard wing of a Su-9. The dark skin panel shows where the integral tank is. Note the cropped inboard end of the flap, the tapered aileron, and the navigation light ahead of it.

28. The GRP fin cap incorporates a wire mesh antenna for the radio. The mass-balanced rudder carried on three brackets is a single-spar structure, and the tip is likewise made of GRP.

The midset *horizontal tail* consists of all-movable slab stabilisers (stabilators) rotating on axles set at 48°30' to the fuselage axis; incidence in neutral position is –2°. Root chord 2.682 m (8 ft., 9³⁹/₆₄ in.), tip chord 0.745 m (2 ft., 5²¹/₆₄ in.), MAC 1.896 m (6 ft., 2⁴¹/₆₄ in.). Each stabilator is a single-spar structure with front and rear false spars, stringers, and ribs. The stabilators feature antiflutter weights projecting beyond the leading edge at the tips.

Landing gear: Hydraulically retractable tricycle type, with a single wheel on each unit; the nose unit retracts forward, the main units inward into the wing roots. All three landing-gear struts have oleo-pneumatic shock absorbers and semilevered suspension. The nose unit is equipped with a shimmy damper; the nose unit is castoring, and steering on the ground is by differential braking.

On early-production Su-9s the nose unit had a 570 × 140 mm (22.4 × 5.5 in.) K-283 nonbraking wheel, while the main units had 800 × 200 mm (31.5 × 7.87 in.) KT-50U brake wheels. Late pro-

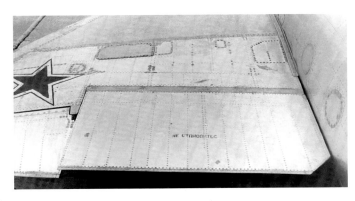

duction batches had a KT-38A brake-equipped nosewheel and KT-89 mainwheels of identical dimensions to the earlier models. Tyre pressure is 9 kg/cm² (128.5 psi) for the nosewheel and 12 kg/cm² (171.4 psi) for the mainwheels.

The nosewheel well is closed by twin lateral doors, the mainwheel wells by triple doors (one segment is hinged to the front spar, one to the root rib, and a third segment attached to the oleo leg). All doors remain open when the gear is down.

Above and *above left*: The vertical tail of a Su-9. These views show the dielectric fin cap, incorporating a radio antenna, the flush ATC/SIF transponder antenna, and the rudder actuator access panel at the base of the fin on the starboard side.

Left, *below*, and *below left*: The stabilators of a Su-9. The tips of the antiflutter weights were often painted red to reduce the risk of injury to the ground personnel.

Above: The nose gear unit of a late-production Su-9 with a KT-38 brake wheel

Above right / far right: These views show the air hoses feeding the nosewheel's pneumatic brake.

Below left: The starboard main gear unit of a Su-9
Below centre / right: The port main gear unit of a Su-9
Bottom: The inboard sides of the main gear units with KT-89 wheels. Note how the fins of the drop tanks overlap because the tanks are so close together; note also the odd-looking fixtures on the tanks.

The mainwheels are equipped with cerametallic disc brakes; the nosewheel has an expander-tube brake. To shorten the landing run, the Su-9 is equipped with a PT-7 or PTZ-7B single-canopy ribbon-type brake parachute (*parashoot tormoznoy*) with an area of 15 m² (161.4 sq. ft.), housed in a bay on the rear fuselage underside. The brake parachute cable is attached to the fuselage by an EPT-055D lock built into the tail bumper at frame 43.

Power plant: One Lyul'ka AL-7F-1 axial-flow afterburning turbojet rated at 6,240 kgp (13,760 lbst) at full military power and 9,200 kgp (20,280 lbst) in full afterburner. Late-production aircraft have an AL-7F-1-100, AL-7F-1-150, or AL-7F-1-200 uprated to 6,800 kgp (14,990 lbst) dry and 9,600 kgp (21,160 lbst) reheat, with a TBO increased to 100, 150, or 200 hours, respectively; the final production batches had a 250-hour TBO. The engine was produced by the 'Salyut' Moscow Engine Production Enterprise and the Rybinsk Engine Factory.

The AL-7F is a single-spool turbojet having an intake assembly with a fixed spinner and 12 radial struts, a nine-stage compressor with a supersonic first stage, an annular combustion chamber with 18 vortex-type flame tubes, a two-stage turbine, and an afterburner with a variable nozzle. The compressor has bleed bands at the fifth and seventh stages. The straight-through afterburner has inner and outer ducts, annular flameholder grids, and antivibration shielding; the two-position convergent-divergent nozzle has 24 petals.

Engine accessories are driven via a ventral accessory gearbox whose power takeoff shaft is located aft of the compressor. There are two ignition units with centrifugal fuel spray nozzles and SPN-4 igniters in two of the combustion chamber's flame tubes. Starting is by means of a TS-19A or TS-20A turbostarter (a small gas turbine engine driving the spool directly via a clutch), which is in turn started by an ST-3PT electric starter. The term 'jet fuel starter' is not applicable, since the starter runs on B-70-grade aviation gasoline; the supply of avgas is 8–9 litres (1.76–1.98 Imp gal.), permitting up to five engine start-ups. The starter is disengaged when the engine speed reaches 35% of the nominal rpm. Engine starting on the ground and in flight is controlled from an APD-21FM control panel, and the sequence is automatic; time from start to idle is no more than 60 seconds. Rundown time from idle rpm is at least 65 seconds. The engine accelerates from idle to full military power in 15–16 seconds and decelerates to idle in 5–6 seconds; afterburner light-up time is up to ten seconds.

The AL-7F has an all-mode hydromechanical fuel control unit (FCU) and a closed-type lubrication system with a fuel/oil heat exchanger.

Engine pressure ratio (EPR) 9.1 (AL-7F-1); mass flow at takeoff rating 114 kg/sec. (251 lbs./sec.), normal turbine temperature at takeoff rating 1,133° K, maximum turbine temperature 1,200° K. Specific fuel consumption (SFC) 2.0 kg/kgp·h (lb/lbst·h) in full afterburner and 0.91 kg/kgp·h in cruise mode; some sources state 2.3 and 0.96 kg/kgp·h, respectively. Length overall (including afterburner) 6,630 mm (21 ft., 9 in.), casing diameter 1,250 mm (4 ft., 1¼ in.). Dry weight 2,010 kg (4,430 lbs.; some sources state 2,050 kg / 4,520 lbs.); weight of fully dressed engine 2,325 kg (5,125 lbs.).

An AL-7F-1 engine with accessories but without the afterburner

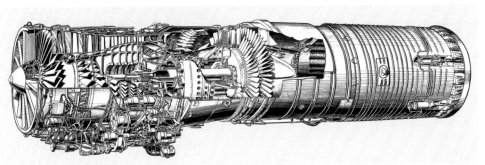

A cutaway drawing of the AL-7F-1 engine, complete with afterburner. Note the nozzle control actuators.

The engine breathes through a circular, supersonic air intake with a movable shock cone and auxiliary inlet doors, both controlled by the ESUV-1 system. The shock cone is in the fully aft position in subsonic flight, gradually moving forward as the Mach number increases, to provide the optimum position of the shock waves, ensuring stall-free engine operation throughout the speed envelope.

Control system: Conventional powered controls with irreversible actuators. Roll control is by means of one-piece ailerons powered by BU-49E actuators (E for *eleron*); pitch control is by means of stabilators powered by two BU-49S actuators (S for *stabilizahtor*: stabiliser), and directional control is by means of a one-piece rudder powered by a BU-49N actuator (N for [*rool'*] *napravleniya*: rudder).

Control inputs are transmitted to the aileron and stabilator actuators by rigid linkages (push-pull rods, control cranks, and levers); a combined linkage utilising both rods and cables is used in the rudder control circuit. Spring-loaded artificial-feel units are provided in all three control circuits; the rudder control circuit features two such units—one for takeoff/landing (disabled by landing-gear extension) and the other for cruise flight. The stabilator control circuit includes an ARZ-1 stick force limiter (*avtomaht reguleerovaniya zagroozki*), which adjusts the stick forces depending on the dynamic pressure, a differential mechanism altering the stick/tailplane gearing ratio, and a trim mechanism. The aileron control circuit features spring-loaded control rods for emergency manual control if one of the actuators fails. Early Su-9s had an AP-106M yaw damper; later aircraft featured a D-3K-110 three-channel damper serving all three control circuits.

Fuel system: On early Su-9s, internal fuel was carried in three fuel cells (two in the forward fuselage and one in the rear fuselage) and two integral tanks in the wing torsion box (aft of the mainwheel wells) holding a total of 3,060 litres (673.2 Imp gal.). The replacement of the no. 1 fuel cell by an integral tank and the provision of two more integral tanks in the wings on late-production aircraft increased the total capacity to 3,780 litres (831.6 Imp gal.). There are provisions for carrying two 620-litre (136.4 Imp gal.) PTB-600 drop tanks on pylons under the centre fuselage.

Refuelling is by gravity via individual filler caps. Fuel grades used are Russian T-1, TS-1, or RT jet fuel for the engine, with a

Two PTB-600 drop tanks under the fuselage of a Su-9

specific gravity of 0.83 g/cm³, 0.78 g/cm³, and 0.778 g/cm³, respectively, and B-70 aviation gasoline for the turbostarter.

Electrics: Main electric power provided by a 12 kW GS-12T DC generator and an SGO-8 single-phase AC generator. Backup DC power provided by a 12SAM-25 (28 V, 25 A.h) silver-zinc battery (or, on the Su-11, a 12-ASAM-23 battery) in the avionics/equipment bay. Stable-frequency AC power for some systems is supplied by four PO-4500 single-phase AC converters (*preobrazovahtel' odnofahznyy*), one PT-1000Ts three-phase AC converter, and one PT-500Ts three-phase AC converter (*preobrazovahtel' tryokhfahznyy*).

Exterior lighting includes port (red) and starboard (green) BANO-45 navigation lights (*bortovoy aeronavigatsionnyy ogon'*: lateral navigation light, 1945 model) on the wing upper surface, close to the wingtips, and a white KhS-39 tail navigation light (*khvostovoy signahl*) on the fin trailing edge. The Su-9 has an FR-100 taxi light (*fara roolyozhnaya*) on the nose gear strut and retractable LFSV-45 landing lights (*lampa-fara samolyotnaya vydvizhnaya*: aircraft-specific, retractable, sealed-beam lamp, 1945 model) in the wing underside. Early-production Su-9s had ultraviolet lights for the instrument panel to make the dials glow in the dark, later replaced by red cockpit lighting.

Hydraulics: Three separate hydraulic systems, each with its own NP-26/1 engine-driven piston pump (*nasos ploonzhernyy*). The *primary system* operates the landing gear, flaps, airbrakes, air-intake shock cone, and auxiliary blow-in doors; it also performs automatic wheel braking during landing-gear retraction. The two *actuator supply systems* (main and backup) exclusively power the aileron, rudder, and tailplane actuators; in addition to the engine-driven pump, the backup system features an NP-27 autonomous emergency pump, ensuring that the system remains operational (and hence the aircraft remains controllable) in the event of an engine failure. All systems use AMG-10 oil-type hydraulic fluid (*aviatsionnoye mahslo ghidravlicheskoye*: aviation-specific hydraulic [system] oil); nominal pressure 210 kg/cm² (3,000 psi).

Pneumatic system: Two subsystems (main and emergency). The pneumatic system operates the wheel brakes and inflatable canopy perimeter seal; it is also responsible for emergency landing gear and flap extension in the event of hydraulics failure. It is charged with nitrogen to 150 kg/cm² (2,140 psi). The Su-9 has three nitrogen bottles with a total capacity of 12 litres (2.64 Imp gal.).

Air-conditioning and pressurisation system: The cockpit is pressurised by air bled from the engine's fifth or seventh compressor stage, depending on rpm, to ensure proper working conditions for the pilot at high altitude. The sliding canopy features an inflatable perimeter seal controlled automatically (or manually in an emergency); the pressure is 1.75 kg/cm² (25 psi). Cockpit pressure is maintained by an ARD-57V automatic pressure governor (*avtomaticheskiy regoolyator davleniya*). It equals sea level pressure up to an altitude of 2,000 m (6,560 ft.); as the altitude increases, so does the pressure differential, reaching a maximum of 0.33 kg/cm² (4.71 psi).

Cockpit air temperature is maintained automatically at +10–20°C (50–68°F) by a TRTVK-45M regulator (*termostaht-regoolyator temperatoory vozdukha v kabine*). The air is fed to the cockpit via nozzles under the canopy transparencies, demisting them at the same time.

Oxygen system and high-altitude equipment: A KKO-2 oxygen equipment set (*komplekt kislorodnovo oboroodovaniya*) is provided for high-altitude operations; it also ensures pilot survival in the event of decompression. The KKO-2 comprises gaseous oxygen bottles, pressure reduction gear, a KM-3-OM oxygen mask (*kislorodnaya mahska*), a KP-34 breathing apparatus (*kislorodnyy pribor*) for normal operation, and a KP-27M breathing apparatus used in the event of an ejection at high altitude.

The pilot is equipped with a VKK-3M pressure suit (*vysotnyy kompenseeruyuschchiy kostyum*: altitude compensation suit) and a GSh-4M full-face pressure helmet (*ghermoshlem*), permitting safe ejection at high altitude.

Fire suppression system: The hot zone of the engine is isolated from the airframe by a titanium firewall at frame 31 and a heat shield around the engine. Fire extinguisher bottles charged with carbon dioxide are provided. System operation is manual; in the event of engine fire, several flame sensors trigger a fire warning light in the cockpit, and the pilot pushes a button, activating pyrotechnic valves and letting out the carbon dioxide into a manifold around the engine.

Avionics and equipment:

a) navigation and piloting equipment: GIK-1 gyro-flux gate compass on early-production Su-9s, replaced by a KSI compass system on later aircraft. RSP-6 instrument landing system including an ARK-5 Amur automatic direction finder with omnidirectional aerial and loop aerial, an RV-UM low-range radio altimeter, and an MRP-56P marker beacon receiver.

b) communications equipment: RSIU-4V two-way VHF radio with a mesh-type antenna built into the dielectric fin cap. The aircraft has a data link receiver forming part of the Lazoor' (ARL-S) ground-controlled intercept (GCI) system.

c) weapons control system: The standard Su-9 is equipped with an RP-9U (TsD-30) fire control radar whose radome is part of the air-intake shock cone; aircraft upgraded to take the R-55 AAM have a modified RP-9UK radar. The weapons control system of the Su-11 is built around a similarly positioned RP-11 fire control radar. An AKS-5 gun camera buried in the starboard wing leading edge records missile launches, and a PAU-457 photo module records the target (and the destruction thereof) on the radar display.

d) flight instrumentation: KUSI-2500 airspeed indicator (*kombineerovannyy ookazahtel' skorosti istrebitelya*: fighter-type combined ASI), VDI-30 altimeter (*vysotomer dvookhstrelochnyy istrebitelya*: fighter-type two-needle altimeter), AGI-1 artificial horizon replaced by an AGD-1 (*aviagorizont distantsionnyy*: remote artificial horizon) on late-production aircraft, EUP-53 turn and bank indicator (*elektricheskiy ookazahtel' povorota*), AM-10 accelerometer (g-load indicator), VAR-300 vertical speed indicator (*variometr*), ARK-5 ADF, GIK-1 gyro-flux gate compass with a common dial for the magnetic gyro compass, and the ADF, M-2,5 Mach meter and AChKh clock (*aviatsionnyye chasykhronometr*: aviation-specific chronometer).

Air data is provided by a primary PVD-7 or PVD-18 pitot on top of the fuselage nose and a backup pitot of the same type on the port wing.

e) IFF equipment: SRZO-2M Kremniy-2M IFF transponder with triple rod aerials located under the nose and under the rear fuselage; SOD-57M air traffic control / secondary IFF (ATC/SIF) transponder with flush aerial in the fin.

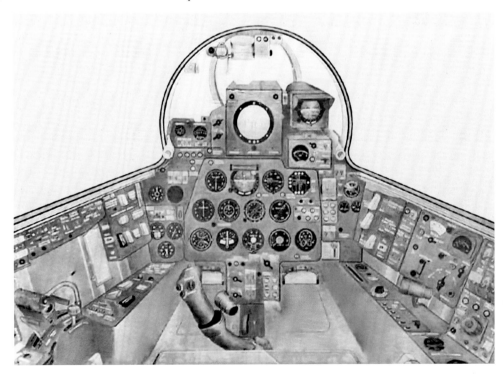

An instructional placard showing the cockpit of an early-production Su-9 with two integral tanks in the wings

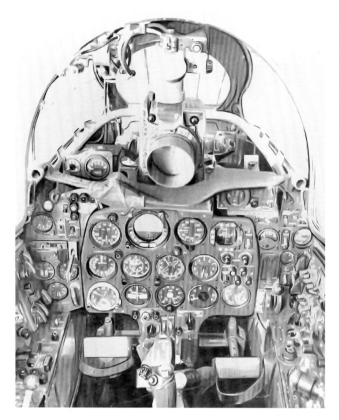

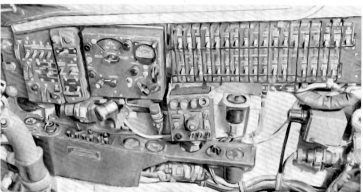

Armament: Originally four RS-2-US beam-riding, air-to-air missiles. On early aircraft these were carried on APU-19 pylons on the inboard (nos. 1 and 2) wing hardpoints and APU-20 pylons on the outboard (nos. 3 and 4) wing hardpoints; late-production Su-9s were fitted with APU-19D and APU-20D pylons. Later the aircraft's weapons system was upgraded by the addition of R-55

Above left: The cockpit of a late production Su-9 with a different radar display

Top: The port cockpit sidewall

Above: The starboard cockpit sidewall with the radio's control panel and system circuit breakers

Left: The starboard APU-19 and APU-20 missile pylons

Below and *below left*: This preserved Su-9 is carrying RS-2-US missiles with nonauthentic nose sections supposed to represent radar seeker heads!

Right: The KS-2 ejection seat of the single-seat Su-9

Centre right and *far right, above*: The cockpit canopy of a Su-9U

Far right, below: The open canopy of a Su-9U

infrared homing AAMs carried on APU-68UM launch rails, and the typical ordnance load came to consist of two RS-2-USs inboard and two R-55s outboard. The missiles can be fired singly, in pairs (with a 0.35-second interval), or all together with a 13-second interval between the pairs; the launch sequence in the latter case is 1-2-3-4.

Crew rescue system: Early-production Su-9s were equipped with a Sukhoi KS-1 ejection seat with an ejection speed limit of 850 km/h (528 mph). On later aircraft it was replaced by a more refined KS-2 seat fired by a TSM-188-52 telescopic ejection gun (*teleskopicheskiy strelyayushchiy mekhanizm*). The seat enables ejections at speeds up to 1,000 km/h (621 mph), the limit being caused by structural integrity reasons; minimum safe ejection altitude at speeds not less than 500 m (1,640 ft.) is 150 m (490 ft.),

which increased the maximum safe ejection speed to 1,000 km/h (620 mph). The final batches featured the improved KS-2A version.

The Su-9U differs from the single-seat Su-9 in the following respects:

Fuselage: The forward fuselage incorporates a 600 mm (1 ft., 11⅝ in.) stretch to accommodate a second cockpit for the instructor. The tandem cockpits are located between frames 4 and 13A and are enclosed by a common canopy with a redesigned fixed windshield (having a plain glass windscreen instead of a bullet-proof windscreen), individual aft-hinged portions operated by pneumatic rams, a glazed intercanopy crash frame in between, and a fixed metal rear fairing. The frames of the windshield, inter-

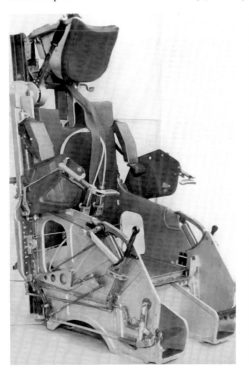

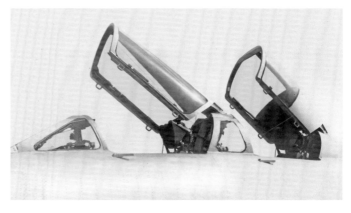

The starboard wing of a Su-9U. The trainer has only two wing pylons.

canopy crash frame, and rear-hinged canopy section are castings made of ML5-T4 magnesium alloy; the frame of the front-hinged canopy section is of riveted duralumin construction.

Wings: As for the Su-9, except that only two missile pylons (one under each wing) are provided at the outboard positions 3.046 m (10 ft., ⁵⁄₆₄ in.) from the centreline.

Landing gear: As for the Su-9, except that a PT-7U brake parachute is used.

Powerplant: One AL-7F-1-100U axial-flow afterburning turbojet.

Control system: Full dual controls.

Avionics and equipment:
b) communications equipment: The Su-9U features an SPU-2 intercom for communication between the trainee and the instructor.

Armament: Two RS-2-US air-to-air missiles carried on pylon-mounted APU-20 launch rails.

Crew rescue system: Two KS-2 ejection seats; the trainee's seat in the front cockpit has a cut-back headrest to improve the instructor's forward view.

The Su-11 differs from the Su-9 in the following respects:

Fuselage: Basically as for the Su-9, except that the number of fuselage frames is increased to 66 (with five more auxiliary frames in the forward fuselage). The forward fuselage diameter ahead of the cockpit is increased and the air-intake centre body is enlarged to accommodate the bigger radar; the air intake shock cone and auxiliary blow-in doors are controlled by the ESUV-2 electrohydraulic intake control system. The forward fuselage features two prominent wiring conduits (port and starboard) located on the upper fuselage sides.

Wings: As for the Su-9, except that only two missile pylons (one under each wing) are provided. Late-production Su-11s have a pneumatic emergency flap extension feature.

Landing gear: Basically as for the Su-9, except that the main units are reinforced and different types of wheels are used. On early-production Su-11s the nose unit had a 570 × 140 mm (22.4 × 5.5 in) KT-100 brake-equipped nosewheel, replaced on later production batches by a 600 × 155 mm (23.6 × 6.1 in) KT-104 wheel; the main units feature 880 × 230 mm (34.6 × 9.0 in) KT-69/4 wheels. Tyre pressure is 10 kg/cm² (142.85 psi) for the nosewheel and 13 kg/cm² (185.7 psi) for the mainwheels.

Powerplant: One AL-7F-2 turbojet with a maximum afterburner rating of 10,100 kgp (22,270 lbst). This version features a modified compressor with titanium first/second stage discs and improved eighth and ninth stages to increase the EPR to 9.3, a modified second turbine stage, a larger-diameter afterburner, a modified control system with turbine temperature and speed limiters, a TS-20B turbostarter and a new oil pump. Mass flow at take-off rating 115 kg/sec (253.5 lb/sec), maximum turbine temperature 1,200° K. SFC 2.0 (some sources say 2.25) kg/kgp·h in full afterburner and 0.89 kg/kgp·h in cruise mode. Length overall (including afterburner) 6,650 mm (21 ft 9⅞ in), maximum diameter 1,300 mm (4 ft 3⅛ in); dry weight 2,100 kg (4,630 lb). The TBO is increased to 300 hours.

The air intake features a pneumatic FOD prevention system, engine bleed air being fed via a pipeline on the port side of the fuselage to twin ejector nozzles under the intake lip to create increased pressure. The system was not used in service.

Control system: Basically as for the Su-9, except that the Su-11 features an AP-28Zh-1B autopilot with RA-16 servos in all three control circuits and a D-3K-110 yaw damper as standard.

Fuel system: The Su-11 has an internal fuel capacity of 4,195 litres (922.9 Imp gal) and carries larger 720-litre (158.4 Imp gal) drop tanks. The rear fuselage tank is an integral tank.

Electrics: Primary power sources as for the Su-9. Back-up DC power provided by a 12-ASAM-23 (28 V, 23 A·h) silver-zinc battery. Stable frequency AC power for some systems is supplied by four PO-750A single-phase AC converters, one PT-125Ts three-phase AC converter and one PT-500Ts three-phase AC converter.

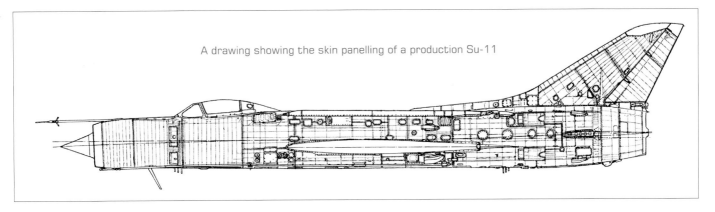

A drawing showing the skin panelling of a production Su-11

Above: The extreme nose and air intake of a production Su-11. Again, an ILS aerial is mounted underneath, with a GCI command link aerial aft of it.

Below: The cockpit canopy of a production Su-11; the opaque rear end of the sliding portion can be seen here.

Below right: Two drop tanks on the fuselage pylons of a Su-11. The tanks are longer than the 600-litre tanks of the Su-9, holding 720 litres each.

An additional PT-1200E AC converter caters for the weapons control system. The separate landing and taxi lights are replaced by two retractable PRF-4M landing/taxi lights (*posahdochno-roolyozhnaya fara*) in the wing underside. Again, early Su-11s had ultra-violet cockpit lighting, later replaced by red cockpit lighting.

Hydraulics: Basically as for the Su-9, except that the Su-11 has an NP34-1T pump in the primary hydraulic system and NP-26/3 pumps in the actuator supply systems, plus an NS-3 emergency pump in the back-up system. The primary system also operates the radar scanner drive and autopilot servos.

Pneumatic system: Basically as for the Su-9, except that the Su-11 has five nitrogen bottles with a total capacity of 21 litres (4.62 Imp gal).

Air conditioning and pressurisation system: On the Su-11 the cockpit air temperature limits are +16-20°C (60-68°F).

Oxygen system and high-altitude equipment: A KKO-3 oxygen equipment set is provided for high-altitude operations. Su-11 pilots used the VKK-3M or VKK-4 suit and GSh-4MS pressure helmet.

Avionics and equipment:
b) communications equipment: RSIU-5 two-way VHF radio with a mesh-type antenna built into the dielectric fin cap. The aircraft has a Lazoor' (ARL-S) data link receiver forming part of the GCI system.

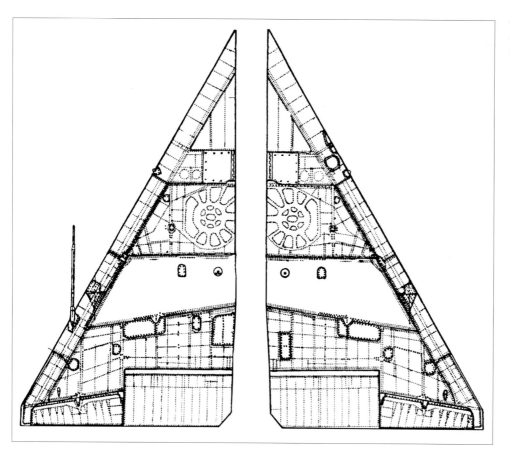

The upper side of the Su-11's wings, showing skin panels. The missile pylons are not shown in this instance.

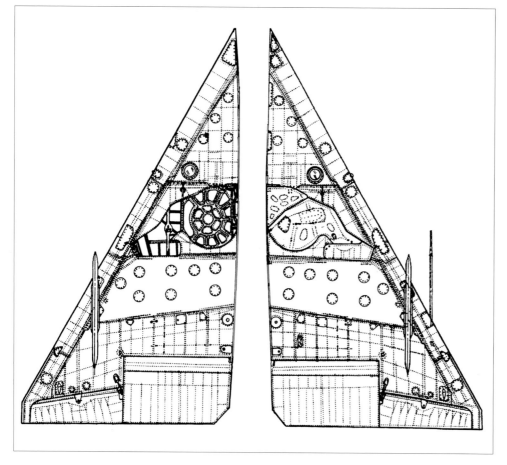

The underside of the Su-11's wings, showing skin panels and the inside of the starboard mainwheel well

c) weapons control system: The WCS is built around an RP-11 fire control radar whose radome is part of the air intake shock cone.

d) flight instrumentation: As for the Su-9, except that the GIK-1 gyro-flux gate compass indicator has a UKL-1 or UKL-2 heading indicator (UK = *ookazahtel' koorsa*), and a KI-13 induction-type compass (*kompas indooktsionnyy*) is added.

Armament: Two R-8M AAMs carried on PU-1-8 launch rails. Usually the complement includes one R-8MR SARH missile and one R-8MT IR-homing missile. The missiles can be fired singly or in a salvo with a 0.5-second interval. Provisions are made for carrying UPK-23-250 cannon pods with twin-barrel 23-mm cannons and 250 rpg on the fuselage hardpoints.

Crew rescue system: The Su-11 features a KS-3 ejection seat which expanded the operational envelope to a maximum speed of 1,100 km/h (683 mph) and a minimum safe ejection altitude of 30 m (100 ft).

Above right: The Su-11's tail surfaces

Right: The cockpit of the Su-11

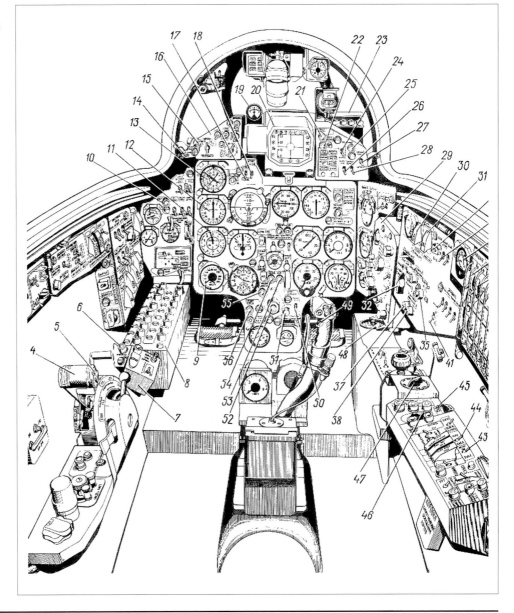

An R-98R missile on the port wing pylon of a Su-11. The canard foreplanes are fixed, control being effected by the inset rudders. The missile on the left photo has a protective cap over the seeker head.

Su-9 and Su-11 specifications

	Su-9	Su-9U	Su-11
Power plant	AL-7F-1	AL-7F-1	AL-7F-2
Takeoff rating, kgp (lbst):			
dry	6,800 (14,990)	6,800 (14,990)	6,800 (14,990)
reheat	9,600 (21,160)	9,600 (21,160)	10,100 (22,270)
Length overall:			
including pitot	18.055 m (59 ft., $2\frac{7}{8}$ in.)	18.655 m (61 ft., $2\frac{1}{2}$ in.)	18.23 m (59 ft., $9\frac{23}{32}$ in.)
less pitot	16.772 m (55 ft., $\frac{5}{16}$ in.) [1]	17.372 m (56 ft., $11\frac{15}{16}$ in.) [1]	17.546 m (57 ft., $6\frac{3}{4}$ in.) [1]
Wingspan	8.536 m (28 ft., 0 in.)	8.536 m (28 ft., 0 in.)	8.536 m (28 ft., 0 in.)
Height on ground	4.82 m (15 ft., $9\frac{3}{4}$ in.)	4.82 m (15 ft., $9\frac{3}{4}$ in.)	4.7 m (15 ft., 5 in.)
Wing area, m^2 (sq. ft.)	34.0 (365.5)	34.0 (365.5)	34.0 (365.5)
Wheel track	4.715 m (15 ft., $5\frac{5}{8}$ in.)	4.715 m (15 ft., $5\frac{5}{8}$ in.)	4.715 m (15 ft., $5\frac{5}{8}$ in.)
Wheelbase:			
no-load condition	4.88 m (16 ft., $\frac{1}{8}$ in.)	5.48 m (17 ft., $11\frac{3}{4}$ in.)	4.88 m (16 ft., $\frac{1}{8}$ in.)
under static load	5.055 m (16 ft., $7\frac{1}{64}$ in.)	5.655 m (18 ft., $6\frac{41}{64}$ in.)	5.055 m (16 ft., $7\frac{1}{64}$ in.)
Empty weight, kg (lbs.)	7,675 (16,920)	n.a.	8,562 (18,875)
Takeoff weight, kg (lbs.):			
normal	11,442 (25,225)	11,773 (25,955)	12,674 (27,940)
maximum (with drop tanks)	12,512 (37,583)	12,863 (28,357)	13,986 (30,833)
Internal fuel load, kg (lbs.)	3,100 (6,835)	3,100 (6,835)	3,440 (7,580)
Top speed at 12,000 m (39,370 ft.), km/h (mph):			
one-minute afterburner engagement	2,230 (1,385)	2,230 (1,385)	n.a.
prolonged afterburner engagement	2,120 (1,315) [2]	2,100 (1,304) [3]	2,340 (1,450)
Service ceiling, m (ft.)	20,000 (65,620)	19,700 (64,630)	18,000 (59,050)
Range, km (miles):			
on internal fuel	1,350 (838)	1,130 (700)	1,260 (780) [4]
with drop tanks	1,800 (1,118)	1,370 (850)	1,710 (1,060) [4]
Takeoff run, m (ft.)	1,200 (3,940)	1,350 (4,430)	1,100–1,250 (3,600–4,100)
Landing run without brake parachute, m (ft.)	1,150–1,250 (3,770–4,100)	1,200 (3,940)	1,000–1,200 (3,440–3,940)

Notes:

1. Air intake shock cone in fully aft position
2. Speed limited to Mach 2.1
3. With two K-5M (RS-2-US) AAMs
4. The Su-11's range is also reported as 1,350 km (838 miles) on internal fuel and 1,800 km (1,118 miles) with PTB-600 drop tanks.

Chapter 5

Defending the Homeland:
The Su-9 and Su-11 in Service

As early as 1959 the Novosibirsk aircraft factory began deliveries of production Su-9s both to the fighter arm of the air defence force (IA PVO) and, strange as it may seem, to the air force. The only air force unit to operate the type was the Tactical Aviation's 4th TsBP i PLS (*Tsentr boyevoy podgotovki i pereoochivaniya lyotnovo sostahva*: Combat Training & Aircrew Conversion Centre), located at Lipetsk-2 airbase immediately northwest of the city of Lipetsk in central Russia. This situation did not last long, though; less than a year later, in May 1960 (even before the type was officially accepted for service), all air force Su-9s were

transferred to the PVO, which thus became the sole operator of the Fishpot.

The Su-9 achieved IOC in 1959, gradually replacing the subsonic, cannon-armed, MiG-17PF all-weather interceptor and the missile-toting supersonic MiG-19PM. Mastering the Fishpot-B proved to be quite a challenge for flight and ground crews alike, owing to the lot of new technology that had gone into the design of the Sukhoi delta-wing jet and the complexity of its equipment.

As already mentioned in chapter 2, the Su-9's production run was rather modest; a total of 1,058 (1,008 single-seaters and 50

This early 1970s publicity photo of early Su-9s is supposed to represent a scramble. However, aircraft on quick-reaction-alert duty would not normally have the cockpit and missiles under wraps!

Left: Su-9 '26 Blue' is being refuelled on a flight line, with several Su-9s in single file. Note the dolly loaded with missiles and the APA-2 ground power unit based on a ZiL-164 general-purpose lorry beside the next aircraft. The base hosts more than one unit, as suggested by the Mil' Mi-6 and Mi-8 transport helicopters and the Ilyushin IL-14 staff transport in the background.

Right: Su-9 '43 Blue' is caught by the camera immediately after lifting off. The absence of missiles indicates this is a practice sortie or a checkout flight. The red star on the tail appears to have vanished altogether.

Far right: '06 Blue', another Su-9 pictured on takeoff with drop tanks but no missiles. Note that the flaps are retracted.

Left: A typical publicity shot from the flight line of an IA PVO unit equipped with Su-9s. The pilots are wearing winter attire and early-model GSh-4 full-face pressure helmets with tinted visors. Typically of PVO aircraft, the tactical codes are blue (in this case, light blue with a black outline). Note the ADF aerial foil strips glued to the canopy and the black antiglare strips on the missile pylon leading edges.

Right: Su-9 '12 Blue' takes off. It is probably from the same unit as '06', depicted above.

Su-9U trainers) had been built when production ended in 1962. Nevertheless, this was enough to equip 31 PVO units at the peak of the type's strength in 1963.

The first PVO unit to reequip with the Su-9 was the 813th IAP (*istrebitel'nyy aviapolk*: fighter regiment), which was then stationed at Novosibirsk-Tolmachovo airport, a stone's throw away from aircraft factory no. 153; it took delivery of the first production interceptors in June 1959. (In the Soviet Union, and later in Russia, quite a few airfields serve[d] a dual purpose, being both civil airports and air force or PVO bases; Tolmachovo was one of them, being originally a fighter base but becoming an airport in 1957.)

This was common practice during the service introduction of a new aircraft, because the close proximity of the manufacturer allowed any problems to be speedily solved. Concurrently the PVO's 148th TsBP i PLS at Savasleyka AB (Gor'kiy Region; now renamed back to Nizhniy Novgorod Region) dispatched a group of highly skilled pilots to the regiment to take conversion training in situ. (Normally it was the 148th TsBP i PLS that would be the first to receive the new hardware, but here the procedure was reversed because of the need to stay close to the factory.) IA PVO commander Air Marshal Yevgeniy Ya. Savitskiy tasked the centre's personnel with mastering the type as quickly as possible and

then participating in the deliveries of brand-new Su-9s to operational units. By early July PVO pilots had made 72 flights in the first eight production fighters; the first six service pilots had received their type ratings, with another three in the training pipeline.

The 813th IAP at Novosibirsk-Tolmachovo AP (which subsequently moved to a new base at Koopino in the west of the Novosibirsk Region) was quickly followed by other PVO regiments stationed far and wide across the nation, from east to west and from north to south. Instead of being delivered in crates by rail, as was often the case, Su-9s built by plant no. 153 were flown to their home bases from Novosibirsk-Yel'tsovka. Due to the interceptor's limited range even with drop tanks, this was no easy task, since it was necessary to stage through airfields located no more than 1,000 km (620 miles) apart—which was often impossible in Siberia and the Soviet Far East, with their huge expanses of woodland. As a way out, the PVO top command proposed fitting the Su-9 with a special nonjettisonable, large-capacity ferry tank instead of the standard 600-litre (132 Imp gal.) drop tanks. In November 1959, Sukhoi OKB engineers proposed a conformal ventral tank fitted to the existing twin fuselage hardpoints in a manner similar to the *Dackelbauch* ('dachshund belly') ferry tank used on the Messerschmitt Bf 110. In Sukhoi OKB parlance this item was dubbed ***bahk-prilipala***: 'remora tank'. Estimated range with this tank was almost doubled as compared to the standard configuration. Ironically, however, it was the military who eventually killed off the idea by demanding that a fuel jettison or emergency tank jettison feature be incorporated—which turned out not to be feasible.

Early-production Su-9s with bag-type fuselage fuel tanks had a limited combat radius; depending on the flight profile, it was approximately 320–450 km (200–280 miles) when intercepting a

Above left: A Su-9 pilot wearing a ZSh-5 'bone dome' helmet and a life vest poses beside his aircraft, which is fully armed with four RS-2-US missiles. Note that the APU-19 and APU-20 pylons had sharp tips, so the ground personnel needed to be extra careful to avoid injury.

Left: This publicity photo gives a good view of an RS-2-US missile from the rear, showing the guidance aerial and the wingtip-mounted tracer flares.

typical target cruising at 20,000 m (65,600 ft.). Later the internal fuel capacity was increased by incorporating an integral no. 1 tank, increasing the combat radius to an acceptable 430–600 km (270–370 miles). The conversion training programme for Su-9 pilots included several typical operational scenarios, and the optimum climb profile and interception tactic were different in each case.

Using the Su-9's weapons had a few peculiarities. In the early days the RP-9U radar had an excessively high minimum altitude at which missiles could be launched and guided—5,000 m (16,400 ft.) or even 8,000 m (26,250 ft.), which imposed limits on the interceptor's operational envelope; later, measures were taken to reduce this altitude significantly. An even-bigger handicap was the inadequate 'kill' range of the RS-2-US AAM. As one PVO pilot put it, *'because of the missiles' short range—3 km [1.86 miles]—to achieve a guaranteed "kill" we were forced to fly up the target's ass. Quite often a pilot fired a missile when apparently within range—and missed because the RS-2-US could not catch up with the target and fell with ignominy.'*

Intercepting a target at medium altitude presented no difficulties even for average-skilled pilots. An interesting 'pass me and die' tactic was developed against supersonic unmanned targets; the Su-9 would be directed to a point ahead of the target on its anticipated course, flying slightly below it, and then fire the missiles as the target overtook it. On the other hand, slow and high-flying targets (such as the famous Lockheed U-2) were a much-tougher nut to crack. In order to reach the Su-9's service ceiling the pilot needed to execute the so-called basic mode—that is, climb to a certain altitude (not less than 10,000 m / 32,800 ft.), then accelerate to Mach 1.6 in level flight and gently put the aircraft into a climb while maintaining an indicated airspeed of 1,100 km/h (683 mph), the Mach number increasing to 1.9 in the process. After that, the aircraft would climb at high angles of attack; the speed needed to be not less than Mach 1.7—otherwise the Su-9 would simply stall at that altitude. Concurrently the pilot had to make constant course corrections as instructed from the ground in order to get a target lock-on—and, since the interceptor was closing in on the target all too fast, the pilot had very little time for making an attack.

Slow-flying Yakovlev Yak-25RV Mandrake high-altitude reconnaissance aircraft were used as the targets for simulated attacks during practice intercepts, as were Tupolev Tu-16 Badger medium bombers and other Su-9s. During live weapons training at target ranges, the Su-9s fired at IL-28M, M-15, and M-17 target drones and purpose-built Lavochkin La-17 jet-powered target drones.

Above right: Lt. A. P. Nikiforov (*left*) and Lt. V. N. Borodin in summer flight suits and ZSh-5 helmets pose with a Su-9 carrying a rarely seen R-55 IR-homing AAM on the port outer pylon.

Right: Another view of the same Su-9 (note the aircraft's tactical code '27' on the drop tank) with Lt. Borodin and another pilot. Note the partially open airbrakes.

Left: Maintenance work on a Su-9 in the middle of the night. Judging by the numbers on the air intake cover, '34 Blue' was previously coded '05'.

Below: 'Though rain may pour and blizzards blow, our vigil still we keep.' This view of a Su-9 coded '39 Blue' on QRA duty illustrates the compound curvature of the intake centrebody's surface.

Right: An unusual 'toad's eye view' of a Su-9. Note the fully open airbrakes.

In addition to aerial-intercept techniques, Su-9 pilots were ordered to practice—wait for it—ground attack techniques, just like their colleagues in the air force's Tactical Aviation. Unlike the latter, this was quite outside their usual line of work, but apparently the decision makers in the Ministry of Defence believed that 'every bit helped'. The only possible way the Su-9 could perform strike duties was to fire RS-2-US AAMs in a dive, with the RP-9U radar working in fixed-beam mode so that the missiles went straight ahead like unguided rockets. Contrary to claims by some sources that 'this was nothing but an isolated test programme', practice strike sorties by Su-9s were flown for quite a while, especially in 1963–64. (Well, actually, the 737th IAP at Sary-Shagan AB did undertake research work of this kind, firing RS-2-US missiles at armoured vehicles on a target range; for want of a proper sight optimised for air-to-ground work, a reference grid was painted on the cockpit windscreen. One of these flights ended in a fatal crash when the Su-9's engine surged after ingesting missile blast gases in the dive. Overruling the range commander, who had told the pilot to eject, fighter division CO Leonid S. Gol'berg ordered the pilot to make an off-field forced landing, which worked out horribly wrong.

Conversion training was something of a problem initially due to the lack of a dedicated trainer version. Future Su-9 pilots first made several flights in a subsonic UTI-MiG-15 trainer; then, having gotten a credit in the theoretical training course, they started mastering the practice part of the course on the single-seat Su-9. This situation persisted until 1962, when MMZ No. 30 started turning out dual-control Su-9Us. Several of these aircraft were delivered to the 148th TsBP i PLS, the first-line units equipped with the Su-9 also taking delivery of one trainer each. Even so, the UTI-MiG-15 (supplanted in the second half of the 1960s by the Su-7U) was still used for Su-9 pilot lead-in training because the Su-9Us were in short supply.

The Su-9 was famed for its 'willingness to fly', and the type's service record includes a few truly amazing incidents. For instance, on 11 June 1964 the crew of a 179th IAP Su-9U, trainee Capt. Mel'nikov and instructor Maj. Nikolayev, lost concentration during the approach to Stryy AB after a training sortie, allowing speed to bleed off dangerously, and ejected, fearing that the trainer would stall and spin. Left to its own devices, the aircraft unexpectedly righted itself, climbed to about 1,300 m (4,265 ft.), and circled around the airbase until it ran out of fuel. It then glided down and landed on its own (!) in a ploughed field; unfortunately the landing was far from perfect, and the aircraft sustained major structural damage, being declared a write-off. Another case when the aircraft displayed more presence of mind than the driver occurred just seven months later. On 25 January 1965, Lt.-Col. Ovcharov, a 737th IAP pilot, took off from Sary-Shagan AB on a night training mission in a single-seat Su-9; soon afterward he discovered a control system malfunction and promptly ejected. Came dawn next day, and the aircraft was discovered 32 km (19¾ miles) from the base in virtually undamaged condition, save for a punctured no. 1 fuel tank! The aircraft was sitting 'in the middle of nowhere' in flat steppeland, resting on its drop tanks, which had been flattened on impact. Investigation showed that the aircraft had not even used up the fuel completely, and it was sheer luck that there had been

no fire. The pilotless Su-9 had touched down in a wings-level attitude at about 400 km/h (248 mph), the crushed drop tanks turning into improvised skis (!) on which it slithered for about 250 m (820 ft.) before coming to a standstill. The bottom line: this unique episode was classed as a 'nonfatal accident / aircraft repairable', and the Su-9 was actually repaired and returned to service!

Nevertheless, the first months of operational service revealed a host of problems and shortcomings. For one thing, early-production AL-7F-1 engines had an appallingly low TBO (a mere 25 to 50 hours), which meant that the interceptors were often grounded by the lack of engines. The TS-19 turbostarter, which ran on petrol, often refused to start at subzero temperatures, turning winter operations into a problem. The AL-7F-1 engine was also prone to surging and flaming out in certain modes; some pilots succeeded in making dead-stick landings more than once.

For another, systems and equipment often failed both in flight and during ground checks, and many equipment items were not easily accessible, requiring the aircraft to be substantially 'undressed'. An incessant stream of claims kept pouring in at the factory and the OKB; the latter took corrective measures, and at times the factory was simply swamped in documents from the OKB requiring this or that modification to be made. This unfortunate situation was eventually resolved, the OKB and the air force agreeing that the manufacturer's teams would perform all necessary modifications in situ. One of the first important

Three Su-9s make a flypast in close formation during the 9 July 1967 parade at Moscow-Domodedovo airport.

Another angle on the same formation over Domodedovo

upgrades was the introduction of the ESUV-1 electrohydraulic system, controlling the air-intake shock cone and auxiliary blow-in doors. In the course of the year 1960, teams consisting of Sukhoi OKB and Novosibirsk aircraft factory personnel had modified more than 120 Su-9s in service.

On the other hand, jet fuel was abundant in those days, and in the days of the Su-9's service introduction period the PVO pilots often logged as many as 150–200 flying hours per year. The service pilots were happy with the fighter's performance and handling; the Su-9 was rock steady at all speeds and had next to no unpleasant peculiarities in transonic flight mode. However, mind-

ful of its initial reliability issues, the pilots used to say: *'Flying the Su-9 is like cuddling a tiger: it feels good but it is dangerous and the outcome is uncertain'*.

Also, the Su-9 had a much-bigger speed and altitude envelope than the predecessors. True enough, its outstanding acceleration characteristics created a few problems in the early days; pilots recalled that the aircraft accelerated very quickly to its maximum landing-gear transition speed during takeoff, and you had to be quick in getting the gear up. Other peculiarities that took some adjusting to included an unusually high angle of attack during climb and landing approach, rapid deceleration from high speeds when the engine was throttled back (in so doing, the sink rate increased, and at best the result was a bumpy landing), and the high landing speed.

Su-9 vs. U-2: The Powers Missions

Meanwhile, the world political situation did not look too good; the First Cold War was gaining momentum. In the late 1950s the US Central Intelligence Agency (CIA) launched a large-scale reconnaissance operation against the Soviet Union, and the Lockheed U-2 strategic reconnaissance aircraft figured most prominently in this operation. The CIA acted on the assumption that the USSR lacked the technical means for intercepting aerial targets flying above 20,000 m (65,600 ft.). Initially the spy missions involving incursions into Soviet airspace were flown from Pakistani territory, the U-2 flying along the Soviet border. Then, as the Americans grew confident they could do it with impunity, the CIA decided to penetrate deep into Soviet territory. The first such intrusion took place on 9 April 1960. A U-2A flown by none other than Capt. Francis Gary Powers took off from the US airbase in Peshawar, Pakistan (alias Badaber Air Station). The intruder was detected belatedly because the AD radars' field of view was obstructed by mountains. Crossing the Soviet border, the U-2 made several passes at 20,000–21,000 m (65,620–68,900 ft.) over the PVO missile test range near Lake Balkhash in Kazakhstan, where the S-75 Dvina (SA-2 Guideline) SAM was being tested; it was not shot down for the simple reason that there were no live SAMs on site at the moment. Next, it overflew the Baikonur space centre in Kazakhstan and escaped into Iran, crossing the border near the town of Maryy (pronounced like the French name 'Marie'), Turkmenia, after spending 6 hours and 48 minutes in Soviet airspace with impunity.

Of course, all hell broke loose; both the PVO's interceptors and the air force's tactical fighters scrambled from several bases, but the MiG-19S Farmer-C and MiG-17F Fresco-C could not reach the

Above right: Technicians prepare to remove the ejection seat from a Su-9 by means of a small crane. Note the partially open airbrakes. An APA-5 GPU based on the Ural-375D 6 x 6 army lorry provides electric power; unusually, this one has a 'ragtop' cab, a rare version.

Right: Technicians swarm like ants over a Su-9 undergoing maintenance. The black hole on the centre fuselage is an air spill grille.

'29 Red', the second preproduction Moscow-built Su-9 (c/n 109000002), served as an instructional airframe at the PVO Junior Technical Specialists' School in Solntsevo. Note the ground safety covers on the stabilators' antiflutter weights.

high-flying U-2. The 735th IAP, which was reequipping with the Su-9 at the time, was also involved. Two Fishpot-Bs scrambled from Khanabad AB, Uzbekistan; however, not being fully familiar with the type and receiving wrong instructions from the command post (which was not yet equipped with the Vozdukh-1 GCI system), flight leader Capt. Doroshenko and wingman Lt. (SG) Kudelya failed to find the U-2. This was the pilots' first experience with pressure suits and pressure helmets, and they climbed straight up instead of accelerating to supersonic speed in level flight as they should have—passing well below the target as a result. The fate of the Su-9, which had only just been recommended for service entry, now hung by a thread; moreover, the reputation of the Sukhoi OKB and the pilots who had tested the Su-9 was in jeopardy. A special commission arrived from Moscow to investigate the incident and find the culprit. The commission included test pilots Vladimir S. Ilyushin (representing the OKB) and Leonid N. Fadeyev (representing GK NII VVS); the latter pilot performed a check flight, using the officially approved climb technique, and reached the required altitude of 20,000 m. Thus the Su-9 was exonerated completely; since the service pilots were really not to blame either, the PVO top command vented its wrath on the PVO Aviation's chief of combat training, Lt.-Gen. Grigoriy F. Pogrebnyak, who was removed from office. For the two weeks that followed, test pilots Ilyushin, Fadeyev, Gheorgiy T. Beregovoy, and Nikolay I. Korovushkin maintained combat duty at the GK NII VVS facility in Akhtoobinsk, ready to stop a new incursion should it occur. On 26 April a squadron of Su-9s flown by service pilots arrived in Akhtoobinsk, relieving the test pilots of this duty.

As the saying goes, the pitcher goes often to the well but is broken at last. On 1 May 1960, Francis G. Powers ran out of luck while flying another spy mission in a U-2A serialled 56-6693 (c/n 360). The mission had been timed to the May Day celebrations in the hope that the Soviets would be less vigilant. This time the route, again originating in Peshawar, lay northward across the central Asian republics to the Urals region; the objective was to reconnoitre the *Mayak* (Lighthouse) Production Association—a plutonium enrichment facility in Ozyorsk, 150 km (93 miles)

southeast of Sverdlovsk—and the Plesetsk missile facility. At first, it looked like the April scenario was going to be repeated. The spyplane entered Soviet airspace near Termez at about 0530 hrs. Moscow time, flying at 20,100 m (65,940 ft.); PVO fighter regiments stationed along the spyplane's route repeatedly but unsuccessfully tried to intercept it, being equipped with MiG-19PMs. Yet, as the U-2 approached Sverdlovsk (now renamed back to Yekaterinburg), it crossed the area covered by the 37th and 57th SAM Brigades, which fired eight S-75 missiles at the target as it cruised leisurely at 21,740 m (71,330 ft.). The first missile, launched at 0846 hrs. Moscow time, nailed the U-2; apparently one more SAM scored a hit, finishing off the job, while the others missed and self-destructed. Powers ejected and was captured after parachuting to safety near Kosoolino railway station, later facing trial and jail.

Here we have to describe the events taking place immediately before and immediately after the shootdown. Again, the only available aircraft that stood a chance of getting at the U-2 was the Su-9. As luck would have it, that very day a pair of factory-fresh Su-9s destined for the 61st IAP at Baranovichi, Belorussia, were staging through Sverdlovsk-Kol'tsovo airport on their westbound delivery flight. (In many accounts of the shootdown these aircraft are mistakenly referred to as 'preproduction T-3s'.) The fighters were flown by Capt. Igor' A. Mentyukov and Capt. Anatoliy N. Sakovich (the latter was a 61st IAP pilot).

Now, the Su-9's armament consisted solely of AAMs, and of course the fighters carried none on the delivery flight. Also, the pilots were not wearing pressure suits as the flight proceeded at low level. Nevertheless, in a gesture of despair, IA PVO commander Col.-Gen. Yevgeniy A. Savitskiy expressly ordered Sakovich to take off and ram the intruder; this was, in effect, a suicide mission, since the pilot would be unable to eject without a pressure suit. Yet, with orders at that level, and in view of the mission's importance, the pilot complied. Sakovich took off at 0740 hrs. and was directed to a spot 150 km south of Troitsk (the name means 'Trinity Town'). However, the guidance proved to be inaccurate and the pilot failed to find the target. After hitting 'bingo fuel' (running critically low on fuel), Sakovich landed at the dirt strip in Troitsk.

Right: A Novosibirsk-built Su-9 on QRA duty in the Moscow PVO District, with a full complement of missiles and drop tanks and the canopy open, ready for the pilot to climb in.

Below: Crews sprint to a pair of Su-9s during a practice scramble (note the absence of missiles on the wing pylons).

(Interestingly, when recounting this episode for the Belorussian MoD monthly magazine **Armiya** (Army), Col. Nikolay P. Filatov (ret.), a former pilot with the 61st IAP, put it as follows: *'Many a time we received unmanned "presents" in the form of drifting reconnaissance balloons. . . . But the balloons are as nothing compared to Capt. A. Sakovich. Here's a might-have-been Talalikhin for you!* [Lt. (JG) Viktor V. Talalikhin was a Red Army air force fighter pilot who, having expended his ammunition, rammed a Heinkel He 111H with his Polikarpov I-16 near Podol'sk on the night of 27 October 1941 to stop the German bomber from reaching Moscow. He lost his life in so doing and was posthumously awarded the Hero of the Soviet Union title.] *Few people are aware of the fact that Sakovich nearly downed the U-2 of* [Francis Gary] *Powers, who had dared to spoil the May Day celebrations for our country in 1960.*

'That day Anatoliy Nikolayevich [Sakovich] *was at one of the military airfields near Sverdlovsk. He was then a flight commander and was ferrying Su-9 supersonic interceptors to his unit's home base from the Novosibirsk aircraft factory. Sakovich was ordered to scramble and intercept, even though his aircraft*

Left: Using an APM-90 mobile search-light mounted on a ZiL-130 general-purpose lorry to provide illumination, technicians prepare a Su-9 for a night sortie at a snow-covered airbase.

Right: An atmospheric dusk shot of Su-9 '15 Red' on a flight line with 'streetlights'. Note the signal lamps on the landing gear, telling ground observers that the gear is down and locked during approach. The red tactical code is unusual.

Below: Su-9s '40 Blue' and '90 Blue' on a floodlit hardstand before a night practice sortie. Neither aircraft carries missiles.

Below right: A publicity photo of two blue-coded Su-9s awaiting a sortie on a winter night

was carrying no missiles; yet, he had orders to attack in any way he could—even ram [the adversary] if necessary! And he would have rammed it if ground control had not bungled: the [GCI] navigators were unable to guide the interceptor properly to the target.

'The intruder then entered the area protected by the SAM guys, who walked away with the prize. This, as you know, had grievous consequences for our aviation. "We do not need aeroplanes like these!" said an angry Nikita Sergeyevich [Khrushchov] and placed his bets on the missiles, ordering the [fighter] air regiments to be disbanded. But, to give the Minister of Defence due credit, Sakovich was not left out in the cold—for his bravery he received a gold watch from the minister.' (A gold watch with an engraved commemorative inscription from the command was no mean reward for the flying personnel in those days, and such gifts were given for saving the aircraft after an in-flight emergency—or for acting properly in exceptional circumstances like these.)

Next, Igor' Mentyukov was ordered up at 0810 hrs. (some sources say 0814 hrs.) with identical orders—'destroy at any cost'. He agreed, asking only that his family be taken care of. The GCI post of the 101st IAD at Uktus (this is now the other airport of Yekaterinburg) did the guidance; yet, once again ground control failed to properly guide the unfamiliar fighter. Accelerating to 2,200 km/h (1,367 mph), Mentyukov climbed to 20,750 m (68,080 ft.) but found himself 10–12 km (6.2–7.5 miles) from the target, which was flying 2,000 m (6,560 ft.) above him, but soon overtook the slow U-2. (Russian MoD records state that the Su-9 came up on the target's anticipated track between Miass and Kyshtym at 0830 hrs., but just then the U-2 changed course, heading north toward Kyshtym.) Attempting to put the situation right, the ground controller ordered the pilot to cancel the afterburner; as a result, the Su-9 lost speed and altitude. Since Mentyukov did not have enough fuel to make a repeat attack, he had no choice but to return to Kol'tsovo and land at 0852 hrs. After being refuelled, at 0952 hrs. he was ordered up once more (!), which was utterly pointless because the U-2 had already been destroyed.

(It may be mentioned that much later, in 1996, Mentyukov came up with a fish story—circulated by the Russian media—that it was he who had downed the target with the wake of his jet by crossing in front of the U-2! Imagine that! Also, he claimed that his aircraft was mistakenly fired upon by the 57th Brigade's SAM

Battalion 1, located at Monetnyy Township and commanded by Capt. Shelud'ko, and that he barely managed to take evasive action. Yet this, too, is a statement open to doubt; Mentyukov was flying at low level and at right angles to the U-2's course, and he could not have seen the incoming missiles.)

Fishpots Far and Wide

Despite the unimpressive initial results (which played into the hands of the 'missile lobby' supported by the head of state, Nikita S. Khrushchov), the events of 1960 demonstrated the need for a high-altitude interceptor. Thus no fewer than 31 PVO units were equipped with the Su-9 at the peak of the type's strength in 1963. Three of them were components of the PVO's 148th TsBP i PLS— the 594th UIAP (*oochebnyy istrebitel'nyy aviapolk*: fighter training regiment) at the centre's main facility, Savasleyka AB, the 592nd UIAP at Klin-5 AB near the town of Klin (Moscow Region), and the 179th GvIAP (*Gvardeyskiy istrebitel'nyy aviapolk*: Guards fighter regiment) in Krasnovodsk (Turkmenia; the city is now called Turkmenbashi). (Note: The Guards units were the elite of the Soviet armed forces, since this title was accorded for special gallantry in combat, indicating the unit had a history dating back to the Great Patriotic War. Some sources state that the 179th GvIAP was not part of the 148th TsBP i PLS, reporting to one of the PVO armies.) The other 28 were ordinary first-line fighter regiments; interestingly, some of them operated a mix of types. These are:

• The 9th *Odesskiy* GvIAP, at Andizhan, Uzbekistan, reporting to the 12th OA PVO (*otdel'naya armiya Protivovozdooshnoy oborony*: Independent Air Defence Army). The unit transitioned to the Su-9 from the MiG-19. The honorary appellation 'Odesskiy' was given for liberating the Ukrainian city of Odessa in 1944.

• The 22nd GvIAP (11th OA PVO), at Tsentral'naya-Ooglovaya AB, Artyom Township, near Vladivostok. The unit converted from the MiG-17; it operated a mix of types (Su-9s in Squadron 1 and Yak-25Ms in Squadron 2).

• The 23rd IAP (Moscow PVO District), at Rzhev, Kalinin Region (now Tver' Region). The unit was later disbanded and is thus not to be confused with the Russian air force's current 23rd IAP, which was established on 1 August 2001.

• The 28th *Leningradskiy* GvIAP (Moscow PVO District), at Andreapol', Kalinin Region. The honorary appellation was given for the unit's part in the defence of the besieged Leningrad.

• The 28th IAP (Moscow PVO District), at Krichev, Mogilyov Region, Belorussia. (Note: There were several cases of two regiments [a regular unit and a Guards unit] confusingly having the same number, and in this case even reporting to the same district.)

• The 47th IAP (11th OA PVO), at Zolotaya Dolina ('Golden Valley') AB, near Nakhodka ('the Find'), Primor'ye Territory. The unit converted from the MiG-15.

• The 57th GvIAP (14th OA PVO), at Noril'sk (Alykel' airport), which also converted from the MiG-15

• The 61st IAP (2nd OA PVO), at Baranovichi, Belorussia— again a former MiG-15 unit. In the 1960s the unit was temporarily deployed at an ice strip on the Zemlya Frantsa-Iosifa (Franz-Joseph Land) archipelago.

• The 90th IAP (8th OA PVO), at Chervonoglinskaya AB, near Artsyz, Odessa Region, the Ukraine

• The 136th IAP (8th OA PVO), at Kirovskiye AB, near Simferopol' in the Crimea, the Ukraine

• The 156th IAP (12th OA PVO), at Maryy-2 AB, Turkmenia. The unit converted from the MiG-17/MiG-17P.

• The 167th GvIAP (Baku PVO District), at Tsulukidze AB (now called Khoni), Georgia. The unit converted from the MiG-17.

• The 177th IAP (6th OA PVO), at Lodeynoye Pol'e AB (Leningrad Region), again a former MiG-17 unit. It was later disbanded but re-formed in February 1994 at the same base. (*Lodeynoye Pol'e* translates as 'shipbuilding field', because vessels similar to Viking ships were built there in olden days; however, the base is jokingly called *Zlodeynoye Pol'e*, 'bad-guy field', in slang!)

Opposite page: Su-9 '21 Red' is pictured a few seconds after takeoff just as the main gear units begin to retract. The nose unit takes longer to retract, moving against the slipstream.

Above: Su-9 '70 Red' uses its quadruple airbrakes to assist the brake parachute after landing. The open brake parachute bay door can be seen below the lower airbrake, and the parachute line is just visible aft of the tail bumper that incorporates the lock.

Right: A fine study of Su-9 '26 Red' basking in the sun on the flight line, with drop tanks but no missiles

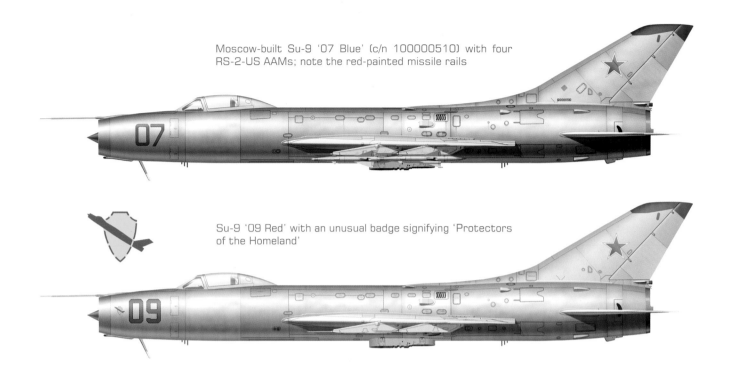

Moscow-built Su-9 '07 Blue' (c/n 100000510) with four RS-2-US AAMs; note the red-painted missile rails

Su-9 '09 Red' with an unusual badge signifying 'Protectors of the Homeland'

• The 179th GvIAP (12th OA PVO), at Krasnovodsk, Turkmenia, a former MiG-17 unit

• The 179th IAP (8th OA PVO), at Stryy AB (L'vov Region, the Ukraine)—another case of unit number duplication

• The 191st IAP (Moscow PVO District), at Yefremov-3 AB (Tula Region)

• The 201st IAP (2nd OA PVO), at Machoolishchi AB, Minsk, Belorussia

• The 209th GvIAP (8th OA PVO), at Privolzhskiy AB, Astrakhan' Region

• The 301st IAP (11th OA PVO), at Desyatyy Oochastok AB (literally 'Land Tract Ten', a.k.a. Kalinka AB), in the Primor'ye Region

• The 350th IAP (14th OA PVO), at Bratsk (Irkutsk Region, Eastern Siberia). The unit converted from the MiG-17.

• The 356th IAP (14th OA PVO), at Zhana-Semey AB, Kazakhstan. This regiment operated a mix of Yak-25s, Su-9s, and Yak-28Ps.

• The 393rd *Baranovichskiy* GvIAP (8th OA PVO), at Privolzhskiy AB, Astrakhan' Region. The appellation was given for the liberation of the Belorussian city of Baranovichi in the Great Patriotic War.

• The 412th IAP (4th OA PVO), at Dombarovskiy AB (Orenburg Region). The unit converted from the MiG-15bis Fagot-B.

• The 415th IAP (Moscow PVO District), at Yaroslavl'-Toonoshna airport. The unit converted from the MiG-15bis.

• The 592nd UIAP, at Klin-5 AB

• The 594th UIAP, at Savasleyka AB

• The 611th IAP (Moscow PVO District), Dorokhovo AB (Bezhetsk, Kalinin Region)

• The 656th IAP (6th OA PVO), Tapa AB, Estonia

• The 683rd IAP (4th OA PVO), Bobrovka AB, Kuibyshev (now renamed back to Samara)

• The 712th *Chernovitskiy* GvIAP (14th OA PVO), at Kansk-Yoozhnyy (= Kansk-South) AB, Krasnoyarsk Region. This regiment converted from the MiG-17. The appellation was given for liberating the Ukrainian city of Chernovitsy.

• The 735th IAP (12th OA PVO), at Khanabad near Karshi, Uzbekistan

• The 737th IAP (12th OA PVO), at Sary-Shagan AB, Kazakhstan. The unit converted from the Yak-25; later it moved to Artsyz (L'vov Region, the Ukraine) and came under the control of the Odessa Military District.

• The 765th IAP (4th OA PVO), at Salka AB near Nizhniy Tagil, Sverdlovsk Region. The unit converted from the MiG-15bis.

• The 790th IAP, at Khotilovo AB, Bologoye (Kalinin Region)

• The 813th IAP (14th OA PVO), at Novosibirsk-Tolmachovo AP. Later the unit moved to Koopino AB because the Ministry of Civil Aviation didn't care about the idea of sharing the airport with a fighter unit and eventually succeeded in getting rid of the military 'neighbours'. The move to Koopino required the existing runway to be extended, because otherwise Su-9 operations would be

The badge that went with the Sniper Pilot skill rating.

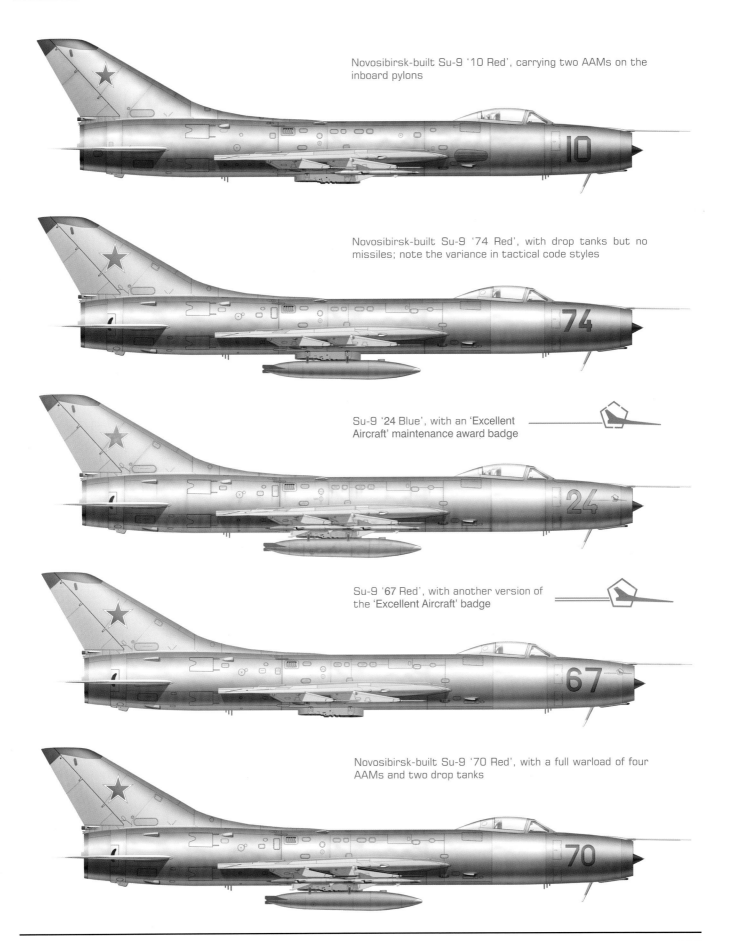

Novosibirsk-built Su-9 '10 Red', carrying two AAMs on the inboard pylons

Novosibirsk-built Su-9 '74 Red', with drop tanks but no missiles; note the variance in tactical code styles

Su-9 '24 Blue', with an 'Excellent Aircraft' maintenance award badge

Su-9 '67 Red', with another version of the 'Excellent Aircraft' badge

Novosibirsk-built Su-9 '70 Red', with a full warload of four AAMs and two drop tanks

impossible. In 1962 the 813th IAP briefly redeployed to Tolmachovo again during the Cuban Missile Crisis, when there was a danger of a US air raid; subsequently the unit continued using Tolmachovo as a reserve airfield.

• The 849th IAP (14th OA PVO), at Koopino AB. The unit converted from the MiG-17.

• The 865th IAP (11th OA PVO), at Yelizovo AP, Petropavlovsk-Kamchatskiy (Kamchatka Region). The unit converted from the Yak-25.

• The 941st IAP (10th OA PVO), Kilp-Yavr AB (Murmansk Region). This was one of the first units to master the Su-9, receiving the first machines in 1959.

• The 976th *Insterburgskiy* IAP, Kuyrdamir, Azerbaijan. This regiment converted from the MiG-17. The appellation was given for the unit's part in the taking of Insterburg Castle in eastern Prussia (which is now the Kaliningrad Region exclave of Russia) in 1945.

As the Vozdukh-1 GCI system gradually found its way to PVO command centres, the Su-9 units began mastering the ground-controlled intercept technique. The pilot would fly the aircraft in flight director mode, continually making course corrections calculated by the command centre and relayed to the aircraft by the Lazoor' data link system. The aircraft was thus guided toward the target along the optimum trajectory, which considerably increased the 'kill' probability.

Unfortunately, like any other aircraft, the Su-9 had its share of accidents (both fatal and nonfatal). The first fatal crash in operational service occurred on 8 March 1960, when a 61st IAP aircraft flown by Lt. (SG) Morgoon suffered an engine failure on takeoff, and the altitude was too low for safe ejection. Despite persistent

An enamel badge marking the 30th anniversary of the 849th IAP (the number is not shown, since it was classified). It shows a Su-9 intercepting an intruder superimposed on the Soviet air force's 'sunburst' flag.

Left: Two 849th IAP pilots wearing leather jackets and ZSh-5 helmets discuss intercept techniques in front of a Su-9 at Koopino AB near Novosibirsk.

A Su-9U trainer pictured at the moment of rotation on takeoff

Right: The hardstand of the Solntsevo ShMAS near Moscow, with Su-9s in the foreground. The fourth aircraft is apparently trestled for a landing gear operation check. A Su-15 is also visible near the far end of the row.

Su-9U '64 Red', with an 'Excellent Aircraft' maintenance award badge

efforts by the OKB and the manufacturing plants to improve reliability, the Su-9's flight safety record was poor, especially between 1961 and 1963, when the type was being fielded en masse by the PVO; the high attrition rate in the early years had a long-term negative effect on the Su-9's service career. According to the air force's attrition statistics, in 1961 alone there were 34 accidents of varying seriousness with the type, including 18 caused by design flaws and poor workmanship. The mean time between accidents was 677 hours overall and 1,278 hours for those caused by manufacturing defects. By comparison, the Su-7 enjoyed a much-better safety record, with only five accidents in 1961 (albeit four out of five were again due to hardware defects); the mean time between accidents was 1,561 and 1,952 hours, respectively.

There were many causes for the Su-9's high accident rate. For instance, no fewer than six crashes were caused by disintegration of the engine's accessory gearbox driveshaft bearings; 30 engines had to be removed prematurely when metal chips were detected in the lubrication system. By 1961 there had been 35 cases of compressor blade failures on AL-7F and AL-7F-1 engines due to foreign object damage (FOD) since the Su-7 fighter, the Su-7B fighter-bomber, and the Su-9 had entered service; turbine blade cracking (often leading to failure) was common too.

The blame did not rest solely with the engine makers; poorly maintained runways at the airbases were a major contributing factor. The Su-7 and Su-9 often operated from old concrete runways that were not designed for the loads generated by the aircraft; the

Above: Maintenance day in a first-line PVO unit, with ground crew in fatigues and characteristic headgear servicing an early Su-9 coded '01' (note the presence of gun blast plates)

Left: A pilot in winter gear poses for a publicity photo on the ladder of his Su-9 parked in an earthen revetment.

Right: Maintenance in progress on a Su-9U trainer coded '25 Red'. Note the blind flying hood in the trainee's cockpit and the safety support placed under the front canopy.

Below: Two generations of interceptors together: Su-11s share the flight line at a PVO base with MiG-17Fs. Since this is winter, all aircraft are kept under wraps when parked to prevent ice and snow from fouling the control surfaces.

Sukhoi jets had a runway loading of about 12 kg/cm² (171 lbs. / sq. in.). The augmented loads, coupled with the jet exhaust, gradually eroded the runway surface, and the top layer disintegrated, whereupon small fragments of concrete were ingested by the engine. The resulting dents on the compressor blades acted as stress concentrators and caused the blades to break—often with fatal consequences. In fact, back in 1959, when serious design flaws had been discovered in the AL-7F-1, someone had proposed throwing this engine out and substituting it with the VK-13 afterburning turbojet, developed by Vladimir Ya. Klimov, since this engine did not require major structural changes. A different solution was found eventually: the paved runways were reinforced and it became standard operational procedure to sweep them before a flying session, using powerful 'vacuum cleaners' mounted on lorries to remove any debris.

Other widespread bugs afflicting the Sukhoi jets included mainwheel tyre explosions, deformation of the wing structure, and the variable nozzle petals. Worst of all, these defects undermined the image of the aircraft as a whole; it was the 'head office'

(that is, OKB-51) that got the blame, not the suppliers of this or that component that had failed.

Alarmed by this situation, the military started 'knocking on every door', demanding that something be done about it. In keeping with orders coming from the Communist Party Central Committee, in February 1961 a special commission—one might say an investigative commission—started working in the IA PVO units, studying the new Sukhoi interceptor's operational peculiarities. The commission established that *'in the course of wide-scale Su-9 operations, new defects and shortcomings adversely affecting . . . the aircraft's reliability and compromising flight safety are still turning up. In 1960–61 there have been three fatal accidents and three nonfatal accidents leading to total hull losses, all caused by engine or engine accessory failures; one fatal accident and three nonfatal accidents / total hull losses caused by failures of off-the-shelf components (AGD-1 and AGI-1 artificial horizons, etc.) and one fatal accident and two nonfatal accidents / total hull losses caused by piloting errors or improper maintenance. . . . The flight and ground crews operating the Su-9, which is, in effect, a "manned*

Above: Su-11s coded '25', '29', and '30' in V formation participate in the 9 July 1967 air parade at Moscow-Domodedovo.

Left: Another trio of Su-11s makes an airshow performance. The aircraft are fully loaded with R-8M missiles and drop tanks.

Above right: A different perspective of the Su-11s from the Domodedovo fly-past

Right: An operational Su-11 coded '68' uses the parachute and air-brakes to shorten the landing run. Note the small drogue parachute extracting the main canopy. The brake parachute was not always deployed because collecting and repacking it afterward was additional work for the ground crews.

Su-11 '36 Red' (c/n 0115301), PVO Junior Tech Specialists' School, Solntsevo

Left: The first production Su-11 in its days as '36 Red', an instructional airframe at the Solntsevo ShMAS. Electric power was distributed to the instructional airframes from the box in foreground.

Right: The same aircraft seen from the other side

Below: Su-9s and Su-11s at the Solntsevo ShMAS

Below right: Curious cadets of the Solntsevo ShMAS swarm around Su-11 '36 Red' during a training session; the aircraft is jacked up for a landing-gear retraction demonstration. Interestingly, the cadets are all carrying gas masks in cloth bags.

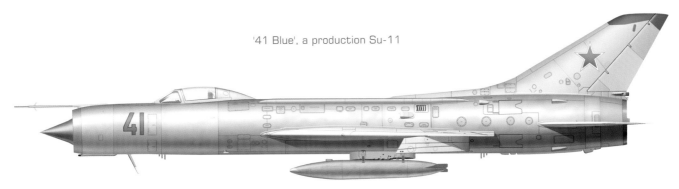

'41 Blue', a production Su-11

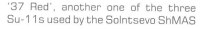

missile" [*sic*], *have the same pay rates as . . . personnel operating
subsonic aircraft, which causes justified complaints and does not
promote the service introduction of new aircraft.'*

'The commission hath spoken', and Su-9 operations came to an
almost complete standstill. The aircraft industry showed no reaction at first, but the accidents continued, and the military finally
ran out of patience. In July 1961 the acting PVO commander in
chief General Gheorgiy V. Zimin reported to Council of Ministers
vice chairman Dmitriy F. Ustinov:

*'Only six to eight pilots in each regiment—the best pilots in the
unit—keep flying, using the best aircraft available, but operations
are still accompanied by a high accident rate due to hardware failures. On 17 June this year, a nonfatal accident occurred . . . due to
disintegration of a bearing in the engine accessory gearbox, with*

Above left: A 'black man', as the
ground crews were dubbed for their
black fatigues, inspects the port tailplane of a Su-11.

Left: An operational Su-11 coded
'34 Red' sits in a revetment at a PVO
base's dispersal area. The aircraft is
partly under wraps; note the ground
cover over the pitch/yaw transducers
on the air data boom.

an ensuing in-flight shutdown. On 11 July, a nonfatal accident occurred . . . due to compressor blade failure and engine surge on takeoff. On 13 July a fatal accident occurred. Immediately after takeoff the pilot reported that smoke was pouring into the cockpit, the afterburner would not shut down, and the aircraft had started rolling uncontrollably; the pilot could not eject due to insufficient altitude and was killed. The VPK ruling of 19 April 1961—specifically, the clause concerning the upgrading of . . . engines installed in operational Su-9s—is disregarded by the factories.'

A total of 21 nonfatal accidents and one fatal crash occurred in 1962, followed by 23 more accidents in 1963. The situation appears odd; considering that the Su-9 and Su-7 shared the same engine and many equipment items, theoretically their operational reliability should be on a comparable level, but this was not the case. Perhaps the answer lies in the fact that the two types were built by different factories; the Su-9, as already mentioned, was built in Novosibirsk and Moscow, whereas the Su-7 and its derivatives were manufactured solely by plant no. 126 in Komsomol'sk-on-Amur in the Soviet Far East, where attention to manufacturing quality may have been higher. Often the accidents were caused by improper operation or maintenance by the flight and ground crews. As the Su-9 matured and the PVO units grew more familiar with it, operational reliability and attrition rates improved to acceptable levels by the late 1960s.

In the summer of 1964 the 393rd GvIAP, based at Privolzhskaya AB, near Astrakhan', began transitioning from the Su-9 to the Su-11 as the first unit to operate the type. The transition to the more advanced interceptor went fairly smoothly, and after stage A of the evaluation programme had been completed by the regiment, the entire production run of the Su-11 was delivered to first-line units in the first half of 1965. Due to its extremely small production run of 100 aircraft, the type served with only three units. Apart from the 393rd GvIAP, these were the 790th IAP at Khotilovo AB 20 km (12.4 miles), south of Bologoye, Kalinin Region (now Tver' Region), and the 191st IAP at Yefremov-3 AB, 8.25 km (5.12 miles) from the town of Yefremov (Tula Region), both of

them in the Moscow PVO District. However, there are reports that the Su-11 was also operated by the 148th TsBP i PLS (more specifically, apparently the 594th UIAP at Savasleyka AB), which certainly makes sense.

Compared to its predecessor, the Su-11 was much more 'user-friendly' and safer to operate—the Sukhoi and Lyul'ka OKBs had learned from experience with the Su-9. The aircraft as a whole and the engine in particular were much more reliable, and there were extremely few accidents caused by hardware failures. On one occasion in 1968, a 191st IAP Su-11 flown by Capt. A. I. Yamnikov ingested a bird, which damaged the first two compressor stages; the AL-7F-2 engine started vibrating violently but kept running, enabling the pilot to make a safe emergency landing.

While Su-11 operational tactics were basically similar to those of the Su-9, an advantage was conferred by the Su-11's greater maximum interception altitude thanks to the more powerful Oryol radar and the R-8M missiles, which allowed the aircraft to attack targets flying far above its own flight level and even gave it a limited 'look-down/shoot-down' capability. Interestingly, the operational tactics developed for the Su-11 included even using the R-8M AAMs for attacks against ground targets and surface ships—probably in an attempt to offset the shortage of guided air-to-surface weapons. In reality, however, this was never done.

In their day the Su-9 and Su-11 more or less topped the bill when it came to combating the nonmanoeuvrable heavy bombers they had been designed to oppose. (We say 'more or less' because, first, there is always an exception to the rule—the Avro Vulcan could fly like a fighter if required; second, the capabilities of the Soviet avionics and weapons imposed certain limits.) It was a totally different story with the latest Western tactical aircraft, which were designed for low-altitude air defence penetration and dogfighting—and the Su-9/Su-11 was designed for neither. This situation was somewhat alleviated by the addition of the R-55 'fire and forget' IR-homing short-range AAM to the Su-9's arsenal in the early 1970s. Also, taking account of the experience gained in the Vietnam War and the Arab-Israeli wars, the Soviet PVO com-

The end of the road. This Su-9 coded '31 Red' ended its days as a ground target at the Groshevo practice range near Astrakhan'. Not only has the hulk suffered several hits, but sections of fuselage skin have been chopped out for some reason.

mand gave due attention to close-in dogfight tactics—even though the Su-9 and Su-11 were ill suited for this kind of combat. A Su-9 from the 656th IAP at Tapa AB is known to have participated in a mock combat session with a MiG-21, and some units (for example, the 136th IAP at Kirovskoye AB) even staged group dogfights.

Deployments to forward-operating locations (FOLs) were also practiced; for example, in March 1966 a group of twenty 14th OA PVO (813th IAP) Su-9s deployed from Koopino AB to an ad hoc ice airfield in Tiksi, Yakutia, staging through Omsk, Kamennaya Tunguska, Noril'sk, and Khatanga. The ground personnel and ordnance were airlifted to Tiksi in advance by Antonov An-8 Camp twin-turboprop transports. Sergey M. Kramarenko, a former 813th IAP pilot, reminisced: *'Our [fighter] regiments were stationed along the Transsiberian Railway and were able to protect only the cities located along this railway. Meanwhile, to the north of it lay a huge expanse with no air cover at all. Hence, a lot of effort was invested in the mastering of the High North. First we would deliver fuel to the chosen FOLs and set up commandant's offices there [to maintain and guard the airfields]. Then we would try redeployments to the FOLs—usually in squadron strength. . . . The results were good, proving the possibility of boosting the efficiency of our aviation. Next, we redeployed a squadron of Su-9s to ice airstrips practically on the coastline of the Arctic Ocean. Supplying the fuel was the biggest problem. The Su-9 was a thirsty aircraft that used a lot of kerosene, . . . and almost all the fuel stocked at the FOL would be used up for refuelling this single squadron. The conclusion was that yes, the Su-9 can indeed operate from the coast of the Arctic Ocean, but supporting such operations is difficult and requires development of the proper means of delivering everything we need for combat operations to these airstrips.'*

In the 1970s the 8th OA PVO practiced Su-9 operations from short tactical strips. In particular, the 179th IAP at Stryy used the nearby FOL at Lyubsha (L'vov Region), which had a 2,200 × 26 m (7,220 × 85 ft.) unpaved runway; compare this to the concrete runway at Stryy AB, which was 2,300 m (7,550 ft.) long and 30 m (98 ft.) wide.

The Su-9 and Su-11 saw a good deal of 'actual combat', intercepting real-life targets. Thus, in the late 1960s, a pair of 976th IAP Su-9s scrambled from Kyurdamir AB, Azerbaijan, to intercept a pair of Iranian air force fighters that had intruded into Soviet airspace. Receiving authorisation from ground control, the flight leader fired a missile at the Iranians, but the radar mistook the two intruders flying in close formation for a single large aircraft and placed the missile dead centre—with the result that the missile passed between the two fighters without hitting either of them.

Far more often, however, Su-9/Su-11 pilots had to deal with drifting reconnaissance balloons; in fact, a special version of the R-8M AAM with a larger warhead, the K-8TSh (the Sh stood for [*vozdooshnyy*] *shar*: balloon), was developed for destroying these targets, since a standard missile was usually not enough to destroy the large balloon. For instance, in 1969, Ye. N. Kravets, a 179th GvIAP Su-9 pilot, fired RS-2-US AAMs at a reconnaissance balloon but succeeded only in shooting off the lower half of the extremely long sensor pack dangling underneath it, so another fighter from a different unit had to be called in to finish it off. In an uncanny replay of this incident, in 1976 the same pilot (now

flying a Su-11 in the 393rd IAP at Privolzhskiy AB) again failed to completely destroy a reconnaissance balloon even with a special 'balloon killer' missile (of which only a handful existed), annihilating only the lower half of the sensor pack 'sausage'.

Curious incidents also occurred from time to time. In the early 1970s, a 393rd GvIAP Su-11 standing on quick-reaction alert (and armed with live missiles, of course) was scrambled to intercept a Su-9 acting as a practice target. In the course of a poorly organised intercept, the Su-11 pilot fired a missile—and shot down his comrade in arms (who fortunately managed to eject and survived). A similar 'friendly fire' incident took place in the 179th IAP at Stryy AB in 1969. Maj. Koorilin, on QRA duty, was ordered to perform a practice intercept of a Su-9 from the same regiment. The pilot successfully found the target, got a good lock-on, and, after receiving authorisation from the ground control centre (!), fired all four missiles. Realising what was about to happen, the aghast pilot pushed the stick forward, putting the aircraft's nose down; the beam-riding missiles followed the radar beam, diving away from the target and self-destructing harmlessly.

In 1979 a 23rd IAP Su-9 making a practice intercept of another fighter was mistakenly vectored toward a Malév Hungarian Airlines Tupolev Tu-134 Crusty short-haul airliner, flying the scheduled Budapest–Moscow service. On approaching within visual range and realising this was the wrong aircraft, pilot Syomkin could not resist the urge to show off. Flying on a parallel course, he overtook the airliner and peeled off spectacularly, demonstrating the four missiles, before leaving the scene. The Hungarian captain was hysterical, sending out a mayday call; the Soviet aviation authorities reacted promptly. The incident was immediately reported to the MoD; it did not take long to identify the culprit, and as soon as Syomkin landed he got it hot!

In the late 1960s the PVO started phasing out the Su-9 as obsolescent; the 14th OA PVO led the way by reequipping three fighter regiments with the Tupolev Tu-128 Fiddler twin-engined heavy interceptor. Col. Eduard M. Yevglevskiy, one of the first service pilots to master the Fiddler, said: *'Pilots who had flown the Su-9 were the most willing to convert to the Tu-128—and were the fastest to master it too. Consider this: the engines were virtually the same, the takeoff and landing speeds were identical, but the Tu-128 had two engines instead of one and nearly three times the Su-9's fuel capacity.'* Other units reequipped with the Su-15; the aircraft freed up in so doing were distributed among the remaining Su-9 units as attrition replacements.

The IA PVO units operating the Su-9 and Su-11 as of 1 January 1970 are listed in the table on page 141; at that time the Fishpot served alongside both newer types, such as the Su-15, and older types, such as the MiG-17 and Yak-25M. (Note: The honorary appellation *Ternopol'skiy* was given for taking the town of Tarnopol' (later renamed Ternopol') during the Great Patriotic War. The appellation **Starokonstantinovskiy** was given for the liberation of the Ukrainian city of Starokonstantinov. The appellation *Transil'vanskiy* was given for the unit's part in the battles in Transylvania, Romania, at the end of the war. The appellation **Amoorskaya** was given for gallantry in the fighting on the Amur River in the Far East. The appellation *Yaroslavskiy* was given for liberating the Russian city of Yaroslavl'. The appellation **El'bingskiy** was

Su-9/Su-11 Units as of 1 January 1970		
Unit	**Base**	**Aircraft type**
Direct Reporting Units		
• Stavropol' VVAULSh * 208th UAP	Sal'sk, Rostov Region	Su-9
Moscow PVO District (HQ Moscow)		
• 2nd PVO Corps, HQ Rzhev, Kalinin Region		
23rd IAP	Rzhev	Su-9
28th IAP	Krichev, Mogilyov Region, Belorussia	Su-9
790th IAP	Khotilovo AB, Bologoye, Kalinin Region	Su-11
• 3rd PVO Corps, HQ Yaroslavl'		
415th IAP	Yaroslavl'-Toonoshna AP	Su-9
• 7th PVO Corps, HQ Bryansk		
191st IAP	Yefremov, Tula Region	Su-11
Baku PVO District (HQ Baku, Azerbaijan)		
• 14th PVO Corps, HQ Tbilisi, Georgia		
167th *Starokonstantinovskiy* GvIAP	Kopitnari AB, nr Kutaïsi, Georgia	Su-9
• 15th PVO Corps, HQ Alyaty, Azerbaijan		
976th *Insterburgskiy* IAP	Kuyrdamir, central Azerbaijan	Su-9
• 16th Guards PVO Division, HQ Krasnovodsk, Turkmenia		
179th *Transil'vanskiy* GvIAP	Krasnovodsk	Su-9
2nd Independent PVO Army (HQ Minsk, Belorussia)		
• 11th PVO Corps, HQ Baranovichi, Belorussia		
61st IAP	Baranovichi	Su-9
201st IAP	Machoolishchi AB, Minsk	Su-9
4th Independent PVO Army (HQ Sverdlovsk)		
• 19th PVO Corps, HQ Chelyabinsk		
412th IAP	Dombarovskiy, Orenburg Region	Su-9
• 20th PVO Corps, HQ Perm'		
765th IAP	Salka, nr Nizhniy Tagil, Sverdlovsk Region	Su-9
• 28th PVO Division, HQ Kuibyshev		
683rd IAP	Bobrovka AB, Kuibyshev Region	Su-9
6th Independent PVO Army (HQ Leningrad)		
• 54th Guards PVO Corps, HQ Taitsy (nr Gatchina, Leningrad Region)		
57th GvIAP	Veshchevo AB, nr Vyborg, Leningrad Region	Su-9

177th IAP	Lodeynoye Pol'e, Leningrad Region	Su-9
• 14th PVO Division, HQ Tallinn, Estonia		
656th IAP	Tapa AB, Estonia	Su-9
8th Independent PVO Army (HQ Kiev, the Ukraine)		
• 28th PVO Corps, HQ L'vov, the Ukraine		
179th *Yaroslavskiy* IAP	Stryy, L'vov Region	Su-9
894th IAP	Ozyornoye AB, Zhitomir, Zhitomir Region	Su-9
• 21st PVO Division, HQ Odessa, the Ukraine		
136th IAP	Kirovskoye AB, Crimea Region	Su-9
10th Independent PVO Army (HQ Arkhangel'sk)		
• 21st PVO Corps, HQ Severomorsk, Murmansk Region		
941st IAP	Kilp-Yavr AB, Murmansk Region	Su-9
11th Independent PVO Army (HQ Khabarovsk)		
• 23rd PVO Corps, HQ Vladivostok, Primor'ye Territory		
22nd GvIAP	Tsentral'naya-Ooglovaya AB, Artyom, nr Vladivostok	Su-9, Yak-25M
47th IAP	Zolotaya Dolina, nr Nakhodka, Primor'ye Territory	Su-9
• 6th PVO Division, HQ Petropavlovsk-Kamchatskiy		
865th GvIAP	Petropavlovsk-Kamchatskiy/Yelizovo AP	Su-9
• 29th *Amurskaya* PVO Division, HQ Belogorsk, Amur Region		
301st GvIAP	Kalinka (Desyatyy Oochastok) AB, Khabarovsk Territory	Su-9
12th Independent PVO Army (HQ Tashkent, Uzbekistan)		
• 7th PVO Division, HQ Alma-Ata, Kazakhstan		
737th IAP	Sary-Shagan AB, nr Karaganda, Kazakhstan	Su-9
• 15th PVO Division, HQ Samarkand, Uzbekistan		
735th IAP	Khanabad AB, Karshi, Uzbekistan	Su-9
• 17th PVO Division, HQ Maryy, Turkmenia		
156th *El'bingskiy* GvIAP	Maryy-2 AB	Su-9, Yak-28P
14th Independent PVO Army (HQ Novosibirsk)		
• 20th PVO Division, HQ Tolmachovo		
849th IAP	Koopino AB, Novosibirsk Region	Su-9

* VVAULSh = *Vyssheye voyennoye aviatsionnoye oochilischche lyotchikov i shtoormanov*: military pilot and navigator college

Su-9/Su-11 Units as of 1 January 1980		
Unit	Base	Aircraft type
Moscow PVO District (HQ Moscow)		
• 2nd PVO Corps, HQ Rzhev, Kalinin Region		
23rd IAP	Rzhev	Su-9
28th IAP	Krichev, Mogilyov Region, Belorussia	Su-9
790th IAP	Khotilovo AB, Bologoye, Kalinin Region	Su-11
• 3rd PVO Corps, HQ Yaroslavl'		
415th IAP	Yaroslavl'-Toonoshna AP	Su-9
• 7th PVO Corps, HQ Bryansk		
191st IAP	Yefremov, Tula Region	Su-11
Baku PVO District (HQ Baku, Azerbaijan)		
• 16th Guards PVO Division, HQ Krasnovodsk, Turkmenia:		
393rd *Baranovichskiy* GvIAP	Privolzhskiy AB, Astrakhan' Region, Russia	Su-11
4th Independent PVO Army (HQ Sverdlovsk)		
• 20th PVO Corps, HQ Perm'		
764th IAP	Perm'-Bol'shoye Savino AP	MiG-25P
765th IAP	Salka, nr Nizhniy Tagil, Sverdlovsk Region	Su-9
• 28th PVO Division, HQ Kuibyshev		
683rd IAP	Bobrovka AB, Kuibyshev Region	Su-9
6th Independent PVO Army (HQ Leningrad)		
• 54th Guards PVO Corps, HQ Taitsy (nr Gatchina, Leningrad Region)		
177th IAP	Lodeynoye Pol'e, Leningrad Region	Su-9
12th Independent PVO Army (HQ Tashkent, Uzbekistan)		
• 7th PVO Division, HQ Alma-Ata, Kazakhstan		
737th IAP	Sary-Shagan AB, nr Karaganda, Kazakhstan	Su-9
14th Independent PVO Army (HQ Novosibirsk)		
• 20th PVO Division, HQ Tolmachovo		
849th IAP	Koopino AB, Novosibirsk Region	Su-9

given for liberating the Polish city of Elbląg (previously known by its German name of Elbing).

By 1975 several more Su-9 units had completed their transition to the Su-15 (the 976th IAP, the 57th GvIAP, the 156th GvIAP, and the 22nd GvIAP) or the Su-15TM (the 941st IAP, the 47th IAP, and the 865th GvIAP). To put things into perspective, at this point the PVO Aviation had 16 regiments of Su-15s *sans suffixe*, 12 regiments of Su-15TMs, three Su-11 regiments, 19 Su-9 regiments, seven MiG-25P regiments, six MiG-19 regiments, two MiG-17 regiments, 12 Yak-28P regiments, and five Tu-128 regiments; the total fighter fleet was around 3,200.

By the end of 1979 the picture had changed somewhat. The number of remaining Su-9 regiments had shrunk to eight; the PVO Aviation also included 14 Su-15/Su-15T regiments, nine regiments and one independent squadron of Su-15TMs, three Su-11 regiments, ten MiG-25P regiments, six MiG-19 regiments, a single MiG-17PF regiment, a single MiG-21*bis* Fishbed-L/N regiment, nine MiG-23M Flogger-B regiments, one MiG-23ML Flogger-G regiment, one MiG-23P Flogger-G regiment, eight Yak-28P/ Yak-28PM regiments, and five Tu-128 regiments. The following units still operated the Fishpot-B/C as of 1 January 1980 (prior to the MoD order dated 5 January 1980, whereby the existing air armies were reorganised into air forces of the military districts in order to improve cooperation with the ground forces).

From 1976 onward the Su-9s were progressively retired as time-expired; units operating the type reequipped with the MiG-23M, subsequently followed by the MiG-23ML and the ultimate MiG-23P tailored to the PVO's requirements. The process was completed in 1981; the Su-9s and Su-11s were concentrated at the storage depots in Rzhev and Kuibyshev, where most of them succumbed to the elements and were ultimately scrapped. A few aircraft were converted into target drones. Others became ground instructional airframes at such locations as the aforementioned Solntsevo ShMAS, the Irkutsk Military Aviation Technical College (IVVAIU: *Irkootskoye vyssheye voyennoye inzhenernoye oochilishche*), and the Daugavpils Military Aviation Technical College (DVVAIU: *Daugavpilsskoye vyssheye voyennoye aviatsionnoye inzhenernoye oochilishche*) in Latvia; they were used both for studying the design and function of aircraft systems and for battle damage repair training (BDRT).

A few Fishpots have been preserved for posterity. The Soviet Air Force Museum (now Central Russian Air Force Museum) in Monino, near Moscow, has Su-9 '68 Red' (now falsely painted as '68 Blue'; c/n 0615308) and Su-11 '14 Red' (similarly masquerading as '14 Blue'; c/n 0115307). A Su-9 coded '05 Red' is preserved at the PVO Museum in Rzhev; another example coded '03 Red' is on display in the North Fleet Air Arm Museum in Safonovo, near Murmansk. Su-9 '07 Blue' (c/n 100000510) was preserved in the base museum at Savasleyka until the museum closed; in 2016 it was transferred to the Patriot Park in Kubinka, near Moscow, and repainted as '52 Blue'. The museum at Moscow-Khodynka (now closed) had Su-9 '10 Red' (c/n 0815348); like most of the surviving exhibits, it was purchased by Vadim Zadorozhnyy's technical museum in Krasnogorsk, near Moscow, but is not currently on display. Su-9 '34 Red' (c/n 1315349) is preserved in a park in Ghenichesk, the Crimea; we may also mention Su-9s '16 Red' in Livny (Oryol Region), '33 Red' (c/n 0715315) in Krasnaya Gorbatka (Vladimir Region), '12 Red' (c/n 1115312) in Chelyabinsk, '27 Red' (c/n 1015382) near Arkhangel'sk-Talagi airport, '05 Blue' (c/n 1415366) in Karmanov (Smolensk Region), '65 Blue' (c/n 1015332) at a test range near Nizhniy Novgorod, and '44 Red' (c/n 1115356) in Tsementnyy Township (Sverdlovsk Region). Two Su-9s are preserved in Belorussia; these are '34 Red' (c/n 1415326) in Krichev (Mogilyov Region) and '50 Red' at Minsk-Machoolishchi AB. Others were preserved at children's summer recreation camps run by the All-Union Pioneer Organisation (the Soviet counterpart of boy scout / girl scout organisations in the West), but most of these have very probably ended up as scrap metal.

Chapter 6

The Experimental Models

In the preceding chapters we have mentioned several versions of the Sukhoi T-3 interceptor family that were destined to remain one-off experimental aircraft. In parallel, however, OKB-51 was working on several single-seat and two-seat interceptors that were stand-alone designs (although they, too, displayed Sukhoi 'family traits'). Some of them at least made it to the flight test phase; others were built in prototype form but never flown, sharing the fate of the first aircraft designated Su-17, or remained paper projects, as described below.

P-1 Experimental Two-Seat Interceptor

In 1954 the Soviet Union began development of its first integrated automatic aerial-intercept system, designated Uragan-1 (Hurri-cane, pronounced *ooragahn*). The system was intended for auto-matic ground-controlled and autonomous vectoring of the interceptor toward the target, followed by automated attack and return to base after the attack. Its ground components were a num-ber of air defence radars with a target acquisition range of 345 km (214 miles), an active interrogator/transponder channel allowing the position of the interceptor attacking an intruder to be deter-mined, a digital guidance control computer, and a GCI guidance station. The system was to enable interception of supersonic bombers doing 1,600–2,000 km/h (993–1,240 mph) at 10,000–25,000 m (32,810–82,020 ft.) while they were still 100–120 km (62–74.5 miles) away from the interceptor's base, providing timely warning was given by the air defence system. A 'kill' probability

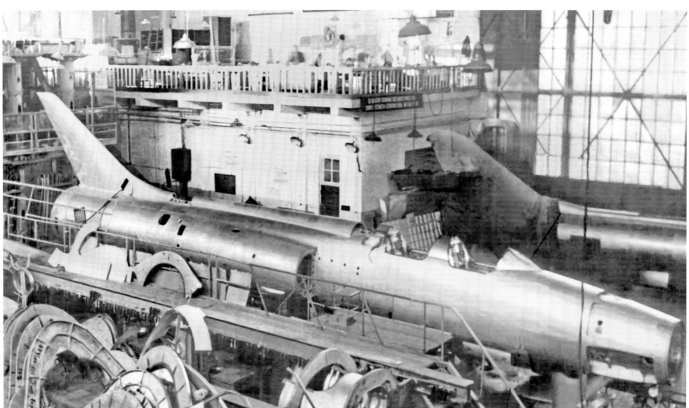

The P-1 during final assembly at MMZ No. 51. The tandem cockpits, air intake trunks, and some of the rocket bay doors around the nose can be seen here.

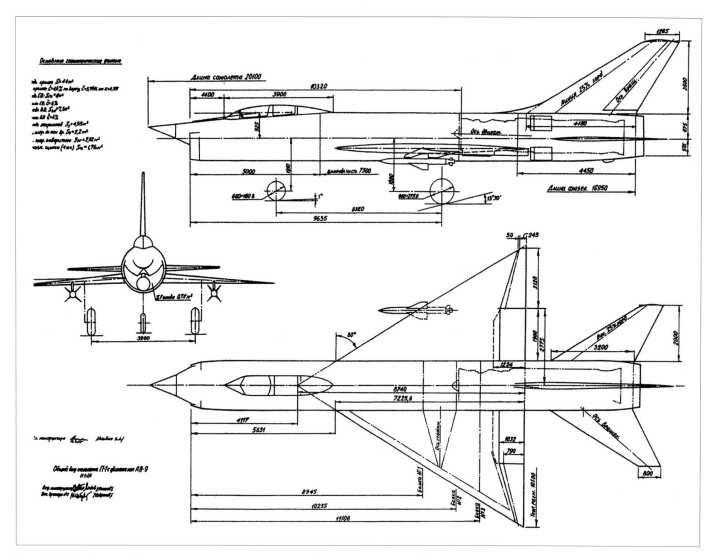

The original project configuration of the P-1, with an Almaz radar and a T-3-style air intake featuring separate radomes for the search and guidance channels. Note the K-7L AAMs under the wings.

of at least 80% in a crossing engagement or in pursuit mode was required. In short, it was a tough bill to top.

In response to an MAP request, at the end of 1954 the Sukhoi OKB initiated project studies on a new fighter. Both single-seat and two-seat versions were considered at this point, as were different armament options (cannons only, missiles only, or a combination of unguided rockets and K-5 AAMs) and different power plants, all of which were 'paper engines' existing in project form (the Lyul'ka AL-9, Klimov VK-9F, Kuznetsov P-2, and Kuznetsov P-4 axial-flow afterburning turbojets). Eventually the choice was narrowed to two configurations; they were single- and twin-engined versions, respectively, of the same design known in-house as *izdeliye* P (this presumably stood for *perekhvatchik*: interceptor).

On 19 January 1955 the Council of Ministers issued directive no. 127-68, ordering the development of these aircraft, among other things. The relevant part of the document said: '[The Sukhoi OKB shall] *1. Design and build a two-seat interceptor equipped with the Uragan-1 automated target acquisition, attack, and disengagement system. . . . The aircraft shall be manufactured in two*

examples; the first one shall be powered by a single AL-9 turbojet and have the following performance: top speed 1,850–1,950 km/h [1,149–1,211 mph], service ceiling 19,000–20,000 m [62,340–65,620 ft]. The armament shall consist of K-7 guided missiles, with unguided rockets as an option. The aircraft shall be submitted for state acceptance trials in the third quarter of 1957.' The unguided rockets were intended as a close-range weapon for use against large and sluggish aircraft such as heavy bombers, not for ground attack. The second example was the twin-engined version, which is described in the next entry. Detailed specifications for the two fighters were developed and approved by all parties concerned in February–March 1955, enabling OKB-51 to begin preliminary design (PD) work on the general arrangement and systems layout.

The design work started in earnest in April 1955. The single-engined version was designated P-1. It shared the basic layout of the T-3 interceptor (which was developed in parallel), having a circular-section fuselage, midset delta wings with 60° leading-edge sweep, and conventional swept tail surfaces with stabilators. However, there were two major differences. First, as noted above,

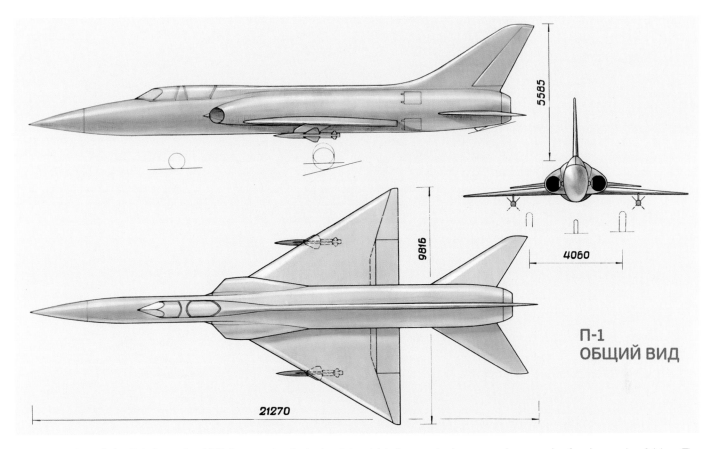

A later version of the P-1 from the ADP documents, featuring lateral intakes, a single nose radome, and a fuselage spine fairing. The wheelbase is short so that the nosewheel stows under the rear cockpit.

the P-1 was to be powered by a new AL-9 axial-flow afterburning turbojet rated at 10,000 kgp (22,045 lbst) in full afterburner; its development had been kicked off by the same directive, no. 127-68. Second, the P-1 was a two-seater flown by a pilot and a weapons systems operator (WSO); the latter's job was to work the radar and use the weapons, leaving the pilot to fly the aircraft. The crew sat in tandem under a common canopy with individual aft-hinged portions and a tapered metal rear fairing. The rear fuselage, which was detachable for engine maintenance/removal, featured four airbrakes in a cruciform arrangement.

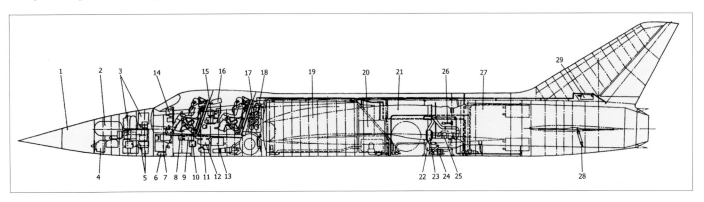

A cutaway drawing of the P-1 from the ADP documents.
1. Radome; 2. The search antenna of the Almaz radar; 3. Modules of the Uragan GCI guidance system; 4. The missile guidance antenna of the Almaz radar; 5. The Khrom-Nikel' IFF interrogator/transponder; 6. RSBN-2S Svod SHORAN and ARK-54 ADF modules; 7. Marker beacon receiver antenna; 8. Tsna approach/landing computer; 9. The rectifier catering for the RSIU-4 radio; 10. RV-5 radio altimeter; 11. RSIU-4 transceiver; 12. PO-1500 and PO-750 AC converters; 13. 12SAM-28 DC battery; 14. The pilot's instrument panel; 15. The amplifier of the Svod SHORAN; 16. The display of the Almaz radar on the WSO's instrument panel; 17. Cooling turbine; 18. Oxygen bottles; 19. The no. 1 fuel cell; 20. The no. 2 fuel cell; 21. Engine inlet duct; 22. Fire extinguisher bottle; 23. Petrol tank for the engine's turbostarter; 24. Oil cooler; 25. Generators; 26. Engine mounting lug; 27. AL-9 afterburning turbojet; 28. Stabilator actuator; 29. Rudder actuator.

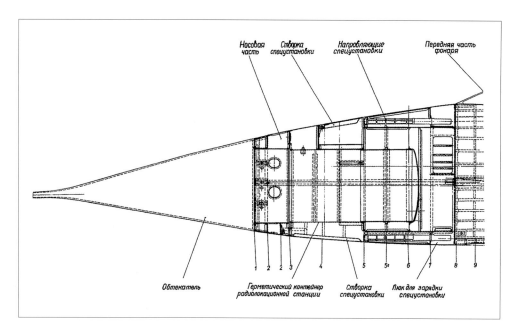

Носовая часть | Створка спецустановки | Направляющие спецустановки | Передняя часть фонаря

Обтекатель | Герметический контейнер радиолокационной станции | Створка спецустановки | Люк для зарядки спецустановки

A drawing from the project documents showing the P-1's nose as actually built. Note the pressurised radar capsule and the FFAR launchers grouped around it.

In its initial project form the P-1 even shared the T-3's air intake design, featuring a 'grinning' nose air intake with an upturned conical radome at the top and a hemispherical radome in the middle; this was because originally the interceptor was to have the Almaz-7 twin-antenna fire control radar. The inlet ducts flanked the cockpits and the centre fuselage fuel tanks, merging ahead of the engine. As in the case of the T-3, the K-7 missiles were carried on short swept pylons outboard of the main gear units.

The aircraft was 20.1 m (65 ft., $11^{11}/_{32}$ in.) long, with a fuselage length of 16.95 m (55 ft., $7^{21}/_{64}$ in.) and a maximum fuselage diameter of 2.044 m (6 ft., $8^{15}/_{32}$ in.); the wingspan was 10.1 m (33 ft , $1^{41}/_{64}$ in.) and the stabilator span 6.044 m (19 ft., $9^{61}/_{64}$ in.). Wing area was 44 m² (473.61 sq. ft.), vertical tail area 8 m² (86.11 sq. ft.), and horizontal tail area 7.1 m² (76.42 sq. ft.). The forward-retracting nose gear unit had a 660 × 150 mm (25.98 × 5.9 in.) wheel, while the inward-retracting main units were fitted with 900 × 275 mm (35.43 × 10.82 in.) wheels; the wheel track was 3.96 m (12 ft., $11^{29}/_{32}$ in.) and the wheelbase 6.32 m (20 ft., $8^{13}/_{16}$ in.). The maximum rotation angle on takeoff was 13°30'.

Soon enough, however, the P-1's appearance changed considerably. The entire forward fuselage section was redesigned to feature a 'solid' nose; the search and guidance antennas of the Almaz-7 radar were placed together in a large conical radome, with the radar set and the Uragan system modules farther aft. The

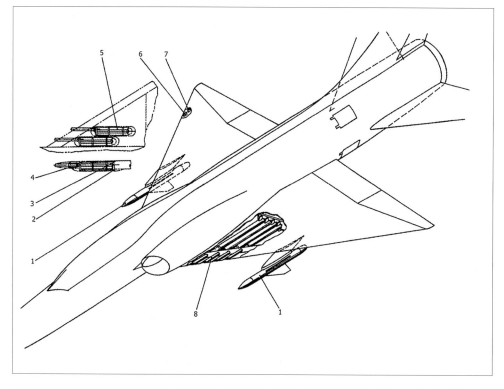

The armament options of the P-1.
1. K-7 AAM;
2. Rear mounting for ARO-70 FFAR launcher;
3. Emergency blast gas chute for ARO-70;
4. Front mounting for ARO-70 FFAR launcher;
5. ARO-70 single-barrel revolver-type FFAR launcher;
6-7 AKS-3 and BM-2 strike cameras;
8. Launch tubes for TRS-85 spin-stabilised unguided rockets.

designers opted for lateral air intakes positioned above the wing roots to protrude beyond the wing leading edge; the circular-section intakes were raked 45° in plan view and stood proud of the fuselage sides, being connected to the latter by small, pointed fairings that spilled the turbulent boundary layer. In the course of 1955 this intake design was studied in detail, allowing the advanced development project to be prepared by the end of the year. Since the radar remained the same for the time being, this drastic redesign may have been dictated by the need to improve the pilot's field of view over the nose.

The forward fuselage cross section in the cockpit area was now elliptical, changing back to circular aft of the cockpit. The canopy now blended into a prominent fuselage spine that ran aft all the way to the fin. The landing gear was considerably revised—the nose unit now retracted aft, stowing under the rear cockpit, while the design of the inward-retracting main units was inspired by the MiG-21 (during retraction the mainwheels rotated around the oleos by means of mechanical linkages to lie vertically in the fuselage rather than horizontally in the wing roots).

While the P-1's primary weapons (the K-7L AAMs) were carried under the wings in normal fashion, the secondary unguided rocket armament was arranged unconventionally. To avoid ruining the interceptor's aerodynamics with bulky rocket pods, two options were proposed. Option 1 was to install a quartet of ARO-70 automatic rocket launchers with a long barrel and a drum holding eight 70 mm (2.75 in.) ARS-70 FFARs. The launchers were buried in the wing roots, two on each side in a staggered arrangement, so that the drums protruded only a little below the lower skin. Option 2 was two 'pan flute' blocks of four launch tubes in the wing roots, with 85 mm (3.34 in.) TRS-85 spin-stabilised rockets, three per tube. The TRS acronym (***toorboreaktivnyy snaryad***: literally, 'turbojet-powered missile') was misleading, since the rocket had a solid-fuel rocket motor with two angled nozzles that caused the finless projectile to rotate like a bullet, stabilising it. Thus the P-1 was to carry 32 ARS-70 rockets or 24 TRS-85 rockets.

The avionics included an RSIU-4 radio, an RSBN-2 Svod (Dome) short-range radio navigation system (***rahdiotekhnicheskaya sistema blizhney navigahtsiï***: SHORAN), an ARK-5 ADF, an MRP-56P marker beacon receiver, an RUP-4 Tsna processor (***reshayushcheye oostroystvo posahdki***: landing computer; Tsna is the name of a Russian river), and Khrom-Nikel' IFF. The second project version of the P-1 was 21.27 m (69 ft., 9^{13}⁄₃₂ in.) long and 5.585 m (18 ft., 3^{7}⁄₈ in.) high when parked, with a wingspan of 9.816 m (32 ft., 2^{29}⁄₆₄ in.) and a wheel track of 4.06 m (13 ft., 3^{27}⁄₃₂ in.).

Yet more changes were to come before the project was finalised. The mockup review commission duly convened in late 1955 to assess the two project versions; both the P-1 and the P-2 (see next entry) were accepted for full-scale development, whereupon the detail design stage began in the first half of 1956. At this point the P-1 underwent major design changes to suit the chosen operational concept. First of all, the rocket launchers buried in the wings were rejected in favour of a different arrangement. Fifty 57 mm (2.24 in.) ARS-57 FFARs were housed in launcher packs located around the circumference of the nose, hidden by six inward-opening doors immediately aft of the radome, in similar manner to the Lockheed F-94C Starfire; they were to be fired in a salvo or a ripple after the doors had been opened. Second, the Almaz-7 radar was replaced by a new *Pantera* (Panther) radar with a single antenna dish developed by NII-17; the radar set was enclosed in a hermetically sealed capsule to prevent it from being affected by the rockets' exhaust gases. Third, the landing-gear wheelbase was increased by moving the nose gear unit forward so that it stowed under the front cockpit. In order to maximise the internal fuel capacity, the designers chose not to area rule the interceptor's fuselage.

Detail design of the P-1 was completed in August 1956, and as soon as the final blueprints were delivered to OKB-51's experimental production facility the latter commenced prototype construction. By the end of the year it became clear that the Lyul'ka OKB was facing major development problems with the AL-9 and would be unable to deliver the engine on schedule. (A different account of the story says that development of the AL-9 was curtailed in favour of the more promising AL-11 afterburning turbojet after only one prototype engine had been built.) Since no other suitable engine was available, as a stop-gap measure it was decided to install the proven, albeit less powerful, 9,600 kgp (21,160 lbst) AL-7F for the initial flight tests; an appropriate order was given by Minister of Aircraft Industry Pyotr V. Dement'yev. This necessitated a redesign of the internal fuselage structure, the inlet ducts, and the air intakes. The latter were now adjustable, featuring movable centre bodies in the shape of a half cone, as on the Lockheed F-104 Starfighter. (Actually the intakes bore but a passing resemblance to those of the Starfighter; they were still circular rather than semicircular, the leading edges were sharply raked instead of being at right angles to the fuselage centreline, forming an elliptical contour in side elevation, and the centre bodies were much more pointed.) According to some sources, on the actual aircraft the number of unguided rockets in the nose was reduced from 50 to 32.

Between May and December 1956, MMZ No. 51 manufactured the static-test airframe of the P-1, which was 92.5% complete by New Year's Day. However, the experimental facility could not cope with the task alone due to lack of capacity. On 4 June 1956, GKAT instructed aircraft factory no. 153 in Novosibirsk, aircraft factory no. 126 in Komsomol'sk-on-Amur, and factory no. 119 in Gor'kiy to help out by supplying, respectively, the wings, tail surfaces, and landing gear for the P-1's flying prototype, but they proved unco-operative, and eventually MMZ No. 51 had to manufacture the wings and tail unit inhouse, commencing final assembly in October. As a result, by 1 January 1957 the aircraft was only 73.6% complete.

Meanwhile, the government wanted higher performance. On 25 August 1956 the Council of Ministers issued a directive requiring the second prototypes of the P-1 and P-2 to be armed with homing missiles. Specifically, the P-1 was to be armed with K-9 AAMs, which were to be developed by the Sukhoi OKB pursuant to the same directive. The directive also required the Novosibirsk factory to build three preproduction P-1s armed with K-9 AAMs in the fourth quarter of 1957.

(To be precise, the missile in question was the K-9-51, the last digits referring to OKB-51; more on this appears under the T-37 heading later in this chapter. Confusingly enough, the Mikoyan OKB was also ordered to develop a similar AAM for its own Ye-150 interceptor as the K-9-155, the digits hinting at OKB-155.

Left: A head-on view of the P-1, showing the elliptical cross section of the fuselage nose

Right: Three-quarters front view of the P-1, showing the air intakes with small semicones on the inboard side. The air intakes' cross section may appear elliptical but is actually circular.

Below right: This side view underscores the P-1's nose-down ground angle and relatively short wheelbase. Note also the wing dogtooth.

A GKAT order dated 4 July 1957 prescribed that for the sake of weapons commonality, the Mikoyan and Sukhoi OKBs were to '*develop launch rails for the Ye-150 and "P" aircraft currently under construction so as to permit carriage of K-9 missiles developed by plant no. 155 and plant no. 51*'.)

At the end of September 1956, General Designer Pavel O. Sukhoi reported thus to I. G. Zagainov, head of GKAT's 7th Main Directorate: '*1. The second prototype of the P-1 two-seat interceptor powered by an AL-9 engine and armed with two homing missiles is intended to reach a top speed of 2,200–2,300 km/h [1,366–1,428 mph] and a service ceiling of 23,000 m [75,460 ft].*

These figures are based on the AL-9 engine's performance estimates supplied by Chief Designer Comrade A. M. Lyul'ka, stating a thrust of 14,900 kgp [32,850 lbst] at 11,000 m [36.090 ft.] and Mach 2.2, thrust losses taken into account. . . .

4. The design bureau has studied the possibility of creating a medium-altitude interceptor based on the AL-9 powered P-1, with the following performance:

top speed at 5,000 m [16,400 ft] in reheat mode, 1,650 km/h [1,025 mph];

top speed at 5,000 m in dry-thrust mode, 1,100 km/h [683 mph];

Left: Rear view of the P-1

Right: Three-quarters rear view of the P-1, showing the anhedral on the horizontal tail

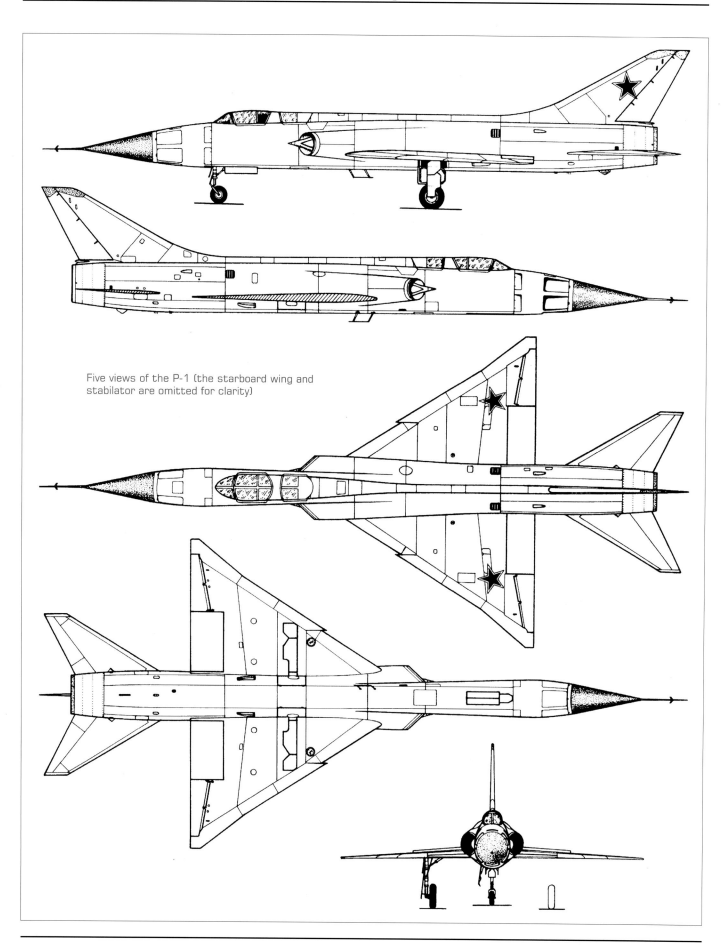

Five views of the P-1 (the starboard wing and stabilator are omitted for clarity)

top speed at 10,000 m [32,810 ft] in reheat mode, 2,200 km/h [1,367 mph];

top speed at 10,000 m in dry-thrust mode, 1,000 km/h [621 mph];

technical range at 5,000 m and 900–950 km/h [559-590 mph] with 7% fuel remaining, 1,400 km [870 miles];

service ceiling in reheat mode, 19,000 m [62,340 ft.];

service ceiling in dry-thrust mode, 12,000 m [39,370 ft];

climb time to 10,000 m, 3 minutes;

armament, K-8 homing missiles plus, in high gross weight configuration, 50 ARS-57 rockets or 30 TRS-85 rockets.

The aircraft can be submitted for joint [state acceptance] *trials in the first quarter of 1959.'* As the reader can see, the Su-11's K-8 missile also came into the picture at this stage!

The static-test article was completed in March 1957, and in May the completed P-1 prototype was rolled out with an AL-7F-1 engine. On 10 June the dismantled aircraft was delivered to the OKB's flight test facility in Zhukovskiy to begin ground checks. M. Goncharov was appointed project engineer.

Wearing no markings other than the national insignia, the P-1 performed its maiden flight on 12 July 1957 with OKB test pilot Nikolay I. Korovushkin at the controls. The engine promptly went unserviceable, and the aircraft was returned to MMZ No. 51 for repairs after the first flight. When a replacement engine had been fitted, the P-1 was again trucked to Zhukovskiy, making a further four flights by the year's end.

Meanwhile, the military kept changing their requirements with respect to the P-1. GKAT's prototype aircraft construction plan for 1957–59, which was drafted in September 1957, contained a clause that the aircraft should be re-engined with either the aforementioned AL-11 afterburning turbojet, rated at 6,800 kgp (14,990 lbst) dry and 10,000 kgp (22,045 lbst) reheat, or the Tumanskiy R15-300 afterburning turbojet, rated at 6,840 kgp (15,080 lbst) dry and 10,150 kgp (22,380 lbst) reheat. With this power plant the interceptor was to have a top speed of 2,800–3,000 km/h (1,739–1,863 mph) at 16,000 m (52,490 ft.), a normal range of 1,250 km (776 miles), a maximum range of 2,000 km (1,242 miles) on internal fuel and 2,500 km (1,552 miles) with a drop tank, a service ceiling of 24,000–25,000 m (78,740–82,020 ft.), and a takeoff/landing run of 850–950 m (2,790–3,120 ft.). The armament was now specified as two K-7 or K-8 AAMs, with options for an additional 50 ARS-57M FFARs; instead of the AAMs, either two 212 mm (8.34 in.) ARS-212 *Ovod* (Gadfly) unguided rockets on PU-21 launch rails or a pair of pods with 24 TRS-57 spin-stabilised unguided rockets each could be carried. A Pantera radar, an autopilot, a SHORAN system, and a GCI system receiver were stipulated. The aircraft was to be submitted for trials in the third quarter of 1959. Moreover, one AL-7F-1-powered P-1 was to be presented for trials in the fourth quarter of 1958 with no fewer than 98 ARS-57M FFARs! Some of these would obviously have to be carried in underwing pods.

The manufacturer's flight tests continued until 22 September 1958 and were performed by Nikolay I. Korovushkin and Eduard V. Yelian. The intended AL-9 and AL-11 engines never arrived, and since the aircraft showed disappointing performance with the provisional power plant, it did not proceed beyond the initial flight test phase.

Curiously, on 13 September 1958 the Council of Ministers issued a directive requiring the P-1 to be converted into an ejection-seat test bed; the Novosibirsk factory was to build two such test beds. In June 1959 the factory's director wrote to the government, requesting that the factory be relieved of the task; he stated that *'at present the P-1 fighter does not exist* [sic!]*; hence there is no basis to build the test beds; the engines and systems for this aircraft have not yet been developed. Moreover, the P-1 is of no interest from a technology standpoint and has no future, which is why GKAT has approached the Council of Ministers, requesting that the P-1 be removed from the plan altogether as an experimental aircraft.'*

For a while, OKB-51 persisted with the P-1 concept, trying to create a viable combat aircraft using the same layout. Pavel O. Sukhoi repeatedly tried, both single-handedly and jointly with the 'subcontractors' responsible for the radar and other equipment, to win air force support for the P-1, but their efforts were thwarted by a singular lack of interest on the part of the prospective customer. In the second half of 1959 the P-1 programme was struck off the Sukhoi OKB's work list in order to allow the OKB to concentrate on higher-priority projects (such as the T-37 heavy fighter). The P-1 was abandoned altogether; the sole prototype was scrapped. The abovementioned three Novosibirsk-built P-1s, which were 50% complete at the end of 1958, were never finished.

The following is a brief structural description of the P-1.

Type: Two-seat supersonic interceptor designed for day and night operation in VMC and IMC. The airframe is of all-metal construction.

Fuselage: Semimonocoque, stressed-skin structure of basically circular cross section and mostly riveted construction; spot welding is used in certain areas. The skin is made mostly of V95 aluminium alloy sheet. Structurally the fuselage consists of three sections: forward (section F-1), centre (section F-2), and rear (section F-3), the latter being detachable for engine maintenance and removal.

The *forward fuselage* is tipped by a conical GRP radome. Its front end incorporates the pressurised radar bay and six unguided rocket launcher bays clustered around it, with inward-opening powered doors enclosing the launchers. Farther aft is the pressurised cockpit section, with the nosewheel well located below the front cockpit. The pilot and WSO are seated in tandem under a common canopy featuring a fixed windshield with a flat elliptical windscreen and curved triangular sidelights, individual upward-hinged sections over the two seats, and an opaque intercanopy frame; the canopy blends smoothly into the fuselage spine.

The cockpit section is flanked by the engine air intakes of circular cross section, blending gradually into the centre portion of the fuselage. The raked supersonic air intakes feature sharp lips and movable shock cones on the inboard side. To prevent boundary layer ingestion, the intakes are set apart from the fuselage, the extended inboard lips acting as boundary layer splitter plates.

The *centre fuselage* is slightly waisted in accordance with the area rule where the two inlet ducts merge at the entrance to the

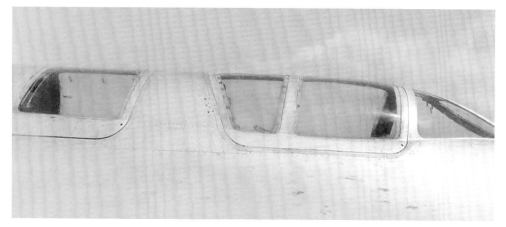

Left: The P-1's cockpit seen from the starboard side. The pilot's canopy has nearly twice the glazing area as compared to the WSO's canopy. The fixed windshield appears to have an ordinary glass windscreen, not a bullet-proof one.

Below left: The open canopies of the P-1 show the curious design with each canopy swinging upward and rearward on three levers. Note the rear canopy's locking handle.

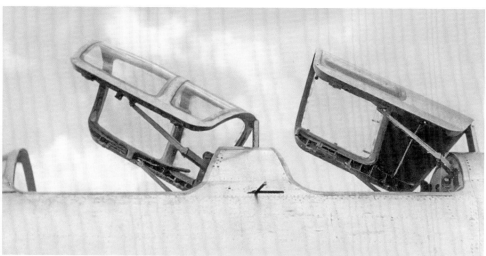

Bottom left: The P-1's nose gear unit

Bottom right: The main gear units (the port one is shown here) had links rotating the wheel to keep it vertical during retraction.

Opposite page, top: The Pantera radar fitted to the P-1

Opposite page, bottom: One of the P-1's ejection seats

engine bay; it incorporates wing attachment fittings and accommodates integral fuel tanks. The *rear fuselage* accommodates the engine and incorporates the tail unit attachment fittings and three airbrakes, one of which is located ventrally and the others laterally.

Wings: Cantilever midwing monoplane with delta wings having 60° leading-edge sweep and a leading-edge dogtooth at half span. The wings feature front and rear spars and three transverse beams (false spars); the skins are chemically milled, with integral stringers. The root portions incorporate integral fuel tanks and provisions for installing unguided rocket launch tubes.

The wings have one-piece constant-chord Fowler flaps, with tapered ailerons outboard of these; the one-piece ailerons are aerodynamically balanced. Two hardpoints for missile pylons are provided outboard of the main gear fulcrums.

Tail unit: Conventional swept-cantilever tail surfaces. The *vertical tail* comprises a fin with a one-piece inset rudder. The fin is a single-spar structure with an internal brace and chemically milled skins with integral stringers; the rudder is of single-spar riveted construction. The *horizontal tail* consists of midset anhedral stabilators with antiflutter weights at the tips.

Landing gear: Hydraulically retractable tricycle type, with a single wheel on each unit; all three landing-gear struts have oleo-pneumatic shock absorbers. The aft-retracting levered suspension nose unit is equipped with a 570 × 140 mm (22.4 × 5.5 in.) K-283 nonbraking nosewheel and a shimmy damper. The telescopic main units retract inward and are fitted with 1,000 × 280 mm (39.37 × 11.0 in.) KT-72 brake-equipped wheels. During retraction the mainwheels are rotated around the oleos by mechanical linkages to stow vertically in the fuselage.

The nosewheel well is closed by twin lateral doors and a small forward door segment attached to the oleo strut; the mainwheel wells are closed by triple doors (one segment is hinged to the front spar, one to the root rib, and a third segment attached to the oleo leg). All doors remain open when the gear is down.

Power plant: One Lyul'ka AL-7F-1 axial-flow afterburning turbojet rated at 6,850 kgp (15,100 lbst) at full military power and 8,950 kgp (19,730 lbst) in full afterburner.

Control system: Powered controls with irreversible hydraulic actuators throughout. Directional control is by means of a one-piece rudder with a BU-49 actuator. Pitch control is by means of stabilators with a BU-51 tailplane actuator. Roll control is by means of one-piece ailerons with BU-52 actuators. Control inputs are transmitted to the aileron and stabilator actuators by push-pull rods, control cranks, and levers; a combined control linkage utilising both rods and cables is used in the rudder control circuit. An AP-28Zh-1B electric autopilot is provided; the tailplane control circuit also features an artificial-feel unit.

Fuel system: The fuel is carried in two bladder tanks located in the centre fuselage between the engine's inlet ducts (the small no. 2 tank is the service tank) and in four integral wing tanks. Internal fuel capacity is 5,450 litres (1,199 Imp gal.), and the internal fuel load 4,470 kg (9,850 lbs.). Provisions are made for carrying a 930-litre (204.6 Imp gal.) centreline drop tank.

Hydraulics: Three separate hydraulic systems, each with its own engine-driven pump. The *primary system* operates the landing gear, flaps, airbrakes, and air-intake shock cones; the two *actuator supply systems* (main and backup) exclusively power the aileron, rudder, and tailplane actuators.

Avionics and equipment:

a) flight and navigation equipment: The avionics include an AP-28Zh-1B autopilot, an ARK-54 ADF, an RV-U low-range radio altimeter, an MRP-56P marker beacon receiver, a GIK-1 gyro-flux gate compass, an AGI-1 artificial horizon;

b) communications equipment: RSIU-4V two-way VHF communications radio (with a wire mesh antenna incorporated into the fin cap) and SPU-2 intercom;

c) targeting equipment: the aircraft is equipped with a Pantera fire control radar and a data link receiver making up part of the *Gorizont-1* (Horizon-1) GCI system;

d) IFF equipment: SRZO-2M Kremniy-2M IFF transponder with aerials under the forward and rear fuselage, plus SOD-57M ATC/SIF transponder with a flush aerial built into the fin;

e) ESM equipment: Sirena-2 radar warning receiver with an aerial at the base of the rudder.

Armament: The principal armament consists of two K-7S semi-active radar homing AAMs carried on underwing pylons.

Additionally, thirty-two 57 mm ARS-57 FFARs are carried in buried launchers around the circumference of the fuselage nose.

Crew rescue system: Sukhoi KS-series ejection seats for the pilot and the WSO.

P-1 Low-Altitude Version (Project)

In March 1958 the Sukhoi OKB proposed a special low-altitude version of the P-1 interceptor optimised for combating low-flying intruders. The aircraft was to be powered by a Klimov VK-13 afterburning turbojet rated at 7,100 kgp (15,650 lbst) dry and 10,000 kgp (22,045 lbst) reheat, and the mission avionics would be revised for low-altitude operations. However, such an aircraft did not fit well into the existing GCI system because communication with ground control centres would be difficult; a special communications relay aircraft would need to be developed for working with it, which was a complex task.

On this pretext the proposal was turned down. In a memo to the Communist Party Central Committee on 29 May 1958, GKAT Chairman Pyotr V. Dement'yev wrote that *'the main task of OKB-51 is the development of high-altitude interceptors. Comrade Sukhoi has suggested tasking him with developing a low-altitude interceptor based on the P-1 aircraft, and tasking plant no. 153 in Novosibirsk with building the aircraft. Plant no. 153 is currently tooling up for T-3 interceptor production; therefore it should not be burdened with the additional task of building the P-1 because this will drain resources from the primary task of building the T-3. Three P-1s will be manufactured by plant no. 153 in keeping with previous rulings, and tasking it with building any more [P-1s] is inexpedient.'*

P-1 Reconnaissance Version (Project)

Another version of the P-1 that briefly came into consideration (in March 1958, it was mentioned in the OKB's work plan for 1958 to 1961) was a reconnaissance aircraft powered by a Lyul'ka AL-11 afterburning turbojet or the R15M-300 afterburning turbojet created by Sergey K. Tumanskiy's OKB-300. Unlike the interceptor, this was to be a single-seater (apparently the WSO's cockpit would be transformed into a mission equipment bay or house an extra fuel tank). The aircraft was to be equipped with vertical and oblique aerial cameras, an *Initsiativa-2* (Initiative) ground mapping radar for navigation and reconnaissance, an RSBN-2S Svod SHORAN system (to be replaced by the Barometr SHORAN), an active electronic countermeasures (ECM) system of the Siren' jammer series (Lilac, pronounced *seeren'*), an RVU radio altimeter, and an RSIU-5 radio.

Performance included a maximum speed of 3,000 km/h (1,863 mph) at 15,000 m (49,210 ft.), a service ceiling of 25,000 m (82,020 ft.), and a takeoff/landing run of 850–900 m (2,790–2,950 ft.). Range depended on the engine type, because the R15M-300 was thirstier. Cruising at 10,000–12,000 m (32,810–39,370 ft.) with a speed of 950–1,000 km/h (590–621 mph), the AL-11-powered aircraft would have a range of 2,500 km (1,552 miles) on internal fuel and 2,900 km (1,801 miles) with drop tanks; for the R15M-300-powered version it would be 2,300 km (1,429 miles) and 2,600 km (1,615 miles), respectively, in the same conditions. The duration of a supersonic dash at 2,800–3,000 km/h (1,739–1,863 mph) would be six minutes at an altitude of 25,000 m, 14 minutes at 24,000 m (78,740 ft.) and 20 minutes at 23,000 m (75,460 ft.).

According to plans, the Novosibirsk aircraft factory was to build a static-test airframe in the fourth quarter of 1958, followed by the prototype in the first quarter of 1959. Of course these plans came to nothing.

P-2 Two-Seat Interceptor (Project)

The P-2 interceptor developed in parallel with the P-1 pursuant to the same C of M directive differed mainly in having a power plant consisting of two Klimov VK-11 axial-flow afterburning turbojets. (By then Nikolay G. Metskhvarishvili had succeeded Vladimir Ya. Klimov as head of the Moscow-based OKB-500, but the VK prefix to the engine designations was still in use for the time being.) This is something of a mystery engine because different sources give widely differing figures on the VK-11's thrust. According to one report, the VK-11 was rated at 4,500 kgp (9,920 lbst) dry and 9,000 kgp (19,840 lbst) reheat; another gives a maximum thrust of only 5,370 kgp (11,840 lbst). A further source quotes 11,250 kgp (24,800 lbst) in full afterburner. Finally, Pavel O. Sukhoi's memo to I. G. Zagainov written in late September 1956 says that the engine maker had quoted the thrust of the VK-11 at 11,000 m (36,090 ft.) as a whopping 20,000 kgp (44,090 lbst)!

The engines were located side by side in the rear fuselage, breathing through air intakes of identical design to those of the P-1 but featuring separate inlet ducts; hence, the centre fuselage was not area ruled. The estimated fuel load amounted to 3,200 kg (7,050 lbs.). According to the PD project the aircraft was 22.75 m (74 ft., 7⁴³⁄₆₄ in.) long and 5.59 m (18 ft., 4⁵⁄₆₄ in.) high when parked, with a wingspan of 9.968 m (32 ft., 8⁷⁄₁₆ in.) and a wheel track of 4.8 m (15 ft., 8³¹⁄₃₂ in.). Due to the higher takeoff weight as compared to the single-engined version, the P-2 was to feature larger and stronger 1,000 × 275 mm (39.37 × 10.8 in.) mainwheels. Estimated performance included a top speed of 2,100–2,200 km/h (1,304–1,367 mph) and a service ceiling of 20,000–21,000 m (65,620–68,900 ft.).

Unlike the P-1, the P-2's principal armament consisted of two 30 mm (1.18 calibre) rapid-firing cannons with 100 rpg installed in the wing roots, the two K-7 AAMs being regarded as additional armament. The cannon type was not specified, but a Council of Ministers directive setting the Sukhoi OKB's work plan for 1955 quotes the rate of fire as 1,300–1,500 rounds per minute; this means it cannot be the Nudelman/Rikhter NR-30 cannon, whose rate of fire was only 850–1,000 rpm. In maximum takeoff weight configuration up to 20 TRS-85 or up to 16 ARS-70, unguided rockets could be carried under the wings.

The P-2 passed the project review together with the P-1 but then started falling behind. According to the initial plans the aircraft was to be submitted for trials in the fourth quarter of 1957, but as of 1 January 1957 the advanced development project was only 55% complete. The aircraft was never built; further work on the P-2 was eventually cancelled by a Council of Ministers directive dated 4 June 1958.

T-3A-9 Aerial-Intercept Weapons System
T-37 (T-3A) Experimental Interceptor

In August 1956 the Council of Ministers let loose with a directive requiring the Soviet 'fighter makers' to increase the performance of the advanced interceptors then under development, boosting the service ceiling to 23,000–25,000 m (75,460–82,020 ft.), and to integrate homing air-to-air missiles on these aircraft. In January

Above: An artist's impression of the P-2 from the ADP documents, showing the constant-width centre fuselage and the forked fairing between the engine nozzles
Below: A three-view drawing of the P-2 from the ADP documents

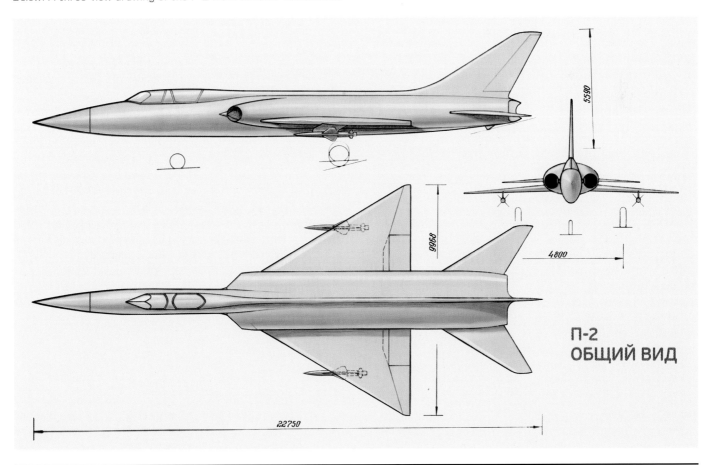

П-2
ОБЩИЙ ВИД

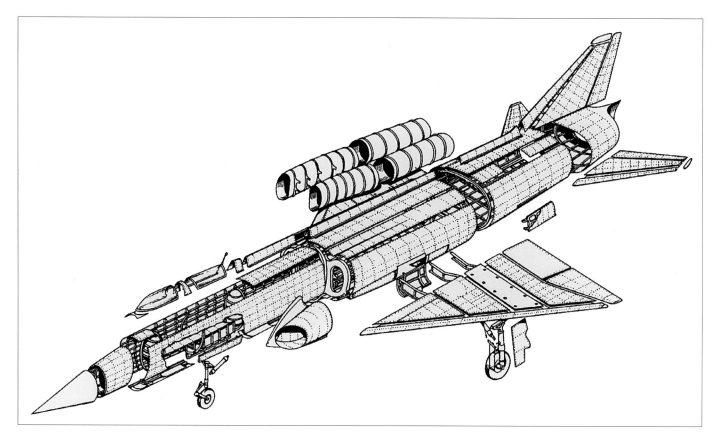

Above: An exploded view of the P-2 interceptor

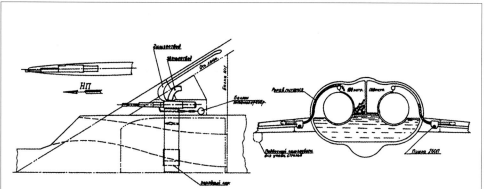

Left: The armament placement of the P-2 as envisaged by the project

A Comparison of the P-1 and P-2 (ADP Data)		
	P-1	**P-2**
Length	21.27 m (69 ft., 9¹³⁄₃₂ in.)	22.75 m (74 ft., 7⁴⁄₆₄ in.)
Wingspan	9.816 m (32 ft., 2²⁄₆₄ in.)	10.25 m (33 ft .,7³⁄₆₄ in.)
Height on ground	5.585 m (18 ft., 3⅞ in.)	5.59 m (18 ft., 4⁵⁄₆₄ in.)
Empty weight, kg (lbs.)	7,710 (17,000)	8,780 (19,360)
Normal takeoff weight, kg (lbs.)	10,600 23,370	12,400 (27,340)
Fuel load, kg (lbs.)	2,360 (5,200)	3,200 (7,055)
Top speed at 15,000 m (49,210 ft.), km/h (mph)	2,050 (1,274)	2,100 (1,304)
Service ceiling, m (ft.)	19,500 (63,980)	20,450 (67,090)
Climb time to 15,000 m, minutes	2.7	2.5
Effective range, km (miles):		
on internal fuel	1,250 (776)	1,400 (869)
with drop tanks	n.a.	2,000 (1,242)

1958, GKAT filed a draft plan of prototype aircraft construction to the Council of Ministers for approval. In particular, OKB-51 was to develop a new version of the T-3 interceptor re-engined with the aforementioned Lyul'ka AL-11 or Tumanskiy R15M-300 afterburning turbojet. The following performance was required:

• top speed at 16,000 m (52,490 ft.), 3,000–3,200 km/h (1,863–1,988 mph);

• service ceiling, 27,000 m (88,580 ft.);

• climb time to 15,000 m (49,210 ft.), 3.5 minutes;

• range at an altitude of 10,000–12,000 m (32,810–39,370 ft.) transonic (950–1,00 km/h; 590–621 mph):

- on internal fuel, 1,000 km (621 miles),

- with drop tanks, 1,600 km (994 miles);

• effective range with drop tanks at an altitude of 20,000 m (65,620 ft.), supersonic (2,000–2,500 km/h; 1,242–1,552 mph), 1,000 km (621 miles);

An artist's impression of the T-37 heavy interceptor with the originally envisaged long multishock intake centre body / radome

Another artist's impression of the T-37. Note the pitot with pitch/yaw transducers at the tip of the radome, the originally planned annular air ejector ahead of the engine nozzle, and the stalky landing gear.

A colour cutaway drawing of the T-37. Note the globular shroud of the TsP-1 radar's antenna inside the radome and the single centreline drop tank.

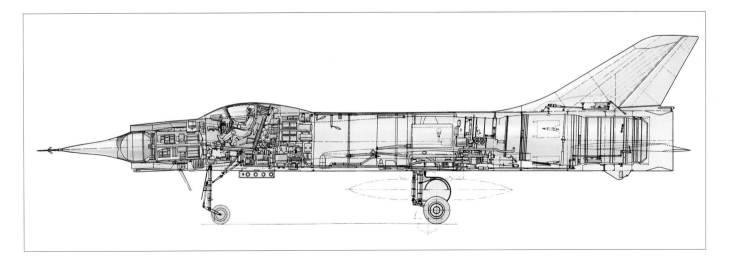

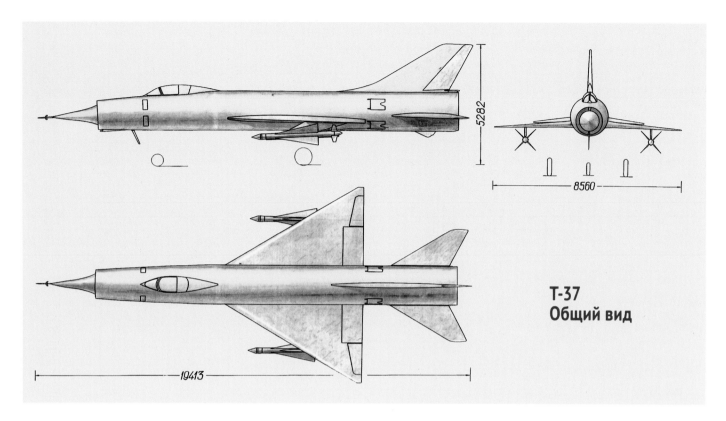

T-37
Общий вид

• endurance at an altitude of 20,000 m, supersonic (2,000–2,500 km/h):
- on internal fuel, 9.0–10.0 km minutes,
- with drop tanks, 15.0–17.0 minutes;
• takeoff/landing run, 750–800 m (2,460–2,620 ft.).

The aircraft was to be armed with two K-9 homing AAMs, with provisions for 32 ARS-57M FFARs or two ARS-212M unguided rockets, and to work with automatic or semiautomatic GCI systems (Uragan-5 or Vozdukh-1), ensuring all-aspect target attack capability and a 'kill' probability of at least 80-90%. Such

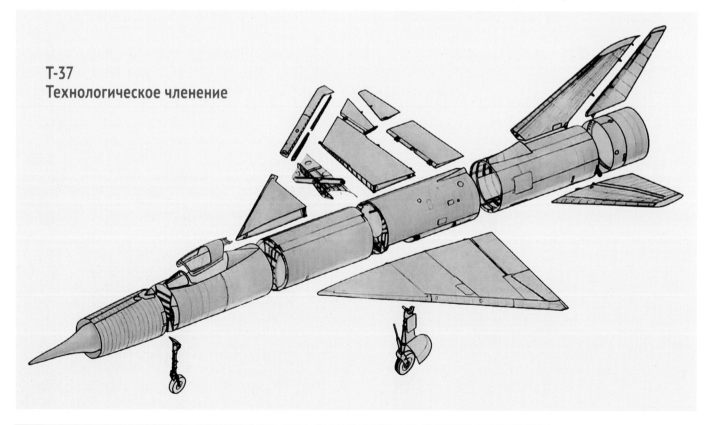

T-37
Технологическое членение

Left: A three-angle view of the T-37 from the ADP documents. Note that there is no longer a gap on the rear fuselage—the annular air ejector has been replaced by flush-fitting doors around the perimeter of the rear fuselage.

Below left: An exploded view of the T-37 from the ADP documents. The upper-wing skin panel in the wheel well area has been omitted to show the shape of the lower panel.

Right: A display model of the T-37 from the Sukhoi OKB museum. It shows the definitive short radome of simple conical shape.

Upper view of the same model, illustrating the T-37's tubular fuselage of almost constant diameter

This lower view shows how the main-wheel wells of the T-37 encroached on the centre fuselage.

tive interceptors. Both OKBs set to work and came up with two very different missiles bearing the same designation (well, not exactly—as already mentioned, Mikoyan's version was designated K-9-155 (NATO AA-4 Awl), while the Sukhoi version was the K-9-51. Confusingly, both missiles have been referred to by the same service designation R-38 (although neither version would eventually enter service!). In both cases the guidance system was the responsibility of KB-1, headed by Konstantin N. Patrookhin, a division of the Ministry of Defence Industry (now known as NPO *Almaz*, 'Diamond' Scientific & Production Association).

The K-9-51 missile, a.k.a. R-38, was a semi-active radar homing Mach 3 missile designed for engagements in both head-on and pursuit modes. The missile used a conventional layout with large cruciform delta wings and cruciform unswept trapezoidal rudders. It carried a 27 kg (59 lb.) directional HE/fragmentation warhead that was detonated by a radar proximity fuse with a maximum detection radius of 25 m (82 ft.). The radar seeker had a detection range of 15 km (9.3 miles). The missile cruised at Mach 3 and was to be capable of destroying targets at altitudes up to 25,000 m (82,020 ft.).

In keeping with the said directive, the K-9-51 was to enter test in the first quarter of 1959. Interestingly, the directive contained a clause requiring the K-9-51 and K-9-155 to be compatible with both Mikoyan and Sukhoi interceptors, and the launch rails were to be designed accordingly.

Actual design work on the T-3A commenced in the spring of 1958, with I. E. Zaslavskiy as chief project engineer; the project was officially sanctioned by a Council of Ministers directive dated 4 June 1958. It soon became apparent that a straightforward adaptation of the existing T-3 to take the K-9-51 missiles and the new powerful TsP fire control radar would not work—the T-3A would have to be a 'clean sheet of paper' aircraft. Such an interceptor was duly developed, receiving the manufacturer's designation T-37.

The engine type was selected quickly. Formally the designers could choose between two engines; however, the AL-11 (*izdeliye* 47) did not yet exist in hardware form (its development had been initiated by a GKAT order issued on 4 June 1958). Eventually, four prototype engines were manufactured for bench testing—and that was it; in early 1959, GKAT issued a new order, suspending all further work on the AL-11. This left the R15-300 (originally developed for the Mikoyan Ye-150 experimental heavy interceptor) as the only option, and this engine was selected to power the T-37. The R15-300 completed its bench test programme at the end of 1959. Starting life as the KR15-300 expendable turbojet for the Tupolev '121' supersonic ground-launched cruise missile, it evolved into a 'normal' fighter engine that powered a series of Mikoyan heavy interceptors (first the experimental Ye-150/Ye-152 series, and later the production MiG-25 Foxbat.

The advanced development project was completed in 1958; three versions of the rear fuselage and two versions of the fuel tanks were tried in the process. The T-37 resembled a scaled-up version of the T-3, featuring an axisymmetrical nose air intake with a massive shock cone that also housed the powerful TsP-1 fire control radar, delta wings with 60° leading-edge sweep, and conventional tail surfaces swept back 55° at quarter chord with all-movable tailplanes. Unlike its predecessors, however, the aircraft

an aircraft was to be presented for state acceptance trials in the first quarter of 1960.

A further C of M directive concerning the bolstering of the Soviet air defence system followed on 4 June 1958. It ordered the creation of the T-3A-9 aerial-intercept weapons system, comprising the T-3A interceptor, two K-9 AAMs and the associated weapons control system, the Looch-1 (Beam-1) GCI system, the Barometr-L data link / navigation / instrument landing system, and the SRZO-2M Kremniy-2M IFF. For the purposes of this document the T-3A was regarded merely as a refined version of the existing T-3 interceptor (hence the designation), with an R15M-300 engine, a new missile armament, and a new fire control radar designated TsP-1. In keeping with the prevailing weapons-systems design ideology of the time, the T-37 was considered as an integral part of a fully automated aerial-intercept system, being equipped with automatic GCI systems, with far-reaching plans to integrate an automated target detection, tracking, and attack system enabling all-aspect engagement (that is, in both pursuit and head-on mode). The pilot's functions were thereby reduced to monitoring the system and taking corrective action if anything went wrong.

The same directive of 4 June 1958 ordered the Mikoyan and Sukhoi design bureaus to develop the K-9 missile for their respec-

featured a monocoque fuselage structure with no longerons (although Sukhoi OKB engineer Eduard S. Samoylovich, who was on the T-37 design team, claims the fuselage was of the usual semimonocoque type). The circular-section fuselage had a maximum diameter of 1.7 m (5 ft., 7 in.). The integral fuel tanks and the inlet ducts were one-piece welded structures made of AMTs aluminium alloy; a similar technology was used for manufacturing the detachable rear fuselage, which was made of titanium and heat-resistant steel. In a departure from normal design practice, the multishock intake centre body was fixed; airflow control was exercised by means of a translating annular sleeve inside the intake (aft of the radome), plus auxiliary blow-in doors on the fuselage sides. Originally, an annular ejector was to be fitted around the engine nozzle to enhance thrust; on the actual aircraft it was replaced by eight air scoops located around the rear fuselage circumference.

The slightly anhedral wings were single-spar, stressed-skin structures with hydraulically actuated, one-piece Fowler flaps and ailerons; a single missile pylon was fitted under each wing. The vertical tail comprised a one-piece, single-spar fin and an inset rudder; the glass fibre fin cap incorporated a wire mesh antenna for the communications radio. The cantilever slab stabilisers, mounted on raked axles, had 5° anhedral; they were differentially controlled by separate hydraulic actuators. The tricycle landing gear had single wheels on all three units; the nose unit retracted aft, the main units inward into the wing roots and centre fuselage. All three struts have levered suspension and oleo-pneumatic shock absorbers. The envisaged maximum speed at 25,000 m (82,000 ft.) was 3,000 km/h (1,863 mph).

As of 1 January 1959 the overall programme was 11% complete. MMZ No. 51 built a full-size mockup of the T-37 and started manufacturing airframe components for the real thing—the prototype and a static-test article. Several more airframe components were manufactured solely for the purpose of verifying the production technology. A set of manufacturing drawings for the T-37 had been issued to the Novosibirsk aircraft factory, which was expected to build the type.

At the detail design stage the project was revised. Most notably, the long, curvilinear radome / intake shock cone with pitch/ yaw transducer vanes at the tip was replaced by a shorter three-shock centre body made up of simple conical sections, with no air data boom at the tip. In so doing, the air intake diameter was slightly increased so that the fuselage nose ahead of the cockpit had a constant diameter instead of tapering gently. The four auxiliary blow-in doors on the sides of the nose were greatly enlarged, their length being doubled so that they had a square shape. The canopy was revised to improve local aerodynamics and make it more suited to the manufacturing technologies of the day at the same time. The originally planned four engine-cooling air intakes on the rear fuselage were replaced by eight suction doors around the rear fuselage circumference a short way ahead of the nozzle, to form an air ejector that served a dual purpose: cooling the afterburner and increasing thrust at the same time.

The ADP duly passed the in-house review in the spring of 1959; detail design continued until the early summer, whereupon prototype construction began. By February 1960 the static-test airframe had been completed and transferred to the static-test shop of MMZ No. 51, while the flying prototype manufactured by plant no. 153 in Novosibirsk was 91.6% complete. The design work on the K-9-51 (R-38) AAM had also been completed, and a set of manufacturing documents had been transferred to plant no. 455, which had manufactured a batch of ten missiles for ballistic launches, with the control surfaces inoperative and a further six in PR-38 configuration as instrumented test rounds, with no seeker head for launches in programmed autopilot control mode. Tests of the missile were performed on the T47-6 development aircraft.

The end came like a bolt out of the blue. On 5 February 1960 the Council of Ministers issued a directive (followed up by an appropriate GKAT order) cancelling all work on the T-3A-9 weapons system (according to some sources, it had been redesignated T-9M by then) and the K-9-51 (R-38) missile effective as of 1 March 1960. All hardware manufactured under this programme was to be destroyed.

The reason was simple—and it was not some underhand scheme of the rival design bureaus. Research undertaken by the R&D establishments of the air force and GKAT throughout 1959 showed that there was no point in increasing the speed of intercep-

Left: Another view of the T-37 model from the company museum

The rear fuselage of the T-37 prototype in the assembly jig at the Sukhoi OKB' prototype construction facility. The recess for one of the four air brakes is visible, as is a fitting for the tail unit.

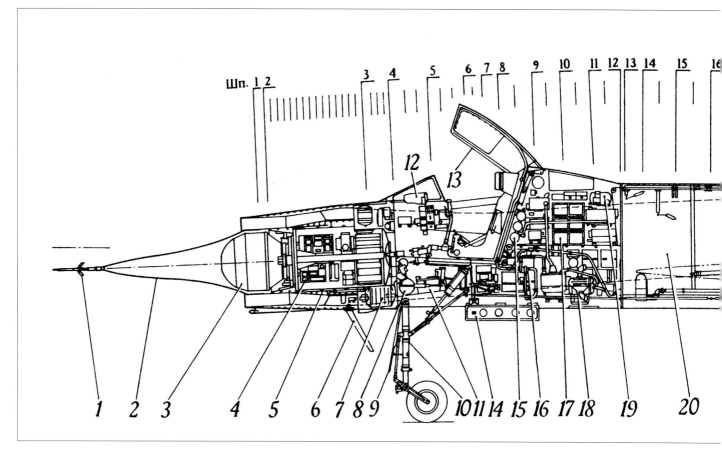

tors to 3,000 km/h and then having to cope with the numerous technical problems arising at such high speeds. This conclusion undermined the position of both the T-37 and the Ye-150/Ye-152 heavy interceptors. In a report to Aleksey N. Kosygin, chairman of Gosplan (the Soviet state economic planning agency), in March

1960, GKAT chairman Pyotr V. Dement'yev noted that designing interceptors to fly at 3,000 km/h would require complete automation of the flight, rendering manned interceptors unnecessary. This was perfectly in line with Khrushchov's notorious 'missilisation' policy—surface-to-air missiles now came to the forefront of air defence. And that was that.

The T-37 prototype's airframe was removed from the assembly jigs and scrapped—a sad end of what might have been a remarkable aircraft. A single PR-38 instrumented test round was saved by transferring it as a teaching aid to the Moscow Aviation Institute, which subsequently returned the unique missile to the Sukhoi OKB for preservation in the company museum.

The following is a brief structural description of the T-37.

Type: Single-seat supersonic heavy interceptor designed for day and night operation in VMC and IMC. The all-metal airframe structure is made mostly of AMG6 aluminium alloy. OT4 heat-resistant titanium alloy, VT3 and VT6 high-strength titanium alloys, D16 and D19A duralumin, and other materials are used in certain areas.

Fuselage: Welded, stressed-skin monocoque structure of circular cross section with no stringers; maximum fuselage diameter 1.7 m (5 ft., 7 in.).

Structurally the fuselage consists of two sections: forward (section F-1) and rear (section F-2), the latter being detachable for engine maintenance and removal.

Basic Specifications of the T-37 (as per ADP; Performance Estimated)	
Length overall (including pitot)	19.413 m (63 ft., 8 ^{19}⁄64 in.)
Wingspan	8.56 m (28 ft., 1 in.)
Height on ground	5.282 m (17 ft., 3 ^{61}⁄64 in.)
Empty weight	7,260 kg (16,010 lbs.)
Takeoff weight:	
normal	10,750 kg (23,700 lbs.)
maximum (with drop tank)	12,000 kg (26,460 lbs.)
Useful load:	
normal TOW	3,490 kg (7,690 lbs.)
high gross weight option (with drop tank)	4,740 kg (10,450 lbs.)
Top speed in afterburner mode (H > 15,000 m / 49,210 ft.)	3,000 km/h (1,863 mph)
Service ceiling in afterburner mode	25,000–27,000 m
	(82,020–88,580 ft.)
Range (H = 12,000 m / 39,370 ft., V = 950–1,000 km/h, 590–621 mph):	
on internal fuel	1,500 km (931 miles)
with drop tank	2,000 km (1,242 miles)
Endurance in level flight (with drop tank):	
at 20,000 m (65,620 ft.)	20 minutes
at 23,000 m (75,460 ft.)	14 minutes
at 25,000 m	8 minutes

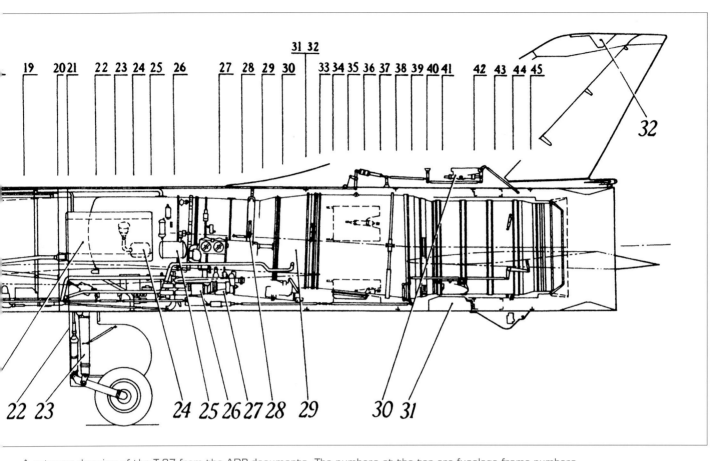

A cutaway drawing of the T-37 from the ADP documents. The numbers at the top are fuselage frame numbers.
1. DUAS-133-1 pitch/yaw transducer; 2. Radome; 3. TsP-1 fire control radar antenna; 4. TsP-1 radar set in forward avionics bay; 5. Translating inlet duct sleeve adjusting the air-intake cross section; 6. Blade aerial for ARL-S Lazoor' GCI command link system; 7. Heat exchanger for pressurised radar bay; 8. Compressed air bottles; 9. Nosewheel well door; 10. Nose gear unit; 11. DC battery; 12. Radar display; 13. Hinged canopy section; 14. Nosewheel well doors; 15. Oxygen bottles; 16. Cooling turbine; 17. Computer; 18. Air / air heat exchanger; 19. KSI compass system modules; 20. No. 1 fuel tank; 21. No. 2 fuel tank; 22. Mainwheel well door; 23. Starboard main gear unit; 24. Petrol tank for the engine's turbostarter; 25. Hydraulic reservoir; 26. GO-16 alternator; 27. GSR-18/105 DC generator; 28. Engine mounting lug; 29. R15M-300 engine; 30. Rudder actuator; 31. Brake parachute housing; 32. Integral wire mesh antenna for RSIU-5V command radio.

The *forward fuselage* (frames 1–31) incorporates 28 auxiliary frames with suffix letters between frames 1 and 16. It begins with an axisymmetrical circular air intake featuring a fixed shock cone / radome. The latter is tipped with a pitot carrying a DUAS-133-1 pitch/yaw transducer (**dahtchik oogla ataki i skol'zheniya**) and carries a translating sleeve (a hydraulically powered annular structure just inside the intake that slides fore and aft, adjusting the intake's cross section). The centre body is attached to a vertical splitter that divides the air intake into two ducts flanking the cockpit, the fuselage fuel tanks, and avionics bays. The radar set is enclosed by a hermetically sealed capsule housed in the no. 1 avionics bay (frames 2–4). The pressurised cockpit is located between frames 4 and 9, with the nosewheel well underneath, and is delimited by two pressure bulkheads, the pressure floor, and the inlet duct walls; the sloping rear bulkhead carries ejection-seat guide rails. The cockpit canopy comprises a fixed windshield with an optically flat windscreen and curved sidelights, an aft-hinged rear portion, and a metal rear fairing. The windscreen is made of special glass; all other transparencies are heat-resistant Perspex.

The no. 2 avionics bay is located immediately aft of the cockpit (frames 9–12). Farther aft are the fuel tanks (no. 1, frames 13–20; no. 2, frames 21–25). The inlet ducts and the integral fuel tanks are welded structures made of AMG6 aluminium alloy. The centre fuselage underside incorporates the mainwheel wells.

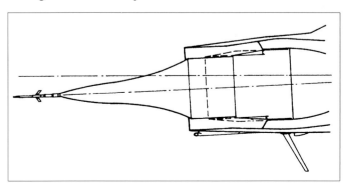

A cutaway drawing of the air intake, showing how the extreme nose was inclined downward to improve the pilot's view

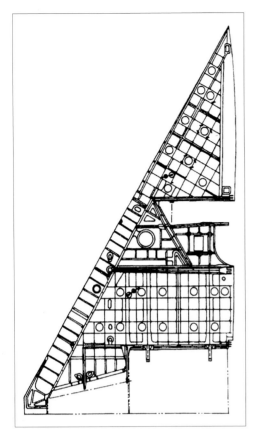

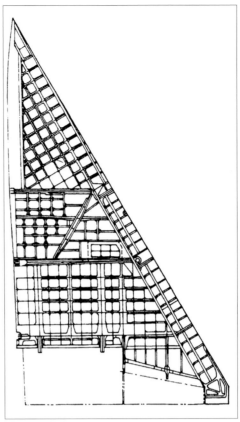

Far left: The T-37's starboard wing underside, showing panel lines

Left: The T-37's starboard wing upper side, showing panel lines

Below left: One of the T-37's stabilators, showing the internal structure

Below: The T-37's vertical tail

Right: The T-37's nose gear unit.

Below right: The T-37's starboard main gear unit

Bottom right: A provisional drawing of the T-37's instrument panel

The *rear fuselage* (frames 32–45) is a one-piece welded structure made of OT4 and VT6 titanium alloys and heat-resistant steel; it accommodates the engine with its extension jet pipe and afterburner (the engine bay begins at frame 26). The rear fuselage incorporates four airbrakes in a cruciform arrangement between frames 33 and 37 and a ventrally located brake parachute container (frames 40–42) closed by clamshell doors. A faired tail bumper is located between frames 42 and 45 to protect the fuselage in the event of overrotation or a tail-down landing. Eight air scoops are located around the rear fuselage circumference aft of frame 45 to enhance thrust and cool the afterburner.

Wings: Cantilever midwing monoplane with delta wings. Leading-edge sweep 60°, anhedral 3° from roots, incidence 0°. The wings are composed of airfoils with a variable thickness/chord ratio of 4.2% to 4.7%.

The wings are of single-spar, stressed-skin construction with three transverse beams (auxiliary spars), which, together with the main spar, form four bays: the leading edge, forward bay, mainwheel well, and centre bay. The structural material is D19A duralumin. The forward and centre bays, delimited by the main spar / no. 1 auxiliary spar and the nos. 2 and 3 auxiliary spars, respectively (plus the root rib), act as integral fuel tanks, with the mainwheel wells in between. The upper and lower wing skins consist of large duralumin panels with integral stiffeners; the leading-edge skins are chemically milled. Additional structural elements are installed between the nos. 1 and 2 auxiliary spars, acting as attachment points for the main gear units and their actuation rams.

The trailing edge is occupied by hydraulically actuated, one-piece Fowler flaps and ailerons; both are made of duralumin. The flaps move on two tracks each. One missile pylon is installed under each wing.

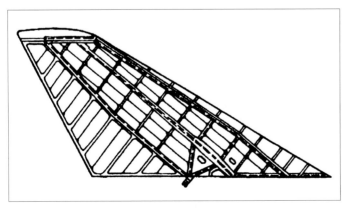

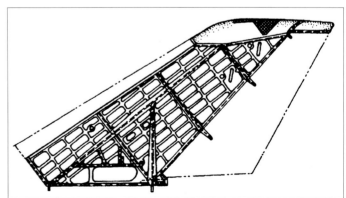

Tail unit: Conventional tail surfaces; sweepback at quarter chord 55°. The *vertical tail* comprises a one-piece fin and an inset rudder; the fin root houses the rudder's hydraulic actuator. The fin is a single-spar structure with a rear auxiliary spar (internal brace), front and rear false spars, and chemically milled duralumin skins with integral stiffeners. The fin incorporates slot aerials for the RSBN-2S SHORAN and the SOD-57M ATC/SIF transponder. The GRP tip fairing incorporates a wire mesh antenna for the communications radio. The mass-balanced rudder is a single-spar structure; it is carried on three brackets.

The cantilever *horizontal tail*, mounted 140 mm (5½ in.) below the fuselage waterline, consists of slab stabilisers (stabilators) rotating on raked axles; anhedral 5°, incidence in neutral position –2°. Each stabilator is a single-spar riveted and spot-welded structure with front and rear false spars and chemically milled duralumin skins with integral stiffeners. The stabilators are differentially controlled by separate hydraulic actuators.

Landing gear: Hydraulically retractable tricycle type, with single wheel on each unit; the nose unit retracts aft to lie under the cockpit, the main units inward into the wing roots and the centre fuselage, contracting during retraction. Wheelbase 6.355 m (20 ft., 10¹³⁄₆₄ in.), track 3.46 m (11 ft., 4⁷⁄₃₂ in.). All three landing gear struts have levered suspension and oleo-pneumatic shock absorbers.

The steerable nose unit is equipped with a 570 × 140 mm (22.4 × 5.5 in.) K-283 nonbraking wheel and a shimmy damper. The main units have 800 × 200 mm (31.5 × 7.87 in.) KT-89 mainwheels equipped with disc brakes. Maximum oleo stroke 440 mm (1 ft., 5²¹⁄₆₄ in.) for the nosewheel and 380 mm (1 ft., 2³¹⁄₃₂ in.) for the mainwheels. The nosewheel well is closed by twin lateral doors and a forward door segment linked to the oleo strut; each main unit has two door segments hinged to the oleo leg. A brake parachute is provided to shorten the landing run; the parachute cable is attached to a lock built into the tail bumper.

Power plant (provisional): One Tumanskiy R15-300 axial-flow afterburning turbojet rated at 6,840 kgp (15,080 lbst) at full military power and 10,150 kgp (22,380 lbst) in full afterburner.

The R15-300 is a single-shaft turbojet with an air intake assembly having a fixed spinner and 30 radial struts, a five-stage compressor, a cannular combustion chamber, a single-stage turbine, and an afterburner with a variable (three-position) nozzle. The compressor has bleed valves at the third stage. The engine is attached to the airframe at five points. Starting is by means of a 150 hp S3 jet fuel starter connected to the ventral accessory gearbox. An electronic engine control system is provided.

EPR at takeoff rating 4.75; mass flow at takeoff rating 144 kg/sec. (317 lbs./sec.), maximum turbine temperature 1,230° K. SFC 2.45 kg/kgp·h in full afterburner and 1.12 kg/kgp·h in cruise mode. Length overall 6,650 mm (21 ft., 9⁷⁄₈ in.), casing diameter 1,640 mm (5 ft., 4½ in.). Dry weight 2,590 kg (5,710 lbs.).

The engine breathes through a circular supersonic air intake with a shock cone, augmented by lateral auxiliary inlet doors. The engine is cooled by boundary layer bleed air, with cooling air intake scoops at frames 25 and 29.

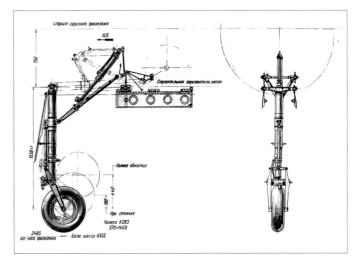

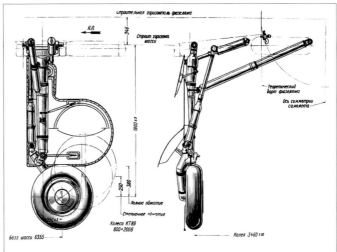

Control system: Powered controls with irreversible hydraulic actuators throughout. The system features an AP-39 autopilot connected via RA-15 servos in all three control channels.

Fuel system: Internal fuel is carried in six integral tanks (nos. 1 and 2 fuselage tanks, plus four wing tanks) and one bag-type tank (the no. 3 fuselage tank); the total capacity is quoted variously as 3,870 litres (851.4 Imp gal.) or 4,800 litres (1,056 Imp gal.). The fuel tanks feature a combined pressurisation/vent system ensuring normal fuel consumption, plus a special tanks allowing the engine to run under negative-g conditions. There are provisions for carrying a 930-litre (204.6 Imp gal.) drop tank under the centre fuse-

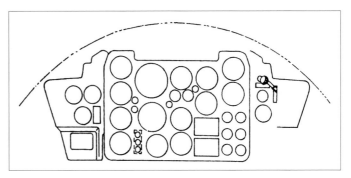

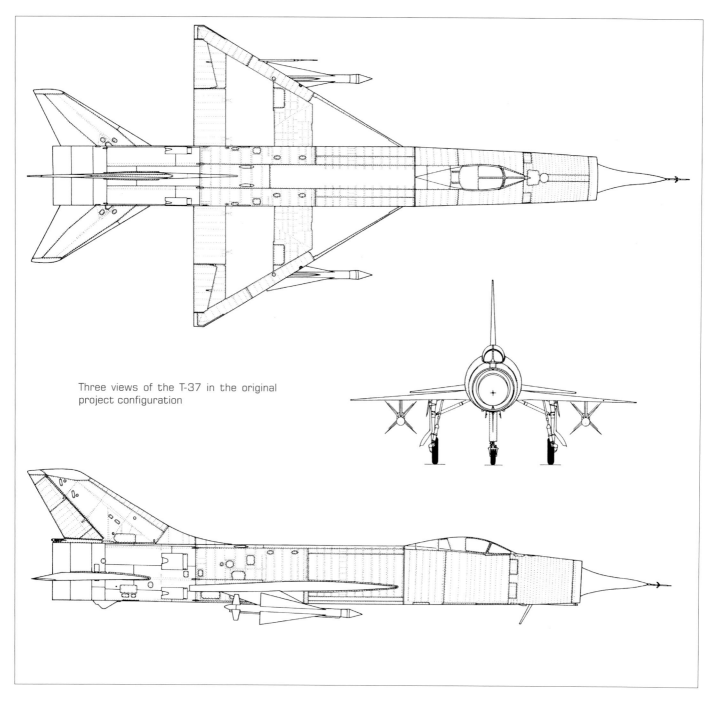

Three views of the T-37 in the original project configuration

lage. Refuelling is by gravity via a filler in the no. 2 tank. The envisaged fuel grades are T-1, TS-1, or T-2 kerosene.

Electrics: Primary DC power is supplied by a GSR-18/105 engine-driven generator, with a DC battery as a backup. Primary single-phase AC power is supplied by a GO-16 engine-driven alternator. AC converters are provided to cater for the avionics.

Hydraulics: Three independent hydraulic systems. The main system operates the air intake adjustment sleeve, landing gear, flaps, and airbrakes; the other two systems cater for the control actuators. Primary hydraulic power is supplied by an engine-driven pump; there is also an electric emergency pump.

Avionics and equipment: The avionics suite includes a TsP-1 fire control radar, an RSBN-2 Svod SHORAN system with flush antennas built into the fin, an RV-U low-range radio altimeter, an MRP-56P marker beacon receiver with a flush antenna built into the fin, SOD-57M DME, a KSI compass system, a Put' (Way) navigation system, an RSIU-5V two-way VHF communications radio with a mesh-type antenna in the fin cap, a Lazoor' data link receiver working with the Looch-1 or Vozdukh-1 GCI system (with a blade aerial on the underside of the nose), an SRZO-2M Khrom-Nikel' IFF transponder, and a Sirena-2 radar-warning receiver.

Armament: Two K-9-51 (R-38) SARH air-to-air missiles carried on underwing APU-28 pylons. Alternatively, 57 mm ARS-57

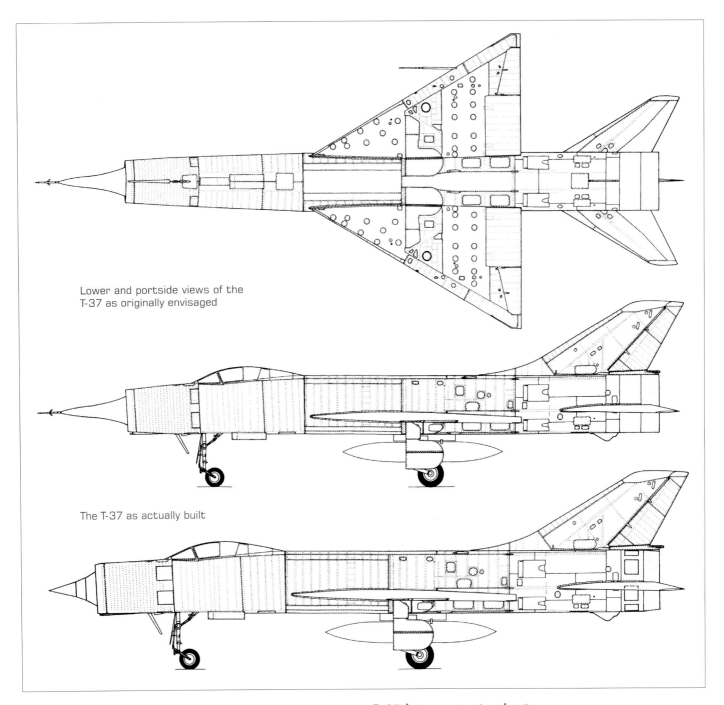

Lower and portside views of the
T-37 as originally envisaged

The T-37 as actually built

FFARs in pods or ARS-212M heavy unguided rockets on launch
rails were to be carried.

Crew rescue system and pilot gear: The aircraft has a
Sukhoi ejection seat with a telescopic ejection gun and a three-
stage parachute stabilisation system. Ejection is initiated by
pulling either of two handles on the seat pan; the canopy is jettisoned without the need to decompress the cockpit first. Safe ejection is possible at speeds up to 1,200 km/h (745 mph). The pilot
is provided with a VKK-4 pressure suit, allowing him to tolerate
g-loads up to +8 g and a GSh-4M full-face pressure helmet
enabling ejection at up to 1,200 km/h IAS. The seat houses a survival kit.

P-37 interceptor (project)

An alternative version of the T-37 featuring lateral air intakes was
developed under the designation P-37. Unfortunately no details are
known of this version, except that the project was 20% complete at
the time of termination and mock-up construction was under way.

T-49 experimental interceptor

Not wishing to put up with the obvious deterioration of the aerodynamics caused by the large radomes of the PT-8 and T-47, the
Sukhoi OKB started investigating alternative radome/air intake
arrangements in 1958. This led to the development of a highly
unconventional and interesting design with two narrow curved
air intakes flanking a conical radome. This arrangement ensured

Left: A head-on view of the T-49, showing the curious sector-shaped air intakes and the elliptical-section nose ahead of them. The dark 'panels' on the sides of the nose are in fact reflections of the intakes in the shiny skin.

Below: The T-49 had an all-metal nosecone instead of the envisaged radome; this carried an air data boom with pitch/yaw vanes. The radome joint line was to be just ahead of the tapered intake lips.

Bottom: This side view illustrates the completely different proportions of the T-49, with its long, pointed nose making the wheelbase appear very short.

Right: Three-quarters rear view of the T-49. The designation is painted on the tail (minus the T prefix).

Below: A three-view drawing of the T-49.

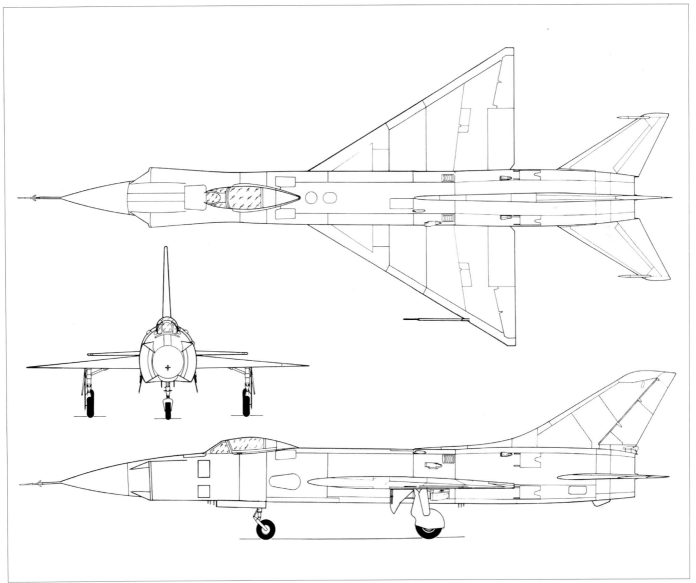

better operating conditions for the radar, which was now unaffected by the movement of the air intake shock cone. In order to minimise aerodynamic losses it was decided to incorporate a so-called isoenthropic air intake with a specially profiled inlet duct throughout its length. This was expected to significantly increase the efficiency of the air intake and hence of the powerplant as a whole; the inlet duct effectively became an 'additional compressor stage', increasing the engine pressure ratio perceptibly. At the same time the unusual intakes left ample space in the fuselage nose for the radar dish.

Bearing the in-house designation T-49, the aircraft incorporating the new intake design was developed in accordance with a GKAT order dated 6th August 1957. It was decided to build the prototype by converting the unfinished T-39, which had been abandoned by 1958 because it had been demoted to experimental status, the programme under which the T-39 had been created becoming the responsibility of the Central Aero Engine Institute (TsIAM).

The conversion involved replacing the entire forward fuselage with a new assembly specially designed and manufactured at

MMZ No.51; the No.3 fuel tank, which had been replaced by a water ballast tank on the T-39, was reinstated in the process. The rebuilt aircraft was rolled out in October 1959 and M. S. Goncharov was put in charge of the test programme. After a period of ground checks OKB-51 test pilot A. A. Koznov successfully performed the T-49's maiden flight in January 1960. He reported that the aircraft handled well, displaying excellent performance; in particular, acceleration had improved considerably, just as the designers had expected.

Unfortunately the T-49's career turned out to be brief. In April 1960 the aircraft was damaged in an accident at Zhukovskiy; after this the T-49 underwent lengthy repairs and modifications but was never flown again.

T-59 interceptor (project)

Another project which owed its existence to the T-37 heavy interceptor programme was the T-59. Like the P-37 described above, it featured lateral air intakes and was intended as a testbed for the

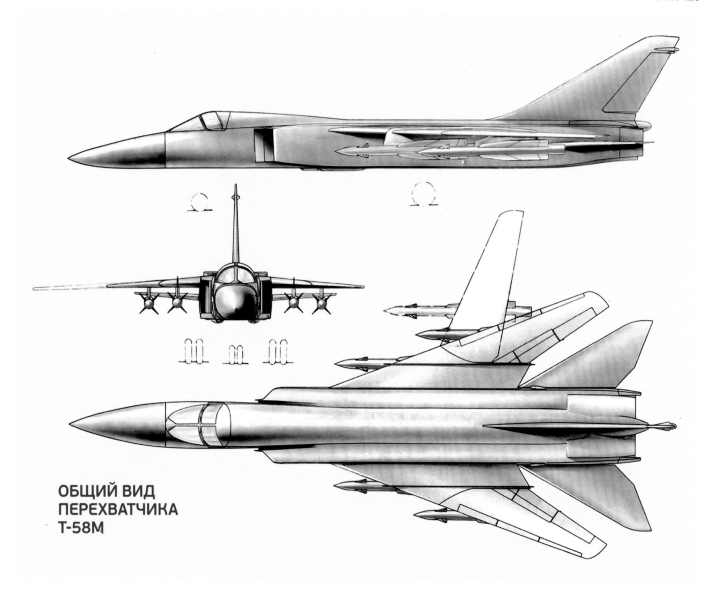

ОБЩИЙ ВИД
ПЕРЕХВАТЧИКА
Т-58М

A three-view drawing of the T-58M interceptor from the ADP documents, showing the pivoting pylons under the movable outer wings

TsP-1 fire control radar. By the end of 1959 the design work was 35% complete and a wooden mock-up was being built; however, the work was halted when the T-37 programme was killed off.

T-58M interceptor (project)

Actually, this should be phrased as 'adaptation of the T-58M as an interceptor'. There is an old adage that you can turn a fighter into a bomber if needs must, but you cannot turn a bomber into a fighter. Well, at one time the Sukhoi OKB actually attempted doing this impossible task.

Development of the Su-24 *Fencer* tactical bomber had started when Nikita S. Khrushchov was king... sorry, head of state. Because of Khrushchov's disdainful attitude towards military aviation, new combat aircraft had a chance only if they were modifications of existing ones – or if they were passed off as such. The Su-24 was a case in point: before being allocated the definitive manufacturer's designation T-6 it was referred to as the T-58M strike fighter – ostensibly a 'modification of the T-58 (Su-15) interceptor'. Well, the irony of it is that in the late 1960s, when Khrushchov had been replaced with Leonid I. Brezhnev (who supported military aviation) and there was no need to pretend any more, the designation T-58M unexpectedly reappeared in the context of an interceptor project based on the Su-24! By then the original delta-wing T6-1, which first flew on 2nd July 1967, had evolved into the T6-2I with variable geometry wings (the prototype of the configuration in which the aircraft entered production as the Su-24). Using the 'swing-wing' configuration as the basis, the Sukhoi OKB and the OKB-339 avionics house then headed by Chief Designer Fyodor F. Volkov came up with the idea of replacing the bomber's PNS-24 Puma-A navigation/attack suite (*pritsel'no-navigatsionnaya sistema*) with a Smerch-100M (Tornado) targeting suite. The latter comprised a fire control radar, an infrared search & track (IRST) unit – both likewise called Smerch-100M in the project documents – and an Argon-100 processor. The radar could detect a medium bomber at 150-170 km (93-105 miles) range in head-on mode and at 54 or 38 km (33.5 or 23.6 miles) range in pursuit mode with the interceptor flying at 20,000 m (65,620 ft) or 10,000 m (32,810 ft) respectively. The IRST unit detected a medium bomber in pursuit mode at a maximum range of 35 km (21.75 miles) in 'look-up' mode or 23 km (14.29 miles) in 'look-down' mode.

Thus modified and armed with four AAMs, the Su-24 could then be used as an interceptor. Such an approach made sense, as it reduced the expenditures involved in prototype construction and testing, expedited the interceptor's production entry, reduced operational costs and simplified conversion training.

The T-58M's principal armament was the K-50 long-range AAM developed by OKB-4 under Chief Designer Matus R. Bisnovat. This large missile had a tail-first layout with delta rudders and long strake-like wings; it was originally intended for the Mikoyan Ye-158 heavy interceptor (a projected precursor of the MiG-31 *Foxhound*) but had lost out to the competing K-33 missile. The K-50, which came in semi-active radar homing and IR-homing versions, acquired the target while still on the wing; it was intended for use against targets flying at up to 32,000 m (104,990 ft) and up to 11,000 m (36,090 ft) above or below the interceptor's

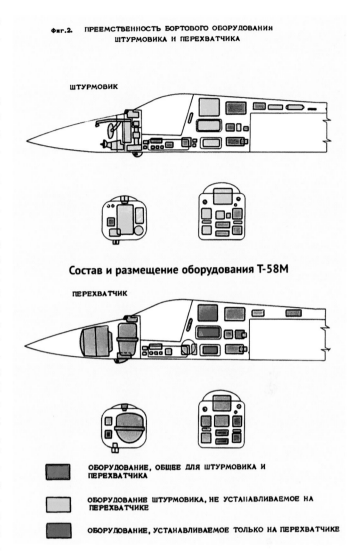

A diagram showing the differences in the avionics of the T-58M's attack version (*yellow*) and interceptor version (*red*). The modules marked in green are shared by both versions.

own level. The SARH version could engage a medium bomber at 50 km (31 miles) range in head-on mode or 20 km (12.4 miles) range in pursuit mode. The IR-homing version was used in pursuit mode only; its 'kill' range was 42 km (26.1 miles). 'Kill' probability in a two-missile salvo was estimated as 90% against an 'A-11 aircraft' (*sic*) and 60% against a North American AGM-28 Hound Dog supersonic cruise missile.

Other missile options were medium-range AAMs – the R-8 and R-8M1 as carried by the Su-11, the R-98 as carried by the Su-15, the K-58, the K-23 (R-23, AA-7 *Apex*) as carried by the MiG-23 – and the ubiquitous K-13 short-range AAM. All four missiles were carried under the wings – two under the fixed inboard sections (the so-called wing gloves) on fixed pylons and two under the movable outer wings on swivelling pylons which were mechanically connected to the wing gloves and stayed parallel to the fuselage axis as the wing sweep changed (a signature feature of the Su-24).

Like the Su-24, the T-58M had a built-in 23-mm (.78 calibre) Gryazev/Shipunov GSh-6-23 (AO-19) six-barrel Gatling cannon with 500 rounds buried in the fuselage underside, offset to starboard; the rate of fire was 10,000 rounds per minute. Surprisingly, some sources state that provisions were made for carrying up to four SPPU-6 gun pod (*s"yomnaya podvizhnaya pushechnaya oostanovka* – detachable movable cannon installation) with GSh-6-23 cannons under the wings; these were part of the Su-24's weapons complement and were designed for strafing ground targets in level flight thanks to their depressable barrels, not for use against aerial targets.

Outwardly the T-58M interceptor differed from the Su-24 in having a longer radome which was slightly drooped and lacked the bomber's distinctive pitot/antenna arrays at the tip which had a distorted 'F' shape and was dubbed *goos'* (goose). Another (and rather surprising) difference was the design of the wing gloves. On the Su-24 their rear portions are cut away at an angle so that the wing gloves are triangular in plan view, the trailing-edge portions of the inboard flap sections fit into special recesses in the centre fuselage sides (provided with spring-loaded inward-opening doors) when the wings are at anything but 16° minimum sweep. In contrast, the T-58M had wing gloves similar to those of the Su-17/Su-20/Su-22 *Fitter-B et seq.* fighter-bomber family – they were designed as hollow bays outboard of the fuselage sides and accommodating the trailing edge of the outer wings at maximum sweep, the gap between the wings and gloves being sealed by special strips. To ensure adequate stiffness of the structure the tip ribs of the wing gloves were load-bearing structures doubling as boundary layer fences; these were in line with the inboard pylons.

A less obvious difference was the powerplant. All Su-24 *Fencer-A/B/Cs* are powered by either two Lyul'ka AL-21F (*izdeliye* 85) afterburning turbojets rated at 6,800 kgp (14,990 lbst) dry and 8,900 kgp (19,630 lbst) reheat, or the uprated AL-21F-3 (*izdeliye* 89) delivering 7,800 kgp (17,200 lbst) dry and 11,200 kgp (24,700 lbst) reheat. The Su-24M *Fencer-D* and subsequent versions are powered by modified AL-21F-3A engines. The T-58M, however, was to be powered by two Tumanskiy R27F2-300 afterburning turbojets – the provisional powerplant used on the original T6-1. The R27F2-300 (*izdeliye* 47) was a two-spool axial-flow turbojet rated at 6,900 kgp (15,210 lbst) dry and

9,400 kgp (20,720 lbst) reheat. The fuel was carried in fuselage and wing integral tanks with a total capacity of 11,500 litres (2,530 Imp gal).

Apart from the Smerch-100M WCS, the avionics unique to the T-58M interceptor were the *Raduga-MB* (Rainbow) active IFF (interrogator/transponder) and the *Zholud'* (Acorn) GCI command link system. Curiously, the T-58M was also advertised as a ground attack aircraft which differed from the interceptor only in certain avionics which were identical to those of the Su-24 bomber; these were the Orion-A pulse-Doppler primary navigation/attack radar and *Rel'yef* (Terrain profile) monopulse ground mapping radar, the TP-23E forward-looking infrared sensor (*teplopelengahtor* – heat seeker or IRST), the *Chaika-1* (Seagull) electro-optical sighting system, the *Filin-N* (Eagle Owl) passive radar homing and identification system supplying target data to anti-radar missiles the *Orbita-58* mainframe computer, the *Molniya* (Lightning) Doppler speed/drift sensor system, the *Yakhta* (Yacht) secure communications system (scrambler/descrambler), the Siren'-F active jammer, the AFA-39 aerial camera (*aerofotoapparaht*) and the Alpha radiation reconnaissance system. The remaining avionics were common for the two versions; they were the PPV-1 head-up display (*pilotazhno-pritsel'nyy vizeer* – flight & sighting display), the *Brilliahnt-M* (Cut diamond) processor, the MIS-P inertial navigation system, the SAU-58M automatic flight control system, the SVS-PN-5-3 air data system (*sistema vozdooshnykh signahlov*), the RSBN-6S Romb-1K (Rhombus) SHORAN, the ARK-15M *Tobol* (a Siberian river) ADF, the MRP-56P marker beacon receiver, the SRO-1P *Parol'-2* (Password) IFF system, the SO-63B ATC transponder, the *Pion-GT-6* (Peony) antenna/feeder system, SPO-10 Sirena-3M passive radar warning receiver (*sistema preduprezhdeniya ob obluchenii*), the R-846 Prizma-Sh (akaProton-2) HF radio, the R-832M *Evkalipt-M* (Eucalyptus) command radio, the SPU-9 intercom etc.

The T-58M in interceptor configuration was intended for destroying targets with a radar cross-section (RCS) of 10 m² (107.64 sq ft) flying at altitudes up to 30,000 m (98,425 ft) and speeds up to 3,700 km/h (2,299 mph). The Smerch-100M suite would also give 'look-down/shoot-down' capability against targets flying as low as 30-50 m (100-164 ft) at up to 1,800 km/h (1,118 mph). With the aircraft operating within the Vozdukh-M GCI system, the probability of intercepting a target with a 10-m² RCS – that is, a bomber – doing 3,600 km/h (2,236 mph) at 30,000 m was estimated as 70-80%; the chances of success against a target with an RCS of 3.5 m² (37.67 sq ft) doing 1,800 km/h at 50 m – that is, a fighter-bomber – were somewhat lower (60-70%). The aircraft could also work with the existing Vozdukh-1 and *Elektron* GCI systems or operate semi-autonomously if there was no uninterrupted AD radar/GCI coverage. Depending on the target's flight level, the attack was to be launched from an altitude of 14,000-20,000 m (45,930-65,620 ft) for high-flying intruders or 8,000-10,000 m (26,250-32,810 ft) for low-flying intruders. Once the radar had achieved target lock-on, the T-58M would make a zoom climb or dive onto the target before firing the missiles. The maximum combat radius in a head-on attack was to be 900 km (559 miles). However the project was not proceeded with, possibly because the K-50 AAM did not materialise.

T-58M Basic Specifications	
Takeoff weight with four K-50 AAMs	25,000 kg (55,120 lbs.)
Maximum speed:	
at sea level	1,450 km/h (900 miles)
at 13,000 m (42,650 ft.)	2,500 km/h (1,552 mph)
Maximum base altitude for attack	20,000 m (65,620 ft.)
Time to altitude with four K-50 AAMs:	
to 10,000 m (32,810 ft.)	2.6 minutes
to 20,000 m (65,620 ft.)	8.3 minutes
Maximum speed:	
at sea level @ 1,100 km/h (683 mph)	1,000 km (621 miles)
ferry range	3,700 km (2,299 miles)
On-station loiter time	2.0 hours
Takeoff/landing run (unpaved runway)	400 m (1,310 ft.)

Chapter 7

Sukhoi Strikes Back

T-58 (T-3-8M3, Su-11M) Single-Engined Interceptor (Project)

In the second half of the 1950s the Western world began fielding new airborne-strike weapons systems, forcing the Soviet Union to take countermeasures. Apart from missile systems, which the Soviet government had a soft spot for during the years when Nikita S. Khrushchov was head of state, new state-of-the-art interceptors possessing longer-range and head-on engagement capability were required for defending the nation's aerial frontiers. Creating such an aircraft appeared a pretty nebulous perspective, considering that many a promising programme for the reequipment of the VVS and the PVO was terminated during the Khrushchov era (including 35 aircraft projects and 21 engine programmes in 1958–59 alone). In 1960 the Council of Ministers issued a directive halting all development work on new aircraft; the design bureaus were authorised to proceed only with upgrades of existing aircraft that had been ordered by prior C of M directives. When the Ministry of General Machinery (MOM: *Ministerstvo obshchevo mashino-stroyeniya*)—the agency responsible for the Soviet missile and space programmes—was created, several major aircraft factories

The Su-15 was the Soviet air defence force's primary interceptor type of the 1970s—and also Sukhoi's most successful fighter until the advent of the Su-27 family.

were transferred to it from GKAT. All aircraft design bureaus were tasked with developing missile systems; the Sukhoi OKB was no exception, being ordered to design a three-stage SAM specifically for Moscow's air defence system (a missile that in the long run never materialised). This was Khrushchov's 'missilisation' at its worst—a blow from which the Soviet aircraft industry took six or seven years to recover.

Still, in this generally troubled climate, the outlook for the Sukhoi OKB seemed quite favourable at first. The Su-7 tactical fighter had been developed and put into production, the Su-7B fighter-bomber version following hot on its heels. The Su-9 interceptor, forming the core of the T-3-51 (Su-9-51) aerial-intercept weapons system, had just sailed through state acceptance trials and entered production at two major factories at once, achieving IOC with the PVO's fighter element. Concurrently the more advanced Su-11 derivative, forming the core of the T-3-8M weapons system, was undergoing trials, and the OKB was hard at work on the new T-3A-9 weapons system based on the T-37 heavy interceptor.

In February 1960, however, the clouds started gathering. As already mentioned, the T-37 and the K-9-51 AAM created for it were cancelled when the prototype was almost complete. By mid-1961 it was obvious that the first-line units of the VVS and the PVO were having big trouble with the recently introduced Su-7B and Su-9, respectively, the appallingly low reliability of the AL-7F-1 engine being one of the worst problems. In the first 18 months of service, 20-plus Sukhoi aircraft were lost in accidents, more than half of which were caused by failures of the aircraft's single engine. Even if they didn't crash, the engine's time between overhauls was initially a mere 25–50 hours, and when it ran out the aircraft had to be grounded for an engine change, which rendered much of the Su-7 and Su-9 fleet unserviceable because no spare engines were available. Not only did this mean a lot of extra work associated with labour-intensive engine changes in the units—it left the aircraft industry out of pocket because hundreds of extra engines had to be manufactured, and the AL-7F-1 was an expensive engine. This situation was insupportable, and the military demanded vociferously that the faults that came to the fore during the two types' service introduction period be corrected.

This situation heightened the air defence force's interest in twin-engined aircraft, which offered higher reliability. The PVO began lobbying for the Yak-28P Firebar interceptor to be put into production—just because it was twin engined, ergo safer. (This is a point open to debate; because of the Yak-28's widely spaced underwing engines, an engine failure and the resulting thrust asymmetry often led to disastrous results.) GKAT amended its production plans accordingly, and in the three years to follow its aircraft factories were to manufacture only twin-engined interceptor types—the Yak-28P and the Tu-128.

Moreover, the rival Mikoyan OKB had begun state acceptance trials of the promising MiG-21PF Fishbed-D, an all-weather, light tactical fighter/interceptor. This aircraft was powered by a single Tumanskiy R11F2-300 afterburning turbojet (*izdeliye* 37F2) rated at 3,900 kgp (8,600 lbst) at full military power and 6,175 kgp (13,610 lbst) in full afterburner, which, while admittedly offering less thrust than the AL-7F, was much more reliable. Consequently, on 27 November 1961 the Council of Ministers issued a directive ordering Su-9 production to be terminated in 1962 and cutting the Su-11's production run dramatically for the benefit of the Yak-28P interceptor, which was to be produced at the same plant no. 153 in Novosibirsk—and, incidentally, was powered by almost identical R11AF2-300 turbojets.

Thus OKB-51 was now facing not merely further cuts in its programmes but the daunting prospect of being closed altogether for a second time as unnecessary. Considering the attitude of the nation's political leaders toward manned combat aircraft, the chances of developing all-new aircraft were close to zero—unless some trickery was involved. All the OKB could do was to modernise existing designs, and then only if state-of-the-art missile armament was integrated did these plans have any chance of success.

This was the situation in which the OKB started development of a new single-engined interceptor at its own risk; the aircraft was known in-house as the T-58. To win support at the top echelon and avoid possible repercussions, the project was disguised as a 'further upgrade of the T-3-8M weapons system'.

The aircraft was to feature a fire control radar with longer detection range and a wider field of view than the RP-11 Oryol, fitted to the production Su-11, and be armed with longer-range and more-lethal missiles. OKB-339 offered two alternative radars for the T-3-8M3—the Oryol-2, developed under chief project engineer Ghedaliy M. Koonyavskiy as an upgrade of the RP-11, and the brand-new Vikhr' (Whirlwind), developed under chief project engineer Fyodor F. Volkov as a scaled-down version of the Smerch fire control radar created for the Tu-128 long-range, heavy interceptor. Both of these radars, however, were too bulky to fit inside the shock cone of an axisymmetrical air intake as used on the Su-11; the only option was to use the entire fuselage nose ahead of the cockpit for accommodating the radar and switch to lateral air intakes.

By then OKB-51 already had some experience with lateral air intakes, having used them on the P-1 and T-49 experimental interceptors; also, such intakes were envisaged for the projected P-37 heavy interceptor. As distinct from all these aircraft, the T-58 featured two-dimensional (rectangular-section) intakes with vertical airflow control ramps—a design that was not yet fully explored in the Soviet Union at the time. Conversely, in the US this type of intake had by then been used on the McDonnell F4H Phantom II and the Convair F-106 Delta Dart—with good results.

Here it should be mentioned that the sector-shaped isoenthropic air intakes used on the T-49 had a staunch supporter at TsAGI, Prof. Gersch L. Grodzovskiy, who once visited the Sukhoi OKB, urging Pavel O. Sukhoi to use them on the T-3-8M3 as well. However, this type of intake, positioned well ahead of the cockpit, required exceptionally long airflow control ramps, which were too difficult to accommodate. Oleg S. Samoylovich, then a designer working in the OKB's general arrangement section, reminisced: *'They had a discussion. Trying to press his point, Grodzovskiy said: "Two theses have been defended on the theoretical design of such intakes"* [ergo, the design is sound]. *Sukhoi replied: "I haven't the slightest doubts about the veracity of the theoretical results, but I cannot put a thesis on my aircraft instead of an air intake."'*

Hence, Sukhoi's instruction to his design staff was to redesign the fuselage structure only as far as the cockpit section, leaving the rest unchanged. This was meant to ensure maximum commonality with the production Su-9 and Su-11, minimising costly changes of the production tooling, and thus make sure that plant no. 153 in Novosibirsk would keep on producing Sukhoi aircraft. The fuselage design also drew on the P-37 PD project, featuring a complex shape; the perfectly conical radome was mated to a circular-section forward fuselage that was flattened from the sides in the cockpit area and flanked by the air intakes. The latter blended smoothly into a centre fuselage that was again of basically cylindrical shape, the inlet ducts merging ahead of the engine. The fuselage structure aft of frame 18 was identical to that of the Su-11; so were the wings, tail unit, landing gear, control system, and power plant—one AL-7F-2 engine rated at 10,100 kgp (22,270 lbst) in full afterburner. (Later, this version of the engine would become standard on the Su-11 in 1962.) The design effort was led by I. I. Tsebrikov, head of the OKB's general arrangement section, and his deputy A. M. Polyakov, though the young designers Rolan G. Martirosov, Oleg S. Samoylovich, A. Voskresenskiy, and Moisey A. Lokshin also had a hand in the matter.

Development work progressed quickly; as early as July 1960 the first metal was cut on the T-58 prototype, and assembly of the forward fuselage began at MMZ No. 51. At the end of 1960 the Sukhoi OKB began testing the T-58's power plant on a special ground rig in order to verify the operation of the lateral air intakes. Meanwhile, construction of the flying prototype and a static-test airframe proceeded at MMZ No. 51. The project was still a 'private venture' at the time, not yet being officially sanctioned by a government directive.

In the meantime, however, the appetites of the military started growing, the customer demanding ever-higher performance. In particular, the new interceptor was required to have all-aspect engagement capability against targets flying at altitudes up to 27,000 m (88,580 ft.) and speeds up to 2,500 km/h (1,550 mph)—that is, be capable of shooting them down in both pursuit and head-on mode.

To appease the nation's missile-minded leaders, two air-to-air missiles were envisaged as the T-58's sole armament. In November 1960 the OKB drafted a Council of Ministers directive that would officially order it to equip the new interceptor with the Vikhr'-P fire control radar and the *Polyot* (Flight) automatic control system [*sic*]; that is, GCI system. The armament was to comprise two K-40 long-range AAMs in SARH and IR-homing versions; the choice of this missile, which was being developed by Matus R. Bisnovat's OKB-4, was dictated by the military, who also envisaged this weapon for the Mikoyan OKB's new interceptors (it would ultimately enter service on the MiG-25P Foxbat-A as the R-40, NATO code name AA-6 Acrid). In this configuration the aircraft was allocated the in-house designation T-3-8M3—that is, 'the third consecutive upgrade of the T-3 aircraft'—and was billed as part of the Su-15-40 aerial-intercept weapons system. Thus the service designation Su-15 came up for the first time (according to established Soviet practice, fighters had odd-numbered designations, but the designation Su-13, which should have followed the Su-11, was skipped for obvious reasons).

Still, time passed but the promised K-40 missile was nowhere in sight, and neither was the anticipated C of M directive concerning

development of the Su-15 with the Vikhr'-P radar (exactly for this reason). Hence, OKB-51 continued development of the interceptor with the alternative Oryol-2 radar and K-8M2 AAMs (likewise a product of OKB-4) pending availability of the intended K-40 missile; the K-8M2 was a refined version of the K-8M, which, unlike its precursor, had all-aspect engagement capability. In the project documents this version of the aircraft was called Su-11M (*modifitseerovannyy*: modified, or *modernizeerovannyy*: upgraded), while the aerial-intercept weapons system based on it was provisionally designated T-3-8M2 because of the missile type.

The flying prototype was due for completion in September 1961, but the work on the T-58 in its single-engined form was suspended in the summer of that year. 'For want of a missile the fighter was lost'? Well, not exactly; see next entry.

T-58D Twin-Engined Interceptor (Project Stage)

As recounted earlier, the Su-9's reputation was seriously marred by its high accident rate, which caused a lot of concern at all levels, including IA PVO commander Air Marshal Yevgeniy Ya. Savitskiy. One of the main contributing factors was the troublesome AL-7F-1 engine; since the Su-11 was powered by the same engine, it was affected by the same problem. The military began considering a possible alternative to the Sukhoi interceptors, and Aleksandr S. Yakovlev, general designer of the rival OKB-115, seized his chance. His previous attempt to build a new interceptor for the PVO had been unsuccessful—the transonic Yak-27 Flashlight-C showed disappointing performance and was rejected. Now, undaunted by the problems OKB-115 was having with the Yak-28 Brewer twinjet supersonic tactical bomber for the VVS, Yakovlev offered it to the PVO as an interceptor. The proposed Yak-28P would share the Su-11's mission avionics and armament (the Oryol radar and two K-8M missiles) but would have a crew of two (a pilot and a WSO); added to this, it offered twin-engine reliability. Yakovlev chose to go for broke—the Yak-28P's advertised performance was truly fantastic, with a top speed of 2,250 km/h (1,397 mph), a service ceiling of 18,000 m (59,060 ft.), and an endurance of 2.5 hours, which was far longer than that of the Sukhoi interceptors. Yakovlev enjoyed a good relationship with the PVO in general and with the IA PVO commander in particular (Savitskiy's personal hack was a Yak-25), and creating an interceptor version of the Yak-28 would help the Yakovlev OKB regain its former strength.

The Yak-28P prototype was built in 1961, making its public debut at the 1961 Aviation Day flypast at Tushino. It caught the attention of the Soviet political and military leaders, and General Designer Yakovlev rode hard on this. Using his influence, he could be very persuasive; also, he had an ally—Air Marshal Savitskiy, who had a favourable impression of the Yak-28P, started lobbying for it in high places. As a result, in October 1961 the MoD top brass sent an official letter to the Communist Party Central Committee, requesting that the Su-9 and Su-11 production plans be slashed in favour of the Yak-28P. Such was the unashamed lobbyism that the Yak-28P was ordered into production in Novosibirsk without waiting even for its state acceptance trials to begin, never mind to end! Added to this, there was the personal factor to contend with; Pavel O. Sukhoi and Aleksandr S. Yakovlev were not just rivals in the professional sense but had a thorough dislike for each other. This animosity dated back to the days when Yakovlev was deputy people's commissar of the aircraft industry, making decisions that benefited or hurt aviation design bureaus.

With the termination of Su-9 and Su-11 production, the Sukhoi OKB was faced with the prospect of losing production capacity altogether. The solution was obviously to develop a new interceptor powered by two afterburning turbojets instead of the single AL-7F. Ironically, it was none other than Air Marshal Savitskiy who first floated the idea of 'replacing one big engine with two smaller ones' with regard to the Sukhoi interceptors, although no documentary evidence of this story exists.

In fact, back in late 1960 the Sukhoi OKB had first considered fitting the T-58 with two engines side by side in the rear fuselage as an insurance policy in case the single-engined T-58 was rejected. The engine envisaged at that point was the new R21F-300 axial-flow afterburning turbojet, rated at 7,200 kgp (15,870 lbst) in full afterburner; this advanced engine was developed by OKB-300 under its new chief designer, Nikolay G. Metskhvarishvili. At the insistence of the PVO's General Headquarters the twin-engined version—likewise known officially as the Su-15—was to be equipped with the Vikhr'-P radar and armed with two K-40 AAMs. The customer was adamant in this issue, even though GKAT pointed out that making use of the Oryol-2 radar and K-8M2 AAMs would allow the new interceptor to enter service much sooner. The PVO also specified that the aircraft should have the proposed general arrangement with lateral intakes and area-ruled fuselage.

The general arrangement and internal layout of the T-58 were finalised in 1961. The power plant was changed at this stage. On the one hand, the single-engined version was indeed rejected, the customer expressly demanding higher reliability, which only a twin-engined aircraft could provide. On the other hand, the R21F-300 turned out to have serious design flaws, and after an uncontained engine failure that led to the loss of the Mikoyan Ye-8/1 development aircraft on 11 September 1962, further development of this engine was terminated. These circumstances prompted the Sukhoi OKB to select the proven R11F2-300 engine to power the T-58. Accommodating the two engines in the rear fuselage presented no problem; OKB-51 already had some experience with a similar installation on the T-5 development aircraft, powered by two R11F-300s (see chapter 2).

In the course of 1961 the OKB completed the detail design of the twin-engined interceptor, whose in-house designation was now amended to T-58D. To this day it is not clear what the *D* suffix stands for; it could mean ***dvig**ateli* (engines), referring to the fact that there were now two engines instead of one, or *dora**botannyy*** (modified or improved). Construction of the prototype and the static-test airframe continued in the meantime—the unfinished airframes of the cancelled single-engined T-58 were modified right in the assembly jigs.

Another important change occurred at this point. Since the K-40 AAM had been selected for the Mikoyan OKB's new Ye-155P heavy interceptor (the future MiG-25P), it was agreed that the T-58D (a.k.a. Su-15) would be armed with upgraded K-8M2 missiles, provided that a further improved version of the Oryol-2 radar was used. This version, featuring a 950 mm (37$\frac{3}{8}$ in.) antenna dish, received a new name, ***Sobol'*** (Sable).

The T-58D, which drew heavily on the detail design project of the original single-engined T-58, utilised the classic layout with

A test rig featuring the Oryol radar on a gimballed mount with 3 degrees of freedom, an Elektron analogue processor, and a remote-target emulator. It was built in 1961 and used for testing the Su-15's weapons control system.

midset and conventional tail surfaces featuring an all-movable horizontal tail. Interestingly, contrary to normal Soviet practice, no chief project engineer was assigned to the T-58D until the mid-1960s. General Designer Pavel O. Sukhoi resolved the key issues related to the interceptor's design, while the problems arising in the course of routine work were handled by his deputy Yevgeniy A. Ivanov.

As already mentioned, to speed up development it was decided to borrow the Su-11's wings and tail unit for the T-58. The prototype and the static-test airframe were built using stock Su-11 wing panels, which were suitably modified to match the different fuselage shape at the wing/fuselage joint and provided with a pair of boundary layer fences. This, in turn, allowed the Su-11's main landing-gear design to be retained as well. The same applied to the tail surfaces; thus the fuselage was the only major component designed from scratch.

In prototype form the T-58D was one of the few Soviet aircraft to make use of the area rule. The fuselage was 'squeezed' in two areas—near the cockpit (that is, just ahead of the air intakes) and at the wing/fuselage joint, where a prominent 'waist' existed, with a minimum width of 1.64 m (5 ft., 4½ in.). This design was meant to minimise interference drag at transonic speed. (It may be said in advance that this 'waist' failed to give the desired effect and was eliminated on the production aircraft.)

The new power plant increased reliability significantly over the single-engined version planned originally. Quite apart from the obvious case of engine failure (the probability of both engines failing for unrelated reasons is virtually negligible), having two engines allowed hydraulic and electric systems to be duplicated, using hydraulic and electric power sources fed by different engines. Thus the T-58D's hydraulic system comprised four separate subsystems—two main circuits (nos. 1 and 2) and two control system circuits (port and starboard) serving solely the control surface actuators; each circuit featured its own hydraulic pump.

Since the new aircraft would obviously be a lot heavier than the Su-11 while having the same wing area, the T-58D's field performance would clearly deteriorate as compared with its precursor. To compensate for the added weight, the engineers decided to use blown flaps (then referred to in Soviet terminology as *reaktivnyye zakrylki*: literally, 'jet flaps'), the air for these being bled from the engine compressors; hence the area-increasing Fowler flaps of the Su-11 were replaced with simple flaps. The landing gear could not be left unchanged after all—it had to be reinforced to cater for the higher weight.

The general belief was that the T-58D would have to deal primarily with single nonagile targets flying at altitudes between 2,000 and 24,000 m (6,560–78,740 ft.) and speeds up to 2,500 km/h (1,550 mph). Without having a significant advantage in speed, the interceptor stood no chance of destroying such targets in pursuit mode—hence, high-speed targets were to be intercepted in head-on mode; both tactics would be used against slower aircraft. The technique of intercepting targets flying at altitudes beyond the fighter's service ceiling had been perfected with the Su-11. It involved climbing to a so-called base altitude, where the fighter would be guided toward the target by GCI centres, subsequently detecting it with its own radar and getting a lock-on; after

coming within missile launch range the fighter would pull up, firing the missiles in a zoom climb. The minimum missile launch altitude was restricted by the performance of the radar, which lacked 'look-down/shoot-down' capability.

The creators of the weapons system intended to maximise its capabilities by automating the intercept procedure insofar as possible. To this end the T-58D was to feature a purpose-built automatic flight control system (AFCS) including heading adjustment command modules and preprogrammed optimum-climb profiles. In the course of GCI guidance and the actual intercept the pilot could choose between three control modes—manual, semiautomatic (flight director mode), and fully automatic. OKB-51 undertook to perform the main part of the design work on the AFCS; until the system was fully up to scratch, the prototypes would be equipped with AP-28T-1 autopilots.

The obligatory in-house review of the ADP and the mockup review commission were dispensed with, since the T-58D was considered to be nothing more than an upgraded version of the Su-11. Only the cockpit section received the attentions of a mockup review commission.

As already mentioned in chapter 2, on 5 February 1962 the Council of Ministers issued a directive clearing the T-3-8M (Su-11-8M) weapons system for service. One of the document's items read: *'For the purpose of enhancing the system's combat capabilities, the Su-11 aircraft is to be upgraded in order to enable attacks in head-on and pursuit mode against targets flying at altitudes of 2,000–24,000 m and speeds up to 2,500 km/h, as well as to further increase the system's reliability, ECM resistance, and automation levels'.* Thus the Su-15 took the first steps toward fully legal status.

All the while, the OKB actively undertook research and development work under the T-58D programme, using various test rigs. Among other things, a series of wind tunnel tests were held at TsAGI; ground rigs were built for testing the T-58D's electric and hydraulic systems, and the static-test airframe was successfully tested to destruction. The creation of the AFCS, which was subsequently designated SAU-58 (*sistema avtomaticheskovo oopravleniya*: automatic control system), was a major R&D effort in its own right; in the course of its development OKB-51 made its first large-scale use of mathematical analysis and simulation. As early as 1961 the OKB built a special simulator for verifying the SAU-58; some of the system's components were tested in flight on the T47-4 development aircraft (see chapter 3).

T58D-1, T58D-2, and T58D-3 Interceptor Prototypes

The first prototype of the new interceptor was built as an aerodynamics test vehicle; hence no radar was fitted, its place being occupied by test equipment, and the conical nose fairing was of metal construction. Designated **T58D-1**, the aircraft was intended for stability/handling trials and performance testing to determine the maximum speed, range, service ceiling, fuel consumption rates, and acceleration characteristics with and without external stores.

The aircraft was rolled out in the first quarter of 1962, sporting a green-painted false radome and the very appropriate but highly unusual tactical code '58-1 Red'. Shortly afterward it was trucked to the LII airfield in Zhukovskiy; Roman G. Yarmarkov was appointed engineer in charge of the test programme. On 30 May 1962, having duly passed the prescribed ground systems checks and taxiing tests, the T58D-1 successfully performed its maiden flight with Sukhoi OKB chief test pilot Vladimir S. Ilyushin at the controls. In the course of manufacturer's flight tests the code was changed to '31 Blue'. By the end of the year the first prototype had made 56 flights under the manufacturer's flight test programme, largely confirming the expectations of its creators.

Even at this early stage the customer demanded installation of a new fire control radar. Accordingly the OKB undertook a redesign of the second and third prototypes' extreme nose and rearranged the cockpit instrumentation on these aircraft. On 17 September 1962, GKAT issued an order specifying that the T-58D should be equipped with a Smerch-AS fire control radar and armed with two K-8M2 missiles in SARH and infrared-homing versions. Thus all three advanced interceptors then under development—the Ye-155P, Tu-128, and T-58D—would share the same radar type.

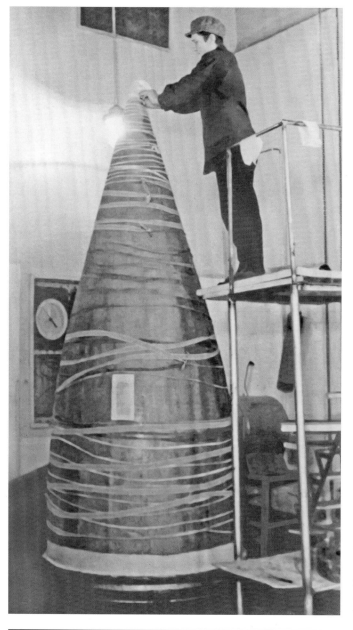

However, a change of radar would necessitate a redesign of the T-58D's forward fuselage; also, no prototype radar was available for installation. Meanwhile, early flight tests had shown that the new Sukhoi interceptor flew well and could be rapidly put into production; integration of a new weapons control system, with all the accompanying test and debugging work, would delay production and service entry for years. The implications were obvious: the Sukhoi OKB had to push for a decision to use the upgraded Oryol radar on the T-58D—initially at least—at all costs. Pavel O. Sukhoi was supported in this view by Matus R. Bisnovat; together they succeeded in making their point not only to GKAT's top executives but also to the commanders in chief of the VVS and the PVO. On 2 March 1963, Sukhoi and Bisnovat wrote to Council of Ministers vice chairman Dmitriy F. Ustinov, explaining the situation. On 13 March, Ustinov wrote back, stating his agreement to use the modified Oryol radar during the first stage of the trials and possibly the initial production stage—with the proviso that the Smerch radar would be integrated eventually. At the same time the military agreed to curb their appetites a little, reducing the target's maximum speed to 2,000 km/h (1,240 mph) and the maximum interception altitude to 23,000 m (75,460 ft.). The state acceptance trials of the T-58D were slated for completion in early November 1963.

Thus the Sukhoi OKB managed to buy some time. The new Sobol' radar specified originally was never installed; instead the second and third prototypes (the T58D-2 and T58D-3) were to feature the Oryol-D radar, the *D* standing for *dorabotannyy* (modified). Changes made at this stage included relocation of the brake parachute container from the rear fuselage underside to the base of the rudder, and provision of a ventral fin that folded sideways during landing-gear extension to provide adequate ground clearance (a feature that later appeared on the MiG-23 tactical fighter). However, the ventral fin was never installed, since the increased-area fin (see below) ensured adequate directional stability. The landing gear featured new wheels—the nose unit had the 600 × 155 mm (23.6 × 6.1 in.) KT-104 wheel replaced with a larger 660 × 200 mm (26.0 × 7.87 in.) KT-61/3 wheel, while the 880 × 230 mm (34.6 × 9.0 in.) KT-69/4 mainwheels of the first prototype were replaced by identically sized KT-117 wheels, featuring more-effective brakes cooled by a water/alcohol mixture.

In early 1963 the T58D-1 underwent modifications to the same standard as the second and third prototypes. At a very early stage of the tests, Vladimir S. Ilyushin had noted that the aircraft had poor directional stability as compared with the Su-11. The problem was cured by inserting a 400 mm (1 ft., 3¾ in.) 'plug' at the base of the fin to increase the vertical tail area; this additional section conveniently allowed the brake parachute to be relocated to a cigar-shaped fairing with clamshell doors below the rudder.

Until the end of the year, OKB test pilots Vladimir S. Ilyushin, Yevgeniy S. Solov'yov, and A. T. Borovkov made a total of 104 flights in the modified T58D-1. New changes were progressively introduced into the design. In particular, to reduce drag the original nosecone was replaced with a longer and more pointed radome featuring a cone angle of 20° instead of 32°. The shape of the 'pen nib' fairing between the engine nozzles was also optimised to cut drag, and the possibility of further reducing drag by forcing air through the engine bays was explored.

Above: The first prototype Su-15 (T58D-1) during final assembly at the MMZ No. 51. Note the short metal nosecone in lieu of a radome.

Right: Three-quarters rear view of the T58D-1. The vertical tail is a stock Su-11 subassembly.

Left: The radome of a T-58 prototype being handcrafted at MMZ No. 51.

Below: The port air intake; the airflow control ramp has yet to be installed.

Below right: The starboard R11F2-300 engine installed in the fuselage of the T58D-1

Due to the delayed decision on the model of radar to be used, the second prototype (**T58D-2**) did not begin its test programme until April 1963; coded '32 Red', it first flew on 4 May in the hands of Vladimir S. Ilyushin, with V. Torchinskiy as engineer in charge. Outwardly it differed from the first prototype in having a real radome that was slightly longer and more pointed, with a cone angle of 28°; the vertical tail was still unmodified and the brake parachute container was accordingly located ventrally. The T58D-2 featured a complete avionics fit, including an Oryol-D58 radar (*izdeliye* 303D).

Tests of the avionics suite on the second prototype as part of the manufacturer's flight test programme continued until the end of June; in early August the T58D-2 was submitted for state acceptance trials, which began in Zhukovskiy on 5 August 1963.

Left: The first prototype after being rolled out at MMZ No. 51, with missiles and drop tanks attached. Note the very appropriate (and very unusual) tactical code denoting the T58D-1. The nose has been painted green to simulate a radome, as the unrealistic shiny finish reveals. Note the 'towel rail' data link aerial under the nose, which is part of the test instrumentation suite.

Left: A side view of the same aircraft, showing the original small tail

Above right: A cutaway drawing of the T-58D from the project documents

Right: A unique picture of the second prototype (T58D-2, '32 Red') during an early test flight at GK NII VVS, with the original short radome. The area ruling of the fuselage is clearly visible.

Below right: '33 Red', the third prototype (T58D-3), sporting six mission markers. Note the new long radome, which became standard on subsequent aircraft and the data link aerial.

Since development of the SAU-58 AFCS was running behind schedule, it was decided to hold a separate trials programme when the system became available. A state commission chaired by IA PVO commander Air Marshal Yevgeniy Ya. Savitskiy was appointed for holding the trials of the AFCS. Interestingly, in official Ministry of Defence documents the T-58D was still referred to at the time as the Su-11M, not as the Su-15.

The main part of the second prototype's state acceptance trials LII was performed by the air Force's project test pilots Stal' A. Lavrent'yev, Leonid N. Peterin, and Vadim I. Petrov, plus Sukhoi

OKB chief test pilot Vladimir S. Ilyushin. Other pilots who flew the aircraft at this stage were GK NII VVS test pilots Andrey A. Manucharov, Pyotr F. Kabrelyov, Vasiliy G. Ivanov, Igor' I. Lesnikov, and Eduard N. Knyazev, as well as state commission chairman Air Marshal Savitskiy and GK NII VVS vice director Lt.-Gen. Anatoliy P. Molotkov. Engineer Zhebokritskiy supervised the ground support and maintenance team, while engineer Lozovoy was in charge of the trials programme.

To speed up the process the state acceptance trials were held in a single stage instead of the usual two. The trials included a

The first prototype (T58D-1) in original configuration

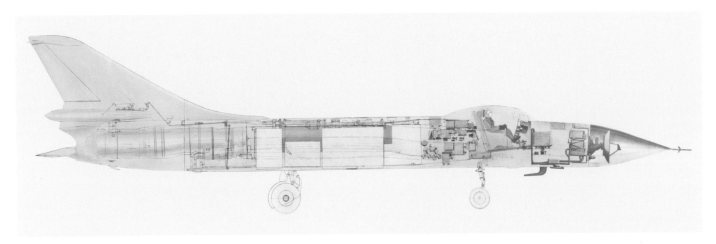

series of spinning tests; this part of the programme, involving seven flights, was performed by LII test pilot Oleg V. Goodkov in September 1963.

On 2 October 1963, OKB-51 test pilot Yevgeniy K. Kukushev took the third prototype (**T58D-3**, '33 Red') up for its first flight; A. Sholosh was engineer in charge of this aircraft's manufacturer's tests. The T58D-3 differed from the two preceding prototypes in having the definitive long radome and tall vertical tail with the brake parachute housing below the rudder, an internal fuel capacity increased by 180 litres (39.6 Imp gal.), and a new AP-46 autopilot fitted.

The air force test pilots were generally pleased with the aircraft's handling but pointed out that aileron authority decreased at low speeds, complicating landings in a crosswind. Another criticism was that the engines tended to run roughly during certain vigorous manoeuvres with a sideslip. The takeoff and landing speeds were rather high too. These shortcomings resulted from the aircraft's chosen layout; thus, the unstable engine operation during manoeuvres with a sideslip was caused by the lateral air intakes—the intake on the opposite side to the direction of the sideslip was blanked off by the fuselage. The high takeoff and landing speeds and unimpressive field performance had a different cause. As already mentioned, the T-58D featured blown flaps, but the bound-

The T58D-3 seen from the other side. The orange-painted K-98 missile on the starboard wing pylon is an instrumented test round.

Another view of the third prototype in early (area-ruled) configuration, the way it looked during the state acceptance trials. The longer nose and larger tail have changed the aircraft's silhouette appreciably. The large air scoops added on top of the rear fuselage are for the nozzles' air ejector system.

Three-quarters rear view of the T58D-3. The rudder is cut away at the base to provide room for ESM and IFF aerials but still has a basically Su-9-style design with three hinges and a large dielectric tip.

ary layer control (BLC) system was inactive during the state acceptance trials because the version of the R11F2-300 engine featuring bleed valves for the BLC system was still unavailable.

The acceleration parameters had deteriorated as compared to the Su-11. On the other hand, no criticism was given of the stability and handling, except for a bit of instability in landing configuration at 340–450 km/h (211–279 mph). Also, remember that the twin-engined T-58D was heavier than the single-engined Su-11; not only the all-up weight but also the empty weight was 1,500 kg (3,306 lbs.) higher—10,060 kg (22,180 lbs.) versus 8,560 kg (18,870 lbs.).

On 8 and 11 October 1963, respectively, the second and third prototypes were flown to the GK NII VVS facility at Vladimirovka AB to continue the state acceptance trials—specifically, to perform live missile launches against real targets. This stage lasted from August 1963 to June 1964. The radar's performance was assessed for starters, using real aircraft as 'targets'; these included Tu-16 and IL-28 bombers, Yak-25RV high-altitude reconnaissance aircraft, and the special Su-9L development aircraft, equipped with an angle reflector to increase the RCS.

Actually the state acceptance trials involved not just the aircraft but the entire aerial-intercept weapons system built around

Here the T58D-3 is seen after extensive modifications to the centre fuselage (the area ruling has been eliminated) and vertical tail. After the conversion the tactical code was changed to '33 Blue' (edged in red!). Note the addition of an undernose aerial pod on a forward-swept pylon ahead of the L-shaped aerial of the ARL-SM Lazoor-M GCI command link receiver.

A side view of the updated T58D-3, with two red-painted dummy missiles

This three-quarters rear view makes an interesting comparison to the picture opposite, showing the revised rudder (still carried on three hinges for the time being) and the new fin cap carrying the bullet-shaped aerial of the Sirena radar-warning receiver. One of the radio altimeter's dipole aerials is visible under the rear fuselage.

it. Designated Su-15-98, the system comprised the Su-15 (T-58D) interceptor, powered by two R11F2-300 engines, its Oryol-D58 fire control radar (weapons control system), and two upgraded K-8M1P AAMs, which were soon redesignated K-98 (*izdeliye* 56). The K-98 featured a new PRD-143 solid-fuel rocket motor with an initial impulse increased to 13,400 kgp (29,540 lbst), upgrades to the autopilot, seeker heads, and proximity fuse. The missile came in two versions—SARH (K-98R/*izdeliye* 56R) and IR-homing (K-98T/*izdeliye* 56T); the latter had a new TGS-14T seeker cooled by liquid nitrogen and giving all-aspect engagement capability. The Su-15-98 system worked with the Vozdukh-1M GCI system.

The trials of the Su-15-98 weapons system proceeded smoothly like never before, the customer voicing almost no criticisms. In December 1963, IA PVO commander Air Marshal Yevgeniy Ya. Savitskiy, who chaired the state commission, endorsed a protocol formulating the preliminary results of the trials. This document stated that by early December a total of 87 flights had been made under the state acceptance trials programme, including 53 flights 'for the record', 13 training flights, 16 flights 'off the record', and five positioning and check flights. The aircraft's flight performance and the operation of its systems and equipment had been fully explored, the performance figures obtained during the trials

The T58D-1 after modifications as '58 Red', with a new radome and a larger tail

The T58D-3 after modifications (with no area ruling) as '33 Blue', October 1963

The T58D-3 as it looked after retirement at Myachkovo airfield

largely matching the manufacturer's estimates. In the course of the manufacturer's flight tests and state acceptance trials, the three prototypes had made more than 300 flights without malfunctions, demonstrating the high reliability of the aircraft as a whole and its systems and equipment.

Being a highly experienced pilot who had seen a lot of action in the Great Patriotic War (hence his 'private' call sign *Drakon*, 'Dragon'), and a representative of the aircraft's customer into the bargain, Savitskiy would be ill advised to squander praise on aircraft that were not worthy of it. Thus his positive appraisal of the T-58D testifies to the undoubted success achieved by the Sukhoi OKB. Later, Sukhoi CTP Vladimir S. Ilyushin gave a similar account of those days, noting that the T-58's trials programme had been remarkably rapid and trouble free.

The first K-8M1P (K-98) missiles were delivered to Vladimirovka AB in early 1964, allowing the T-58D's armament trials to begin; these included missile attacks in head-on mode. The missile basically met its specifications, except for the inability to score guaranteed 'kills' against high-speed targets because the proximity fuse could not detonate the warhead in time at high closing speeds. The verdict was that in a head-on attack, the interceptor's missile armament enabled it to destroy targets doing up to 1,200 km/h (745 mph). The maximum interception range (combat radius) and effective range were shorter than expected, ferry range

at optimum altitude with two drop tanks being only 1,260 km (780 miles) instead of the required 2,100 km (1,300 miles). Hence the state commission recommended that the internal fuel supply be increased even before the Smerch-AS radar envisaged for the second stage of the development programme was integrated.

The Sukhoi OKB decided to increase the fuel capacity by eliminating the 'waist' of the area-ruled fuselage. Within a short time the T58D-1 was modified in the first quarter of 1964 by riveting on a sort of 'corset' over the narrow portion of the centre fuselage between frames 12 and 31, so that the fuselage now had constant width determined by the distance between the outer faces of the air intakes. This increased the internal volume sufficiently to provide an internal fuel capacity of 6,860 litres (1,509 Imp gal.) or 5,600 kg (12,345 lbs.)—more than the total premodification fuel capacity *with* drop tanks. Moreover, it actually reduced drag, improving the acceleration characteristics on a par with those of the Su-11! Additionally, to improve stability and handling the aileron travel was increased from 15° to 18°30', and the air intake ramp adjustment time was reduced from 12 seconds to five or six seconds.

Between 2 and 16 June 1964 the converted T58D-1 (now coded simply '58 Red') underwent a special test programme at GK NII VVS to check the effect of the modifications; these received a positive appraisal and were recommended for introduction. The T58D-3 was later modified in the same fashion and recoded '33

Blue' in so doing. On 19 June, Yevgeniy Ya. Savitskiy made two flights in the T58D-2, and the state acceptance trials were officially completed on 25 June. By then the three prototypes had made a total of 250 flights between them, including 194 flights under the state acceptance trials programme (146 flights for the record, and 30 practice, positioning, and checkout flights) and 26 demonstration flights. The trials included 45 missile launches, in which nine target drones (seven IL-28Ms, one Yak-25RV-II, and one MiG-15M) were destroyed, and two emergency ordnance drops.

The final report of the state acceptance trials (which referred to the weapons system as the 'Su-11-8M: stage I upgrade') said that the new aircraft offered significant advantages over the production Su-11, especially as far as head-on engagement capability was concerned. Other strong points included greater flight safety, longer target detection / lock-on range, a lower minimum operational altitude, and the new radar's better ECM resistance. The report went on to say that the T-58 could intercept targets at medium and high altitudes round the clock and in adverse weather, and that the aircraft was easy to fly and could be mastered by the average pilot; the aircraft basically met the air force's operational requirements and was recommended for service entry. (The military pilots who flew the T-58, however, were somewhat less enthusiastic about the aircraft.) The upgraded T58D-3 was recommended by the state commission as the *etalon* (pattern aircraft for production). It was recommended to explore the possibility of operating the Su-15 from unpaved runways after the wheels had been replaced with skids (this will be discussed later).

Subsequently, all three prototypes were used as 'dogships' for testing new systems and equipment. Among other things, OKB-51 undertook a major programme aimed at refining the new interceptor's power plant jointly with OKB-300, LII, and GK NII VVS. Under this programme the T58D-1 and T58D-2 were used in 1964–65 to verify a new air-intake control system intended to lift certain restrictions on power plant operation when the engines were throttled back. The lengthy efforts turned out to be fruitless, and the restrictions stayed in force throughout the Su-15's service career.

In early 1965 the first prototype was modified for testing new cranked delta wings of increased area and 720 mm (2 ft., 4³⁄₈ in.) longer span, with the leading-edge sweep on the outer portions reduced from 60° to 45°. The purpose of this modification was to increase aileron efficiency at low speeds. Vladimir S. Ilyushin made the first postmodification flight on 22 February; by June, three versions of the modified wings had been tried, the designers settling for a version on which the outer-wing leading edge was extended forward and cambered 7°. The new wings had a positive effect on both stability/handling and field performance and were subsequently incorporated on late-production Su-15s.

Later the T58D-1 was modified even more extensively to become the T-58VD short takeoff and landing (STOL) technology demonstrator described later in this chapter. The T58D-2 was also modified, becoming the T-58L development aircraft. The T58D-3 was used to test a new technique involving the use of flaps for takeoff (until then, the normal procedure was to deploy the flaps for landing only). The new flap settings were 15° for takeoff and 25° for landing; this technique reduced the unstick speed by 20 km/h (12.5 mph) and the takeoff run by an average 150 m (490 ft.), and the modification

The T58D-3 after the modification, showing the lack of area ruling

was recommended for production. Boundary layer control was necessary to reduce the approach/landing speed, but the modified engines featuring BLC bleed valves were still unavailable. The T58D-3 was also used for perfecting the SAU-58 AFCS and the upgraded Oryol-D58M radar between 1965 and 1968.

The following brief structural description applies to the T58D-1 prototype as originally built.

Type: Single-seat supersonic interceptor designed for day and night operation in VMC and IMC.

Fuselage: Semimonocoque, riveted, stressed-skin structure built in two sections, with a break point. The *forward fuselage* has circular cross section immediately aft of the conical metal nose fairing; it features detachable lateral panels for access to the no. 1 avionics bay. The latter is followed by the cockpit enclosed by a bubble canopy of similar design to that of the Su-9/Su-11, except that the sliding portion has a transparency divided by a centreline frame member. The no. 2 avionics bay is located aft of the cockpit.

The forward fuselage is flanked by two-dimensional supersonic air intakes with sharp lips. Each intake features a two-shock vertical airflow control ramp with a movable panel governed by

Top and *above*: The T58D-3 sits at Myachkovo airfield, a short way west of Zhukovskiy, after the completion of the trials. The tactical code is again '33 Red' (albeit in a different presentation). Note the open auxiliary blow in door aft of the code.

Left: Another view of the retired T58D-3 sitting on the grass at Myachkovo

Right: The same aircraft some time later; half the fuselage is under wraps, but these are duly marked '33'.

the UVD-58D engine/intake control system ([*sistema*] *oopravleniya vozdukhozabornikom i dvigatelem*), plus a rectangular auxiliary blow-in door on the outer face. To prevent boundary layer ingestion, the intakes are set apart from the fuselage, the inner lip acting as a boundary layer splitter plate; V-shaped fairings spilling the boundary layer connect the splitter plates to the fuselage.

The centre fuselage is area ruled at the wing/fuselage joint, narrowing markedly between frames 14B and 28; it incorporates S-shaped engine inlet ducts, with fuel tanks in between. The *rear fuselage* is detachable for engine maintenance and change, accom-

modating the engines. It incorporates four airbrakes located in a cruciform arrangement, and a brake parachute bay with clamshell doors located ventrally between the engine's jet pipes.

Wings and tail unit: The wings and tail surfaces are identical to those of the Su-11, except for the changes to the wings to match the area-ruled fuselage and the provision of two wing fences.

Landing gear: Hydraulically retractable tricycle type, with single wheel on each unit; all three units have levered suspension and oleo-pneumatic shock absorbers. The forward-retracting nose unit is equipped with a 600 × 155 mm (23.6 × 6.1 in.) KT-104 brake wheel and a shimmy damper. The main units retracting inward into the wing roots have 880 × 230 mm (34.6 × 9.0 in.) KT-69/4 wheels.

Power plant: Two Tumanskiy R11F2S-300 axial-flow after-burning turbojets rated at 3,900 kgp (8,600 lbst) at full military power and 6,175 kgp (13,610 lbst) in full afterburner. (For a detailed description of this engine, see chapter 9.) Provisions were made for installing R11F2SU-300 engines features bleed valves for the flaps' boundary layer control system.

Fuel system: Internal fuel is carried in four integral tanks—two fuselage tanks and two wing tanks. The total capacity is 5,120 litres (1,126 Imp gal.), and the fuel load 4,200 kg (9,260 lbs.). There are two 'wet' hardpoints under the centre fuselage, permitting carriage of 600-litre (132 Imp gal.) drop tanks that increase the total to 6,320 litres (1,390 Imp gal.) or 5,180 kg (11,420 lbs.).

Armament: Two K-8M2 (K-98) medium-range air-to-air missiles with semi-active radar homing or IR homing carried on pylon-mounted PU-1-8 launch rails under the wings, as on the Su-11.

Avionics and equipment: The avionics suite includes an RSIU-5 (R-802V) two-way VHF communications radio, an ARK-10 ADF, an RV-UM low-range radio altimeter, an MRP-56P marker beacon receiver, SOD-57M DME, a Lazoor' (ARL-S) command link receiver working with the Vozdookh-1M GCI system, an SRZO-2M Kremniy-2M IFF transponder, and (provisionally) a Sobol' fire control radar.

Crew escape system: A Sukhoi KS-3 ejection seat.

Su-15 Production Interceptor
(T-58, *izdeliye* 37 or '*izdeliye* 37 Srs D')

On 30 April 1965 the Council of Ministers issued a directive formally including the Su-15-98 aerial-intercept weapons system into the PVO inventory. The aircraft officially received the service designation Su-15 (thus, it was recognised as a new type, not an 'upgraded Su-11'), while the K-98 missile was redesignated R-98. The directive required the Novosibirsk aircraft factory no. 153 to launch production of the new interceptor in early 1966.

Back in the second half of 1964 the Sukhoi OKB had completed detail design work on the T-58D's production version, incorporating the changes requested by the state commission (e.g., increased fuel capacity), transferring the blueprints to the Novosibirsk aircraft factory. In the course of 1965, the plant, which had been building the Yak-28P since the termination of Su-11 production, geared up to build the Su-15, which received the product code *izdeliye* 37. (Later, when the Su-15T/Su-15TM entered production [see below], the original model was sometimes referred to in official documents as *izdeliye tridtsat' sem' serii D* (product 37 Srs D)

in order to discern it from the new version, or *izdeliye tridtsat' sem' serii M*; the *D* probably referred to the original designation, T-58D.) Construction of the first two aircraft in the preproduction batch (batch 00) began at the end of the year. As already mentioned, initially the Su-15 had no official chief project engineer; it was not until it had entered production that OKB-51 engineer N. P. Polenov was assigned overall responsibility for this aircraft.

Aircraft designers are only human, and one can hardly blame them for wishing to promote their own products—unless they resort to dirty tricks, of course. Alarmed by the steady progress of the Su-15's state acceptance trials and perceiving it as a threat to the Yak-28P (to which the new Sukhoi interceptor was clearly superior), OKB-115 general designer Aleksandr S. Yakovlev urgently set about developing a modernised version of his interceptor, with

similar air intakes. Actually 'similar' is a rather mild way of putting it; in fact, the chief of OKB-115 urgently despatched his elder son, Sergey A. Yakovlev, to Novosibirsk to have a close look at the section of the Su-15's manufacturing drawings referring to the air intakes. Yet, the radically but hastily redesigned Yak-28-64 (alias Yak-28N) featuring buried R11F2-300 engines and Su-15-style two-dimensional lateral intakes turned out to be a complete flop—the first few flights revealed it was inferior to the standard Yak-28 with wing-mounted engines, never mind the Su-15! The programme was abandoned and the Sukhoi OKB regained control over the Novosibirsk plant. 'The empire strikes back'?

Building the Su-15 did not involve a complete change of manufacturing technology, since the aircraft had considerable structural commonality with the Su-9 and Su-11, which the factory had

Far left: 'Toad's-eye view' of the first preproduction Novosibirsk-built Su-15 (c/n 0015301), showing the outward-canted air intakes. The aircraft is carrying two R-98T IR-homing missiles.

Left: Three-quarters rear view of the same aircraft, showing the revised tail with a new rudder carried on two hinges and a neater dielectric fin cap. The starboard missile is in fact a dummy (note the lack of the rocket motor nozzle), while the port one is an instrumented test round.

Left: The tactical code '34 Red' of the first preproduction Su-15 continued the sequence begun with the prototypes.

Below left: This side view illustrates the classic appearance of the production-standard Su-15 *sans suffixe*.

Right: This aspect of '34 Red' shows the wing planform and the fuselage 'pinched' ahead of the air intakes. Note the larger antiglare panel ahead of the canopy, and the additional antiglare panels on the air intake trunks.

built earlier; it also shared a lot of systems components and equipment with both the Su-11 and the Yak-28P. Yet, a few changes were made before the aircraft entered production. In particular, as mentioned earlier, on the prototypes the vertical tail was a stock Su-9 subassembly with an insert at the base to accommodate the brake parachute container at the base of the rudder, so as not to redesign the fin. On the production model, however, the structure was redesigned after all; the forward fin attachment fitting was moved forward from fuselage frame 38 to frame 35, and the fin spar was kinked to accomplish this. The new rudder was carried on two brackets instead of three and had no dielectric tip, and the dielectric fin cap was also revised.

As a result, the first preproduction aircraft (c/n 0015301; the abbreviated form 0001, as stencilled on the actual aircraft, is sometimes used) took a long time to complete. Coded '34 Red', it was rolled out at Novosibirsk-Yel'tsovka on 21 February 1966, several months late. On 6 March the aircraft made its first flight with factory test pilot Ivan F. Sorokin at the controls; in late April it was

'34 Red', the first preproduction Novosibirsk-built Su-15

Above: The first preproduction Su-15 recoded '01 Red' sits at the OKB compound upon completion of all trials. Note the open no. 2 avionics bay access hatch and the black and yellow 'Danger, air intake' stripes on the splitter plates.

Left and *below*: The second production Su-15 ('67 Red', c/n 0115302) was used for unpaved runway tests.

The second production Su-15 as it appeared during unpaved runway tests

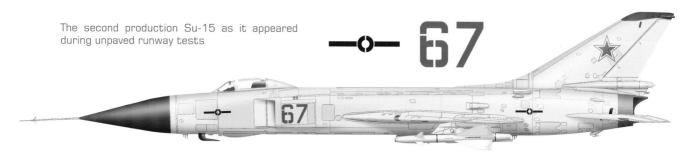

Su-15 '69 Blue' (c/n 0315306) was one of the ten aircraft that underwent service trials in the 611th IAP, the first regular PVO unit to receive the type. It is pictured here at the unit's home base, Dorokhovo AB.

'69 Blue' is depicted with live missiles—an IR-homing R-98T to port (with a ground cover over the IR seeker) and a radar-homing R-98R to starboard.

ferried to the Sukhoi OKB's flight test facility in Zhukovskiy. The second preproduction Su-15 (c/n 0015302) was completed in June 1966, joining the first aircraft on 21 July.

As mentioned earlier, in early 1965 the OKB had tested new cranked delta wings on the first prototype. However, the factory refused to build the fighter with this wing design on the pretext that no verdict from GK NII VVS existed on the soundness of this design. In reality the reason was more down to earth but nonetheless plausible: the jigs and tooling for the Su-15's original delta wings had already been manufactured; modifying them would mean further delays in the production schedule, which was in jeopardy as it was.

Speaking of which, in 1965 the abbreviation GK NII VVS was changed to GNIKI VVS, which basically means the same. From 1967 onward the institute was officially called GNII-8 VVS.

Full-scale production of the Su-15 gradually gained momentum from mid-1966 onward; 17 production aircraft had been assembled by the end of that year. The production model featured an internal fuel capacity of 6,860 litres (1,509 Imp gal.) or 5,600 kg (12,345 lbs.) thanks to the constant-width centre fuselage patterned on the postmodification T58D-3, but the number of fuselage tanks was reduced to three. Production aircraft were powered by R11F2S-300 (*izdeliye* 37F2S) engines rated at 3,900 kgp (8,600 lbst) dry and 6,175 kgp (13,610 lbst) reheat. The SAU-58 automatic flight control system took some time coming, passing its state acceptance trials only in 1968. The trials revealed that the AFCS required major changes, and it was decided to postpone its introduction until the aircraft's next upgrade. Still, the installation of the SAU-58 had been planned from the outset, and space for its modules was reserved in the avionics bays. As a result, the aircraft had neither the AFCS nor the simpler AP-28 autopilot fitted to the prototypes; the road to hell is paved with good intentions! Worse, the production Su-15 did not even have dampers in any of the con-

Su-15 '69 Blue', 611th IAP, Dorokhovo AB
Moscow-Domodedovo airshow, 9 July 1967

trol circuits, the ARZ-1 artificial-feel unit in the tailplane control circuit being the only stability augmentation system. Curiously, the military never demanded changes in this area, since the stability and handling characteristics of production aircraft during pre-delivery tests appeared adequate.

Right from the start, the production aircraft featured an improved UVD-58M air-intake control system and the Sukhoi KS-4 ejection seat, permitting safe ejection at altitudes up to 20,000 m (65,620 ft.) and speeds up to 1,200 km/h (745 mph) IAS. The seat had a KSM-S two-stage ejection gun (*kombineerovannyy strely-ayushchiy mekhanizm*) and a PS-S three-canopy parachute system functioning in accordance with any of four operating programmes, which was selected automatically depending on speed and altitude. Programme 1 was for ejection above 3,000 m (9,840 ft.) and 550 km/h (341 mph) IAS; programme 2 was for altitudes below 3,000 m and speeds above 550 km/h, and programme 3 was for altitudes above 3,000 m and speeds below 550

Top: The detached radome reveals the antenna of the Oryol-D (RP-15) radar.

Above: This view shows the radar's hydraulic antenna drive and the removed access panels exposing the radar set.

km/h. Finally, programme 4 was for ejection below 3,000 m and 550 km/h, including the takeoff and landing run, providing the speed was 160 km/h (99 mph) or higher. On the minus side, the KS-4 seat was heavy, weighing 167–170 kg (368–375 lbs.) together with the parachute and the NAZ-7 survival kit (*nosimyy avareey-nyy zapahs*: portable emergency supplies).

The avionics fit of early-production Su-15s included an RSIU-5V (R-802V) VHF communications radio, an MRP-56P marker beacon receiver, an RV-UM low-range radio altimeter, an ARK-10 ADF, a Lazoor' (ARL-S) command link receiver, an SRZO-2M IFF transponder, an SOD-57M ATC/SIF transponder, a Sirena-2 radar-warning receiver, a KSI-5 compass system, and an AGD-1 artificial horizon. Production aircraft were equipped with the Oryol-D58 radar, which, in its production form, was officially designated RP-15 (as a reference to the Su-15). Increasing the radar's ECM resistance and perfecting the missiles' proximity fuses was the responsibility of other bureaus. This, too, proved to be a protracted affair, and the trials of the improved RP-15M (Oryol-D58M) radar held jointly by the manufacturer and the air force were not completed until 1967, when the Su-15 was already in service. New-build Su-15s were henceforth completed with the modified radar, while previously built examples were upgraded to the new standard in situ.

A typical production Su-15 had an empty weight of 10,220 kg (22,530 lbs.). The production rates built up gradually; in 1968 the factory turned out 150 Su-15s versus 90 in 1967.

Between 7 July 1967 and 25 September 1968, GNIKI VVS held check trials of a batch 2 Su-15 (c/n 0215301) to see if the performance figures matched those obtained during the state acceptance trials. The results were disappointing, and the causes were traced to two main problems. The first problem lay with the engines. The R11F2S-300 engine was produced by two factories, no. 500 in Moscow and no. 26 in Ufa, Bashkir ASSR. In the course of the tests, Su-15 c/n 0215301 flew consecutively with three sets of engines, two of which were manufactured in Moscow and the third in Ufa; the Moscow-built engines provided the required performance, but the Ufa-built ones did not (this concerned, first and foremost, interception range in pursuit mode).

Between 10 June and 30 August 1969 the same aircraft underwent further tests with a new pair of Ufa-built engines. This time the performance improved to an acceptable level, except that the interception range in pursuit mode against a target doing 1,400 km/h (870 mph) at 23,000 m (75,460 ft.) turned out to be 25 km (15.5 miles) less than required. GNIKI VVS immediately solved the problem by a bit of trickery: the next mission was flown with a single drop tank instead of two to reduce drag, and the required interception range of 195 km (121 miles) was obtained.

The other nasty surprise was that in certain flight modes, the stick forces increased abruptly all of a sudden—the stick seemed to bump into invisible stops. The problem was traced to the control surfaces' hydraulic actuators, which were not powerful enough. The OKB and the military turned to LII for help; at the end of 1968 the institute held a special research programme that was performed by test pilot Aleksandr A. Shcherbakov in the fourth production Su-15 (c/n 0115304). In parallel the OKB investigated the problem on its own, using the second preproduction

Top, *top right*, and *above*: Three aspects of an early-production (pure delta) Su-15 armed with R-98 AAMs on PU-1-8 pylons

Below: This Su-15 has been upgraded with PU-2-8 outboard pylons and PD-62 inboard pylons / APU-60 launch rails for R-60 AAMs.

Su-15 '21 Red', 302nd IAP, Pereyaslavka AB, 1978

Su-15 (c/n 0015302) and the second production aircraft ('67 Red', c/n 0115302), but soon pressure of higher-priority programmes caused the issue to be put on hold.

Concurrently the Su-15 underwent service trials in the PVO. Ten aircraft (mostly batch 3 machines) were evaluated by the 611th IAP of the Moscow PVO District, based at Dorokhovo AB, near Bezhetsk (Yaroslavl' Region)—the first regular PVO unit to reequip with the new interceptor. Between 29 September 1967 and 15 May 1969 the ten Su-15s made a total of 1,822 flights, including 418 under the actual evaluation programme; two live weapons training sessions were held with the expenditure of 58 R-98 AAMs. The service tests basically corroborated the results of the state acceptance trials. However, a number of serious shortcomings were discovered; among other things, the service ceiling fell short of the specifications because engine thrust decreased in the course of the engines' service life, and the interception range was again shorter than expected.

The Su-15 and its systems underwent constant refinement in the course of production. The biggest number of upgrades was made in 1968, when the new wings with the cranked leading edge and the BLC system were introduced after all. In early 1968, OKB-51 received the first shipset of R11F2SU-300 (*izdeliye* 37F2SU) engines; the *U* in the designation stood for *oopravleniye* [*pogranichnym sloyem*]: BLC. After that, the first preproduction Su-15 was re-engined and rewinged. After a brief initial flight test programme performed by OKB pilots, the fighter was flown to the GNIKI VVS facility in Akhtoobinsk to undergo more-extensive testing. The military test pilots observed that the extended-chord outer-wing portions had a positive effect on stability. On the minus

side, the double-delta wings caused a slight reduction in performance at supersonic speeds and a reduction of the service ceiling; yet, there was no cause for alarm, since the performance figures obtained were still within the limits specified by the military.

Regarding the blown flaps, the air force test pilots noted that the BLC caused a forward shift in the aircraft's CG, which complicated the landing procedure because stabilator authority was insufficient. On the other hand, the 40 km/h (25 mph) reduction in approach/landing speed was an undoubted asset. The final conclusion was a thumbs-up, and the modifications were recommended for incorporation on the production fighter.

Later, between 1968 and 1970, the Sukhoi OKB used the second production Su-15 for further tests on unpaved runways. The aircraft was fitted with a test equipment suite but was outwardly unmodified, save for photo calibration markings on the nose.

In 1969 the blown flaps were introduced on production Su-15s from c/n 1115301 onward, but the old pure delta wings were retained for the time being; the first production Su-15 to be completed with double-delta wings was c/n 1115331. From c/n 1115336 onward, all Su-15s had provisions for installing Gavrilov R13-300 engines, rated at 4,100 kgp (9,040 lbst) dry and 6,600 kgp (14,550 lbst) reheat. Another change introduced on batch 11 was the addition of a 'black box'—the SARPP-12V-1 FDR.

Predelivery tests of production Su-15s showed that the new wings reduced the service ceiling by an average 400 m (1,310 ft.). As a result, the PVO temporarily stopped accepting new Su-15s; Pavel O. Sukhoi's aide Yevgeniy A. Ivanov, who was responsible for the Su-15 programme, received a dressing-down from the 'head office' at GKAT. Several batch 11 aircraft were urgently delivered to GNIKI VVS for the purpose of holding check trials, and a Sukhoi OKB delegation flew to Akhtoobinsk to attend them. The trials confirmed the reduction; yet, both the military and the OKB were well aware that nothing could be done to increase the service ceiling. Hence, a protocol of agreement was signed in which the PVO conceded that the service ceiling of the rewinged Su-15 would be 18,100 m (59,380 ft.) versus 18,500 m (60,695 ft.) for the original 'pure delta' version.

The issue of the 'invisible stops' hampering stick travel was addressed after the double-delta version had entered production, and the remedy was to install more-powerful hydraulic actuators. Tests held in 1970 showed that on aircraft featuring the new BU-220 actuators the phenomenon recurred only when the airbrakes were deployed or if one of the control system's hydraulic circuits failed. From then on, identical BU-220 actuators were installed in all three control circuits on production Su-15s.

A pure-delta/six-pylon Su-15 carrying UPK-23-250 cannon pods on the fuselage hardpoints

The power plant and some other systems also had their share of bugs. While being more reliable than the AL-7F, the R11F2S-300 engines powering the Su-15 were not immune against surging or flaming out at high altitude, and relighting them after a flameout was not always easy. Actual Su-15 operations in the PVO's first-line units added new details to the picture; among other things, it turned out that the engines were prone to catching fire, while the fire-warning and fire suppression systems were unreliable. In 1968–69 alone, two accidents and six incidents (in the Russian terminological sense—that is, near accidents or damage not grave enough to be rated as a nonfatal accident / partial loss) occurred in PVO fighter units for the reasons stated above. Sukhoi OKB test pilots also found themselves in such dangerous situations. Thus, on 30 September 1969, when Vladimir S. Ilyushin was making yet another flight in Su-15 c/n 0015302 with the objective of testing the SAU-58 AFCS, he discovered that the nozzle petals on one of the engines would not close when the afterburners were switched off. He chose to abort the mission and return to base urgently—and not a minute too soon, as it turned out. Examination of the failed engine showed that the afterburner chamber had burned out near one of the flameholder's attachment points. The escaping hot gases destroyed the hydraulic lines feeding the nozzle actuators, and started burning through the rear fuselage structure; at the moment of touchdown the rear fuselage was a hair's breadth away from failing catastrophically. On 12 June 1972 a similar failure resulted in the crash of Su-15 c/n 1115342—incidentally, the sole

'company-owned' example to be lost in an accident. Test pilot Aleksandr S. Komarov was making a routine flight to establish the aircraft's roll stability characteristics and measure the temperature inside the rear fuselage. He was less lucky than Ilyushin; when the afterburner failed, the fire burned through the control runs, leaving him no choice but to punch out. Komarov sustained serious injuries in the ejection, breaking both legs and his left arm; it was another two years before the doctors decided that he was fit to fly again.

Production of the initial version with no suffix letters to the designation (or 'Su-15 *sans suffixe*') peaked in 1969, when 165 examples were built. In 1971 the Su-15 *sans suffixe* was succeeded on the Novosibirsk production line by the more advanced Su-15TM; total production of the initial version stood at 564, making it the most widespread version.

The production-standard Su-15 made its public debut on 9 July 1967 at the grand air show at Moscow-Domodedovo airport. After that the ASCC allocated the reporting name 'Flagon' to the new interceptor; this was changed to Flagon-A when new versions became known. The R-98 missile was code-named AA-3A Anab.

***

Several production Su-15s were used in various research and development programmes between 1966 and 1975, mostly as avionics or equipment test beds, verifying items that found use on later versions of the Su-15. In total, 26 such programmes were completed between 1966 and 1969 alone. For instance, in 1969 and

Two views of the T-58L development aircraft on wheels; the tall twin-wheel nose gear gives it a strongly nose-up ground angle. The tail has been revised but the fuselage is still area ruled; note the new '58-L' tail titles and the unusual location of the tactical code.

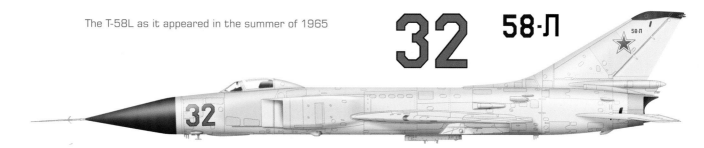

The T-58L as it appeared in the summer of 1965

32 **58-Л**

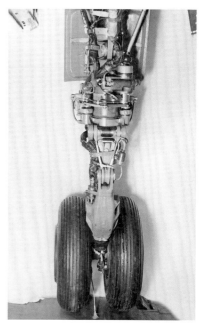

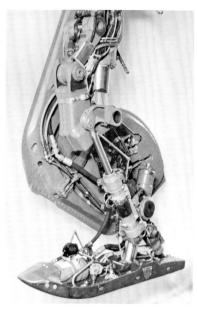

Top: Here the T-58L is shown with skids, making a high-speed run on packed snow. Note the nosewheel mudguard and the many faired or podded cameras recording the snow spread patterns.

Above: The skid-equipped T-58L leaves ruts on a loose snow surface.

Top right and *above right*: Close-ups of the nose gear and the main gear with the extra shock absorber and skid lubrication system

1971 the first preproduction example (c/n 0015301) was used to test new shapes of the fairing between the engine nozzles; in 1970 the same aircraft served to determine the field performance with the engines in minimum afterburner mode. Other development aircraft are listed below.

T-58L Development Aircraft

In the early 1960s, when the Cuban Missile Crisis put the two superpowers on the brink of an all-out nuclear war, the Soviet armed forces paid much attention to dispersing troops (including air force units) in order to make them less vulnerable to enemy strikes. The reason was that such aircraft needed ever-longer paved runways, which would surely be targeted by enemy aviation in the opening stage of a war, leaving the aircraft firmly grounded. Building lots of concrete runways on the eve of an impending war would not be feasible, not to mention costs. This meant operations from unpaved tactical and reserve airstrips—for which, as it turned out, the units of the VVS and the IA PVO were totally unprepared. This led the military to demand insistently that all tactical aircraft types should be capable of operating from semi-prepared dirt strips. This was not easy—the ever-growing weight of tactical aircraft necessitated an increase of the tyre pressure to 10–12 kg/cm² (142–171 psi), which caused the wheels to sink into the soft ground of such airstrips, meaning the aircraft were confined to paved airfields. Something had to be done to reduce the aircraft's ground pressure. There was also the issue of preventing ingestion of dust and debris from unpaved runways into the engine air intakes, which could cause FOD.

Upon completion of the Su-15's state acceptance trials, the Sukhoi OKB followed the recommendations of the state commission, developing a special skid landing gear for the Su-15 with a view to exploring the possibility of operating the new interceptor from unpaved strips. This work was initiated by a VPK ruling issued on 1 April 1964. By then the OKB had accumulated considerable experience in this field with the S22-4, S-23, and S-26 development aircraft, all of them versions of the Su-7B featuring different versions of skid landing gear. Thus the optimum layout could be chosen and the design work completed within a short time frame. The engineers selected a mixed arrangement with skids on the main units and a wheeled nose unit, as on the S-26.

Modification work on the second prototype (T58D-2, '32 Red') was completed in the first half of 1965, whereupon the aircraft was redesignated T-58L (the designation is sometimes rendered as T58-L), the *L* standing for *lyzhnoye shassee*: skid landing gear. The conversion involved installing new main gear units that could be quickly reconfigured from wheels to skids and back again, with appropriate modifications to the mainwheel wells and gear doors. The skids had a stamped aluminium frame and a running surface made of titanium sheet; the latter was necessary because the temperature of the running surface could reach 450°C–500°C (842°F–932°F) due to the enormous friction. The running surface was detachable and could be replaced when it became worn out. A pneumatic ram was mounted ahead of the axle to absorb the jolts when taxiing and align the skid properly for touchdown. For braking at the start of the takeoff run and on landing, each skid had a titanium 'claw' deflected by another pneumatic ram. To prevent the skids from sticking to mud in the spring/autumn or freezing to the snow-covered surface in the winter, an alcohol/glycerine mixture stored in special bottles was forced through slits in the skids' undersides by compressed air from bottles in the mainwheel wells. The standard castoring nose gear unit was replaced by a steerable unit, as on the S-26 (normally the T-58 was steered on the ground by differential braking, which was impossible with skids); the nosewheel was equipped with a mudguard. Provisions were made for installing jet-assisted-takeoff (JATO), solid-fuel rocket boosters, changes were made to the forward fuselage and cockpit, and a new KS-4 ejection seat was fitted.

Vladimir S. Ilyushin performed the T-58L's first flight on 6 September 1965. From 1966 until the mid-1970s the aircraft underwent extensive testing on various semiprepared grass, dirt, and snow strips in various climatic zones; GNIKI VVS also participated in these tests. Apart from Ilyushin, the aircraft was flown by OKB test pilots Yevgeniy K. Kukushev, Yevgeniy S. Solov'yov, Vladimir A. Krechetov, et al., as well as GNIKI VVS pilots.

The test programme included measurement of the vibration loads affecting the avionics and weapons. The vibrations turned out to be too strong; as a result the PU-1-8 missile pylons were provided with a longer nose section and an additional support for the missile, the modified version being designated PU-1-8A.

In one of the test flights with Kukushev at the controls on 8 September 1967, the aircraft started rocking to and fro during the takeoff run, and at the moment of rotation the antiflutter weight on one of the stabilators dug into the ground, ripping away together with a portion of the skin. To prevent a repetition of this incident, the antiflutter weights were angled up 15° on the Su-15T, Su-15TM, and Su-15UM. Another change brought about by the tests was that the ventrally located cooling-air scoops, which got clogged with mud, were relocated to dorsal and lateral positions.

In 1967 the T-58L was refitted with a new, taller nose gear unit featuring twin 620 × 180 mm (24.4 × 7.0 in.) KN-9 wheels (*koleso netormoznoye*: nonbraking wheel). The purpose of this change was to increase the angle of attack on takeoff (thereby increasing lift and shortening the takeoff run), raise the air intakes higher above the ground (thereby reducing the risk of FOD), and improve ground manoeuvrability. During winter tests on a snow-covered runway, the T-58L was literally festooned with cameras recording the snow spray patters. Two faired cameras were mounted on each side of the cockpit section, looking aft at the nosewheels and the air intakes; two more were suspended in pods under the nose, just aft of the radome, two more were mounted aft of the nose gear (looking forward), and the final two were carried under the wings.

Further tests at GNIKI VVS followed in 1968, and the verdict was unambiguous: the skid landing gear was unsuitable for an interceptor. The tests of the T-58L revealed major problems associated with operations from unpaved strips. The vibrations experienced on uneven runways subjected the avionics and armament to augmented loads that could ruin them; also, the missiles' IR seekers were liberally spattered with dirt, rendering the missiles 'blind' and useless. It should be noted that production Su-15s with a standard landing gear also underwent tests on unpaved runways; these tests ultimately led to the introduction of a twin-wheel, steerable nose gear unit on the Su-15TM.

Upon completion of the test programme in 1974, the T-58L was donated to the air force academy named after Yuriy A. Gagarin (VVA: *Voyenno-vozdooshnaya akademiya*), in Monino, Moscow Region, as an instructional airframe with 209 hours of total time since new. Fortunately it was not 'vivisected', as ground instructional airframes often are; later it moved to the colocated Soviet Air Force Museum (now Central Russian Air Force Museum).

Su-15/R11F3-300 Engine Test Bed

The fourth production Su-15 (c/n 0115304) was used by LII as a test bed for the Tumanskiy R11F3-300 engine, featuring a contingency rating. Actually this term was used in a nonstandard way, since it referred to increasing thrust at low altitudes to improve performance, not to an automatic power reserve activated in the event of an engine failure.

T-58-95 Engine Test Bed

In keeping with MAP and air force orders issued in October 1967 and May 1968, respectively, several production Su-15s were modified for testing the new Gavrilov R13-300 afterburning turbojets. The R13-300 (*izdeliye* 95) was a derivative of the R11F-300 developed by the Ufa-based *Soyooz* (Union) engine design bureau, led by Sergey A. Gavrilov. At that time the young OKB had little design experience of its own and thus ran into major problems with the R13-300, which differed significantly from the precursor; among other things, the number of high-pressure compressor stages was increased from three to five, and a second afterburner stage was added. Thanks to these changes, the engine delivered 4,100 kgp (9,040 lbst) at full military power and 6,600 kgp (14,550 lbst) in full afterburner versus 3,900 kgp (8,600 lbst) and 6,175 kgp (13,610 lbst), respectively, for the R11F2S-300.

Upon completion of the bench tests, a flight-cleared R13-300 was installed on Su-15 c/n 0415302 by August 1967, replacing the starboard R11F2S-300; the resulting 'lopsided' aircraft was known at the Sukhoi OKB as the T-58-95, the last two digits referring to the development engine's product code. Suitably fitted out with data-recording equipment, the T-58-95 made 11 flights under the initial flight test programme before being transferred to LII, where the manufacturer's tests of the R13-300 engine were held in 1967–68.

Su-15/R13-300 Engine Test Beds

By mid-December 1968 the Sukhoi OKB had installed a complete shipset of R13-300 engines in a production Su-15 coded '51 Blue' (c/n 0715311). After completing manufacturer's flight tests in March 1969 the aircraft was flown to the GNIKI VVS facility in Akhtoobinsk for state acceptance trials of the new engine and the re-engined interceptor as a whole. The trials programme, involving 53 flights, showed that the service ceiling, acceleration time, effective range, combat radius, and field performance had improved thanks to the new engines.

Between November 1969 and February 1970, Su-15 '51 Blue' underwent additional testing to explore the R13-300's resistance to surging; the test programme was performed by Vladimir S.

Left: Su-15 '51 Blue', a propulsion test bed with two R13-300 engines, at Akhtoobinsk. Outwardly it is a perfectly standard Flagon-A.

Below: Another view of the same test bed during trials at GNIKI VVS

Two views of Su-15 '37 Red' (c/n 1115337), another test bed for the R13-300 engines, at Zhukovskiy

The instrument panel and starboard cockpit console of '37 Red'. Note that no radar display is fitted to this test bed.

Ilyushin. Another Su-15 coded '37 Red' (c/n 1115337), an aircraft owned by LII and one of the first examples powered by R13-300 engines, joined the test programme in December 1969. In the course of the tests, engine flameouts at high Mach numbers were experienced on both aircraft when the engines were running in full afterburner. It turned out that the engines were simply not getting enough air because the air intakes were too small. To eliminate this dangerous phenomenon, the air intakes had to be widened, but this was impracticable in mass production at the time, since it required major structural changes and hence changes to the tooling. Therefore it was decided simply not to engage the second afterburner stage on Su-15s *sans suffixe* with R13-300 engines, since the first afterburner stage provided an adequate increase of flight performance.

Nevertheless a third production Su-15 (identity unknown) was re-engined with R13-300s, undergoing tests in 1970–71. This aircraft featured wider air intakes to cater for the engines' greater mass flow; this intake design, together with the R13-300 engines, was later introduced on the ultimate Su-15TM.

Su-15 ECM/IRCM Equipment Test Bed

From 1969 onward, LII used a specially equipped early-production Su-15 ('16 Blue', c/n 0615316) to study the reflection of radar echoes from targets, clouds of chaff, and the ground. Later this aircraft was used as a test bed for passive electronic countermeasures (ECM) and infrared countermeasures (IRCM) equipment, serving to verify almost all chaff/flare dispenser types used by the Soviet air force. These included the APP-50 (*avtomaht postanovki [passivnykh] pomekh*: automatic passive jammer), developed by PKB *Gorizont* (*priborno-konstrooktorskoye byuro*: 'Horizon' Instrument Design Bureau), in Ramenskoye, Moscow Region, which was tested successfully in 1978–79. The APP-50 *Avtomaht-F* (Automatic device; a.k.a. L029) fired 50 mm (1.96 in.) PPI-50 magnesium flares (*peeropatron infrakrasnyy*: infrared flare) to decoy IR-homing missiles or PPR-50 chaff bundles (*peeropatron rahdiolokatsionnyy*) to jam radars and the radar seekers of AAMs. During tests of PPI-50 flares, the APP-50s were mounted in a converted drop tank carried on the starboard fuselage pylon, firing at

different angles (vertically, horizontally, or 45° down); a different type of pod was used for the PPR-50s. Photo calibration markings were applied to the nose and the fin. In some cases the Su-15 test bed was firred with podded AKS-16 cine cameras (*apparaht kino-syomochnyy*) on various pylons, but in other cases these were omitted and the tests were filmed from a chase plane.

SL-15R (T-58R) Avionics Test Bed

Since the Sukhoi T-6 (Su-24) tactical bomber was designed for automatic terrain-following flight during low-level air defence penetration and strike, the Leningrad-based LNPO *Leninets* (Leninist), formerly NII-131 of the Ministry of Electronics Industry (MRP: *Ministerstvo rahdioelektronnoy promyshlennosti*),

Above left: LII's Su-15 '16 Blue' in standard configuration with AAMs

Left: The same aircraft as a test bed, with a pod for PPR-50 chaff bundles

Below left and *bottom*: Here, '16 Blue' is fitted with an IRCM flare pod, camera pods on the port fuselage pylon, and three of the four wing pylons (the port outer pylon carries a counterweight). Note also the angle reflector aft of the nose gear (to assist radar tracking from the ground) and the photo calibration markings on the fuselage and fin.

Top right and *above right*: Front and rear views of the same test bed

Right: Close-up of the pod for launching flares at three different angles

Far right, top: Photo calibration markings on the wings

Far right: Su-15 '16 Blue' fires PPI-50 IRCM flares.

Below right: '16 Blue' dispenses chaff.

Su-15 '16 Blue' (c/n 0615316) with an experimental IRCM flare dispenser pod and camera pods, LII

developed the PNS-24 Puma-A navigation/attack suite (*pritsel'no-navigatsionnaya sistema*) for it. The suite included the *Orion-A* primary radar and the *Rel'yef* (Surface profile) terrain avoidance radar, located above one another inside a common radome. (LNPO = *Leningrahdskoye naoochno-proizvodstvennoye obyedineniye*: Leningrad Scientific & Production Association. This company, which was one of the Soviet Union's leading avionics houses, is now the Leninets Holding Company.)

To put the Rel'yef radar through its paces, in May 1972 LNPO Leninets converted the abovementioned Su-15 c/n 0715311 into an avionics test bed designated SL-15R or T-58R. SL stood for *samolyot-laboratoriya* ('laboratory aircraft' or test bed), in keeping with LNPO Leninets's system of designating its avionics test beds, while the *R* suffix referred to the Rel'yef radar. The Oryol-D58M radar was replaced with a prototype Rel'yef radar; outwardly the SL-58R was no different from any production Su-15, since the experimental radar fitted well into the standard radome. The aircraft was equipped with a KT-61/3 nosewheel and KT-117 mainwheels. The tactical code was now changed to '11'.

Tests of the T-58R continued until 1975, whereupon the Rel'yef radar was verified on the actual Su-24 prototypes. Afterward the T-58R was relegated to the aforementioned PVO Junior Aviation Specialists' School (ShMAS) in Solntsevo as a ground instructional airframe.

Su-15 Communications Equipment Test Bed
Another Su-15 (identity unknown) was used in 1968–69 to test the new R-832M *Evkalipt-SM* (Eucalyptus-SM) command radio.

Su-15 Avionics Test Bed with IRST Unit
A production Su-15 (exact version unknown) was used as a test bed for an infrared search-and-track (IRST) unit designed as part of a fighter's weapons control system. The IRST enables the fighter to acquire and track a target covertly without switching on its radar and thereby revealing itself to the target, which may then take evasive action.

Su-15 Aerodynamics Research Aircraft for Spinning Tests and Uncontrollable-Roll Research
Two specially modified Su-15s were used for extensive aerodynamics research to investigate the aircraft's stability and control characteristics in certain flight modes. Thus the Flight Research Institute twice held spinning tests of the Su-15—in 1968, using an unidentified early-production aircraft with pure delta wings, and

in 1973, using the second production example of the double-delta version (the aforementioned '37 Red', c/n 1115337). Oleg V. Goodkov was project test pilot in both cases, but Igor' P. Volk performed part of the test programme on Su-15 c/n 1115337. A while earlier, in 1970, this aircraft was used to check the flight performance in minimum afterburner mode; in 1971 it was used to verify landing techniques developed for a fully forward-CG configuration. It was not until 1972 that Su-15 c/n 1115337 was equipped with PPR-90 spin recovery rockets (*protivoshtopornaya porokhovaya raketa*) under the wings, enabling high-alpha and spinning tests to be held. A similar spinning test programme was performed by GNIKI VVS, with Norair V. Kazarian as project test pilot.

The tests showed that considerable vibration set in when the aircraft approached critical AOAs, warning the pilot that he was 'pushing it too far'. Actually, the Su-15 could enter a spin only due to a grave piloting error or if the spin was intentional. The spinning characteristics of the two versions were similar, but the double-delta version was more stable during the spin.

Another test programme was held in response to a series of accidents in which the aircraft suddenly started rolling uncontrollably during vigorous manoeuvres at supersonic speeds, the pilots perceiving this as a critical control system failure. The second production Su-15 ('67 Red', c/n 0115302), which still had a test equipment suite from an earlier trials programme, was set aside to investigate the problem. In 1970–71 the Sukhoi OKB and LII held a joint test programme to determine the conditions in which this phenomenon occurred—first at subsonic speeds and then beyond Mach 1; Yevgeniy S. Solov'yov and Igor' P. Volk were the OKB's and LII's project test pilots, respectively. It was established that there were no control system failures at all—the cause was traced to a specific relationship of inertia forces along different axes; the pilots provoked the uncommanded roll by pulling negative g. The correct course of action in this situation was to reduce speed and set the controls to neutral.

T-58K Aerodynamics Research Aircraft with Modified Wings
In 1968 the Sukhoi OKB started work on modified wings featuring a sharp leading edge. By April 1973 this work reached the practice stage— the fourth production Su-15 (c/n 0115304) was converted into the T-58K research vehicle (the *K* stood for [*modifitseerovannoye*] *krylo*: [modified] wings). The boundary layer fences and missile pylons were deleted, the hardpoints being enclosed by special fairings, and a new extended leading-edge section with a more pointed profile was fitted. The BU-220 hydraulic actuators in the

tailplane control circuit were replaced by BU-250 units, and part of the standard avionics was replaced by test equipment and ballast. The T-58K underwent trials at LII in 1973–74.

Su-15 Cannon Armament Test Beds

Originally the Su-15's armament consisted solely of two air-to-air missiles, yet the military kept requesting that cannon armament be incorporated as well. At first the Sukhoi OKB intended to use a single GP-9 centreline cannon pod housing a 23 mm (.90 calibre) Gryazev/Shipunov GSh-23 twin-barrel cannon with 200 rounds. GP denotes *gondola **push**echnaya*, which translates (and is very conveniently deciphered) as 'gun pod'. The GP-9 was developed by OKB-134 (GMKB Vympel) for the MiG-21PFM Fishbed-F fighter, entering production at MMZ *Kommunar* ('member of the Paris Commune') in 1967. On the MiG-21 the pod was conformal, the flat top adhering to the fighter's fuselage underside. On the Su-15, however, for some reason the GP-9 was attached via a tapered adapter, the pod's rear end hanging in thin air.

After a series of tests on Su-15 c/n 0515328, the GP-9 was found suitable for the Su-15, and the Novosibirsk aircraft factory even built ten batch 12 aircraft with the appropriate attachment fittings and connectors. These ten fighters served with the 166th GvIAP—a PVO unit at Sandar AB in Marneuli, Georgia. However, no more GP-9 pods were delivered to Su-15 units—a strange fact, considering that the VVS's tactical fighter units equipped with the MiG-21S (which, too, was originally armed only with two AAMs) received these pods.

By then, however, the military had changed their requirements; the UPK-23-250 pod, containing the same cannon but with 250 rounds instead of 200, became the Su-15's standard cannon armament. In addition to the greater ammunition supply, the UPK-23-250 could be fitted and removed easily (unlike the GP-9); most importantly, two such pods could be carried on the Su-15's fuselage hardpoints instead of drop tanks, giving twice the firepower.

A production Su-15 (c/n 1115342) was set aside for cannon armament tests, passing its state acceptance trials between March and September 1971. Even though aiming accuracy with the Su-15's standard K-10T sight left a lot to be desired, the cannon pod installation was recommended for use against both air and ground targets. Since production of the basic Su-15 *sans suffixe* had ended by then, these aircraft were retrofitted with UPK-23-250 pods in service.

Su-15 with Wing Cannons (Project)

In 1968–69 the Sukhoi OKB first considered the idea of equipping the Su-15 with a built-in cannon. A bay envisaged in the starboard wing root was to house a 23 mm *izdeliye* 225P cannon freshly developed by Aron A. Rikhter at OKB-16 in Tula, a city renowned for its armourers. (OKB-16 is now called KB Tochmash, *Konstrooktorskoye byuro tochnovo mashinostroyeniya*: Precision Machinery Design Bureau, named after Aleksandr E. Nudelman.) Code-named *Kartech* (Buckshot), the *izdeliye* 225P revolver cannon was an experimental derivative of the production Rikhter R-23 (*izdeliye* 261P), from which it differed in having a cylinder with five chambers instead of four and using standardised rounds rather than unique ones. It was a fairly compact cannon with a high rate

Top and *above*: A GP-9 cannon pod fitted experimentally to Su-15 c/n 0515328. Note the adapter between the pod and the fuselage.

of fire. Yet, accommodating the ammunition supply proved to be an insurmountable task; the engine inlet duct rendered a fuselage location of the ammo box impossible, and there was no room for it inside the Su-15's thin wing, and eventually the idea was dropped.

T-58VD Experimental STOL Aircraft

In early 1965, when the T58D-1 had completed a brief flight test programme with the new double-delta wings, the OKB decided to use this aircraft as a propulsion systems test bed and a STOL technology demonstrator in conjunction with the development of the T-58M low-altitude attack aircraft. (The latter designation proved to be short lived; the T-58M, which later became the T-6, was a totally unrelated design and a much-larger aircraft that evolved into the Su-24 tactical bomber and lies outside the scope of this book.) This involved installing small turbojet engines vertically inside the fuselage to generate lift. The lift-jet concept was quite popular then both in and outside the Soviet Union. Western development aircraft making use of lift engines included the Dassault Balzac supersonic fighter and the Short SC.1 technology demonstrator, although both of them were vertical takeoff and landing (VTOL), not STOL, aircraft.

On 6 May 1965, MAP issued an order requiring the Sukhoi OKB to build and test a proof-of-concept vehicle in order to verify the STOL technology using lift jets. The engineers set to work; by midyear they had completed the project documents for converting the T58D-1 into such a vehicle. The extensive conversion involved remanufacturing

Above left: The specially built ground test rig at MMZ No. 51 for preliminary testing of the T-58VD's power plant, seen in the winter of 1966. It featured an NK-12 turboprop with AV-60 contrarotating props to emulate the slipstream.

Above: The T-58VD parked behind the rig beneath a special shed, hiding it from surveillance satellites

Left: This view of the T-58VD with safety nets in front of the cruise engine air intakes for a ground run shows well the redesigned wide fuselage, the lift engine air intake doors, and the double-delta wings.

Here the T-58VD is shown parked at Zhukovskiy.

the centre fuselage to accommodate three 2,350 kgp (5,180 lbst) RD36-35 turbojets developed by the Rybinsk-based OKB-36 under Pyotr A. Kolesov; some sources state the thrust as 2,540 kgp (5,600 lbst) each. The lift engines were installed in a bay between the cruise engines' inlet ducts, with the shafts inclined forward 10°, breathing through two large scoop-type intakes on the fuselage's upper surface (the forward intake served the foremost engine, and the rear intake the other two). The exhaust aperture featured louvres that had two operational settings, directing the jet exhaust aft on takeoff (to add a measure of forward thrust) or forward on landing (to slow the aircraft down). In cruise flight (in 'clean' configuration) the lift jets' intakes and exhaust louvres closed flush with the fuselage skin.

A rare colour photo of the T-58VD undergoing unpaved runway tests at Zhukovskiy. The open lift engine air intakes are visible.

The T-58VD development aircraft in early colours

The same aircraft in an interim finish with no code

The T-58VD in late colours, as it appeared at the Domodedovo airshow on 9 July 1967

To make room for the lift engine bay, the cruise engines were shifted outward, but the afterburners stayed put and were connected to the engines by adapters in the form of dogleg ducts made of heat-resistant steel. For the same reason the upper pair of airbrakes were built into large fairings, finding themselves outside the normal fuselage contour. The conversion also included modifications to the wings, relocation of various equipment and piping, etc.

All fuel was now carried in the wing tanks—and that means less fuel and three more engines guzzling away at it. But then, range and endurance were not crucial for a pure technology demonstrator that was not meant to operate far away from its base.

Designated T-58VD (for *vertikahl'nyye dvigateli*: 'vertical engines'; that is, lift jets), the rebuilt aircraft was completed at the

end of 1965, commencing tethered tests on a purpose-built ground rig on the Sukhoi OKB's premises; Roman G. Yarmarkov retained his assignment as this aircraft's engineer in charge of the tests. The rig featured an 'open-air wind tunnel'—a 12,000 ehp Kuznetsov NK-12 turboprop engine driving ducted AV-60 contrarotating propellers emulated the slipstream at simulated speeds up to 400 km/h (248 mph), creating proper operating conditions for the lift engines. The pad on which the aircraft sat was rigged with pressure sensors to record the off-loading of the landing gear and thus assess the efficiency of the lift engines.

The tethered tests allowed the T-58VD's aerodynamics, with the lift engines running, to be explored and the operation of all principal systems to be checked. Unfortunately they were marred

Here the T-58VD is seen in 1966 or early 1967, showing a revised colour scheme with a sloping colour division line on the nose and no tactical code or photo calibration markings. Note the 'towel rail' data link aerial.

Below: A side view of the T-58VD. Note the bulged fairings on the rear fuselage sides, to which the upper pair of airbrakes have been displaced by the more widely spaced cruise engines.

Left: A three-quarters rear view of the T-58VD

Below left: This view with all engines running illustrates the lift engine air intakes and the narrower-than-usual cruise engine blow-in doors.

Below: A further series of unpaved runway tests, with the T-58VD in its definitive colour scheme

Opposite page, above / above right: The T-58VD makes a demo flight at Domodedovo on 9 July 1967.

Right and *far right*: The T-58VD as an teaching aid at MAI in the 1970s

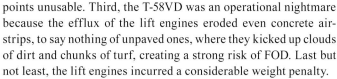

by a tragic incident in February 1966. A mechanic from the OKB's propulsion laboratory was careless enough to approach the aircraft's forward fuselage when the blower was running; the powerful stream of air immediately swept him off his feet and hurled him savagely against the aircraft, killing him.

On 26 April 1966, upon completion of the ground test phase, the aircraft was trucked to LII. After a series of high-speed runs and short hops, on 6 June the T-58VD made its first flight in the hands of Yevgeniy S. Solov'yov on the power of the cruise engines only. Flights with the lift jets running began at the end of June. Later, the T-58VD was flown by both Solov'yov and Sukhoi OKB chief test pilot Vladimir S. Ilyushin; by the end of the year it had made 37 real flights and 19 taxi runs and short hops, including high-speed runs on a dirt strip at Zhukovskiy. The manufacturer's flight tests showed that the lift created by the auxiliary engines reduced the unstick speed from 390 to 285 km/h (from 242 to 177 mph) and the landing speed from 315 to 225 km/h (from 195 to 139 mph). The takeoff run was shortened from 1,170 to 500 m (from 3,840 to 1,640 ft.), and the landing run from 1,000 to 560 m (from 3,280 to 1,840 ft.)—an impressive result.

On the other hand, it became apparent that the chosen location of the lift jets was not the optimum one, since the thrust of the forward lift engine caused a strong tendency to pitch up during landing approach. The problem was solved by using only the centre and rear lift jets for landing. Second, the lift jets caused strong heating of the adjoining structure and rendered the fuselage hard-

points unusable. Third, the T-58VD was an operational nightmare because the efflux of the lift engines eroded even concrete airstrips, to say nothing of unpaved ones, where they kicked up clouds of dirt and chunks of turf, creating a strong risk of FOD. Last but not least, the lift engines incurred a considerable weight penalty.

On 9 July 1967 the T-58VD participated in the airshow at Moscow-Domodedovo, giving a short takeoff and landing demonstration with Yevgeniy S. Solov'yov at the controls. After that, the STOL version received the reporting name 'Flagon-B' in the mistaken belief it was an operational version.

The results of the T-58VD's flight tests gave the Sukhoi OKB valuable experience in designing, building, and testing STOL aircraft and allowed the test pilots to master the technique of flying such aircraft. This knowledge was incorporated into the design of the delta-wing T6-1 strike aircraft prototype. However, once again the trade-off for the good short-field performance turned out to be too high; the lift engines dramatically reduced the space available for fuel while significantly increasing fuel consumption on takeoff and landing. Also, running the lift jets impaired longitudinal stability somewhat, and in cruise mode they were just a lot of useless weight, reducing the payload. Hence, the second prototype, the T6-2I, was radically reworked to feature variable-geometry wings, which gave the desired results, and this configuration was cleared for further development and production as the Su-24.

Upon completion of the test programme the T-58VD was retired. In 1976 it was donated to the Moscow Aviation Institute

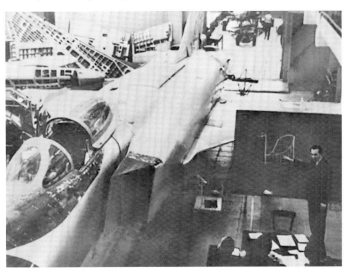

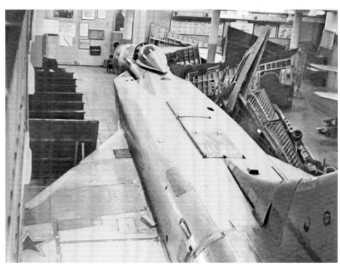

(MAI), where it served as an instructional airframe for a while— or, as local wits put it, an illustration of how not to build an aircraft. Sadly, in 1980 this unique aircraft was scrapped to free up space for new teaching aids in the MAI hangar; it could, and should, have found a place in a museum.

Su-15 CCV with a Side Stick

In 1980 the Sukhoi OKB converted a production Su-15 (c/n 1115328) into a control configured vehicle with variable in-flight stability and controllability parameters. For the first time in Soviet aircraft design practice, the CCV featured a side-stick controller. The standard centrally mounted stick was retained and the pilot was able to switch the control system from one stick to the other as required.

The aircraft underwent tests at LII in 1981–82; it was flown by LII test pilots Vladislav I. Loychikov, Rimantas-Antanas A. Stankeavicius, Anatoliy S. Levchenko, Igor' P. Volk, Aleksandr V. Shchookin, Viktor V. Zabolotskiy, and Yuriy A. Oosikov. Unfortunately, on 11 November 1982 the CCV crashed and was destroyed before the test programme could be completed. A malfunction in the control system caused the aircraft to start rolling crazily; Oosikov ejected but sustained serious injuries that forced him to give up flying.

Su-15 Multirole Test Bed ('Aircraft 0009')

As already mentioned, tests of the R13-300 engines on Su-15 c/n 0715311 revealed a tendency to flame out at high Mach numbers, because the air intakes were too small. Hence, in 1970 the Sukhoi OKB modified a further production Su-15 (c/n 1315340) to feature widened air intakes, which were later incorporated on the production Su-15TM. For security reasons this aircraft was referred to at the OKB as 'aircraft 0009' (possibly with a view to fooling would-be spies into thinking it was the aircraft's c/n). After fairly lengthy manufacturer's tests the aircraft was turned over to GNIKI VVS, making 44 test flights there between mid-May and August 1971 as part of the Su-15TM's state acceptance trials. The aircraft showed encouraging performance in comparison with the Su-15TM prototype ('37 Red', c/n 0115305), which featured narrow intakes (see later); acceleration at supersonic speeds was improved, the service ceiling increased from 17,600 to 18,500 m (from 57,740 to 60,695 ft.), and effective range increased to 1,680 km (1,040 miles).

In June 1972, 'aircraft 0009' was used to test the new ogival radome developed for the Su-15TM.

Su-15 Missile Armament Test Beds

When the Su-15TM, armed with R-98M missiles, entered service, it was decided to adapt existing Su-15s *sans suffixe* equipped with the Oryol-D58 radar for using this missile, which was originally designed for use with the *Taifoon* (Typhoon) radar. To this end a late-production Su-15 (c/n 1415301) was modified in 1975, successfully passing a special test programme.

By the early 1970s the **Molniya** (Lightning) OKB had completed development of the R-60 agile short-range AAM, and the air force selected it as the main close-in weapon for all Soviet fighter types. After the R-60 had been tested on the Su-15TM, it

was decided to arm the Su-15 *sans suffixe* with this missile as well. A suitably modified early-production Su-15 (c/n 0615327) was tested successfully in 1978–79; the air force's aircraft overhaul plants started upgrading Su-15s with launch rails for two R-60s. A configuration with four R-60s on APU-60-2 paired launchers (*aviatsionnoye pooskovoye oostroystvo*: aircraft-mounted launcher) was also tested but did not find its way into service.

T-58N Experimental Nuclear-Strike Aircraft

Until the 1970s the Soviet air force required virtually all Soviet fighter types to be capable of carrying small-calibre (that is, tactical) nuclear bombs—originally because no supersonic tactical bombers existed, and then probably as an insurance policy in case the bombers were destroyed by enemy strikes. Fighters adapted for the 'nuke 'em' role received the suffix letter *N* to the designation, standing for *nositel'*: literally, 'carrier'; that is, delivery vehicle for *special stores* (*spetsizdeliya*), as the nuclear munitions were coyly referred to in Soviet terminology.

The Su-15 also 'fell victim' to this trend. It is known that a single Su-15 was modified as the T-58N tactical nuclear-strike aircraft. No details have been disclosed to date, except that when the aircraft was written off upon completion of the tests, its wings were used for building the U-58B combat trainer prototype.

Su-15UT Conversion Trainer (U-58T, *izdeliye* 42)

It so happened that dual-control trainer versions of Soviet combat aircraft usually appeared much later than the baseline single-seaters for some reason. The Su-15 was no exception.

The first project studies of a two-seat trainer version of the T-58 dated back to 1961–62, but the design work had to be suspended due to pressure of higher-priority programmes. Hence, in keeping with the well-established tradition, the Su-15 had to be mastered by service units without the benefit of a trainer. Officially, development of the trainer version was initiated only on 30 April 1965 by a special item of the aforementioned C of M directive clearing the Su-15 for service. The appropriate MAP order appeared on 20 May 1965, requiring OKB-51 to build two prototypes and a static-test airframe; all three were to be manufactured by the Novosibirsk aircraft factory, and the prototypes were to commence state acceptance trials in the second quarter of 1967. In similar manner to the Su-9U trainer, which had the in-house designation U-43 (*oochebnyy* [*samolyot*]) to identify it as a trainer version of the T-43), the new two-seater received the manufacturer's designation U-58 (that is, trainer version of the T-58).

Design work on the trainer version continued for the greater part of 1965; the in-house project review and the sessions of the mockup review commission took place in October. Since the U-58 was intended for training pilots both in flying the aircraft and in combat tactics, it was to retain the complete avionics and armament fit of the single-seater and have similar performance.

The trainer differed from the basic version in having a second cockpit for the instructor; this required a 450 mm (1 ft., 5¾ in.) fuselage stretch to be made aft of the existing cockpit, and the capacity of the no. 1 fuselage fuel tank to be reduced. The cockpits were enclosed by a common canopy similar to that of the Su-9U, with individual aft-hinged portions and a fixed section in between.

Right: The Su-15UT trainer prototype (U58T-1) at Zhukovskiy during manufacturer's tests. The R-98 missiles are dummy versions. Note also the lack of the 'hockey stick' aerial of the ARL-SM GCI data link receiver.

Below: The U58T-1 ('01 Red') had pure delta wings. The front cockpit was glazed much more extensively than the rear one. Note the 'towel rail' data link aerial of the test equipment suite beneath the air intake.

Each cockpit featured a full set of controls and flight instruments and a KS-4 ejection seat. Importantly, the canopy of the rear cockpit incorporated a retractable periscope to give the instructor a measure of forward view during takeoff and landing; the Su-9U had no such luxury. Changes were made to certain other systems.

The avionics and equipment were to match those of the late-production (double delta) Su-15. Thus the trainer was meant to be armed with R-98 AAMs and equipped with a *Korshun-58* (Kite, the bird) fire control radar, an advanced derivative of the Oryol-D58.

A full set of manufacturing documents for the U-58 were delivered to the Sukhoi OKB's Novosibirsk branch office by September 1966. By then it was obvious that the manufacture of the trainer airframes at the plant was running behind schedule, and the delivery dates were slipping (hence the deadlines of the state acceptance trials would have to be moved). Also, in 1967 the air force demanded that the new Taifoon fire control radar be integrated on the upgraded (double delta) Su-15 instead of the Korshun radar; this meant the Taifoon would have to be fitted to the trainer as well, causing further delays. Hence the OKB suggested splitting the U-58 programme into two stages to speed up progress—a suggestion gladly accepted by MAP. Stage 1 involved developing a simplified conversion trainer lacking radar and some other equip-

The Su-15UT trainer prototype (U58T-1)

Above and *left*: An uncoded production Su-15UT (c/n 0815311) with double-delta wings. The aircraft was involved in a test programme of some sort.

Opposite page: Three views of a production Su-15UT coded '02'. The wing planform is clearly visible in the upper view.

ment items; these would be integrated during stage 2 to create a fully capable combat trainer.

The downgraded conversion trainer variant received the manufacturer's designation U-58T and the service designation Su-15UT (*oochebno-trenirovochnyy*: for [conversion and proficiency] training) to indicate it had no combat capability. The aircraft featured the single-seat Su-15's standard navigation and communications suite but lacked the fire control radar, ARL-SM Lazoor'-M GCI command link system, radar-warning receiver, and missile-arming / launch system modules. On the other hand, the avionics were augmented by the addition of an SPU-9 intercom and an MS-61 cockpit voice recorder. The bottom line was that the trainer's avionics fit was rather basic. Like the single-seater, the Su-15UT had wing pylons, but the trainer could carry only dummy weapons— even though, in theory, there were no obstacles to making it capable of using IR-homing AAMs. The addition of a second cockpit reduced the capacity of the no. 1 fuselage fuel tank by 900 litres (198 Imp gal.); by way of partial compensation, a fifth fuel tank holding 180 litres (39.6 Imp gal.) was added in the rear fuselage beneath the engines. All of this caused a rearward shift in the CG position, which was restored by installing a counterweight in the forward fuselage. Empty weight increased to 10,660 kg (23,500 lbs.); this, together with a reduction of the fuel load to 5,100 kg (11,240 lbs.), entailed a substantial reduction in range.

The static-test example of the U-58T was completed in late 1967. Designated **U58T-1**, the prototype (c/n 0015301) followed in the summer of 1968; the aircraft had pure delta wings, and the BLC system was inactive. A group of Sukhoi OKB specialists headed by engineer in charge L. A. Ryumin arrived from Moscow in early August to take charge of the aircraft. Yevgeniy K. Kukushev was

appointed project test pilot, performing the maiden flight on 26 August; sometime before 16 September he flew the aircraft to Zhukovskiy. The OKB was unable to hold a full-scale manufacturer's test programme there because MAP kept urging that state acceptance trials begin as soon as possible; thus, as early as 2 October the U58T-1 was ferried to GNIKI VVS at Vladimirovka AB. Manufacturer's tests continued there, proceeding in parallel with the state acceptance trials and ending on 12 December 1968.

Between 15 and 19 October 1968 the U58T-1 was test flown by a number of service pilots from operational PVO units, including the new IA PVO commander in chief Lt.-Gen. Anatoliy L. Kadomtsev. The actual flights under the state acceptance trials programme did not begin until 16 November. GNIKI VVS project test pilots Mikhail I. Bobrovitskiy, Gheorgiy A. Bayevskiy, and Nikolay V. Rukhlyadko did the testing, additional test flights being made by Stepan A. Mikoyan, Andrey A. Manucharov, Vasiliy S. Kotlov, and Vyacheslav V. Mayorov. The programme included performance testing, assessment of field performance, stability, and handling; part of it was performed by OKB test pilots, as was customary. One of the flights on 20 January 1969 nearly ended in an accident; after a mission involving a series of high-g manoeuvres, OKB test pilot Yevgeniy K. Kukushev discovered that the main landing-gear units would not extend. The pilot again resorted to vigorous manoeuvring, and the g-force wrenched the gear loose on the fifth try, after which the aircraft landed normally. It turned out that the gaps between the main gear doors and the wheel well walls were too small; this had not caused any trouble until then, the defect surfacing only when the aircraft was subjected to high g-loads.

The state acceptance trials were completed on 26 February 1969. Predictably, the two-seater's performance was inferior

to that of the single-seater: range had dropped to 1,390 km (863 miles) and the service ceiling had decreased to 17,700 m (58,070 ft.). The stability and handling were deemed acceptable, except that some directional instability set in above Mach 1, which was a serious drawback. Generally, however, GNIKI VVS stated that the Su-15UT was suitable as a pilot trainer except for weapons training, which was beyond the aircraft's capabilities.

The final protocol of the state commission was signed in the summer of 1969, whereupon the OKB set to work eliminating the deficiencies discovered in the course of the trials. These included the instability mentioned above, and the cause was clear—the vertical tail area was too small, now that the fuselage was stretched and the area ahead of the CG had increased. Increasing the vertical tail area by inserting another 'plug' at the root, as had been the case in the Su-15's early flight test days, was impossible for reasons of structural strength. The OKB decided to try equipping the Su-15UT with ventral fins. In the spring of 1970, OKB test pilots Yevgeniy S. Solov'yov and A. N. Isakov performed a special test programme in the suitably modified U58T-1, comparing the aircraft's handling with and without ventral fins. It turned out that the fins did not give any major improvement; therefore the OKB and the air force compromised, limiting the trainer's maximum permissible speed to Mach 1.75. Consequently the service ceiling further decreased to

16,700 m (54,790 ft.), since the above figure of 17,700 m had been obtained at Mach 1.9, using the standard climb technique.

The Su-15UT entered full-scale production in 1969 under the in-house product code *izdeliye* 42. The first production aircraft (c/n 0115301, often shortened to 0101) was completed in October, making its first flight on 10 December with factory test pilots Vladimir T. Vylomov and V. A. Belyanin at the controls. Production examples differed from the prototype in having double-delta wings and an operational boundary layer control system. The first

The one-off U-58B combat trainer prototype, '70 Blue', as it appeared during flight tests

five Su-15UTs were delivered to operational units in the spring of 1970; in July that year the aircraft was officially included into the inventory pursuant to Ministry of Defence order no. 0115.

Shortly afterward the Su-15UT passed a separate spinning test programme. Since the trainer's directional stability parameters were different from those of the single-seater, it was thought that the spinning characteristics might be different too.

The Su-15UT remained in production until the end of 1972; a total of 148 were built. The final batches featured a new R-832M Evkalipt-SMU command radio, replacing the earlier R-802V; also, in the course of production the rear aerials of the SRO-2 IFF transponder were relocated from the top of the fin to the base of the rudder (above the brake parachute container). The empty operating weight of the production model grew to 10,750 kg (23,700 lbs.).

In addition to first-line units, a number of Su-15UTs were delivered to the PVO's Stavropol' Military Pilot College (SV VAUL: ***Stav***ropol'skoye **vys**sheye **vo**yennoye aviatsion*noye oochilischche lyot*chikov) and the Test Pilots School in Zhukovskiy (ShLI: ***Shko***la lyot*chikov-ispytah*teley), the Soviet/Russian counterpart of the UK's Empire Test Pilots' School (ETPS). Unfortunately, on 17 April 1987 a Su-15UT operated by ShLI suffered a critical failure; the crew ejected but cadet A. V. Chechoolin lost his life.

The Su-15UT had the NATO reporting name 'Flagon-C'.

U-58B Combat Trainer Prototype (*izdeliye* 37UB)

Completed much later than intended due to late deliveries of the mission avionics, a single Su-15 was built as a fully capable combat trainer designated U-58B (*boyevoy*: combat, used attribu-

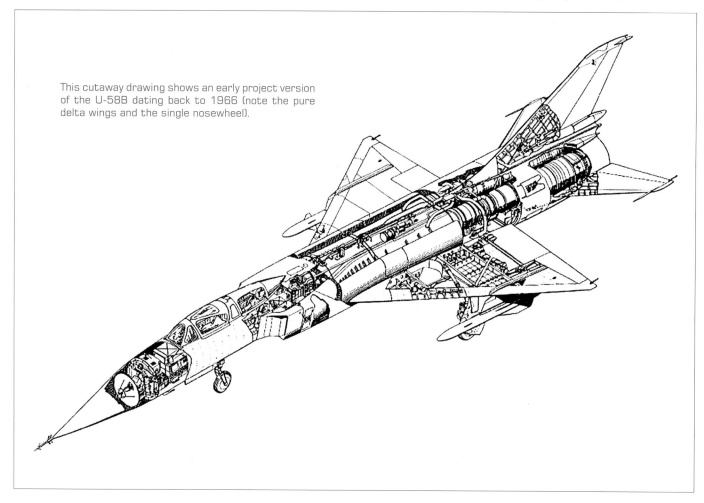

This cutaway drawing shows an early project version of the U-58B dating back to 1966 (note the pure delta wings and the single nosewheel).

Above and *above right*: Rare pictures of the U-58B in flight during trials

Right: Another air-to-air view of the U-58B

Below right: A rare colour photo of the U-58B as an instructional airframe at the Solntsevo ShMAS, showing the twin-wheel nose gear unit

Bottom right: The U-58B in derelict condition after the closure of the school

tively). It was known at the Novosibirsk aircraft factory as *izdeliye* 37UB (*oochebno-boyevoy* [*samolyot*]: combat trainer); somewhat surprisingly, the product code was derived from that of the single-seater, not of the Su-15UT. Bearing the tactical code '70 Blue' and the nonstandard alphanumeric c/n 0003UB86, the aircraft entered flight test in the summer of 1970. On 24 June the U-58B made its first flight in the hands of factory test pilot Aleksey S. Gribachov and was ferried to the OKB's flight test facility in Zhukovskiy on 2 August. Originally it was powered by R11F2S-300 engines, but these were replaced by R11F2SU-300s in May 1971, allowing the BLC system to be activated.

Outwardly the U-58B was identifiable by the reinforced nose gear unit with twin KN-9 wheels, identical to that of the T-58L development aircraft. Unlike the latter, however, the purpose of this modification was to cater for the higher weight on the nose gear due to the installation of the radar in the forward fuselage. The main gear units featured KT-117 wheels, and the wings were taken from the T-58N development aircraft, which had been cannibalised after completing its flight test programme. A further identification feature was the cine camera in a pylon-mounted pod, offset to starboard under the nose, to capture missile launches.

As already mentioned, the Su-15UT was 'tail heavy', requiring the provision of ballast in the nose. The U-58B, on the contrary, was 'nose heavy' due to the combination of the second cockpit and the fire control radar; with the CG located well forward, it was as sluggish as a wet sponge and generally disappointing in its performance. At the initiative of the OKB, with MAP's formal consent, the U-58B's development programme was suspended; a while later the military also agreed with this decision. After sitting in storage at the OKB's flight test facility for a while, the aircraft was transferred to the Solntsevo ShMAS as a ground instructional airframe, the tactical code being amended to '70 Red'.

Su-15UT Research Aircraft for Exploring Weather Minima

In 1973 LII used a suitably modified Su-15UT (c/n 0815315) to conduct research for the purpose of determining the weather minima in which aircraft could take off and land safely. For example, the Su-15's weather minima were 250 × 2,000 m (that is, cloudbase 250 m / 820 ft. and horizontal visibility 2,000 m / 1.24 miles) in the daytime, and 350 × 3,000 m (1,150 ft. × 1.86 miles) at night; for the Su-15TM interceptor, equipped with the RSBN-5S short-range radio navigation system (and described later in this chapter), the minima were 60 × 800 m (200 ft. × 0.5 mile).

Tragically, one of the test missions on 29 October 1975, aimed at reducing the type's weather minima, ended in a crash in which LII test pilot Ivan V. Makedon and 148th TsBP i PLS pilot Rudol'f N. Zoobov were fatally injured. Landing with the blind-flying hood closed and a simulated control system actuator failure, Zoobov (who was the pilot in command) inadvertently increased the sink rate from the required 5–6 m/sec. (980–1,180 ft./min.) to 10 m/sec. (1,970 ft./min.) and then to 15 m/sec. (2,950 ft./min.). Despite corrective action the aircraft landed hard between the outer and inner marker beacons, undershooting by 1,400 m (4,590 ft.); next thing, it collided with the elevated edge of a concrete road and burst into flames, both pilots being thrown clear of the cockpit before the machine came to a halt. The crew were rushed to hospital but Zoobov was dead on arrival; Makedon succumbed to his injuries on 23 November.

Su-15T Interceptor (T-58T, Su-15 Stage II Upgrade, *izdeliye* 37M or '*izdeliye* 37 Srs M', *izdeliye* 38)

As already noted, the military were not completely happy with the performance of the production Su-15; the type was due for a midlife update. Such an upgrade was developed in due course, and in contemporaneous documents the upgraded aircraft was referred to as the ***Su***-*pyatnadtsat' vtorovo etapa* ('Su-15 stage II'). The requirements for this version were outlined by the aforementioned C of M directive of 30 April 1965. At that time the Sukhoi OKB was swamped with work, being busy with such programmes as the T-4 (*izdeliye* 100) Mach 3 missile strike aircraft, the S-22I 'swing-wing' fighter-bomber (the Su-17 prototype), the T-58M attack aircraft project (soon to be redesignated T-6), etc., so it was less than overjoyed at the prospect of having to upgrade the Su-15.

Most of the design work on the Su-15 upgrade proceeded on a 'time permitting' basis due to the programme's low-priority status. Actually, the work did not begin in earnest until early 1966, and even then for the first two years it made painfully slow progress. The reason was that the type of radar to be fitted was not decided on for a long time.

In mid-1966 the OKB started detail design work on incorporating the new advanced Korshun-58 fire control radar, the SAU-58 AFCS, the RSBN-5S *Iskra* (Spark) short-range radio navigation system (RSBN = ***rahdiotekhnicheskaya sistema blizhney navigahtsiï***: SHORAN), a new communications radio, and a skid landing gear on the Su-15. Later the military belatedly discovered that the Korshun radar could not provide the required performance; the attention now focused on the Smerch radar designed for installation in the Mikoyan Ye-155P heavy interceptor (the future

MiG-25P). As a result, in October 1967, when the OKB had all but completed the project documents for the installation of new systems and equipment on the Su-15, it was greeted by a joint ruling by several ministries to the effect that all work on the Korshun-58 radar be stopped and the fighter be equipped with the Taifoon fire control radar (a scaled-down derivative of the Smerch) instead. Officially this change was documented by a ruling of the Military Industry Commission on 22 March 1968. Thanks a bunch. It was back to the drawing board for Sukhoi.

The upgrade programme was divided into two stages. Stage 1 involved state acceptance trials of the aircraft with the existing R-98 AAMs in November 1968; during the second stage, scheduled for the third quarter of 1969, the aircraft was to be armed with the new K-98M missile (which had not yet passed its state acceptance trials either). The aircraft modified to stage 1 specifications was to be designated Su-15T, the suffix letter referring to the Taifoon radar, while the stage 2 aircraft would be designated Su-15TM, the *M* denoting *modernizeerovannyy* (updated). This gave the avionics and defence industry a respite, allowing the aircraft's new avionics and armament to be put through their paces.

The Sukhoi OKB had no choice but to rework the project documents all over again. The advanced development project of the Su-15T interceptor (known in-house as the T-58T) was completed by early September 1968, the in-house project review and the sessions of the mockup review commission taking place in October. The aircraft was to be powered by the new and more powerful Gavrilov R13-300 engines; changes to the hydraulics and electrics were also envisaged.

The military demanded that both the Su-15T and the Su-15TM should have a secondary strike capability that would make them usable by the Soviet air force's tactical arm (FA: *Frontovaya aviahtsiya*). The weapons options in strike configuration were one or two 500 kg (1,102 lb.) bombs; up to four 100 or 250 kg (220 or 551 lb.) bombs; one or two UB-16-57U rocket pods (*oonifitseerovannyy blok*: standardised [rocked] pod), each holding sixteen 57 mm (2.24 in.) S-5 FFARs; one or two S-24 heavy unguided rockets; and two UPK-23-250 cannon pods (these were to be carried under the wings, not on the fuselage hardpoints). The possibility of incorporating an internal cannon was also considered.

The control system was also to be modified by incorporating the servo drives of the SAU-58 AFCS, which was finally nearing the end of its development at the Sukhoi OKB. Apart from the usual speed/altitude/angle stabilisation and 'panic button' (automatic restoration of straight and level flight) functions typical of any automatic flight control system, the SAU-58 was to enable automatic flight along several preset trajectories and automate the main stages of the interception process. Additionally, the AFCS was to enable automatic low-level terrain-following flight. This totally new feature was not meant for air defence penetration, of course; rather it resulted from the customer's new stringent requirement that the upgraded Su-15 was to be capable of intercepting targets flying at altitudes right down to 500 m (1,640 ft.). Since the Taifoon radar still lacked 'look-down/shoot-down' capability, the intention was to 'paint' the targets from below, flying at altitudes less than 500 m. This meant flying dangerously close to the terrain at speeds close to 1,000 km/h (620 mph), and the pilot had to work the radar all the while! Hence, the OKB opted for a simpler version of the

Su-15T '37 Red'

AFCS, using the radio altimeter, not the radar, as the primary source of data; this made flight level stabilisation possible, but the feature was usable only over flat or very moderately hilly terrain.

The 'Su-15 stage II' was to feature a new R-832M Evkalipt-SM command radio, replacing the earlier R-802V, a Pion-GT (Peony, pronounced *pee on* . . . sorry) antenna / feeder system combining the receiver and transmitter antennas of various avionics into a single ensemble for greater reliability, built-in test equipment (BITE), and an RSBN-5S Iskra-K SHORAN. The latter enabled semiautomatic landing approach down to 50–60 m (165–200 ft.), improving the aircraft's all-weather capability considerably.

An early-production pure-delta Su-15 (c/n 0515348) was converted as the Su-15T prototype; for security reasons this aircraft was referred to at the OKB as **'aircraft 0006'**. With the air force's consent, the prototype entered test with an incomplete avionics fit, lacking the BITE and SHORAN, among other things; nor were the R13-300 engines (the prototype was powered by R11F2S-300s), skid landing gear, and strike armament installed. On the other hand, the aircraft was rewinged, receiving double-delta wings; a prototype Taifoon radar, the SAU-58 AFCS, and a twin-wheel nose gear unit were installed.

On the night of 4 January 1969 the modified aircraft was trucked to the flight test facility in Zhukovskiy. Vladimir A. Krechetov was appointed project test pilot for the manufacturer's test phase, with M. L. Belen'kiy as engineer in charge. According to some documents, the Su-15T made its maiden flight on 27 January; however, Krechetov's flight log says 31 January. As the mili-

tary kept pushing the Sukhoi OKB to submit the fighter for state acceptance trials, the manufacturer's tests were suspended after only eight flights, and on 6 March 1969, Krechetov flew the Su-15T prototype to GNIKI VVS.

The acceptance procedure dragged on until the end of May; meanwhile the OKB carried on with the manufacturer's flight tests. IA PVO vice commander Col.-Gen. Fyodor I. Smetanin was chosen to chair the state commission, while R. N. Lazarev headed the air force's flight test team. The latter included GNIKI VVS test pilots Stal' A. Lavrent'yev, Eduard M. Kolkov, Vadim I. Petrov, and Stepan A. Mikoyan, as well as OKB test pilot Vladimir A. Krechetov. The trials proceeded in two stages, the first of which was to be completed in the first quarter of 1970.

The state acceptance trials of the Su-15T prototype were a far cry from those of the original T-58D, proceeding slowly and laboriously. The main objective of the trials was to assess the interceptor's combat capabilities with the new radar. Here there would appear to be no pitfalls, since fire control radars broadly similar to the Taifoon had been verified on the production Tu-128 heavy interceptor and the Ye-155P, which had passed its trials successfully. Nevertheless the Taifoon radar turned out to be rather troublesome. By the end of the year the prototype had made 64 flights, but only 40 of them counted, the other 24 missions apparently being aborted due to malfunctions (or being training flights and the like). To avoid delaying the Su-15T's production entry, GNIKI VVS decided to issue a so-called preliminary report; in February 1970, stage A of the trials was discontinued altogether. The report

'77 Red', a production Su-15T, shows the combination of the conical radome and the tall twin-wheel nose gear unit. Note that the nose probe carries the aerials of the Pion-GT antenna / feeder system at the root but no pitch/yaw transducers closer to the tip.

said that only 63 of the 87 flights made had proceeded in accordance with the plan of the trials, the remainder being devoted to refining the radar and the AFCS. Eventually the OKB managed to get the interceptor's principal systems up to scratch, and the aircraft was ready for stage B of the trials.

Here we have to go back a bit. In December 1969 the Sukhoi OKB completed the second T-58T prototype converted from the fifth production Su-15 (c/n 0115305); A. Sholosh was appointed engineer in charge of this aircraft's test programme. This aircraft was actually not a Su-15T but the Su-15TM prototype and featured an almost complete avionics and equipment fit, including R13-300 engines and an upgraded RP-26 Taifoon-M radar, compatible with K-98M missiles instead of the basic Taifoon. Since the state acceptance trials of the first prototype Su-15T were running late, it was decided that the second prototype should join the programme at this stage. Due to development problems with a number of systems, it was more than three months before the second prototype could enter flight test; the aircraft first flew on 7 April 1970 with Vladimir A. Krechetov at the controls. Four days later it was ferried to GNIKI VVS at Vladimirovka AB. By then the institute had been conducting live weapons tests and combat tactics verification with the first aircraft for more than three weeks, in accordance with stage B of the trials. The availability of the second prototype powered by the intended engines made it possible to determine the aircraft's flight performance.

The K-98M (*izdeliye* 57) was a growth version of the K-98, an all-weather missile with round-the-clock/all-aspect engagement capability. Logically enough, it came in SARH and IR-homing versions designated K-98MR (*izdeliye* 57R) and K-98MT (*izdeliye* 57T), respectively. As part of the weapons system, the K-98MR was capable of engaging targets at 2,000–21,000 m (6,560–68,900 ft.) in head-on mode and 500–24,000 m (1,640–78,740 ft.) in pursuit mode; the target could be up to 6,000 m (13,120 ft.) above the interceptor's flight level. The target's speed in these cases was 500–2,500 km/h (310–1,552 mph) and 500–1,800 km/h (310–1,118 mph), respectively. Maximum 'kill' range was 24 km (15 miles) in head-on mode and 16 km (10 miles) in pursuit mode. The R-98MT ensured the same attack parameters in pursuit mode only.

The state acceptance trials ended in mid-June 1970; stage B was not completed in full either, since the MAP and air force top brass demanded the beginning of the Su-15TM's state acceptance trials pronto (this was exactly what the second prototype was intended for). In the course of stage B the two aircraft made 58 and 14 flights, respectively. The final report of the trials said that generally the weapons system met the specifications, even though the new equipment, first and foremost the Taifoon radar (no pun intended), proved rather unreliable.

The Novosibirsk aircraft factory was to complete the first 20 production Su-15Ts in the second half of 1969; yet, the first production example of the new model (referred to initially as *izdeliye* 37M or *izdeliye* 37 Srs M) was flown by the factory's CTP Vladimir T. Vylomov only on 20 December 1970. As the trials of the more advanced Su-15TM progressed, the interest of the military in the interim Su-15T waned, and the production run was limited to a mere 21 aircraft (c/ns 0115301–0115310, 0215301–0215310, and 0315301). Confusingly, the new version had a separate batch num-

bering sequence. Later, when the Su-15TM (likewise designated *izdeliye* 37M) entered production, the interim Su-15T's product code was changed to *izdeliye* 38 to discern it from the newer model.

The avionics suite of the production Su-15T included the Taifoon radar, the SAU-58 AFCS, the R-832M Evkalipt-SM radio, the RSBN-5S Iskra-K SHORAN, the ARL-SM (Lazoor'-SM) GCI command link receiver, the ARK-10 ADF, the RV-5 low-range radio altimeter, the SPO-10 Sirena-3 radar-warning receiver, and the Pion-GT antenna / feeder system. The latter's aerials were mounted on the main pitot at the tip of the radome and in a small fairing above the brake parachute container (which required the rudder to be cut away at the base). The nose gear unit featured twin KN-9 nonbraking wheels. The production Su-15T was powered by the old R11F2SU-300 engines.

On 25 January 1971, GNIKI VVS commenced check trials of the 1st and 15th production Su-15Ts (c/ns 0115301 and 0215305), with the objective of assessing the operation of the armament. The former aircraft made only three flights under this programme, the other machine making 23. The programme was completed within a month, and the results were disheartening: the aircraft was incapable of intercepting low-flying targets. In five test flights at an altitude of 500 m (1,640 ft.), the radar tracked the target on two occasions only, and then at very close range—a matter of 3 km (1.86 miles), which was totally unsatisfactory. Worse, neither could the radar reliably capture and track the target at higher altitudes almost throughout the permitted missile launch range. Besides, poor electromagnetic compatibility (EMC) of various avionics was discovered, landing with the BLC system on was complicated due to the limited tailplane travel, and so on.

As a result, the delivery of the production Su-15Ts dragged on for more than 12 months due to the need to rectify these defects. The aircraft did not become operational until the summer of 1972. Most of them were eventually transferred from active duty to the Stavropol' VVAUL with the air force's and MAP's approval, serving on as trainers. A few were transferred to MAP for use in various R&D programmes.

The Su-15T's NATO reporting name was Flagon-E.

Su-15T Multirole Test Bed

The 16th production Su-15T (c/n 0215306) was one of the above-mentioned research vehicles. In 1972 the Sukhoi OKB and LII held a joint programme with this aircraft to explore the EMC parameters of the avionics and test a trim mechanism in the roll control circuit. At the end of the year the aircraft was fitted with increased-area tailplanes, undergoing a special test programme in 1972–73 with a view to improving the handling in landing mode with the BLC activated. In 1973, Su-15T c/n 0215306 served as a test bed for the new Tester-U3 FDR, which later became standard on many Soviet combat aircraft.

Buddies: The Sakhalin Experience

The Sukhoi OKB's first involvement with in-flight refuelling (IFR) dates back to 1971. The need to master IFR techniques was caused by the necessity to increase the range and combat radius of the T-6 (Su-24) tactical bomber, which was undergoing trials at the time. By the end of the year the OKB prepared a set of project documents envisaging the installation of an IFR system on the bomber.

Unlike the Sukhoi OKB, which was breaking new ground with in-flight refuelling, the Flight Research Institute and the *Zvezda* (Star) design bureau (formerly OKB-918), under Guy Il'yich Severin, were old hands at this technique. By the early 1970s these two establishments had accumulated a wealth of experience in developing, testing, and using various IFR systems. In the 1950s and 1960s, such systems were created in the Soviet Union both for heavy bombers and for tactical aircraft, although it would be a while before the latter would actually benefit from in-flight refuelling.

The Zvezda OKB had been working on IFR systems since the late 1960s, and the programme was code-named *Sakhalin* after an island in the Soviet Far East. (Perhaps the implication was that 'with this system, our aircraft will be able to reach Sakhalin nonstop'!) Between 1971 and 1973 the OKB's specialists designed and tested the principal components of a probe-and-drogue refuelling system.

The preliminary design project of the T-6, featuring an IFR system with a retractable refuelling probe, was assessed at a session of MAP's Scientific & Technical Council. In keeping with the council's recommendations, the Sukhoi OKB decided to hold a series of tests in advance so that the system would be fully mastered by the time the bomber was ready to take it. The Su-15 was selected for conversion into IFR system test beds, one aircraft acting as the tanker and the other as the receiver. In October 1973 the VVS issued a specification in which three Sukhoi types—the Su-15TM, the Su-17M/Su-17M2, and the T-6 (Su-24)—were envisaged as possible tanker aircraft fitted with 'buddy' refuelling pods. The pod itself, or hose drum unit (HDU), was designated UPAZ (*oonifitseerovannyy podvesnoy agregaht zaprahvki*: 'standardised suspended [that is, external] refuelling unit').

Pursuant to a joint MAP / air force ruling, the Sukhoi OKB allocated two Flagons—the first preproduction Su-15 *sans suffixe* ('34 Red', c/n 0015301) loaned from the air force and a production Su-15T (c/n 0215306)—for testing the Sakhalin-1A IFR system. Both aircraft had a long history as company 'dogships', having been used for testing various systems and equipment. Additionally, LII allocated one of its Su-15s *sans suffixe* ('37 Red', c/n 1115337) for testing the Sakhalin-1A system and evolving IFR techniques. Since each of these aircraft served a different purpose, they will be described separately hereunder, followed by an account of the trials.

1. Su-15 IFR System Test Beds ('Buddy' Tankers)

By December 1972, Su-15 c/n 0015301 had been modified as the first of two aircraft fitted with a dummy UPAZ-1A (Sakhalin-1A) pod for aerodynamic testing; actually, the pod featured a functional hose drum allowing the drogue to be deployed and rewound. On 19 December, OKB test pilot Vladimir A. Krechetov performed the first test flight for the purpose of assessing the aircraft's stability and handling with this rather bulky external store.

In 1973 the OKB issued a set of documents for the adaptation of the production-standard Su-15's fuel system to accept the UPAZ pod. This involved installation of additional fuel pumps in the nos. 1, 2, and 3 fuselage tanks; modifications to the electric system; and replacement of the standard TRV1-1A fuel metering kit with a new TRK1-1 kit. The display of the Oryol fire control radar was removed to make room for the HDU's control panel.

The UPAZ-1A had a 26 m (85 ft., 3 in.) hose and a flexible 'basket' drogue. The hose drum was powered by a ram air turbine (RAT) with an intake scoop on the port side, which was normally closed flush. A second air intake at the front, closed by a movable cone, was for an RAT driving a generator for the electric transfer pump. Normal delivery rate was 1,000 litres (220 Imp gal.) per minute, but this could be increased to 2,200 litres (484 Imp gal.) in case of need. In an emergency the hose could be severed by a special guillotine. 'Traffic lights' were installed at the rear end of the pod to indicate fuel transfer status to the pilot of the receiver aircraft. The pod was attached to the airframe via a so-called standardised piping/wiring connector (UURK: *oonifitseerovannyy oozel razyoma kommunikatsiy*) and could be jettisoned pyrotechnically in an emergency. A test equipment suite was fitted.

The conversion was performed from April to July 1974 by the OKB's Novosibirsk branch. Outwardly the aircraft, which received a new tactical code ('01 Red') after the conversion, differed from its standard sister ships in having an egg-shaped pod housing an AKS-5 camera, fitted to the starboard PU-1-8 missile launch rail. The aft-looking camera captured the moments when the receiver aircraft made and broke contact.

On 4 July 1974, Sukhoi OKB test pilot Aleksandr S. Komarov made the first check flight from Novosibirsk-Yel'tsovka, whereupon the modified aircraft was ferried back to Zhukovskiy for testing.

The second aircraft to be fitted with a dummy UPAZ-1A pod was the aforementioned Su-15 '37 Red' (c/n 1115337), which was loaned from LII. Manufactured on 13 February 1970 and delivered new to LII for spin tests, this aircraft had double-delta wings, an operational BLC system, and provisions for fitting R13-300 engines instead of R11F2SU-300 engines. In late 1973 the fighter was modified in-house by LII to permit installation of an operational UPAZ-1A. Apart from testing the HDU as such, Su-15 c/n 1115337 was intended for verifying the approach and contact technique. Contact would be made in 'dry' mode (that is, without actual fuel transfer); hence the scope of the modification work on this aircraft was much smaller as compared to Su-15 c/n 0015301. The conversion involved removing the radar, which was replaced by ballast, and installing the HDU control panel, the UURK 'wet' centreline pylon, and the appropriate data-recording equipment. The missile launch rails were removed for the duration of the Sakhalin test programme.

In 1974, LII test pilots held a series of tests on this aircraft, checking the operation of the HDU (hose deployment/retraction and the operation of the pod's other systems). Afterward, Su-15 '37 Red' continued in use with the institute, participating in several research programmes. Unfortunately, on 24 December 1976 it crashed near Lookhovitsy, Moscow Region, killing LII test pilot Leonid D. Rybikov. Five (some sources say three) minutes after taking off from Tret'yakovo airfield (the factory airfield in Lookhovitsy) on a positioning flight to Zhukovskiy, which is about 90 km (56 miles) away as the crow flies, the aircraft inexplicably entered a shallow dive with considerable bank, descending at

100–120 m/sec. (19,685–23,622 ft./min.). The pilot briefly regained control at the last moment and even had time to query the tower (*'Do you have me on radar?'*) a second before the fighter impacted in a field 39.5 km (24.5 miles) from the point of origin, disintegrating utterly. Examination of the crash site and analysis of the wreckage showed that the aircraft had been perfectly serviceable up to the point of impact. At the final section of the flight path, the aircraft had been levelled out but continued losing altitude due to the high sink rate, hitting the ground in a wings-level attitude; the pilot was thrown clear of the cockpit and killed instantly. The exact cause of the crash was never determined, but temporary pilot incapacitation was cited as a likely cause.

Shortly after the completion of the Sakhalin IFR system's trials, Su-15 c/n 0015301 was returned to the PVO as time-expired. Actually, the aircraft could have been returned to service after an overhaul and a service life extension, but in view of the extensive conversion it had undergone, using it as a combat aircraft was inexpedient. Hence, after making its final flight on 9 July 1976, '01 Red' was transferred to the Solntsevo ShMAS as a ground instructional airframe. After the closure of the school in 1991 the Su-15 was returned to the OKB for preservation and, after cosmetic repairs, joined the collection of the open-air aviation museum at Moscow-Khodynka, established in 1994. When the airfield and the museum closed in 2003, the exhibits were left largely unguarded and the aircraft was in serious danger, especially considering that greedy real-estate developers had plans for the property on which the museum was located. Fortunately, the Su-15 'tanker' was saved from destruction by the Sukhoi OKB and is now preserved at the company's premises on the other side of the former airfield.

2. Su-15T IFR System Test Bed (Receiver Aircraft)

In late 1973 the Sukhoi OKB started converting the abovementioned Su-15T c/n 0215306, another long-serving 'dogship', into the receiver aircraft under the Sakhalin programme. Here the conversion was the most extensive of the three aircraft involved, since the aircraft had to be equipped with an IFR system ensuring the correct fuel transfer sequence (the fuel tanks needed to be topped up in a specific order to keep the CG within the allowed limits).

The uncoded aircraft was equipped with a new TRK1-1 fuel-metering kit and a fixed L-shaped refuelling probe offset to starboard ahead of the cockpit windshield; the tip of the probe was located 4.25 m (13 ft., $11^3/_8$ in.) aft of the tip of the radome, 0.9 m (2 ft., $11^1/_2$ in.) to the right of the fuselage centreline and 0.8 m (2 ft., $7^1/_2$ in.) from the fuselage surface. A forward-looking AKS-5 cine camera was installed in a cigar-shaped fairing, replacing the dielectric fin cap of the communications radio antenna for filming the contact with the tanker's drogue; hence, the R-832M radio's usual antenna, built into the fin cap, was replaced by a nonstandard ASM-1 blade aerial on the centre fuselage. An MSL-2 (a.k.a. KhS-62) flashing beacon was installed on the upper centre fuselage for synchronising the operation of all photo and cine cameras capturing the refuelling sequence. Since the refuelling operation imposed considerable stress on the pilot of the receiver aircraft, Su-15T c/n 0215306 was fitted with special *Koovshinka* (Water lily) medical equipment recording the pilot's physiological parameters (pulse and breath) and the distribution of his concentration

during various stages of the process. Finally, a PAU-467 cine camera was fitted inside the cockpit windshield to give a pilot's-eye view of the process.

3. The Course of the Sakhalin Test Programme

Apart from the three aircraft described above, the tests involved a MiG-21U Mongol-A trainer owned by LII, which acted as a chase plane and camera ship. According to plan, the first stage of the tests (performed jointly by the Sukhoi OKB and LII) was devoted to evolving and perfecting the optimum approach and contact technique. Yevgeniy S. Solov'yov was the OKB's project test pilot, with M. L. Belen'kiy as engineer in charge; LII appointed engineers V. D. Koorbesov and Yu. N. Goonin to the programme.

Before the joint flights and attempted contacts with the tanker could begin, the probe-equipped Su-15T made a series of test flights to see if and how the refuelling probe affected the aircraft's stability and handling. The actual IFR flight test programme commenced on 31 May 1974, when the first two flights were made, but these were not a success. The approach to the tanker and attempted contacts were made at 8,200 m (26,900 ft.) on the first occasion and about 6,000 m (19,680 ft.) on the second occasion; the speed was 550 km/h (340 mph) in both cases. Both attempts ended in failure, since the pilot of the receiver aircraft found it hard to keep formation because of wake turbulence, and no contact was made; moreover, on the second try the receiver aircraft missed the drogue, and the fuel transfer hose ensnared the IFR probe and broke as the receiver aircraft manoeuvred.

A pause was then called while the engineers made corrections to the piloting technique during the final approach phase. The pause turned out to be a long one, the flights resuming only on 24 December 1974. During this period the Zvezda OKB revised the UPAZ-1A pod, increasing the length of the hose to 27.5 m (90 ft., 2 in.). In the meantime, Yevgeniy S. Solov'yov took special training on a purpose-built simulator at the OKB and in the actual aircraft (the approach to the tanker was simulated on the ground, and special reference lines were applied to the Su-15T's cockpit canopy to mark the drogue's position at different ranges). It was decided that the tanker aircraft would deploy the flaps and that the dampers in the receiver aircraft's control circuits would be switched on. The flight altitude was reduced to 4,000 m (13,120 ft.), and the tanker approach technique was revised accordingly.

The effect of the additional training taken by the pilots was felt immediately; as early as 14 January the modified Su-15T made the first stable contact with the tanker, maintaining refuelling formation for a while. This flight marked the end of the phase involving LII's 'buddy tanker' (Su-15 c/n 1115337), since the OKB's own 'buddy tanker' (Su-15 c/n 0015301) had been completed by then.

Solov'yov remained the receiver aircraft's project test pilot at this stage; the other aircraft was flown by Vladimir S. Ilyushin, Aleksandr S. Komarov, Vladimir A. Krechetov, and Yuriy A. Yegorov. M. L. Belen'kiy likewise continued in his capacity as engineer in charge of the tests.

Duly prepared and endorsed at all levels, the test schedule for the summer of 1974 envisioned 70 flights, 29 of which would be made by the two aircraft together. Yet, the beginning of the programme's main phase involving contacts with the tanker was

Su-15 *sans suffixe* '01 Red'—the Sukhoi OKB's 'buddy tanker' modified under the Sakhalin R&D programme. It is seen here at Zhukovskiy with the bulky UPAZ-1A hose drum unit under the fuselage and a camera 'egg' on the starboard pylon.

LII's similarly configured Su-15 *sans suffixe* '37 Red'. Note the open air intake of the drum drive ram air turbine on the HDU.

The uncoded Su-15T c/n 0215306 modified as the receiver aircraft, with a fixed IFR probe. It is seen here at Zhukovskiy.

This view of the same aircraft shows well the photo calibration markings and the AKS-5 cine camera atop the fin.

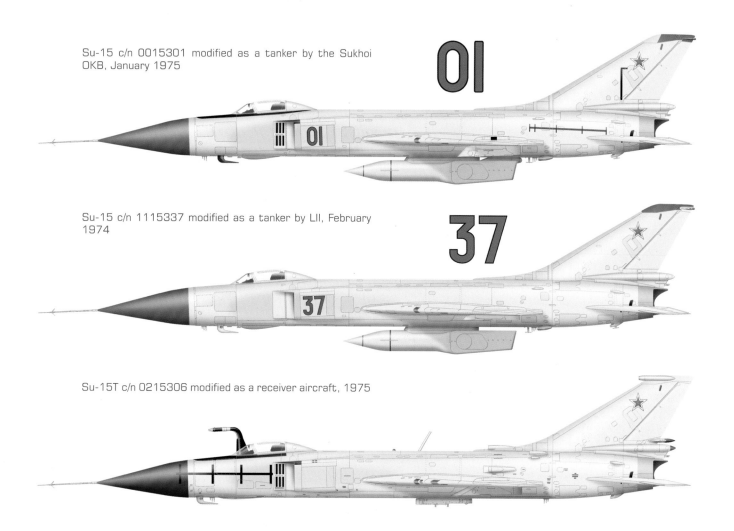

Su-15 c/n 0015301 modified as a tanker by the Sukhoi OKB, January 1975

Su-15 c/n 1115337 modified as a tanker by LII, February 1974

Su-15T c/n 0215306 modified as a receiver aircraft, 1975

delayed until 21 January 1975. The first contacts were made in 'dry' mode (without fuel transfer). The missions were flown at 2,000–7,500 m (6,560–24,600 ft.) and 480–660 km/h (300–410 mph); each mission involved two to seven attempts at making contact. This stage continued until the end of February, after which another lengthy hiatus followed due to the need to analyse the results obtained and prepare for the next phase. This was devoted to testing and perfecting the UPAZ-1A HDU proper and the associated equipment of the carrier aircraft during refuelling missions.

The work resumed in June 1975. Again, initially contacts were made in 'dry' mode; in early July, however, the plug closing the orifice of the HDU's drogue was removed, allowing fuel to be

The modified Su-15T in refuelling formation with Su-15 '01 Red'. The HDU's nose appears blunt because the forward RAT air intake is open. Note the reference stripes on the hose, showing how much has been paid out.

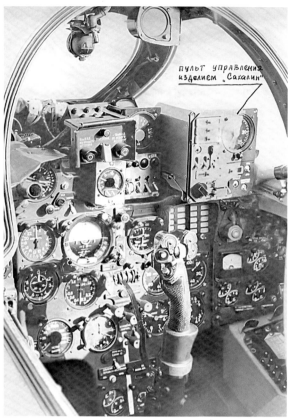

Top: The cockpit of the Su-15 tanker '01 Red'; the HDU control panel is centrally located, replacing the radar display.

Top right: The cockpit of the Su-15 tanker '37 Red'; the HDU control panel is on the right-hand side.

Right: The cockpit of the receiver aircraft, Su-15T c/n 0215306

Above: Su-15 '37 Red' begins to unreel the hose.

Below: The receiver aircraft, with the probe locked into the tanker's drogue

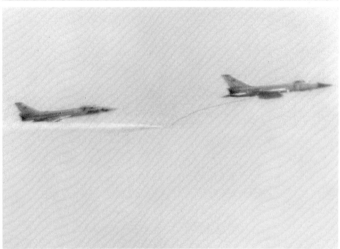

Left: Stills from the footage taken by the tail-mounted camera of Su-15T 0215306 as it approaches the drogue and makes contact

Top and *above*: Things get out of hand. The receiver aircraft misses the drogue, whereupon the hose ensnares the IFR probe and then breaks, spewing fuel.

Below: The former tanker '01 Red' at the Solntsevo ShMAS, with photo calibration markings still in evidence

transferred. An immediate problem arose: on 2, 4, and 18 July, fuel was seen to be leaking from the drogue after the receiver aircraft's probe had locked into position. It turned out that the drogue had been manufactured inaccurately, making it impossible to seal the joint properly; a new, higher-quality drogue took care of the problem. The first successful transfer of 250 kg (550 lbs.) of fuel took place on 30 July 1975; the next day, Su-15T c/n 0215306 made two more fuel top-ups, receiving 500 and 1,000 kg (550 and 1,100 lbs.) of fuel, respectively.

By early December 1975 the Sukhoi OKB and the Zvezda OKB had rectified all the bugs discovered in the course of the preceding tests. After that, another four flights involving three fuel top-ups were made between 10 and 23 December; on the latter date the receiver aircraft 'hit the tanker' twice in a single mission, taking on 400 and 250 kg (880 and 550 lbs.) of fuel, respectively. Thus the test programme was successfully completed in full.

The test report said, *'The in-flight refuelling system and technique verified . . . can be recommended for use primarily on the Su-24 aircraft'.* Further tests of the Sakhalin-1A IFR system were done, using Su-24M Fencer-D bombers.

L.10-10 Weapons Test Bed

At the suggestion of Yevgeniy A. Fedosov, director of the State Research Institute of Aircraft Systems (GosNII AS: *Gosudarstvennyy naoochno-issledovatel'skiy institoot aviatsionnykh sistem*), by October 1978, Su-15T c/n 0215306 was modified yet again, becoming a weapons test bed as part of the Su-27 fourth-generation fighter's development effort. (GosNII AS was the leading Soviet integrator of avionics and aircraft weapons.) The test bed was designated L.10-10 (that is, 'flying laboratory' no. 10 under the T-10 programme). It was one more of the assorted test beds under the Su-27 programme with designations in the L.XX-10 series (the L.01-10 and L.07-10 were mentioned in chapter 2).

The aircraft served for testing the new K-27E advanced medium-range AAM developed by GMKB Vympel as the Su-27's main weapon. Hence the standard PU-1-8 missile launch rails were replaced with APU-470 launch rails, which were also a GMKB Vympel product. The missiles fired by the L.10-10 were instrumented test rounds equipped with a simple autopilot and data link (*izdeliye* 474-3A3E).

In December 1978 the aircraft was ferried to the main facility of GNIKI VVS at Vladimirovka AB, in Akhtoobinsk, where the tests began in April 1979, with B. V. Zakharovskiy as engineer in charge. The first launch took place on 6 April 1979, Sukhoi OKB test pilot Aleksandr S. Komarov firing a K-27E at 15,300 m (50,200 ft.) and Mach 1.55. However, the first few launches showed the missile to be unstable and the tests were suspended, resuming in December, when the K-27's control system had been revised; a total of 24 flights and 11 launches had been made by year's end. The tests continued in 1980 with another 35 flights and 14 launches of the IR-homing version; this time the results were positive, allowing test launches from the Su-27 prototypes to begin. Manufacturer's tests of the K-27E were completed in November 1981, the missile entering production as the R-27 (AA-10 Alamo).

Su-15TM Interceptor
(T-58TM, *izdeliye* 37M or '*izdeliye* 37 Srs M')

As already mentioned, the Su-15TM version of the 'Su-15 stage II upgrade' commenced state acceptance trials in September 1970, when the prototype (c/n 0115305) joined the programme. The aircraft was flown by GNIKI VVS test pilots Eduard M. Kolkov, Valeriy V. Migoonov, Valeriy I. Mostovoy, and Stal' A. Lavrent'yev; R. N. Lazarev continued in his capacity as engineer in charge.

Stage A, comprising 40 flights, was to verify the operation of the aircraft's principal systems. Progress was terribly slow, with only six flights 'for the record' being made by the end of 1970. On 3 February 1971 the original Su-15T prototype, or 'aircraft 0006' (c/n 0515348), which had been refitted with an upgraded RP-26 Taifoon-M radar in the meantime, was added to the first aircraft in the hope of speeding up the trials, but it did little good. During

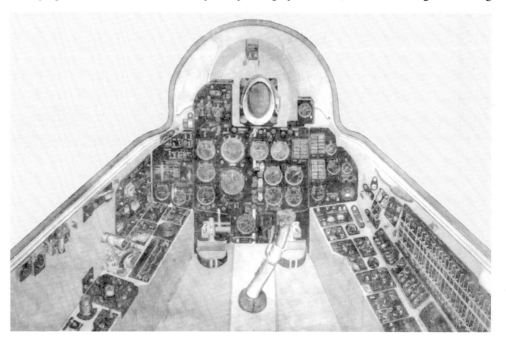

An image from an instructional placard showing the cockpit of an early Su-15TM

the first three months of the year, the two aircraft made a mere 42 flights between them, only three of these 42 missions being accepted 'for the record'. Neither aircraft had the widened air intakes envisaged for the production version, which, as noted earlier, had been tested successfully on Su-15 c/n 1315340 ('aircraft 0009'). A third aircraft (c/n 0115309) joined the trials programme in 1971, making 19 test flights with the objective of exploring the structural-strength limits.

Meanwhile, plant no. 153 was already preparing to build the Su-15T; therefore, as mentioned earlier, GNIKI VVS decided to issue a so-called preliminary report on the trials results in order to avoid holding up production of the updated fighter. To this end

a special test schedule was drawn up, flights under this programme commencing on 20 May 1971. By the end of June the prototypes had made a total of 123 flights under stage A of the state acceptance trials (including 35 'for the record'). Still, radar operation and the guidance of the radar-homing AAMs at low altitudes were unstable, and the air force suspended the testing of 'aircraft 0006'. The other prototype kept flying for a while, but on 17 June 1971 a fire broke out just as the aircraft was taxiing out for takeoff; due to the danger of an explosion, test pilot Valeriy I. Mostovoy vacated the cockpit without even bothering to shut down the engines. The fire, which had been caused by a malfunction in the oxygen system, inflicted heavy damage on the aircraft, which, though not a

Left: '74 Blue', the first production Su-15TM, at GNIKI VVS. Note that the aircraft has an ogival radome and four wing pylons; both features were then experimental and took a while to introduce on the Su-15TM production line.

Below: Another view of the same aircraft, with dummy R-60s on the inboard pylons

Bottom: Su-15TM '75 Blue', the second production aircraft

total loss, could be repaired only by the manufacturer in Novosibirsk.

Thus the state acceptance trials of the Su-15TM effectively stopped altogether; they resumed on 26 August, when 'aircraft 0006' reentered flight test after the Taifoon-M radar had been updated. In December it became clear that the rebuild of the first prototype was taking longer than expected, and 'aircraft 0006' would have to shoulder the remainder of the state acceptance trials. The OKB and GNIKI VVS attempted to widen the scope of the trials work by using the first two production Su-15TMs, '74 Blue' (c/n 0315302) and '75 Blue' (c/n 0315303), which fully conformed to the 'Su-15 stage II upgrade' standard as far as both airframe and

Above right: The stabilators of Su-15TM '75 Blue' still featured straight antiflutter weights (not angled upward, as on mass production aircraft).

Right: This ogival-nosed Su-15TM, '06 Blue' (c/n 0515306), was used for tests; hence the S-13 camera under the nose.

Below: Another aspect of Su-15TM '06 Blue'

avionics were concerned. The two aircraft arrived at Vladimirovka AB on 15 December; however, they had been handed over to the air force in such haste that the obligatory predelivery tests had not been performed, and these had to be done at GNIKI VVS instead of the factory. As a result, the two production Su-15TMs did not actually join the programme until March 1972. By then the rebuilt first prototype had returned to Vladimirovka AB, but it was a case of too little, too late—stage A of the trials ended on 31 March.

The report on the results of stage A said that the four participating aircraft had made 289 flights between them; of these, 81 flights (including 42 'for the record') were made under the stage A programme proper, and 91 (including 47 'for the record') under the 'preliminary report' test schedule. Nearly all performance tar-

gets had been met, with the exception of the weapons system's low-altitude performance. The maximum speed of the target being intercepted and the radar's target detection range were shorter than expected. The strong points noted by the pilots included the presence of the SAU-58 automatic flight control system and a short-range radio navigation system, both of which facilitated flying and landing, and, most importantly, the Su-15TM's greatly enhanced combat potential as compared to the in-service Su-15 *sans suffixe*. The insufficient tailplane travel was cited as the main shortcoming. Eventually the strengths outweighed the weaknesses, and the Su-15TM was recommended for production.

Stage B of the state acceptance trials began on 17 April 1972. The greater part of it was to be performed using the first two pro-

Top: Su-15TM '65' (c/n 0915326), with two wing pylons, was used in a test programme. Note the 'Excellent Aircraft' badge below the windshield.

Above: Su-15TM '76' (c/n 1015307) carries a UKPEV cargo pod (used during redeployments) on a BD3-57M pylon under the starboard wing.

Left: The same aircraft loaded with R-98M AAMs and drop tanks

Below: Close-up of the drop tanks on Su-15TM c/n 1015307

duction Su-15TMs, which were fitted with production Taifoon-M radars manufactured by LNPO Leninets, the other two aircraft being set aside for special test programmes. The radars proved fairly reliable; also, they featured a new module increasing the radar set's ECM resistance. At this stage the OKB had to tackle the complex task of increasing intercept efficiency at low altitudes (the aircraft did not meet the air force's requirements in this respect, and only one of five such missions performed by the end of April had been successful). A new GCI guidance algorithm had to be developed, and the result was felt immediately; 12 of the 16 low-altitude intercept missions that followed were successful, albeit they were flown over level terrain.

Stage B ended in April 1973, by which time a third production Su-15TM (c/n 0315304) had joined the test fleet. All in all, the five

Top: '23 Red', a six-pylon Su-15TM, with a TS-27AMSh rearview mirror on the canopy, introduced on batch 13.

Above: '76 Blue' (c/n 1015307) was used by GNIKI VVS to check the Su-15TM's suitability for strike missions. Here it is seen with UB-32A FFAR pods under the wings and cannon pods under the fuselage.

Right: Three-quarters front view of the same aircraft, showing the S-13 camera under the nose

aircraft made 256 flights, including 143 as part of the programme of state acceptance trials (92 of them 'for the record') and another 103 under various special test programmes. A total of 46 K-98M missiles were fired at La-17M, M-17 (MiG-17M), M-28 (IL-28M), and M-16 (Tu-16M) target drones, some of which featured active and passive ECM gear, as well as at RM-8 and PRM-1 paradroppable targets and KRM high-speed targets (*krylataya raketa-mishen'*: cruise missile-based target drone). Three of the target aircraft received direct hits, and three others were destroyed by proximity detonation; in the other cases the missiles were instrumented inert rounds used for trajectory measurements.

The final report on the results of the state acceptance trials (stage B) did not point out any major shortcomings; on the other hand, it effectively outlined a plan for the further upgrade of the Su-15TM. Among other things, in the future the aircraft was to be re-engined with the new Gavrilov R25-300 afterburning turbojets (see Su-15*bis* below). New wings and stabilators of increased area were to be incorporated, and an automatic lateral-stability augmentation system and a pitch trim mechanism were to be provided.

The Su-15TM had entered production back in October 1971, superseding the Su-15T on the Novosibirsk production line. Curiously, c/n 0315302 was the first production aircraft; since the two models had a lot in common, the Su-15TM's batch numbering continued that of the Su-15T (that is, Su-15TM production started with batch 3). The in-house product code (*izdeliye* 37M or *izdeliye* 37 Srs M) remained unaltered. This was the last of the Su-15's production versions. Concurrently, plant no. 153 produced the Su-24 tactical bomber, which took up a lot of the production capacity;

Left: A full frontal of a production Su-15TM with six pylons and a canopy mirror

Below: Side view of the same machine. Late-production Su-15TMs lacked the large air scoops on top of the rear fuselage that were so typical of early examples and previous versions.

Bottom: A plan view of the same Su-15TM

Right: This Su-15TM parked on a rain-soaked taxiway wears tactical camouflage, indicating it has been transferred from the PVO to the air force.

Below: This camouflaged six-pylon Su-15TM with a white-outlined tactical code has been retrofitted with a V-shaped rain deflector in front of the cockpit windshield. The radar-warning receiver aerial has been relocated from the top of the fin to a place above the brake parachute housing.

hence, the Su-15TM's production rates were not particularly high, peaking at 110 aircraft per year.

The upgraded Su-15-98M aerial-intercept weapons system, based on the Su-15TM, was officially included into the inventory by a Council of Ministers directive on 21 January 1975. It enabled manually or automatically controlled interception of single targets flying at altitudes of 500–24,000 m (1,640–78,740 ft.) and speeds up to 1,600 km/h (990 mph) in pursuit mode, and targets flying at altitudes of 2,000–21,000 m (6,560–68,900 ft.) and speeds up to 2,500 km/h (1,550 mph) in head-on mode. The weapons control system had enhanced ECM resistance; on the downside, the service ceiling had decreased from 18,500 m (60,690 ft.)—the figure obtained in the course of the state acceptance trials—to 17,970 m (58,960 ft.). After service entry the Taifoon-M radar received the

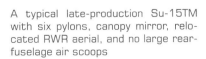

A typical late-production Su-15TM with six pylons, canopy mirror, relocated RWR aerial, and no large rear-fuselage air scoops

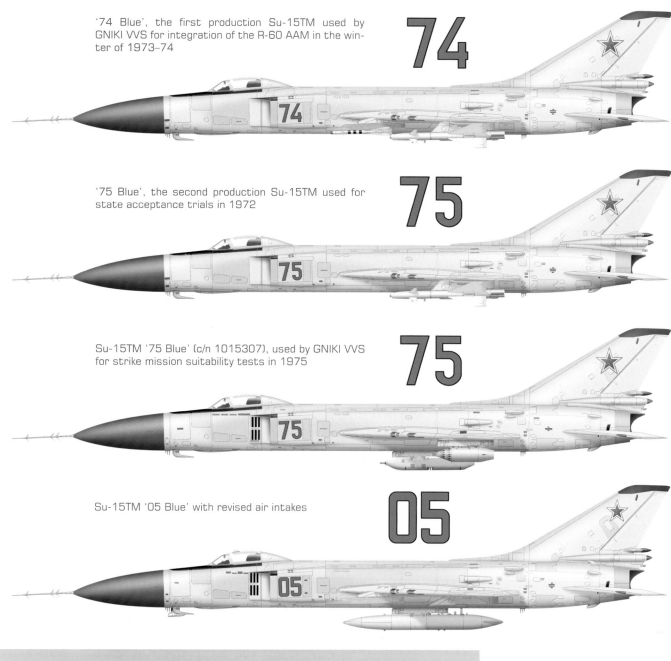

'74 Blue', the first production Su-15TM used by GNIKI VVS for integration of the R-60 AAM in the winter of 1973–74

'75 Blue', the second production Su-15TM used for state acceptance trials in 1972

Su-15TM '75 Blue' (c/n 1015307), used by GNIKI VVS for strike mission suitability tests in 1975

Su-15TM '05 Blue' with revised air intakes

Su-15TM '05 Blue' was an aircraft of the 14th and final production batch, featuring revised air intakes with a cut-back upper lip to improve performance at negative AOAs. It is seen here during tests.

official designation of RP-26, while the K-98M missile was renamed R-98M (its NATO code name was again AA-3A Anab).

The first lot of production Su-15TMs was handed over to the military in the spring of 1972. Apart from the radar, production Su-15TMs were almost identical to the Su-15T as regards avionics and equipment. Empty weight increased to 10,870 kg (23,960 lbs.) versus 10,220 kg (22,530 lbs.) for the Su-15 *sans suffixe*; the fuel capacity was 6,775 litres (1,490.5 Imp gal.), and the fuel load 5,550 kg (12,235 lbs.).

One of the deficiencies the Sukhoi OKB and LNPO Leninets had to rectify together was the clutter on the radar display arising from internal reflections of the radar pulse inside the radome. The avionics house suggested fitting an ogival radome to cure the problem. After a series of tests on Su-15 c/n 1315340 at LII in June 1972, involving several differently shaped radomes, such ogival radomes were fitted to the first two production Su-15TMs—'74 Blue' (c/n 0315302) and '75 Blue' (c/n 0315303), which underwent additional tests. The latter showed that the annoying echoes were gone, but the service ceiling, base altitude, effective range, and interception range had decreased somewhat due to the extra drag created by the new radome. (Contrary to popular belief, the ogival radome was not a measure aimed at improving the Su-15TM's aerodynamics—in fact, it made them worse.) Upon completion of the check trials at GNIKI VVS in the autumn of 1973, the new radome was cleared for production. By then, however, a considerable number of Su-15TMs had been built with the old 'pencil nose'; new-build 'TMs received the ogival radome from batch 8 onward, and the previously manufactured aircraft were progressively updated in service.

The Su-15TM received the NATO reporting name 'Flagon-F'.

The service tests of the new variant were held by one of the PVO's first-line units between 1 February 1975 and 20 July 1978, with good results. Like most aircraft, the aircraft was not immune to accidents; the first total loss was on 7 February 1973, when Su-15TM c/n

0815320 suffered a critical failure during predelivery tests in Novosibirsk, forcing factory test pilot Ivan M. Gorlach to eject.

In the course of production the Su-15TM was constantly updated. Some of the changes are listed below.

From batch 6 onward the Su-15TM was equipped with the upgraded SAU-58-2 AFCS, enabling automatic interception of low-flying targets (which was beyond the capabilities of the earlier SAU-58). In-service aircraft were retrofitted with a V-shaped rain deflector ahead of the windshield to improve the pilot's view in rainy weather.

Aircraft up to and including c/n 0915310 had the same PU-1-8 wing pylons with a kinked leading edge as the Su-11 and Su-15 *sans suffixe*. From Su-15TM c/n 0915311 onward, these were replaced with PU-2-8 pylons having longer, sharper noses, and appropriate changes were made to the electric system. The PU-2-8 pylons could be easily replaced with BD3-57M bomb racks (**bahlochnyy derzhahtel'**: beam-type rack for group 3 ordnance; that is, up to 250 kg / 551 lb. calibre, 1957 model, updated) for carrying air-to-ground weapons. From c/n 1315331 onward. the weapons complement was augmented with two R-60 'dogfight missiles' carried on PD-62 pylons with PU-60-1 (P-62-1) launch rails under the inner wings; earlier Su-15TMs were upgraded accordingly. The missile passed its trials on the first production Su-15TM, '74 Blue', in late 1974 / early 1975; the new weapon was integrated in situ from 1979 onward.

Despite the different engines, Su-15TMs up to and including c/n 1015329 retained the engine-nozzle air ejector system seen on the Su-15 *sans suffixe*. From c/n 1015330 onward this system was deleted; its characteristic large air scoops on top of the rear fuselage were removed and replaced by much-smaller air scoops. Older Flagon-Fs were updated accordingly during scheduled overhauls.

On late-production aircraft the pitch/yaw transducers were deleted from the nose probe and replaced by a DUA-3 pitch transducer (**dahtchik oogla atahki**) on the port side of the cockpit. From

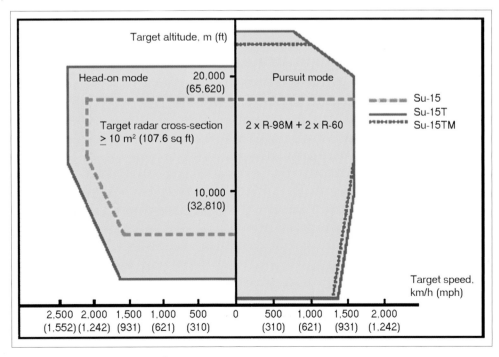

This graph provides a comparison of the various Su-15 versions' target intercept envelope in head-on and pursuit modes.

batch 13 onward, a TS-27AMSh faired periscopic rearview mirror was added to the lengthwise frame member of the sliding-canopy section; it was developed by the State Optical Institute, named after Sergey I. Vavilov (GOI: *Gosudarstvennyy optich̄eskiy insti-*

toot). On batch 14 (the final batch) the upper lips of the air intakes were cut away at about 45° to the centreline, beginning halfway along the boundary layer splitter plates; this change was meant to improve the intakes' performance at negative angles of attack.

Two more updates were part of the large-scale measures taken by the VVS and the PVO to mitigate the damage done by Lt. Viktor I. Belenko's notorious defection to Japan in a MiG-25P on 6 September 1976. First, the SRO-2M Khrom-Nikel' IFF suite, which had been compromised by the defection, was replaced by the new *Parol'-2* (Password) IFF suite, comprising an *izdeliye* 623-1 interrogator and an *izdeliye* 620-20P transponder. Outwardly the new system could be identified by the distinctive triangular blade aeri-

Table 1. The Su-15TM's Interception Range

Interception range, km (miles)	Cruise mode	Power plant operation mode full afterburner	full military power
head-on mode	504 (313)	360 (223)	300 (186)
pursuit mode	450 (279)	240 (149)	55 (34)

Table 2. Specifications of the Su-15TM's Missile Armament

	R-98	R-98M	R-60
Design g-load	14	14	42
Operational on-wing g-load	3	3	5
Launch range, km (miles):			
head-on mode	8–18 (5–11)	5–24 (3.1–14.9)	–
pursuit mode	2–14 (1.24–8.7)	2–15 (1.24–9.3)	0.2–16 (0.12–9.93)
at low altitude	–	2–3.5 (1.24–2.17)	0.3–1.5 (0.18–0.93)
Target elevation, m (ft.):			
head-on mode	3,000–4,000 (9,840–13,120)	4,000–5,000 (13,120–16,400)	2,000 (6,560)
pursuit mode	–	–	–
at low altitude	–	–	–

Table 3. Radar Performance Comparison

	Su-15TM	Su-15
Radar type	Taifoon-M	Oryol-D58
Target detection range, km (miles):		
at high altitude	65 (40.3)	35 (21.7)
at low altitude	15 (9.3)	15 (9.3)
Target tracking range, km (miles):		
at high altitude	45 (27.9)	30 (18.6)
at low altitude	10 (6.2)	10 (6.2)
Scan limits:		
azimuth	±70°	±60°
elevation	+30°/–10°	+31°/–15°

Table 4. Performance Comparison of Soviet Interceptors of the 1970s

	Su-15TM	Su-15	MiG-25PD/MiG-25PDS
Indicated airspeed at sea level, km/h (mph)	1,300 (807)	1,100 (683)	1,200 (745)
Maximum true airspeed at 11,000 m (36,090 ft.), km/h (mph)	2,230 (1,385)	2,230 (1,385)	3,000 (1,863)
Service ceiling, m (ft.)	18,000 (59,050)	17,650 (57,900)	20,500 (67,260)
Endurance	1 hr., 41 min.	1 hr., 27 min.	1 hr., 37 min.
Base altitude:			
head-on mode	17,000 (55,770)	15,000 (49,210)	20,000 (65,620)
pursuit mode	16,000 (52,500)	n.a.	n.a.
Climb time to base altitude, minutes	n.a.	n.a.	9.7
Maximum range, km (miles)	1,380 (860)	1,120 (695)	1,320 (820)
Operational g-limit	+6.5	+6.0	+4.4
Maximum thrust/weight ratio	0.82	0.63	0.7
Wing loading, kg/m^2 (lbs. / sq. ft.)	397 (81.39)	395 (80.98)	490 (100.46)

Table 5. Performance of Some Soviet and US Interceptors

	MiG-25P	MiG-23M	Su-15TM	McDD F-15A	GD F-16A
Thrust/weight ratio	0.66	0.85	0.7	1.15	1.4
Top speed, km/h (mph):					
at sea level	1,200 (745)	1,350 (838)	1,300 (807)	1,470 (913)	1,490 (925)
at 11,000 m	3,000 (1,863)	2,500 (1,550)	2,230 (1,385)	2,650 (1,645)	2,100 (1,300)
Maximum Mach number	2.83	2.35	2.1	2.5	2.0
Service ceiling, m (ft.)	20,500 (67,260)	17,800 (58,400)	18,000 (59,050)	19,200 (62,990)	18,000 (59,050)
Minimum control speed, km/h (mph)	400 (248)	400/450 (248/279)	450 (279)	350 (217)	350 (217)

als mounted under the nose and under the rear fuselage, replacing the equally characteristic triple aerials of the SRO-2M (which accounted for the NATO code name of Odd Rods). Second, the Taifoon-M radar was upgraded at the insistence of the military; the modification was a success (see below), but it is not known with certainty if operational Su-15TMs were thus upgraded.

Su-15TM production ended in late 1975, when the final 116 were completed. A total of 420 were built, making the Flagon-F the second-largest version in terms of numbers.

Su-15TM Development Aircraft for Soft-Field Tests

A late-production Su-15TM coded '31 Blue' (c/n 1415331), which had been used for tests in the strike configuration with unguided air-to-ground weapons, was also used for tests on semiprepared (dirt or snow) runways with various weapons loads, including a combination of four AAMs (two R-98Ms and two R-60s) under the wings and two 270 kg (595 lb.) OFAB-250-270 high-explosive/fragmentation bombs under the fuselage. Outwardly a perfectly standard Flagon-F, the aircraft was obviously fitted a test equipment suite for measuring vibration loads.

Right and *below*: Su-15TM '31 Blue' (c/n 1415331) illustrates the late-style air intakes with cut-back upper lips.

Bottom: The same aircraft with OFAB-250-270 bombs on the fuselage pylons during strike mission suitability tests

Su-15TM Control System Test Bed

Service pilots kept complaining that the Su-15's lateral stability was poor, especially during the landing approach. The Sukhoi OKB worked in several directions, trying to eliminate this shortcoming. Eventually the second production Su-15TM ('75 Blue') was fitted with a trim mechanism in the aileron control circuit and a lateral-stability augmentation system. This aircraft was turned over to GNIKI VVS for testing in 1974; the new features received a positive appraisal and were introduced on the production line.

Left: Here the same Su-15TM '31 Blue' is pictured during tests on a grass runway with a load of four missiles.

Below: This Su-15TM coded '61 Red' (c/n 1015310) was an avionics test bed with the experimental Ozon IFF transponder and BAN-75 GCI data link. The experimental transponder was served by the curved aerial just aft of the radome.

Later the same aircraft was used to test an increased-area horizontal tail meant to address the insufficient stabilator authority problem. The test programme included 29 flights; the new horizontal tail was likewise recommended for production. This time, however, it was too late, since Su-15TM production had ended by then.

Su-15TM Strike Armament Test Bed

The incorporation of bomb armament on the Su-15 for use as a tactical-strike aircraft had been repeatedly delayed ever since the beginning of the state acceptance trials. Finally, by August 1974 a production Su-15TM coded '76 Blue' (c/n 1015307) was modified to feature four BD3-57M bomb racks instead of the standard mis-

Su-15TM '31 Blue', used for strike mission suitability tests with OFAB-250-270 bombs

Su-15TM '61 Red', with the experimental Ozon IFF and BAN-75 Raduga-Bort GCI data link

sile and drop tank pylons, with appropriate changes to the electrics. The K-10T sight was equipped with a tilting mechanism enabling attacks against ground targets.

The state acceptance trials proceeded in two stages; stage A (October 1974 through May 1975) was to verify the bomb armament, while stage B (June–December 1975) was concerned with the cannon and rocket armament. The aircraft was flown by GNIKI VVS test pilots Yevgeniy S. Kovalenko, Vladimir A. Oleynikov, and Valeriy N. Moozyka. The results were good, the report stating that the armament fitted under test rendered the aircraft suitable for use against pinpoint ground targets. Hence, late-production Su-15TMs were equipped with PU-2-8 launch rails, which could be easily exchanged for BD3-57M racks.

Su-15TM Avionics Test Beds with Modified Radars

On 6 September 1976, Lt. Viktor I. Belenko, a pilot of the PVO's 530th IAP stationed in the Far East, defected to Japan in a MiG-25P Foxbat-A, landing at Hakodate airport and laying the latest state of the art in Soviet interceptor design wide open for inspection by the West. In response to this, the Soviet Council of Ministers issued a directive in November 1976 requiring measures to be taken in order to minimise the damage done by Belenko's treason. The MiG-25P received the greatest attention, undergoing a complete change of the weapons control system, which resulted in the advent of the MiG-25PD/MiG-25PDS Foxbat-C. The Su-15TM, on the other hand, would make do with a modest upgrade of the radar.

In early 1977, two production Su-15TMs (c/ns 1315349 and 1415307) were set aside for modification under this programme, undergoing tests between June and October that year. It took another 12 months to perfect the modified weapons control system, and in 1978 the modifications received approval for incorporation on in-service aircraft.

Su-15TM Avionics Test Bed with Ozon IFF and BAN-75 Data Link

In 1974 another production Su-15TM coded '61' (c/n 1015310) was modified for testing the new *Ozon* (Ozone) IFF suite. Its presence was revealed by a nonstandard forward-curving aerial under the nose, ahead of the L-shaped aerial of the GCI command link system. The latter was also new—the standard ARL-SM Lazoor'-M receiver was replaced with the BAN-75 *Raduga-Bort* receiver (≈ Rainbow-Onboard; BAN = *bortovaya apparatoora navedeniya*: onboard guidance equipment, 1975 model). This worked with the Raduga-SPK-75P radar (*stahntsiya peredachi komahnd*: command transmitter station), and both items were part of the Looch-1 (Beam, or Ray) GCI system that replaced the earlier Vozdukh-1 system.

The aircraft underwent trials at GNIKI VVS. The Ozon IFF suite turned out to be unsatisfactory and did not progress beyond experimental status. The BAN-75 receiver, on the other hand, performed well and was recommended for production, becoming standard on such Soviet interceptors as the MiG-23 and MiG-25PD.

Su-15TM Weapons Test Bed with Internal Cannon

The Sukhoi OKB did not give up on the idea of fitting an internal cannon to the Su-15; now a production GSh-23L cannon was to be buried in the Su-15TM's fuselage underside (aft of the nosewheel well) and enclosed by a neat fairing à la MiG-23 or MiG-21S et seq. The third production example, coded '23 Red' (c/n 0315304), one of the five involved in the state acceptance trials, was modified for testing this cannon installation.

The 'cannon saga' continued for almost three years, the modified aircraft eventually undergoing a separate state acceptance trials programme in 1973. The results were very similar to those obtained with the standard UPK-23-250 pods; thus the built-in cannon was recommended for production. Yet, gunnery accuracy was still rather poor because the standard K-10T sight was ill suited for working with cannons; since a specialised gunsight could not be fitted due to space limitations, the built-in cannon never found its way to the Su-15 production line.

Su-15*bis* Experimental Interceptor (T-58*bis*)

On 25 February 1971, shortly after the completion of stage A of the Su-15TM's state acceptance trials, the Council of Ministers issued a directive followed by a joint MAP / air force ruling. These documents required the Sukhoi OKB to re-engine the Su-15TM with Gavrilov R25-300 afterburning turbojets, rated at 4,100 kgp (9,40 lbst) dry and 6,850 kgp (15,100 lbst) reheat, with a contingency rating of 7,100 kgp (15,650 lbst) up to an altitude of 4,000 m (13,120 ft.).

Development work began in 1972, the aircraft receiving the in-house designation T-58*bis* and the provisional service designation Su-15*bis*. The prototype was converted from the fifth production Su-15TM, coded '25 Blue' (c/n 0315306), at the Novosibirsk aircraft factory in the first half of the year, making its maiden flight on 3 July with Sukhoi OKB chief test pilot Vladimir S. Ilyushin at the controls. V. Vasil'yev was engineer in charge of the tests.

LII test pilot Aleksandr A. Shcherbakov, who specialised in spin tests, boards the Su-15*bis* prototype coded '25 Blue'. Note the Sukhoi OKB 'winged archer' emblem, rarely seen on the Su-15.

Left and *below*: The one-off Su-15*bis* at Zhukovskiy with dummy R-98M AAMs under the wings. The Sukhoi badge was painted on both sides of the nose.

Three-quarters rear view of the same aircraft. Outwardly the Su-15*bis* was no different from a standard Su-15TM.

The Su-15*bis* prototype, '25 Blue'

Sukhoi OKB engineers and ground crew watch with interest as a LII test pilot writes his comments in the test log after a high-altitude flight in the Su-15*bis*.

The manufacturer's flight tests continued until 20 December; the aircraft was also flown by OKB test pilots Aleksandr N. Isakov and Vladimir A. Krechetov. As compared to the standard R13-300-powered aircraft, the Su-15*bis* had markedly better acceleration characteristics and a higher top speed at low and medium altitudes, especially with the engines at contingency rating. The service ceiling and interception range in head-on mode were also improved.

The Su-15*bis* underwent state acceptance trials between 5 June and 10 October 1973; GNIKI VVS test pilots Nikolay I. Stogov, Valeriy I. Mostovoy, and Yevgeniy S. Kovalenko made a total of 79 flights. The trials report said that performance below 4,000 m was improved over the Su-15TM, and using the contingency rating (or rather power boost perhaps) allowed targets flying at up to 1,000 km/h (620 mph) to be intercepted in pursuit mode. The Su-15*bis* was recommended for production, but it never achieved production status; conversely, the R25-300 engine did, powering the mass-produced MiG-21*bis* Fishbed-L/N tactical fighter.

Su-15UM Combat Trainer (U-58TM, *izdeliye* 43)

In late 1974 the OKB started design work on a new combat trainer that received the manufacturer's designation U-58TM. Developed to meet an air force requirement for a trainer version of the Su-15TM, the aircraft was intended for training PVO pilots in fly-ing techniques, aerobatics, and combat tactics. In accordance with a joint MAP/MRP ruling agreed on by the air force, the Sukhoi OKB was to develop a set of project documents for a combat trainer version of the Su-15TM within the shortest possible time, where-upon the Novosibirsk aircraft factory would build a prototype. The project documents were transferred to plant no. 153 in the spring of 1975, but it was not until 16 July 1975 that MAP finally issued an order officially initiating development of the U-58TM.

The parties concerned chose not to build a prototype, perform-ing the required trials on the first production aircraft. The trainer was based on the airframe of the late-production Su-15TM; unlike the Su-15UT, there was no fuselage stretch, the overall length being the same as the single-seater's. The twin-wheel nose gear unit was also retained.

Remarkably, the provision of a second cockpit did not incur a reduction in fuel capacity, the space for it being provided by deleting some of the avionics. The internal fuel capacity was 6,775 litres (1,490.5 Imp gal.), and the fuel load was 5,550 kg (12,235 lbs.); addi-tionally, two 600-litre (132 Imp gal.) drop tanks could be carried.

In addition to a full set of controls and flight instruments, the rear cockpit featured a special control panel allowing the instruc-tor to deactivate some of the instruments in the trainee's cockpit, simulating hardware failures. The canopy was similar to that of

Above: '01 Blue', the Su-15UM prototype, pictured during state acceptance trials with a load of dummy missiles

Left: Front view of the same aircraft. The nose probe carries neither pitch/yaw transducers nor Pion-GT aerials.

Opposite page: Photos from the state acceptance trials report, showing the cockpits of the Su-15UM prototype. *Left row, top to bottom*: The instrument panel, port, and starboard consoles in the trainee's cockpit *Right row, top to bottom*: The instrument panel, port, and starboard consoles in the instructor's cockpit

The Su-15UM prototype as it appeared during state acceptance trials in 1976

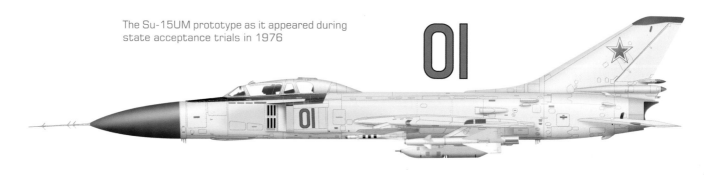

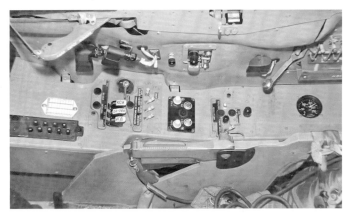

the Su-15UT, the instructor's section incorporating a retractable periscope. The area of the horizontal tail was increased slightly to address the elevator authority problem typical of the Su-15.

Equally remarkably, the U-58TM's empty weight of 10,635 kg (23,445 lbs.) was lower than the single-seater's. This was accomplished by deleting the radar, the SAU-58-2 AFCS, the Lazoor'-M command link system, the SPO-10 RWR, and the RSBN-5S SHORAN. The avionics included an R-832M radio, an ARK-10 ADF, an RV-5 low-range radio altimeter, an MRP-56P marker beacon receiver, a KSI-5 compass system, and an AGD-1 artificial horizon, as well as an SPU-9 intercom and an MS-61 CVR.

The customer required the trainer to retain a measure of combat capability so that weapons training could be performed. Given the lack of radar, this requirement could be met by using heat-

seeking missiles; thus the U-58TM had a weapons control system compatible with the R-98T medium-range AAM and the R-60 short-range AAM. Also, UPK-23-250 gun pods could be carried.

The 'second-generation' trainer variant received the service designation Su-15UM (*oochebnyy, modernizeerovannyy*: trainer [version], upgraded). Aptly coded '01 Blue', the first Su-15UM (c/n 0115301) was rolled out at Novosibirsk-Yel'tsovka in the spring of 1976; Yuriy K. Kalintsev was appointed engineer in charge of the tests. The maiden flight took place on 23 April with factory test pilots Vladimir T. Vylomov and V. A. Belyanin at the controls. Five days later the aircraft was flown to Zhukovskiy, where OKB test pilots Yevgeniy S. Solov'yov and Yuriy A. Yegorov performed an abbreviated manufacturer's test programme comprising only 13 flights.

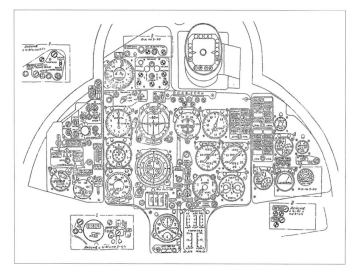

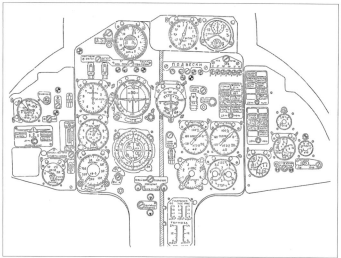

Above left: A production Su-15UM coded '20'; note the black-painted rear canopy frame.

Left: Upper view of the same aircraft

Below, far left: The instrument panel of the production Su-15UM's front cockpit

Below, left: The instrument panel of the production Su-15UM's rear cockpit

Above: '50', another production Su-15UM

Below: A schematic three-view with dimensions from the Su-15UM's structural manual (marked 'Classified')

On 23 June the Su-15UM production prototype was turned over to the military for state acceptance trials; these were rather brief, lasting only five months, and were completed on 25 November with good results. At this stage the aircraft was flown by GNIKI VVS test pilots Yevgeniy S. Kovalenko, Valeriy S. Kartavenko, Oleg G. Tsoi, and V. Ye. Kostyuchenko, who made a total of 72 flights, including 60 'for the record'. The state commission's report said that the two-seater was suitable for training aircrews in takeoff and landing techniques, all flight elements, and certain elements of combat tactics; the Su-15UM was recommended for production and service.

The Novosibirsk aircraft factory produced the new trainer between 1976 and 1980 under the product code *izdeliye* 43; a total of 119 were built in four batches, which numbered up to 50 aircraft

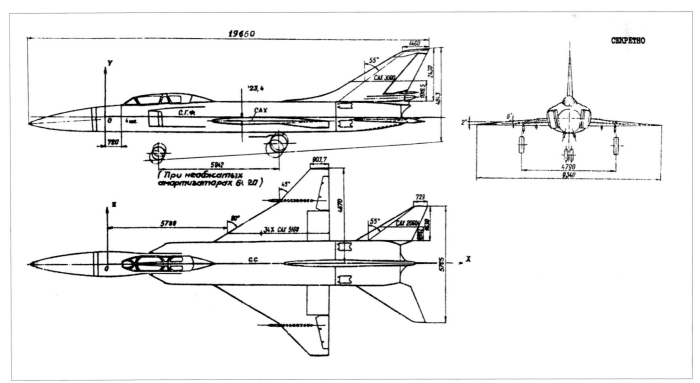

each. The type was cleared for service without the usual Council of Ministers directive—a Ministry of Defence order was all it took. The Su-15UM's NATO reporting name was Flagon-G.

Deliveries commenced in 1978. The only major change made to the Su-15UM in the course of production was that the RSBN-5S Iskra-K SHORAN was added after all; new-build examples were equipped with the system on c/n 0315344 and from batch 4 (c/n 0415301) onward; accordingly, the aerials of the Pion-GT antenna / feeder system were added to the root of the air data boom and the base of the rudder. The final three trainers off the line were delivered fairly late; two of them (c/ns 0415343 and 0415344) left the plant in February 1981, while Su-15UM c/n 0415345—the very last Flagon built—did not make its first flight until 14 February 1982, a full year after the rollout. The honour of making the 'last first flight' of a Su-15 fell to NAPO test pilots Igor' Ya. Sushko and Yuriy N. Kharchenko. In service the Su-15UM was retrofitted with a rain deflector in front of the canopy, a TS-27AMSh rear-view mirror on the front canopy, and the SRO-1P Parol' IFF suite.

T58D-30 Interceptor (Project)

In February 1966, the Sukhoi OKB considered re-engining the Su-15 with D-30 turbofans; the project was provisionally desig-
nated T58D-30 to indicate the engine type. Developed by OKB-19 under General Designer Pavel A. Solov'yov in Perm', the D-30 was a commercial engine created for the Tu-134 short-haul airliner. It had a bypass ratio of 1; the basic version was rated at 6,800 kgp (14,990 lbst), which was more than the R13-300 could provide even in full afterburner (4,100 kgp / 9,040 lbst dry and 6,600 kgp / 14,550 lbst reheat). Moreover, its SFC was 0.62 kg/kgp·h at takeoff power and 0.786 kg/kgp·h in cruise mode, versus the R13-300's 2.25 kg/kgp·h in full afterburner and 0.96 kg/kgp·h in cruise mode; thus, the more fuel-efficient D-30 could increase the Su-15's range and endurance.

However, installing D-30 engines would entail a massive redesign. For one thing, the D-30 had a larger inlet diameter— 0.963 m (3 ft., 2 in.) versus 0.907 m (2 ft., 11¾ in.)—and nearly twice the mass flow at takeoff rating— 126 kg/sec. (277 lbs./sec.) versus 66 kg/sec. (145 lbs./sec.); this would necessitate new air intakes and inlet ducts, which meant designing the entire centre/rear fuselage anew. For another, the D-30 was heavier, weighing 1,550 kg (3,420 lbs.) versus 1,134 kg (2,500 lbs.), which would cause a rearward shift of the aircraft's CG. Last but not least, such radical changes would require new production tooling, which would disrupt production, and the T58D-30 project was abandoned.

T-58Sh Attack Aircraft (Project)

In the summer of 1969 the Sukhoi OKB looked into the possibility of transforming the T-58 into a fully fledged attack aircraft. The idea was triggered by engineer Oleg S. Samoylovich's initiative to design an all-new ground attack aircraft, which was initially known as the SPB (*samolyot polya boya*: battlefield aircraft) before becoming the T-8 (the Su-25 Frogfoot). The SPB unexpectedly ran into an in-house competitor: A. M. Polyakov, the chief project engineer of the Su-7 and Su-17, proposed a version of the T-58 interceptor designated T-58Sh (*shtoormovik*: attack aircraft).

Billed as an 'in-depth upgrade' of the interceptor, the T-58Sh was for all intents and purposes a new aircraft. The forward fuselage up to frame 10 was new, being drooped to provide adequate downward visibility. The wings were also new, featuring a trapezoidal planform with reduced leading-edge sweep and greater area. The cockpit section and the engines were protected by armour, and

the fuel tanks were self-sealing for higher survivability. The radar and other mission avionics associated with the interceptor role were replaced by an ASP-PF gunsight, a PBK-2 bombsight optimised for lob bombing (*pritsel dlya bombometaniya s kabreerovaniya*), and a Fon (Background) laser rangefinder.

The aircraft featured eight weapons hardpoints and a built-in *izdeliye* 225P cannon. The ordnance options included bombs of up to 500 kg (550 lbs.) calibre, unguided rockets of assorted calibres, Kh-23 (AS-7 Kerry) air-to-surface missiles, UPK-23-250 cannon pods, and SPPU-17 pods with movable cannons for strafing ground targets in level flight. For self-defence the T-58Sh would carry K-55 and K-60 AAMs. At a 17.5-ton (38,580 lb.) takeoff weight, the aircraft was to lug 4 tons (8,820 lbs.) of ordnance.

Eventually the T-8 was selected as the more promising design; the T-58Sh did not progress beyond the general arrangement drawing stage.

Left: '50 Blue', a Su-15UM operated by Squadron 3 of the 681st IAP at Danilovo AB, near Yoshkar-Ola, Mari ASSR

Below left: A production Su-15UM coded '30' shows the raised instructor's periscope and the added rain deflector in front of the windshield.

Right: A drawing of the T-58Sh attack aircraft from the ADP documents, showing the new trapezoidal wings with six pylons and the drooped radarless nose improving the pilot's view downward at low altitude

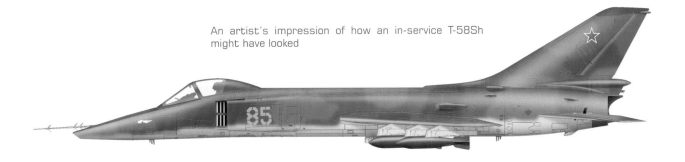

An artist's impression of how an in-service T-58Sh might have looked

A drawing of the Su-19 from the ADP documents, showing the ogival wings with six pylons and the integral cannon on the centreline

Su-19 (T-58PS) Advanced Interceptor (Project)

In 1972–73 the Sukhoi OKB proposed an in-depth upgrade of the Su-15, striving to enhance the interceptor's performance by radically improving the aerodynamics. Since the OKB placed high hopes on the ogival wings developed for the T-10 Flanker-A fighter (the precursor of the Su-27), the intention was to use such wings on the Su-15 (T-58) as well. The rewinged interceptor bore the in-house designation T-58PS; the meaning of the suffix is unknown.

A series of wind tunnel tests was held at TsAGI, followed by more-detailed research into layouts utilising ogival wings. Estimates showed that the interceptor's performance and agility would be enhanced dramatically; also, the new wings provided room for two additional hardpoints, allowing more short-range AAMs to be carried— a real asset in a dogfight, in which the more manoeuvrable fighter could now engage.

Later the T-58PS was referred to in the Sukhoi OKB's official correspondence with MAP and the air force as the Su-19.

Su-19M Advanced Interceptor (Project)

The next step toward improving the performance of the prospective Su-19 (T-58PS) was to install advanced R67-300 engines rated at 7,500 kgp (16,530 lbst). The Sukhoi OKB submitted a technical proposal for an R67-300-powered version to MAP and the air force for appraisal. According to this document the rewinged aircraft (the basic Su-19) could enter flight test in the fourth quarter of 1973, the re-engined version designated Su-19M following in the first quarter of 1975. Yet, the military showed a complete lack of interest; what they needed more was a new radar giving the fighter 'look-down/shoot-down' capability.

Su-15M Advanced Interceptor (Project)

Failing to get the go-ahead for Su-19/Su-19M development, the OKB proposed fitting the Su-15TM with a new *Poorga* (Blizzard) fire control radar to give it 'look-down/shoot-down' capability. The PVO top command, which favoured the Su-15, supported this idea. In addition to the new radar, the proposed upgrade (provisionally designated Su-15M) involved installation of Lyul'ka AL-21F-3 afterburning turbojets, rated at 7,800 kgp (17,195 lbst) dry and 11,215 kgp (24,725 lbst) reheat, and integrating K-25 AAMs. Yet, MAP regarded this project with a jaundiced eye, and all further work on upgrading the Su-15 had to be abandoned.

***

All Su-15 production was concentrated at MAP aircraft factory no. 153, in Novosibirsk, which manufactured 1,272 aircraft of all versions between 1966 and 1980. The by-model/by-year breakdown of Su-15 production is given in the table on this page.

Pages 256–258 show the principal Sukhoi OKB, GNIKI VVS, LII, and Novosibirsk aircraft factory test pilots involved in the testing of the Su-15.

	1966	1967	1968	1969	1970	1971	1972	1973	1974	1975	1976–1980*	Total
Su-15	17	90	150	165	105	37						564
Su-15UT			5	30	60	53						148
Su-15T				20	1							21
Su-15TM					24	60	105	115	116			420
Su-15UM										119		119
Total	17	90	150	170	155	122	113	105	115	116	119	
Grand total												**1,272**

* No information is available on the year-by-year breakdown of Su-15UM production.

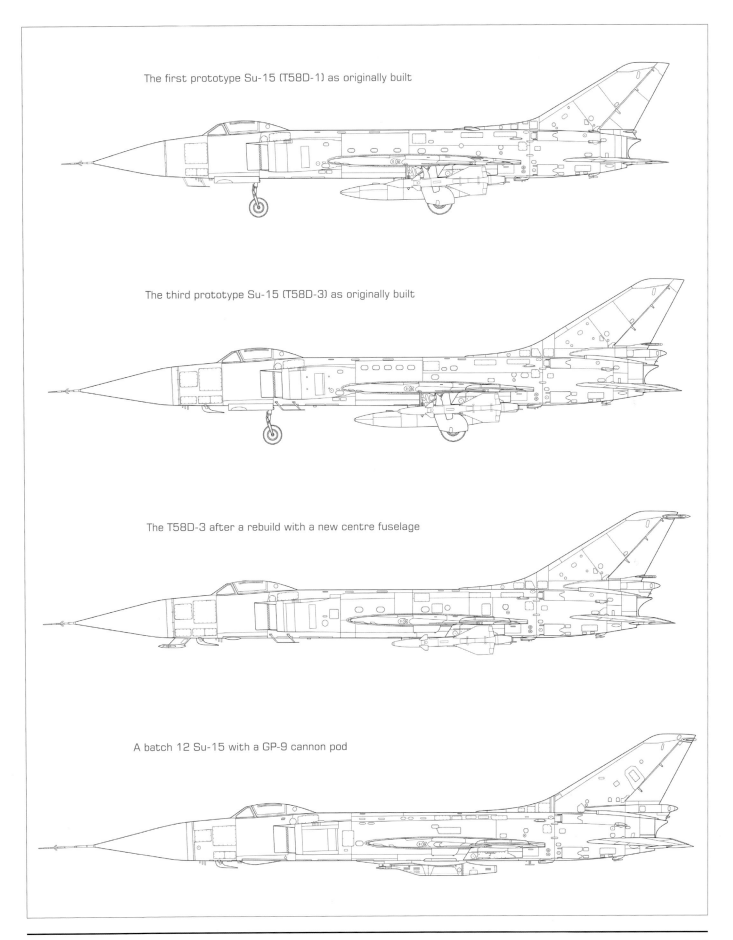

The first prototype Su-15 (T58D-1) as originally built

The third prototype Su-15 (T58D-3) as originally built

The T58D-3 after a rebuild with a new centre fuselage

A batch 12 Su-15 with a GP-9 cannon pod

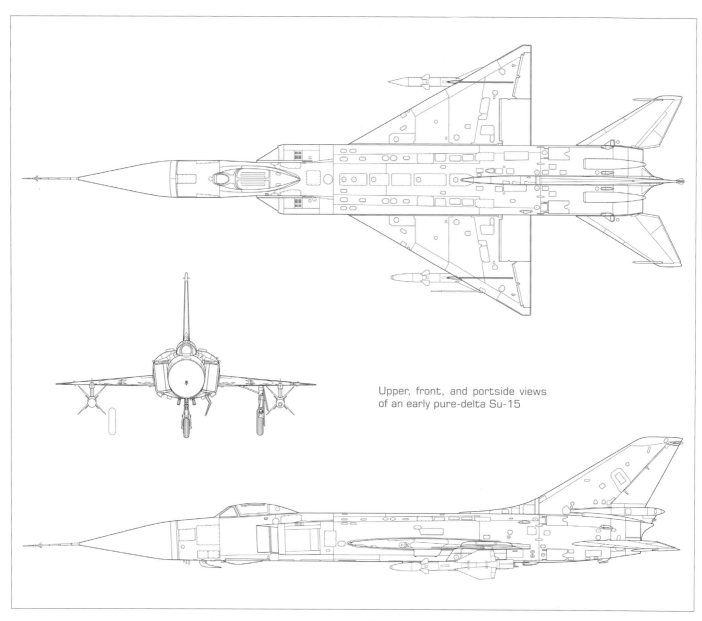

Upper, front, and portside views
of an early pure-delta Su-15

This early-production pure-delta Su-15 is a gate guard at the Russian air force's 514th Aircraft Repair Plant in Rzhev, Russia.

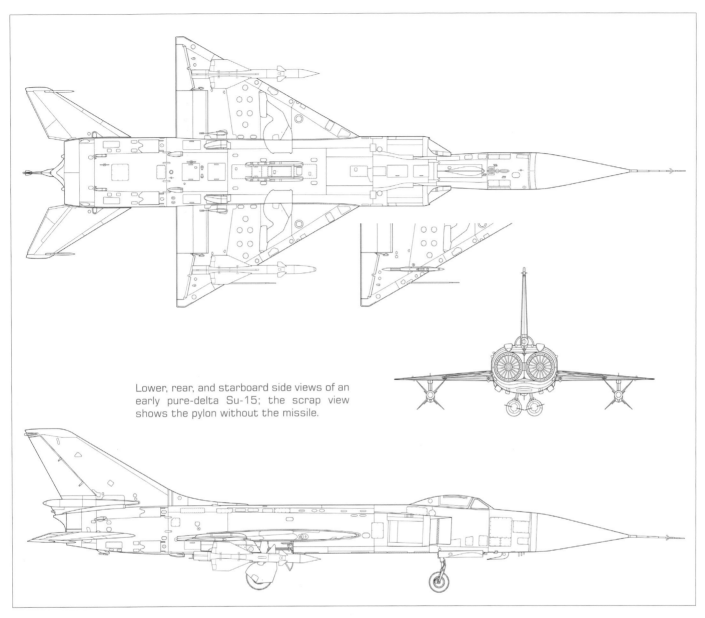

Lower, rear, and starboard side views of an early pure-delta Su-15; the scrap view shows the pylon without the missile.

Su-15 *sans suffixe* '42 Red' (with the radome detached to show the radar drish) in the now-defunct museum at Moscow-Khodynka

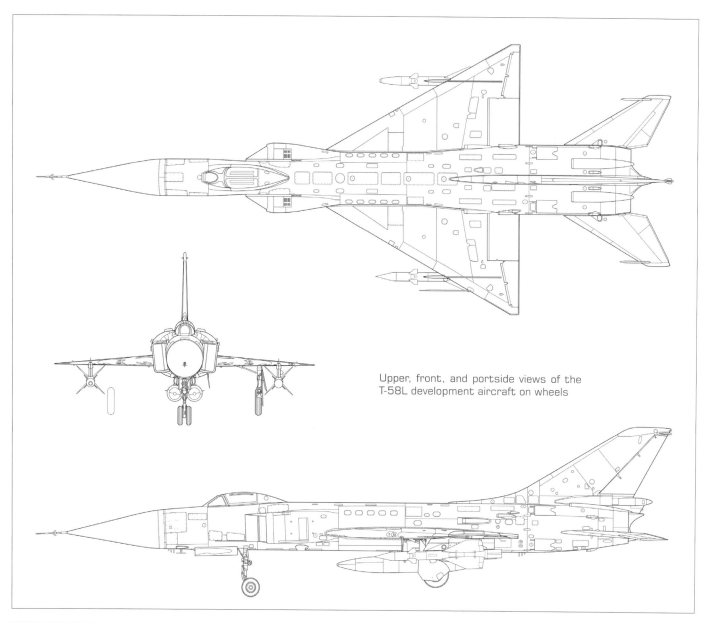

Upper, front, and portside views of the
T-58L development aircraft on wheels

The T-58L (with normal wheeled main gear units) in the Central Russian Air Force Museum in Monino

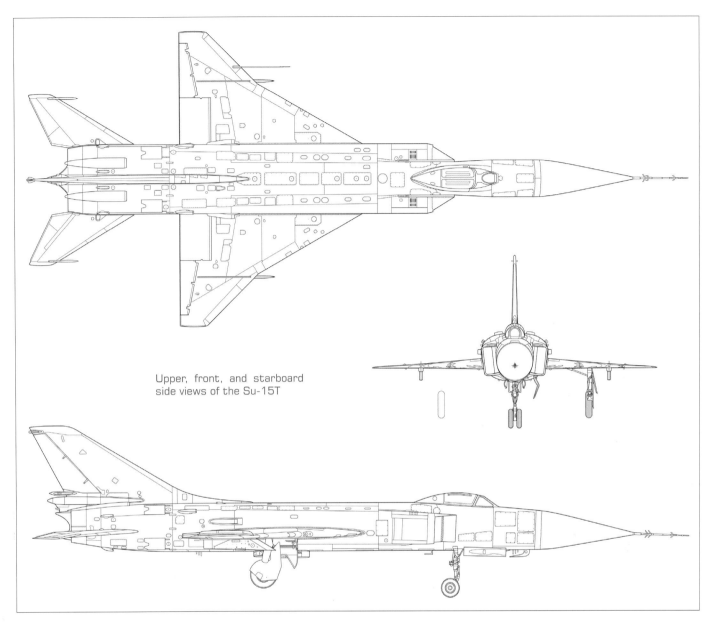

Upper, front, and starboard
side views of the Su-15T

This (unfortunately vandalised) double-delta Su-15 *sans suffixe* was preserved in front of the officers' lodge in Yuzhno-Sakhalinsk.

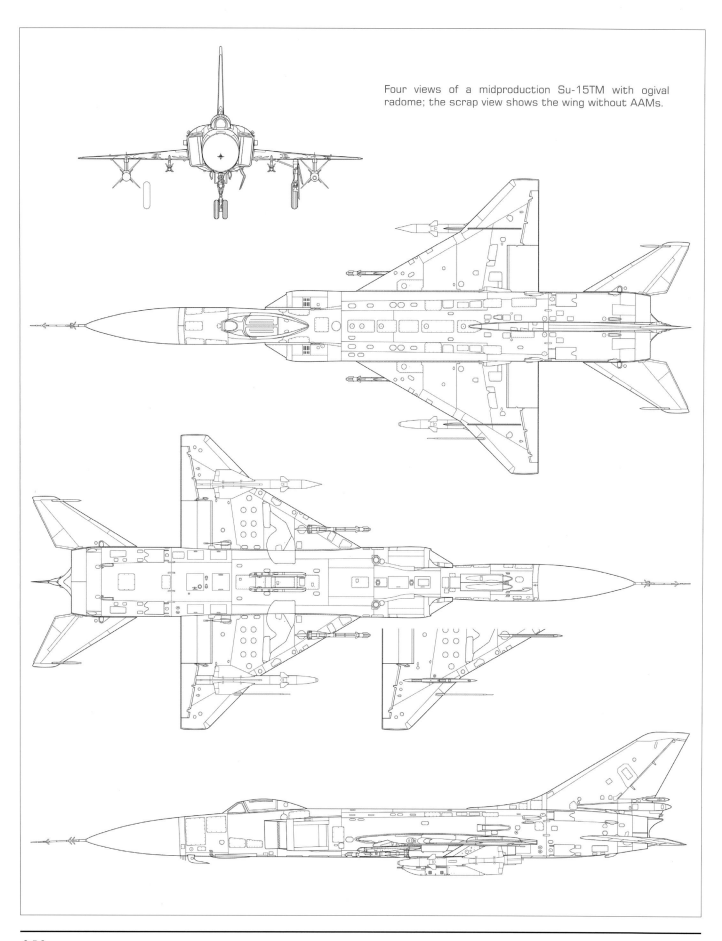

Four views of a midproduction Su-15TM with ogival radome; the scrap view shows the wing without AAMs.

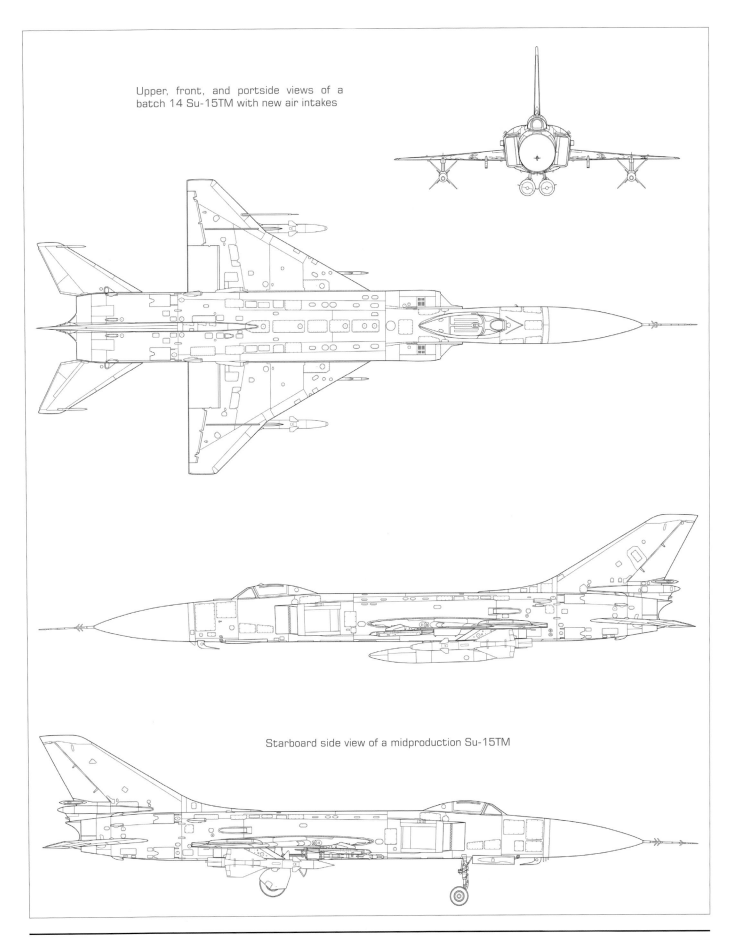

Upper, front, and portside views of a batch 14 Su-15TM with new air intakes

Starboard side view of a midproduction Su-15TM

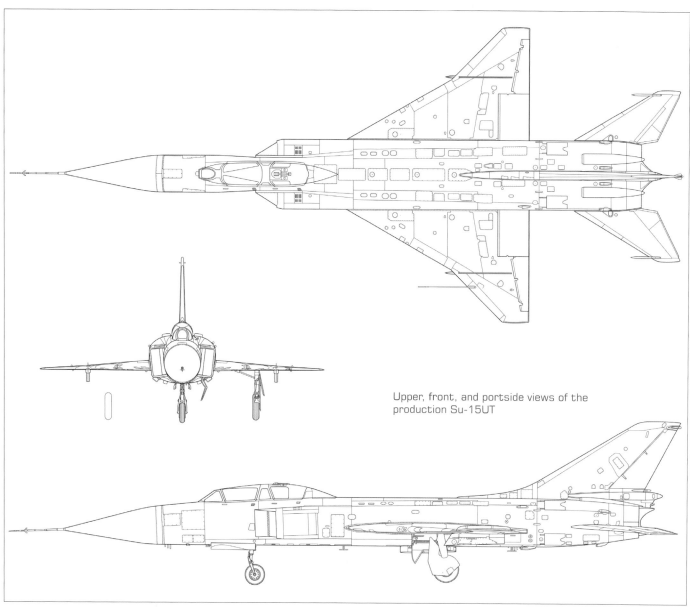

Upper, front, and portside views of the production Su-15UT

Su-15UT '50 Red' seen during its days at Khodynka. It is now at Vadim Zadorozhnyy's technical museum, awaiting restoration.

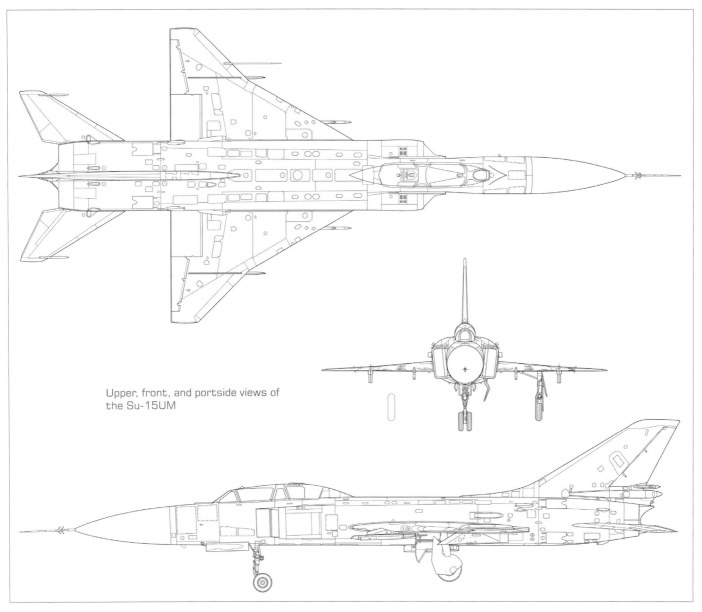

Upper, front, and portside views of
the Su-15UM

Su-15UM '30 Blue' in the now-defunct base museum at Savasleyka AB

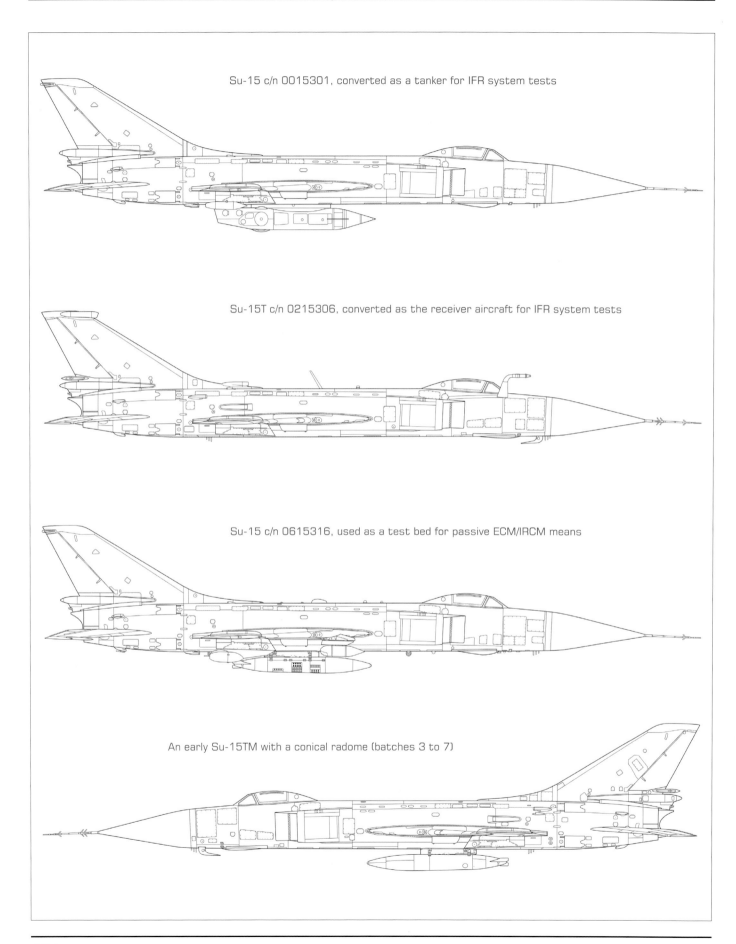

Su-15 c/n 0015301, converted as a tanker for IFR system tests

Su-15T c/n 0215306, converted as the receiver aircraft for IFR system tests

Su-15 c/n 0615316, used as a test bed for passive ECM/IRCM means

An early Su-15TM with a conical radome (batches 3 to 7)

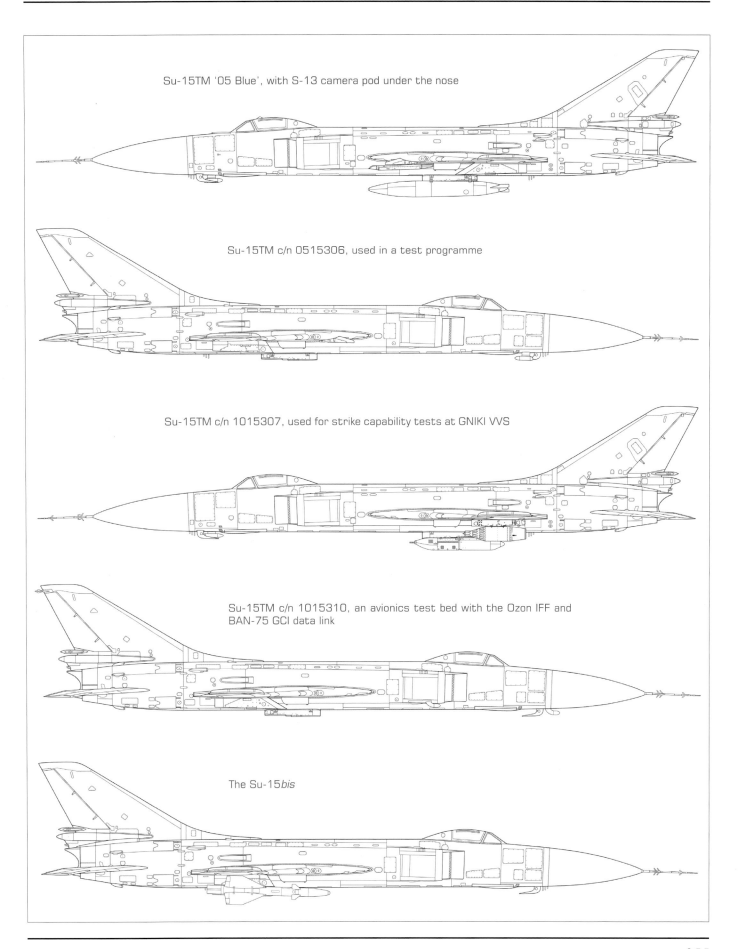

Su-15TM '05 Blue', with S-13 camera pod under the nose

Su-15TM c/n 0515306, used in a test programme

Su-15TM c/n 1015307, used for strike capability tests at GNIKI VVS

Su-15TM c/n 1015310, an avionics test bed with the Ozon IFF and BAN-75 GCI data link

The Su-15*bis*

Sukhoi OKB test pilot Vladimir S. Ilyushin

Sukhoi OKB test pilot Aleksandr N. Isakov

Sukhoi OKB test pilot Vladimir A. Krechetov

Sukhoi OKB test pilot Yevgeniy K. Kukushev

GNIKI VVS test pilot Gheorgiy A. Bayevskiy

GNIKI VVS test pilot Vasiliy G. Ivanov

GNIKI VVS test pilot Pyotr F. Kabrelyov

GNIKI VVS test pilot Norair V. Kazarian

GNIKI VVS test pilot Valeriy S. Kartavenko

GNIKI VVS test pilot Eduard N. Knyazev

GNIKI VVS test pilot Eduard M. Kolkov

GNIKI VVS test pilot Yevgeniy S. Kovalenko

GNIKI VVS test pilot Igor' I. Lesnikov

GNIKI VVS test pilot Valeriy V. Migunov

GNIKI VVS test pilot Vladimir N. Moozyka

GNIKI VVS test pilot Vladimir A. Oleynikov

GNIKI VVS test pilot Leonid N. Peterin

GNIKI VVS test pilot Vadim I. Petrov

GNIKI VVS test pilot Nikolay V. Rukhlyadko

GNIKI VVS test pilot Stal' A. Lavrent'yev

GNIKI VVS test pilot Nikolay I. Stogov

GNIKI VVS test pilot Oleg G. Tsoi

GNIKI VVS test pilot Valeriy I. Mostovoy

GNIKI VVS test pilot Andrey A. Manucharov

LII test pilot Anatoliy S. Levchenko

LII test pilot Ivan V. Makedon

LII test pilot Aleksandr V. Shchookin

LII test pilot Yuriy A. Oosikov

LII test pilot Vladislav I. Loychikov

LII test pilot Viktor V. Zabolotskiy

Novosibirsk aicraft factory test pilot Ivan M. Gorlach

Novosibirsk aicraft factory test pilot Aleksey S. Gribachov

Novosibirsk aicraft factory test pilot Yuriy N. Kharchenko

Novosibirsk aicraft factory test pilot Igor' Ya. Sushko

Novosibirsk aicraft factory test pilot Vladimir T. Vylomov

Novosibirsk aicraft factory test pilot Ivan F. Sorokin

Chapter 8

The Su-15 in Detail

The following brief structural description applies to the standard Su-15 *sans suffixe*. The differing design features of the other versions are indicated as appropriate.

Type: Single-seat supersonic interceptor designed for day and night operation in VMC and IMC. The airframe is of all-metal construction; D16-series duralumin is the primary structural material, with V95 and AK4-1 aluminium alloys used in some areas. Highly stressed structural components are made of 30KhGSA-, 30KhGSNA-, and 30KhGSL-grade high-strength steel, while some components of the rear fuselage structure subjected to high temperatures are made of OT4 heat-resistant titanium alloy.

Fuselage: Semimonocoque, riveted, stressed-skin structure with frames and stringers. The frames can be regular or reinforced (mainframes). The cross section changes along the fuselage length.

Structurally the fuselage consists of two sections: forward (section F-1) and rear (section F-2), with a break point that allows the rear fuselage to be detached for engine maintenance or removal. The two sections are held together by bolts and anchor nuts.

The *forward fuselage* (frames 1–34) includes seven auxiliary frames with duplicate numbers (8/8A/8B, 13/13A/13B, 14/14A/14B, and 28/28A). It begins with the detachable conical radome tipped with the main pitot, which carries pitch and yaw transducer vanes. The dielectric radome is of GRP construction, with a metal attachment 'skirt' fixed to frame 1 at 12 points; it is followed by the no. 1

Overall view of an early-model pure-delta Su-15 *sans suffixe*

Top: The radome and main pitot of a Su-15 *sans suffixe*. Note the pitch/yaw transducer vanes on the pitot.

Centre: The forward fuselage of a Su-15 *sans suffixe*, showing the no. 1 avionics bay access panels

Left and *above*: The cockpit canopy of a Su-15. The stencil reads *Na stoyanke fonar' zachekhlyat'* (Cover the canopy when aircraft is parked).

Above left: The rear end of an early Su-15 with afterburner cooling air intakes

avionics/equipment bay (frames 1–4), which houses the radar set, with six detachable access panels secured by screws on each side.

The pressurised cockpit (frames 4–9) is contained by pressure bulkheads, the fuselage skin, and the pressure floor, with the nose-wheel well located underneath. The sloping rear bulkhead (frames 8B–9) carries ejection-seat guide rails. The cockpit is enclosed by a bubble canopy of similar design to that of the Su-9/Su-11, except that the aft-sliding-canopy portion (frames 7–13) has the transparency divided into port and starboard halves by a frame member. Aft of the cockpit is the no. 2 avionics/equipment bay (frames 9–14A), accessed via two ventral hatches. The forward fuselage is area ruled, the cross section changing from circular aft of the radome to elliptical, with the longer axis vertical in the cockpit section, which is flanked by the engine air intake assemblies (frames 8B–14). The intake trunks are rectangular-section structures blending gradually into the centre fuselage, where the fuselage cross section is almost rectangular. The intakes have sharp lips, and the leading edges are vertical in side elevation. To prevent boundary layer ingestion, the intakes are set apart from the fuselage, the inboard lips acting as boundary layer splitter plates, which are attached to the fuselage by V-shaped fairings spilling the boundary layer. To improve performance at high angles of attack, the air intake trunks are canted outward 2°30'. Each intake features a three-segment vertical airflow control ramp and a rectangular auxiliary blow-in door (frames 13A–13B) on the outer face.

The rear half of section F-1 (frames 14A–34) accommodates three integral fuel tanks, the engine inlet ducts (whose cross section changes smoothly from rectangular at frame 11 to oval at frame 14 to circular at frame 21), and the engine bays; the latter are located between frames 28 and 34, featuring engine-mounting beams and ventral access hatches (frames 28A–30 and 31–33). The inlet ducts incorporate dorsal inspection hatches between frames 21 and 23. Mainframes 16, 21, 25, 28, and 29 feature wing attachment fittings. The rear end of section F-1 mounts the fin fillet (frames 26–34), attached to the skin by special plates with anchor nuts. There are two 'wet' hardpoints side by side under the centre fuselage for carrying drop tanks or cannon pods.

The *rear fuselage* (frames 35–45) is of elliptical cross section, with the longer axis horizontal. It is built in three portions, with a detachable tail fairing constructed of titanium and stainless-steel sheet featuring a 'pen nib' fairing between the engine nozzles. The rear fuselage incorporates the vertical tail attachment fittings and the stabilator-mounting axles at mainframes 38, 42, and 43; it accommodates the engine's jet pipes and the tailplane actuators. The rear fuselage carries four small ventral air scoops for cooling the engine bays, and two large dorsal air scoops for cooling the afterburners. Four airbrakes with a total area of 1.32 m² (14.19 sq. ft.) are located between frames 35 and 38, opening in a cruciform arrangement; maximum deflection is 50°.

Wings: Cantilever midwing monoplane. Most production Su-15s *sans suffixe* (up to c/n 1115330) have pure delta wings similar to those of the Su-9/Su-11, with constant 60° leading-edge sweep, 2° anhedral, and zero incidence. The wings are of two-spar, stressed-skin construction; they are one-piece structures joined to the fuselage at frames 16, 21, 25, 28, and 29. Each wing

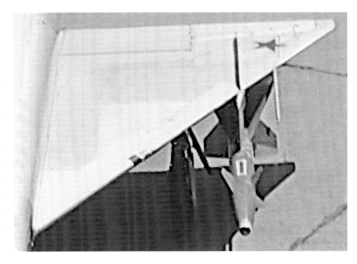

The original pure delta-wing version. Note the wing fence in line with the missile pylon and the backup pitot on the port side.

has 17 ribs, 28 rib caps, and three transverse beams (auxiliary spars), which, together with the front and rear spars, form five bays: the leading edge, forward bay, mainwheel well (between the nos. 1 and 2 auxiliary spars), rear bay, and trailing edge. The rear bays between the nos. 2 and 3 auxiliary spars function as integral fuel tanks, whose skin panels are stamped integrally with the ribs and stringers; ordinary sheet-metal skins are used elsewhere.

Aircraft from c/n 1115331 onward have wings of greater span and area featuring a leading-edge kink at 2.625 m (8 ft., 7³⁄₈ in.) from the centreline, with 60° leading-edge sweep inboard and 45° outboard; the outer portions feature 7° negative camber. The dou-

The port wing of a late-production Su-15 or a Su-15T/Su-15TM. This view shows the cranked leading edge, with 60° leading-edge sweep inboard and 45° outboard. Note the position of the wing fence just outboard of the leading-edge kink and the longer aileron.

ble-delta-version edge has an extra auxiliary spar, 18 ribs, and 29 rib caps per wing.

The wing trailing edge is occupied by one-piece blown flaps, with ailerons outboard of these. There are no leading-edge devices on either version of the wings. The constant-chord flaps are hydraulically actuated, with pneumatic emergency extension, moving on two tracks. Flap settings are 15° for takeoff and 25° for landing when the boundary layer control system (BLCS) is activated, or 25°/45° with the BLCS inactive. The tapered ailerons, carried on three brackets each, are aerodynamically balanced and mass balanced, with a maximum deflection of ±18°30'.

The wings have two hardpoints for missile pylons located approximately 3.05 m (10 ft., ⁵⁄₆₄ in.) from the centreline. Two boundary layer fences are located on the wing upper surface in line with the hardpoints. The port wing carries the backup pitot, mounted just outboard of the hardpoint.

Tail unit: Conventional cantilever tail unit of riveted, stressed-skin construction; sweepback at quarter chord 55° on all tail surfaces. The *vertical tail* comprises a one-piece fin and an inset rudder. The fin is a single-spar structure with a rear auxiliary spar (internal brace), front and rear false spars, stringers, and ribs; it

features a root fillet and a GRP tip fairing. The mass-balanced rudder is a single-spar structure; it is carried on two brackets.

The low-set cantilever *horizontal tail*, mounted 110 mm (4³⁄₈ in.) below the fuselage waterline, consists of slab stabilisers (stabilators); anhedral 6°, incidence in neutral position –4°10'. Each stabilator is a single-spar structure with a rear auxiliary spar (internal brace), front and rear false spars, stringers and ribs, and sheet duralumin skins; it rotates around its axle in two ball bearings. The stabilators feature antiflutter weights projecting beyond the leading edge at the tips; originally the weights were straight but then were angled upward 15° on the production aircraft.

Landing gear: Hydraulically retractable tricycle type, with pneumatic emergency extension. All three landing-gear struts have levered suspension and oleo-pneumatic shock absorbers; the nose unit is equipped with a shimmy damper. The nose unit is castoring through ±60°; steering on the ground is by differential braking.

The forward-retracting nose unit has a single 660 × 200 mm (26.0 × 7.87 in.) KT-61/3 brake wheel. The main units retracting inward into the wing roots are equipped with 880 × 230 mm (34.6 × 9.0 in.) KT-117 brake wheels.

Far left: The starboard tailplane of a very early Su-15 (note the straight antiflutter weight)

Left: The vertical tail of a Su-15, showing the dielectric fin cap, the flush ATC/SIF transponder antenna below it, and the rudder actuator access panel

Far left, below: The nose gear unit of a Su-15 *sans suffixe*, showing the nosewheel brake mechanism and the bulges on the wheel well doors to accommodate the nosewheel

Below left: The starboard main gear unit of a Su-15

Right: An R11F2S-300 engine, showing the ventral oil tank, oil filter, and engine-driven accessories

The nosewheel well is closed by twin lateral doors, the main-wheel wells by triple doors (one segment is hinged to the front spar, one to the root rib, and a third segment attached to the oleo leg). All doors remain open when the gear is down.

All three wheels have pneumatically actuated disc brakes with bimetal and cerametallic brake pads. A PT-15 ribbon-type brake parachute with an area of 25 m² (268.8 sq. ft.) is housed in a fairing at the base of the fin, with vertically split clamshell doors.

Power plant: Two Tumanskiy R11F2S-300 (on early aircraft with no BLCS) or R11F2SU-300 axial-flow afterburning turbojets, rated at 3,900 kgp (8,600 lbst) at full military power and 6,175 kgp (13,610 lbst) in full afterburner. (Some sources give different figures: 4,200 kgp [9,260 lbst] dry and 6,120 kgp [13,490 lbst] reheat.) Aircraft from c/n 1115331 onward have provisions for installing more-powerful R13-300 engines, described under the Su-15T/Su-15TM heading below.

The R11F2S-300 is a two-spool turbojet featuring a three-stage low-pressure (LP) compressor, a three-stage high-pressure (HP) compressor, an annular combustion chamber, single-stage HP and LP turbines, and an afterburner with an all-mode variable nozzle. The transonic-flow compressor has no inlet guide vanes, which facilitates replacement of the first LP stage in the event of damage; the second-stage blades have snubbers to prevent resonance vibrations. Bleed valves are provided to prevent surge. The R11F2SU-300 version additionally features air bleed valves for the boundary layer control system; the bleed rate does not exceed 2.5 kg/sec. (5.5 lbs./sec.); the BLCS operates with the engines in dry-thrust mode.

Engine accessories are driven via a ventral accessory gearbox whose power takeoff shaft is located aft of the HP compressor. The engine has a closed-type lubrication system. Starting is electric, the starter-generator using DC power from onboard batteries or a ground power source. An oxygen feed system is provided to facilitate in-flight restarting. The engine has a closed-type lubrication system using MK-8P mineral oil. Engine-mounting fixtures are located at the top and on both sides of the engine casing.

EPR at takeoff rating 8.7; mass flow at takeoff rating 66 kg/sec. (145.5 lbs./sec.), maximum turbine temperature 1,175° K. SFC 2.37 kg/kgp·h (lb/lbst·h) in full afterburner and 0.93 kg/kgp·h in cruise mode; the said sources give alternative figures of 2.2 and 0.94 kg/kgp·h, respectively. Length overall (including afterburner) is 4.6 m (15 ft., 1 in.), casing diameter 0.825 mm (2 ft., 8½ in.). Dry weight 1,088 kg (2,400 lbs.).

The engines are located side by side in the centre/rear fuselage, breathing through two-dimensional supersonic air intakes located on the centre fuselage sides. The intakes are fully adjustable, with airflow control ramps and auxiliary blow-in doors governed by the UVD-58M electrohydraulic engine / intake control system.

Control system: Conventional powered controls with BU-49 or BU-220D irreversible hydraulic actuators. Roll control is by means of one-piece ailerons, pitch control is by means of stabilators powered by individual actuators, and directional control is by means of a one-piece rudder.

Control inputs are transmitted to the aileron and stabilator actuators via push-pull rods, control cranks, and levers; in the rudder control circuit, cables are used up to frame 31, with rigid linkage farther aft. Artificial-feel units are provided. The tailplane control circuit includes an ARZ-1 stick force limiter, a differential mechanism, and a trim mechanism.

Fuel system: Internal fuel is carried in five integral tanks: three fuselage tanks (no. 1, frames 14A–18; no. 2, frames 18–21; no. 3, frames 21–28) and two wing tanks located immediately aft

PTB-600 drop tanks suspended under the fuselage of a Su-15

of the mainwheel wells. The total capacity is stated variously in different documents, the figures ranging from 8,675 to 8,860 litres (1,907 to 1,949 Imp gal.)—possibly due to the differing specific gravity of different grades of jet fuel. The distribution for the former figure is as follows: no. 1 fuselage tank, 2,350 litres (517 Imp gal.); no. 2 tank, 1,150 litres (253 Imp gal.); no. 3 tank, 2,740 litres (602.8 Imp gal.); and 615 litres (135.3 Imp gal.) in the wing tanks. The internal fuel load is 5,600 kg (12,350 lbs.). The two 'wet' hardpoints under the centre fuselage enable carriage of two 600-litre (132 Imp gal.) PTB-600 drop tanks. Fuel grades used are T-1, TS-1, or RT kerosene.

Electrics: Main 28.5 V DC power is provided by two 12 kW GSR-ST-12000VT engine-driven starter-generators (*ghenerahtor samolyotnyy, s rassheerennym diapazonom skorostey vrashcheniya, so startyornym rezhimom raboty*: aircraft-specific generator with an expanded rpm range, with starter mode); two 15-STsS-45A silver-zinc batteries (22.5 V, 45 A.h) as a backup. 115 V/400 Hz single-phase AC is provided by two SGO-8TF engine-driven alternators (*samolyotnyy ghenerahtor odnofahznyy*: aircraft-specific single-phase [AC] generator). Two ground power receptacles for AC and DC power are located low on the port side of the fuselage, near the wing trailing edge. The electric system uses a single-wire layout (that is, the airframe acts as the 'minus' wire).

The exterior lighting equipment includes port (red) and starboard (green) BANO-45 navigation lights on the wings' upper

The L-shaped aerial of the ARL-SM Lazoor'-M GCI data link system, with the forward IFF aerials ahead of it

surface, close to the wingtips; a KhS-39 white tail navigation light on the fin trailing edge, near the top; identical KhS-39 lights on all three landing-gear struts to confirm to the ground personnel that the gear is 'down and locked' during night operations; and two retractable PRF-4M landing/taxi lights in the wing roots.

Hydraulics: Four separate hydraulic systems (two primary and two actuator supply systems), each with its own NP-34 and NP-26/1 engine-driven piston pump. The *no. 1 primary system* operates the landing gear, flaps, airbrakes, artificial-feel-unit switch mechanism, the port air intake ramp and auxiliary blow-in door, and the port engine's nozzle actuators. It also performs automatic wheel braking during landing-gear retraction. The *no. 2 primary system* powers the radar dish drive, the starboard air intake ramp / auxiliary blow-in door, and the starboard engine's nozzle actuators. The two *actuator supply systems* (main and backup) power the aileron, rudder, and tailplane actuators; in addition to the engine-driven pump, the port system features an NS-3 electrically driven, autonomous emergency pump (*nasosnaya stahntsiya*: 'pumping station'), ensuring that the aircraft remains controllable in the event of a dual engine failure. All systems use AMG-10 oil-type hydraulic fluid; nominal pressure 215 kg/cm^2 (3,070 psi).

Pneumatic system: The pneumatic system performs normal and emergency wheel braking as well as emergency landing-gear and flap extension and operates the inflatable canopy perimeter seal. The system is charged with compressed air to 200 bars (2,857 psi), featuring three 6-litre (1.32 Imp gal.) air bottles. There is also a separate pneumatic system charged to 150 bars (2,140 psi), which operates the stabilising gyros of the R-98 (or R-8M) missiles' seeker heads.

Air conditioning and pressurisation system: Similar to that of the Su-9/Su-11. The cockpit is pressurised by engine bleed air; cockpit air pressure and temperature are maintained automatically. The canopy has an inflatable perimeter seal.

Oxygen system and high-altitude equipment: The oxygen equipment includes a breathing apparatus for normal operation and a separate breathing apparatus used in the event of an ejection.

For operations at altitudes up to 10,000 m (32,810 ft.) and speeds up to 900 km/h (560 mph), the pilot is equipped with a KM-32 oxygen mask, a ZSh-3 'bone dome' flying helmet, and a VK-3 or VK-4 ventilated flying suit (*ventileeruyemy kostyum*). For missions involving supersonic flight, the pilot wears a VKK-4M, VKK-6, or VKK-6P pressure suit and a GSh-4MS, GSh-4MP, or GSh-6M full-face pressure helmet.

Fire suppression system: Titanium firewalls and heat shields are provided in the engine bays to contain possible fires. The Su-15 has an SSP-2I fire-warning system (*sistema signalizahtsii pozhara*; the *I* means *istrebitel'nyy variahnt*: fighter version), a single 6-litre (1.32 Imp gal.) UBSh-6-2 fire extinguisher bottle (*oonifitseerovannyy ballon sharovoy*: standardised spherical [fire extinguisher] bottle) charged with Khladon™ (114V$_2$-grade chlorofluorocarbon) extinguishing agent, and pyrotechnical valves for the port and starboard engines, pipelines, and spray manifolds around the engines. The system has a single-shot operating algorithm.

Avionics and equipment:

a) navigation and piloting equipment: KSI-5 compass system, RSP-6 instrument landing system (including an ARK-10 ADF), an RV-UM low-range radio altimeter, and an MRP-56P marker beacon receiver. An RSBN-5S SHORAN system (with aerials on the nose probe and at the base of the rudder) and an SAU-58 or SAU-58-2 automatic flight control system are fitted.

b) communications equipment: RSIU-5V (R-802) two-way VHF command radio with a wire mesh antenna built into the dielectric fin cap. A Lazoor'-M (ARL-SM) data link receiver with an L-shaped aerial under the nose is fitted for working with the ground-controlled intercept system.

c) weapons control system: The Su-15 is equipped with an RP-15 Oryol-D58 or RP-15M Oryol-D58M fire control radar in a conical radome. A K-10T collimator gunsight is provided.

d) flight instrumentation: KUSI-2500 airspeed indicator, VDI-30 altimeter, AGD-1 artificial horizon, EUP-53 turn and bank indicator, AM-10 accelerometer (g-load indicator), DA-200 combined vertical speed indicator/turn and bank indicator, VAR-300 vertical speed indicator, UKL-2 heading indicator for the KSI-5 compass system, KI-13 compass, M-2,5 Mach meter, ARK-10 ADF indicator, critical angle-of-attack warning system, and AChS-1 chronometer

Air data is provided by main and backup PVD-7 pitots, located at the tip of the radome and on the port wing, respectively.

e) IFF equipment: SRZO-2M Kremniy-2M IFF transponder with triple rod aerials under the forward and rear fuselage and SOD-57M ATC/SIF transponder with flush aerial in the fin

f) ESM equipment: Sirena-2 radar-warning receiver

g) data-recording equipment: From batch 11 onward, the Su-15 is equipped with an SARPP-12V-1 flight data recorder. The FDR continuously records six analogue parameters (barometric altitude, indicated airspeed, vertical g-load, tailplane deflection, and port/starboard engine rpm), as well as 12 single actions (e.g., gear/flap transition), on photo film.

Armament: The standard armament of the Su-15 consists of two R-98 medium-range air-to-air missiles carried on pylon-mounted PU-2-8 launch rails; the missile comes in SARH (R-98R) and IR-homing (R-98T) versions. The older R-8MR and R-8MT can also be used, but only when the target is attacked in pursuit mode. The missiles are fired singly or in a salvo with a 0.5-second interval. Su-15s *sans suffixe* that have received a midlife update can additionally carry two R-60 short-range IR-homing AAMs on PD-62 pylons, with APU-60-1 launch rails (also called P-62-1) retrofitted inboard of the standard pylons in similar manner to the Su-15TM.

The two fuselage hardpoints with BD3-57M pylons (fitted instead of the original BD3-59FK pylons) can be used for carrying UPK-23-250 pods, each housing a Gryazev/Shipunov GSh-23 twin-barrel 23 mm (.90 calibre) cannon with 250 rounds, for use against ground or aerial targets.

Top and *above*: The cockpit of a Su-15 *sans suffixe* (the radar display is unfortunately missing)

Below: The radome of this Su-15 has been detached, exposing the antenna dish of the RP-15 Oryol-D radar.

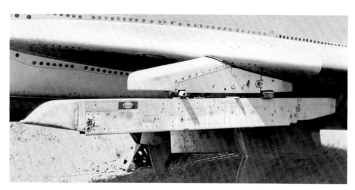

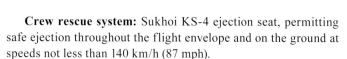

Above left: Early Su-15s were fitted with PU-1-8 launch rails featuring a kinked leading edge for carrying R-98 or R-8M AAMs.

Left: The PU-2-8 missile launch rail on the starboard outer-wing pylon of a late-production Su-15TM; it is characterised by an unbroken leading edge.

Above: An APU-60 launch rail on the inboard missile pylon of a Su-15TM. These are used for carrying R-60 AAMs.

Crew rescue system: Sukhoi KS-4 ejection seat, permitting safe ejection throughout the flight envelope and on the ground at speeds not less than 140 km/h (87 mph).

The Su-15T and Su-15TM differ from the Su-15 *sans suffixe* in the following respects:

Fuselage: Structural changes associated with the installation of the Taifoon radar are made to the forward avionics/equipment bay (frames 1–4), which has differently sized access hatches (three on each side). The detachable radome still has a simple conical shape on the Su-15T (identical to that of the Su-15 *sans suffixe*). In contrast, the Su-15TM has a new ogival radome (fitted to new-build aircraft from batch 8 onward and retrofitted to older examples), again tipped with the main pitot, and further structural changes in the no. 1 avionics bay area associated with the Taifoon-

M radar. The nosewheel well is extended forward to accommodate the taller strut, commencing at frame 3.

A V-shaped spray dam is installed ahead of the cockpit canopy as a midlife update to keep rainwater off the windscreen. Su-15TMs from batch 13 onward have a TS-27AMSh periscopic rearview mirror on the sliding-canopy portion.

The Su-15TM has air intakes of greater area to cater for the greater mass flow of the R13-300 engines; from batch 14 onward the upper lips are cut away to improve intake performance in negative-g manoeuvres. The rear fuselage is aerodynamically cleaner, with six small cooling-air scoops and no large dorsal air scoops.

Wings: Double-delta wings (identical to those of late-production Su-15s *sans suffixe* from c/n 1115331 onward). The Su-15TM has two additional wing hardpoints halfway between the main gear fulcrums and the fuselage.

An R-98 AAM (with a ground cover protecting the seeker head) on the port pylon of a Su-15

A pair of UPK-23-250 cannon pods under the fuselage of a Su-15

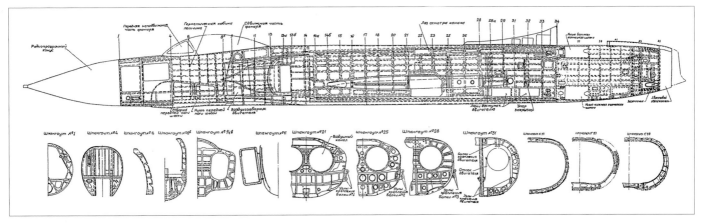

Landing gear: Similar to that of the Su-15 *sans suffixe*, except that the nose unit is taller and is equipped with twin 620 × 180 mm (24.4 × 7.0 in.) KN-9 wheels (*koleso netormoznoye*: nonbraking wheel) to cater for the new and heavier radar, and the nosewheel well is closed by three doors. The main units are again fitted with 880 × 230 mm (34.6 × 9.0 in) KT-117 wheels.

Power plant: Two Tumanskiy R13-300 axial-flow afterburning turbojets rated at 4,100 kgp (9,040 lbst) at full military power and 6,600 kgp (14,550 lbst) in full afterburner. (Some sources state the Su-15TM's engine type as the R13F2-300.) This is likewise a two-spool turbojet with a three-stage LP compressor, a five-stage HP compressor, an annular combustion chamber, single-stage HP and LP turbines and an afterburner with an all-mode variable nozzle. The afterburner features three annular/radial flameholders and a perforated heat shield.

EPR 9.15 at full military power and 9.25 in full afterburner; mass flow at take-off rating 66 kg/sec, maximum turbine temperature 1,223° K. SFC 2.25 kg/kgp·h in full afterburner and 0.96 kg/kgp·h in cruise mode. Length overall (including afterburner) 4.6 m (15 ft 1 in), casing diameter 0.907 m (2 ft 11¾ in). Dry weight 1,134 kg (2,500 lb).

Avionics and equipment:

b) communications equipment: RSIU-5V (R-802) two-way VHF radio (or an R-832M Evkalipt radio on the Su-15TM).

c) weapons control system: The Su-15T is equipped with a Taifoon fire control radar, while the Su-15TM has an RP-26 Taifoon-M radar. A K-10T collimator gunsight is provided.

e) IFF equipment: SRO-1P Parol' IFF transponder with triangular aerials under the forward and rear fuselage and SOD-57M ATC/SIF transponder with flush aerial in the fin.

f) ESM equipment: (Su-15TM) SPO-10 Sirena-3 radar warning receiver.

Armament: The Su-15TM is armed with two R-98MR (SARH) or R-98MT (IR-homing) medium-range AAMs on the outboard pylons and two R-60 short-range IR-homing AAMs on the inboard pylons; later the Su-15T underwent a similar upgrade, being retrofitted with two extra pylons for R-60s. In addition to UPK-23-250 cannon pods, the Su-15TM's fuselage hardpoints can be used for carrying free-fall bombs during strike missions.

Above: A drawing from the Su-15TM's structural manual, depicting the fuselage structure. The scrap views at the bottom are fuselage cross sections at frames 1, 4, 6, 8B, 14B, 11, 21, 25, 28, 31, 35, 37, and 39.

Below: The nose of the Su-15T, showing the twin-wheel nose gear unit and the differently sized avionics access panels

Bottom: The cockpit canopy of a Su-15TM

The Su-15UT and Su-15UM trainers differ from the Su-15 *sans suffixe* in the following respects:

Fuselage: The Su-15UT has a 450 mm (1 ft 5¾ in) longer forward fuselage (Section F-1) with tandem cockpits enclosed by a common canopy similar to that of the Su-9U, with a redesigned windshield (having a plain glass windscreen instead of a bulletproof one), individual aft-hinged portions operated by pneumatic

rams, a glazed inter-canopy crash frame in between and a fixed metal rear fairing. The instructor's cockpit canopy has a pop-up periscope to give a measure of forward view. The empty radome has the same conical shape as on the Su-15 *sans suffixe*.

In contrast, the Su-15UM does not feature this fuselage stretch, having the same dimensions as the single-seat Su-15TM; the instructor's cockpit was accommodated by deleting part of the equipment in the No.2 avionics/equipment bay. The trainee's cockpit canopy has a a spray dam in front of the windshield and a TS-27AMSh periscopic rear-view mirror on the hinged portion. On most aircraft the radome has an ogival shape, as on the Su-15TM (early Su-15UMs still had the conical radome). Also, the Su-15UM has increased-area engine air intakes and a 'cleaner' rear fuselage with fewer cooling air scoops.

Landing gear: (Su-15UT) Basically as for the Su-15 *sans suffixe*, with single KT-61/3 nosewheel and KT-117 mainwheels, except that the wheelbase is longer because of the fuselage stretch; (Su-15UM) as for the Su-15TM, with twin KN-9 nosewheels.

Power plant: (Su-15UT) two R11F2S-300 or R-11F2SU-300 engines; (Su-15UM) two R13-300 engines.

Top left: The twin-wheel nose landing-gear unit of the Su-15T

Top centre: Another view of the Su-15T's nose gear unit with KN-9 nonbraking wheels. Note the shimmy damper above the torque link.

Top right: The starboard air intake of a Su-15T. The stencils between the black/yellow stripes on the boundary layer splitter plate read *Opasno, vozdukhozabornik* (Danger, air intake). Note the perforated forward segment of the airflow control ramp.

Above left: The open port engine bay access doors of a Su-15TM

Left: The R13-300 engine

Avionics and equipment:

a) navigation and piloting equipment: KSI-5 compass system, RSP-6 instrument landing system including an ARK-10 ADF, an RV-5 low-range radio altimeter, an MRP-56P marker beacon receiver. The SHORAN system and SAU-58 (SAU-58-2) automatic flight control system are omitted.

b) communications equipment: (Su-15UT) RSIU-5V (R-802) two-way VHF radio or (Su-15UM) R-832M Evkalipt radio. The two-seat versions have an SPU-9 intercom. The Lazoor'-M (ARL-SM) data link system is omitted.

c) weapons control system: No radar is fitted; however, the Su-15UM does have appropriate controls for using IR-homing AAMs and a K-10T collimator gunsight.

f) electronic support measures equipment: none.

g) data recording equipment: SARPP-12V-1 FDR and MS-61B cockpit voice recorder (*magnitofon samolyotnyy* – 'aircraft-specific tape recorder' or CVR).

Armament: The Su-15UT has no live armament, carrying only dummy AAMs. The Su-15UM can carry R-98MT and R-60 IR-homing AAMs for live weapons training.

Crew rescue system: Two KS-4 ejection seats.

Su-15 Acceleration Time from Mach 1.5 in Full Afterburner at 15,000 m (49,210 ft.) with Two R-98 AAMs			
Time, minutes	AUW 12,500 kg (27,560 lbs.)	AUW 13,000 kg (28,660 lbs.)	AUW 13,500 kg (29,860 lbs.)
to Mach 1.6	0.8	1.0	1.15
to Mach 1.7	1.5	1.8	2.0
to Mach 1.8	2.1	2.4	2.7
to Mach 1.9	2.7	3.0	3.3
to Mach 2.0	3.1	3.5	3.9

Su-15 Target Intercept Parameters with Two R-98 AAMs			
	Cruise mode	Mixed mode*	Afterburner mode
Target flight level, m (ft.)	12,000 (39,370)	20,000 (65,620)	21,000 (68,900)
Target speed, km/h (mph)	1,000 (621)	2,500 (1,552)	2,500 (1,552)
Interceptor's flight level, m (ft.)	9,500 (31,170)	15,000 (49,210)	17,000 (55,770)
Interceptor's speed, km/h (mph)	900 (559)	2,000 (1,242)	2,000 (1,242)
Intercept range from base, km (miles)	590 (366)	400 (248)	295 (183)
Time to intercept range, minutes	36.4	21.4	11.4

* part of the climb is in cruise mode (full military power) and part in afterburner mode

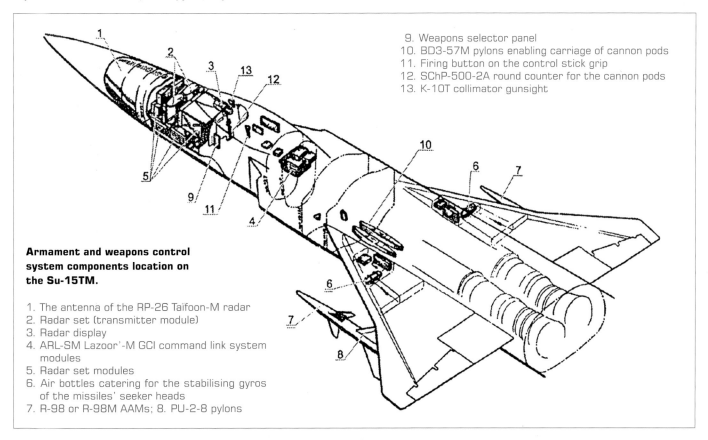

9. Weapons selector panel
10. BD3-57M pylons enabling carriage of cannon pods
11. Firing button on the control stick grip
12. SChP-500-2A round counter for the cannon pods
13. K-10T collimator gunsight

Armament and weapons control system components location on the Su-15TM.

1. The antenna of the RP-26 Taïfoon-M radar
2. Radar set (transmitter module)
3. Radar display
4. ARL-SM Lazoor'-M GCI command link system modules
5. Radar set modules
6. Air bottles catering for the stabilising gyros of the missiles' seeker heads
7. R-98 or R-98M AAMs; 8. PU-2-8 pylons

Top: A Su-15TM with the radome and a hatch cover removed to show the Taifoon-M radar's antenna and radar set

Centre: The radome of a Su-15TM

Above: The landing gear of a Su-15TM

Top: The starboard air intake of a Su-15UM. This design with a cut-back upper lip was also used on batch 14 Su-15TMs.

Centre: The starboard main gear unit and PU-2-8M wing pylon of a Su-15UM

Above and *above right*: The main gear units of a Su-15UM

Top: The port wing of a Su-15TM

Above: Another angle on the Su-15TM's port wing. The apparent double kink of the leading edge is an illusion caused by the wing camber.

Left: The port stabilator of a Su-15TM, showing the upward-angled antiflutter weight

Top: The nose gear unit of a Su-15UM, showing the rear door segment of the nosewheel well. Since the trainer has no radar, the nose gear is lightly loaded and the oleo strut is fully extended.

Centre: This shot gives a view of the starboard main gear unit's inboard side.

Above: The tail of a Su-15UM, showing how the rudder is cropped at the base to provide room for the rear aerials of the RSBN-5 SHORAN and the radar-warning receiver aerial.

Above right: Close-up of the brake parachute container and the cluster of aerials above it

Above: The instrument panel of a Su-15TM

Top left: This Su-15TM is from a different production batch and has a subtly different instrument panel.

Above left and *left*: The outer PU-2-8M and inner PD-62 pylon (with APU-60-1 missile rail) of a Su-15TM

Below left: An R-98MT IR-homing missile carried by a Su-15TM

Below: An R-98MR radar-homing missile carried by a Su-15TM

Above: The trainee's cockpit of a Su-15UM trainer, complete with a dummy radar display

Above right: The instructor's cockpit of a Su-15UM

Right: The cockpit section of a Su-15UT

Below: R-98MT and R-60 IR-homing AAMs carried by a Su-15TM

The cockpit section of a Su-15UM, with a TS-27AMSh rearview mirror on the front canopy. Note the black antiglare panels.

Su-15 Specifications

	Su-15	Su-15TM	Su-15UT	Su-15UM
Power plant	2 × R11F2S-300	2 × R13-300	2 × R11F2S-300	2 × R13-300
Length (less pitot)	20.54 m (67 ft., 4⅝ in.)	20.54 m (67 ft., 4⅝ in.)	20.99 m (68 ft., 10⅜ in.)	19.66 m (64 ft., 6 in.)
Wing span	8.616 m (28 ft., 3¼ in.)	9.34 m (30 ft.,7¾ in.)	8.616 m (28 ft., 3¼ in.)	9.34 m (30 ft., 7¾ in.)
Height on ground	5.0 m (16 ft., 4⅞ in.)	4.843 m (15 ft., 10⅝ in.)	5.0 m (16 ft., 4⅞ in.)	4.843 m (15 ft., 10⅝ in.)
Landing-gear track	4.79 m (15 ft., 8½ in.)	4.79 m (15 ft., 8½ in.)	4.79 m (15 ft., 8½ in.)	4.79 m (15 ft., 8½ in.)
Landing-gear wheelbase	5.887 m (19 ft., 3¾ in.)	5.942 m (19 ft., 6 in.)	6.337 m (20 ft., 9 31/64 in.)	5.942 m (19 ft., 6 in.)
Wing area, m^2 (sq. ft.)	34.56 (371.6)	36.6 (393.54)	34.56 (371.6)	36.6 (393.54)
Aileron area, m^2 (sq. ft.)	1.126 (12.1)	1.51 (16.23)	1.126 (12.1)	1.51 (16.23)
Aileron balance area, m^2 (sq. ft.)	0.34 (3.65)	0.326 (3.5)	0.34 (3.65)	0.326 (3.5)
Horizontal tail area, m^2 (sq. ft.)	5.58 (60.0)	5.58 (60.0)	5.58 (60.0)	6.43 (69.1)
Vertical tail area, m^2 (sq. ft.)	6.951 (74.74)	6.951 (74.74)	6.951 (74.74)	6.951 (74.74)
Empty weight, kg (lbs.)	10,220 (22,530)	10,874 (23,970)	10,750 (23,700)	10,635 (23,445)
Takeoff weight, kg (lbs.):				
normal	16,520 (36,420) [1]	17,194 (37,905) [1]	16,690 (36,795) [2]	17,200 (37,920) [1]
maximum	17,094 (37,685) [3]	17,900 (39,460) [4]	17,200 (37,920) [3]	17,900 (39,460) [4]
Landing weight, kg (lbs.)	12,040 (50,790)	12,060 (26,590)	n.a.	13,314 (29,350)
Fuel load, kg (lbs.)	5,600 (12,345)	5,550 (12,235)	5,010 (11,045)	5,550 (12,235)
Thrust/weight ratio	0.92	0.92	0.88	n.a.
Top speed, km/h (mph):				
at sea level	1,200 (745)	1,300 (807)	1,200 (745)	1,250 (776)
at high altitude	2,230 (1,385) [5]	2,230 (1,385) [6]	1,850 (1,150) [5]	1,875 (1,164) [7]
Mach number at high altitude	2.13	2.16	1.753	1.758
Unstick speed, km/h (mph)	395 (245)	370 (230)	n.a.	340–350 (211–217)
Landing speed, km/h (mph)	315 (195)	285–295 (177–183)	330–340 (204–211)	260–280 (161–174)
Service ceiling, m (ft.)	18,500 (60,695)	18,500 (60,695)	16,700 (54,790)	15,500 (50,850)
Climb time to 16,000 m (52,490 ft.), minutes	13	n.a.	12	n.a.
Range, km (miles):				
on internal fuel	1,270 (790)	1,380 (860)	1,290 (800)	n.a.
with drop tanks	1,550 (960)	1,700 (1,055)	1,700 (1,055)	1,150 (715)
Endurance	1 hr., 54 min.	n.a.	n.a.	n.a.
Takeoff run, m (ft.)	1,100 (3,600)	1,000–1,100 (3,280–3,600)	1,200 (3,940)	n.a.
Landing run, m (ft.):				
without brake parachute	1,500 (4,920)	1,050–1,150 (3,440–3,770)	n.a.	n.a.
with brake parachute	1,000 (3,280)	850–950 (2,790–3,120)	1,150–1,200 (3,770–3,940)	n.a.
G-limit	5	5	5	5
Armament:				
missiles	2 × R-98R/T (R-8MR/MT, R-8MR1/MT1)	2 × R-98MR/MT (R-8MR1/MT1)	2 × R-98MT 2 × R-60	2 × R-98MT 2 × R-60
cannons	2 × UPK-23-250	2 × UPK-23-250	–	–
Ordnance load, kg (lbs.)	586	1,135	–	–

Notes:

1. With two R-98 missiles; 2. With two dummy R-98 missiles; 3. With two drop tanks / no missiles; 4. With two drop tanks, two R-98Ms, and two R-60s
5. At 15,000 m (49,210 ft.); 6. At 13,000 m (42,650 ft.); 7. At 11,500 m (37,730 ft.)

Chapter 9

The Su-15 in Service

On the morning of 9 July 1967, huge crowds of Muscovites and visitors to the capital came flocking to Moscow's Domodedovo airport, where a spectacular airshow—the first after a six-year pause—was to take place. After the hardships of the Khrushchov era, the Soviet aircraft industry and the air force were eager to show the nation's new leaders (and the public at large) that in spite of the battering they had taken due to Khrushchov's 'missile itch', they were still very much alive and had considerable potential. Hence it was decided to display almost everything the industry had to offer, including aircraft that were still undergoing trials at the time or were just about to enter production, service, or both. The latter included the Sukhoi OKB's latest product, the Su-15

interceptor, which received the honour of opening the flying display of the show. Right on schedule, a group of five Su-15s flown by 148th TsBP i PLS pilots and led by Col. P. P. Fedoseyev made a high-speed pass over the improvised grandstand and pulled into a spectacular formation climb, fanning out at the top. The display also included a short takeoff and landing demonstration by the experimental T-58VD piloted by OKB test pilot Yevgeniy S. Solov'yov. A while later, Sukhoi OKB chief test pilot Vladimir S. Il'yushin made a flypast in a production Su-15 coded '47 Red' and painted black overall for sheer effect.

From the number of Su-15s participating in the show, Western military analysts concluded that the Soviet Union had fielded a new

Technicians inspect the nose gear of an early (pure-delta) Su-15 *sans suffixe* parked in front of a jet blast deflector. An APA-5 ground power unit is parked alongside.

Left: This Su-15, painted black overall to create a menacing effect and coded '47 Red', gave a solo performance at the Moscow-Domodedovo airshow on 9 July 1967.

Three of the five Su-15s *sans suffixe* that opened the flying display at the airshow on 9 July 1967. The fighters carry dummy R-98 missiles.

interceptor, and the Su-15 was allocated the NATO reporting name 'Flagon'. Western aviation experts made a fairly accurate guess as to the fighter's performance and correctly guessed that the aircraft was powered by Tumanskiy R11 afterburning turbojets. The advent of the Su-15TM with its ogival nose, however, confused the Western experts; they decided that the aircraft was fitted with a new radar (which was correct) and powered by Lyul'ka AL-21F engines (which was absolutely wrong). Code-named Flagon-F, the new version was referred to in the Western press as the 'Su-21'; it was quite some time before the correct designation became known.

As mentioned in chapter 7, the Su-15-98 aerial-intercept weapons system was formally included into the Soviet air defence force inventory in April 1965 upon completion of the state acceptance trials. The system was capable of intercepting targets flying at

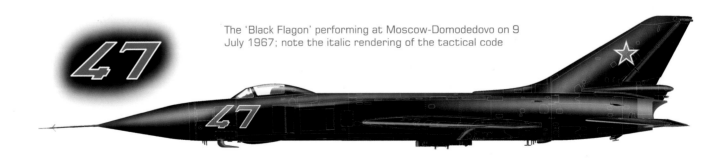

The 'Black Flagon' performing at Moscow-Domodedovo on 9 July 1967; note the italic rendering of the tactical code

Right: Su-15 *sans suffixe* '01 Blue' taxies in after a sortie (note the open brake parachute doors). The aircraft has been upgraded with two extra pylons for R-60 AAMs. Note that the flight line features centralised refuelling, obviating the need for fuel trucks.

Opposite page, bottom: Another view of the Su-15s at Domodedovo; note the DAP-67 smoke generator pods on the fuselage pylons.

Below right: A late-production Su-15 *sans suffixe* with double-delta wings

speeds of 500–3,000 km/h (310–1,860 mph) and altitudes of 500–23,000 m (1,640–75,460 ft.). The interceptor was guided toward the target by the Vozdukh-1 automated GCI system until the target came within range of its fire control radar.

The Soviet Ministry of Defence in general, and the PVO top brass in particular, had a lot riding on the new interceptor which was to replace several obsolete aircraft types in the PVO inventory. Following the usual practice, the 148th TsBP i PLS was the first unit to master the new type; the centre's 594th UIAP at Savasleyka AB started conversion training for the Su-15 in early 1966. Su-15 production in Novosibirsk had a slow start, and practical training on the type could not begin until Sukhoi OKB test pilot Vladimir S. Ilyushin had ferried the second preproduction aircraft (c/n 0015302) from Zhukovskiy to Savasleyka AB on 28 October 1966. By the end of the year the centre's pilots had made 14 flights in this aircraft.

Deliveries of production Su-15s to the 594th UIAP began in January 1967. Since no dual-control trainer version of the Su-15 existed yet, single-engined Su-9U trainers had to be used as the next-best thing. Even so, the Su-9U was in short supply and was badly needed by the operational units flying the Fishpot, so the decision was taken to use swept-wing Su-7U trainers instead. In May 1967 service pilots started taking their conversion training in the Su-7U before flying solo in the Su-15.

In the spring of 1967 an ad hoc display team was formed at the 148th TsBP i PLS for the abovementioned Moscow-Domodedovo airshow, which was to take place in July; the team included 594th UIAP pilots, pilots from the centre's Command & Control Squadron, and a few service pilots. To rehearse the display the team temporarily relocated to Zhukovskiy together with its aircraft. (According to some sources, the Su-15s came from the 611th IAP—see below.) Training flights were made with dummy R-98 missiles and did not go without incident; on 4 July, five days before the show, one of the fighters (c/n 0315304) lost a missile *together with the pylon* after pulling into a steep climb. Investigation of the incident showed that the aircraft had exceeded its operational g-limit by far, and it was no wonder that the pylon had broken off. Detailed examination of the airframe revealed substantial permanent structural deformation, and the aircraft was declared a write-

off; thus the whole affair was actually a nonfatal accident. To prevent further incidents, the actual display flight at the show was performed sans missiles and with DAP-67 smoke generator pods (*dymovoy aviatsionnyy pribor:* aircraft-specific smoke generator device) on the fuselage hardpoints instead of drop tanks.

Deliveries to first-line PVO units began in the spring of 1967. The 611th IAP of the Moscow PVO District, based at Dorokhovo AB near Bezhetsk (Yaroslavl' Region), was the first to reequip, receiving ten Su-15s (mostly batch 3 aircraft). The pilots took their training at the 148th TsBP i PLS, while the ground personnel studied the Su-15 directly at the Novosibirsk plant. As mentioned in

chapter 7, the 611th IAP was entrusted with the obligatory service trials of the new interceptor, which proceeded from 29 September 1967 to 15 May 1969. The 62nd IAP, based at Bel'bek AB on the Crimea Peninsula, the Ukraine, followed in July 1967; the 54th GvIAP, at Vainode AB, Latvia, reequipped shortly afterward.

Under the conversion training programme, one pilot for each Su-15 would be trained within a six-month period to perform combat duty in visual and instrument meteorological conditions in the daytime and in VMC at night. This proved difficult to accomplish; to hasten the training process, qualified flying instructors (QFIs) were seconded to first-line PVO units from the 148th TsBP i PLS.

Unlike the Su-7 and Su-9, the Su-15's service introduction period was not characterised by soaring accident rates; this was no doubt partly due to the added safety of the twin-engined fighter versus a single-engined aircraft. Still, the first total loss in operational service occurred as early as 16 August 1967, when Capt. N. I. Nazarov of the 611th IAP was forced to eject from Su-15 c/n 0315301 after both engines quit on final approach at an altitude of 270 m (885 ft.). Fuel starvation was found to be the cause; the aircraft had not been refuelled adequately and the flow meters had been working incorrectly. The share of accidents caused by design flaws and manufacturing defects did not exceed 30%.

The strategic bombers in service with the US Air Force (primarily the Boeing B-52 Stratofortress) and the Royal Air Force (the V-Bombers), as well as the North American AGM-28 Hound Dog (USAF) and Avro Blue Steel (RAF) supersonic air-to-surface missiles carried by these aircraft, were envisaged as the principal

Above left: A PVO pilot poses for a publicity shot with his Su-15. This view shows well the *Flagon-A*'s conical radome.

Left: Three late-production (double-delta) Su-15s with extra wing pylons at the dispersal area of a PVO airbase. Note that the national insignia have no white filling between the star itself and the red outline.

Right: 'Can't find the darn place on the map . . . just point your finger!' This view illustrates the Su-15's distinctively splayed air intakes.

Right: A Su-15 coded '50 Blue' in flight, carrying an IR-homing R-98T on the port pylon and a radar-homing R-98R on the starboard pylon

Below right: 'No malfunctions.' A Su-15 pilot writes his comments in the maintenance log after a sortie for the aircraft's crew chief. Note the early-style maintenance award in the form of the legend '*Otlichnyy*' (Excellent) on the nose.

targets that the Su-15 would have to deal with. As a dogfighting machine the Su-15 was no good, of course, since it lacked the agility—but then, it was not designed with dogfights in mind. The addition of R-60 heat-seeking, short-range AAMs when the Su-15TM came on the scene (and earlier Flagons were upgraded) did not increase the interceptor's chances in the event of an encounter with enemy fighters but still improved the chances of a 'kill' if the R-98 medium-range AAMs missed their target.

By June 1968, eight fighter regiments had taken delivery of 130 Su-15s; a total of 149 pilots had the Su-15 type rating but fewer than half of them were fully trained to fly combat sorties in daytime IMC, and only two pilots (!) were able to fly night sorties. Apart from the units of the 148th TsBP i PLS, Su-15 pilots were trained at the Stavropol' Military Pilot & Navigator College (SVVAULSh: *Stavropol'skoye vyssheye voyennoye aviatsionnoye oochilischche lyotchikov i shtoormanov*). Special attention was given to engagements in head-on mode during conversion training, since this type of attack was new for Soviet interceptor pilots—the capabilities of the Su-9 and Su-11 simply did not enable head-on engagements. Live weapons training at a target range near Krasnovodsk involving missile launches commenced in April 1967; the 611th IAP's pilots were the first to do so, firing 47 missiles at various practice targets.

The Su-15T, featuring a new Taifoon radar and an SAU-58 automatic flight control system (which enabled flight along preset trajectories and automated the main stages of the intercept), entered production in December 1970. However, the Flagon-E was beset by numerous problems associated with the weapons control system and the new blown flaps. As a result, the production run was limited to a mere 21 aircraft, which did not become operational until the summer of 1972 due to the need to rectify various defects. With the air force's and MAP's consent, most of them were eventually transferred to SVVAUL, serving on as trainers.

The Su-15T was just an interim type, since the Sukhoi OKB had by then brought out the more advanced Su-15TM, which, together with the R-98M missile and the Vozdukh-1M GCI system, formed the upgraded Su-15-98M aerial-intercept weapons system. The first lot of production Su-15TMs was delivered in the spring of

Su-15 Units as of 1 January 1970		
Unit	**Base**	**Aircraft types**
Direct reporting units		
• 148th TsBP i PLS, Savasleyka AB		
592nd UIAP	Klin-5 AB	Su-15
594th UIAP	Savasleyka AB	Su-15, Yak-28P
• Stavropol' VVAULSh		
218th UAP	Sal'sk, Rostov Region	Su-9, Su-15, MiG-17
Moscow PVO District (HQ Moscow)		
• 2nd PVO Corps, HQ Rzhev (Kalinin Region)		
28th Leningradskiy GvIAP	Andreapol', Kalinin Region	Su-15
• 3rd PVO Corps, HQ Yaroslavl'		
611th IAP	Dorokhovo AB, Bezhetsk, Kalinin Region	Su-15
• 16th PVO Corps, HQ Bryansk		
153rd IAP	Morshansk, Tambov Region	Su-15
2nd Independent PVO Army (HQ Minsk, Belorussia)		
• 27th PVO Corps, HQ Riga, Latvia		
54th Kerchenskiy GvIAP	Vaïnode, Latvia	Su-15
4th Independent PVO Army (HQ Sverdlovsk)		
• 28th PVO Division, HQ Kuibyshev		
681st IAP	Danilovo AB, nr Yoshkar-Ola, Marii ASSR	Su-15
8th Independent PVO Army (HQ Kiev, the Ukraine)		
• 1st PVO Division, HQ Sevastopol', the Ukraine		
62nd IAP	Bel'bek AB, Sevatopol', Crimea Region	Su-15
• 21st PVO Division, HQ Odessa, the Ukraine		
90th IAP	Chervonoglinskaya AB, Artsyz, Odessa Region	Su-15
10th Independent PVO Army (HQ Arkhangel'sk)		
• 5th PVO Division, HQ Petrozavodsk, Republic of Karelia, Russia		
265th IAP	Poduzhem'ye, nr Kem', Karelia	Su-15
11th Independent PVO Army (HQ Khabarovsk)		
• 8th PVO Corps, HQ Komsomol'sk-on-Amur		
60th IAP	Komsomol'sk-on-Amur/Dzyomgi	Su-15
302nd IAP	Pereyaslavka-2 AB, Khabarovsk Territory	Su-15
• 24th PVO Division, Sakhalin Island		
777th IAP	Sokol AB, Sakhalin	Su-15
12th Independent PVO Army (HQ Tashkent, Uzbekistan)		
• 7th PVO Division, HQ Alma-Ata, Kazakhstan		
9th Odesskiy GvIAP	Andizhan, Uzbekistan	Su-15

1972, and the new version was officially included into the inventory on 21 January 1975. The Flagon-F enabled manually or automatically controlled interception of targets flying at altitudes of 500–24,000 m (1,640–78,740 ft.) and speeds up to 1,600 km/h (990 mph) in pursuit mode, or 2,000–21,000 m (6,560–68,900 ft.) and up to 2,500 km/h (1,550 mph) in head-on mode. The weapons control system had enhanced ECM resistance; on the downside, the service ceiling had decreased from 18,500 m (60,690 ft.)—the figure obtained in the course of the trials—to 17,970 m (58,960 ft.).

Gradually, together with the MiG-25P heavy interceptor, the Su-15 replaced the outdated Su-9, Su-11, Yak-28P, and MiG-21PFM in the PVO inventory. The Flagon saw service with units stationed in almost all borderside regions of the Soviet Union, the High North and the Far East receiving the highest priority. By the end of 1975 the PVO intended to reequip 41 fighter regiments with the Su-15, whereupon the new interceptor would make up nearly 50% of the service's aircraft fleet. However, by the time production of the Su-15's combat versions ended in early 1976, the type was operational with only 29 units, 18 of them equipped with Su-15s *sans suffixe* and 11 units flying Su-15TMs. These were the following:

• The 9th *Odesskiy* GvIAP at Andizhan, Uzbekistan, reporting to the 12th OA PVO (Independent Air Defence Army). The unit previously operated the Su-9.

• The 22nd *Khalkhingol'skiy* IAP (14th OA PVO), at Bezrechnaya AB (Chita Region, East Siberia). The unit converted to the Su-15TM from the Yak-28P; it is not to be confused with the 22nd GvIAP, at Tsentral'naya-Ooglovaya AB. The honorary appellation was given for the unit's part in the war with Japan on the Khalkhin Gol River, Manchuria (a.k.a. the Nomonhan Incident), in 1939.

• The 47th IAP (11th OA PVO), at Zolotaya Dolina AB, near Nakhodka, Primor'ye Territory. The unit consecutively operated the Su-15 *sans suffixe*, Su-15T, and Su-15TM, having converted from the Su-9.

• The 54th GvIAP (6th OA PVO), at Vainode, Latvia, which was established with the type

• The 57th GvIAP (14th OA PVO), at Noril'sk (Alykel' airport), Krasnoyarsk Region, which also converted to the Su-15TM from the Su-9. This unit disbanded in 1978, its number and regalia being transferred to the former 911th IAP, which see.

• The 60th IAP (11th OA PVO), at Komsomol'sk-on-Amur/ Dzyomgi airfield, Primor'ye Territory, which converted to the Su-15TM from the MiG-17PF

• The 62nd IAP (8th OA PVO), at Bel'bek AB near Simferopol', Crimea Region, which consecutively operated the Su-15 *sans suffixe*, Su-15T, and Su-15TM. The unit had the honorary appellation *imeni pyatidesyatiletiya VLKSM* (named after the 50th anniversary of the All-Union Lenin Young Communist League); such lofty names were not uncommon at the time.

• The 90th IAP (8th OA PVO), at Chervonoglinskaya AB, near Artsyz (Odessa Region, the Ukraine), operating the Su-15 *sans suffixe* and Su-15TM, which previously flew Su-9s.

• The 153rd IAP (Moscow PVO District), at Morshansk, Tambov Region. The unit converted from the Yak-28P, consecutively operating the Su-15 *sans suffixe*, Su-15T, and Su-15TM.

• The 156th El'bingskiy IAP (12th OA PVO), at Maryy-2 AB, Turkmenia. The unit converted from the Su-9.

Right: A Soviet serviceman acts as ground marshaller, giving hand signals (for want of flags) to the pilot of a Su-15T taxiing in after landing. The aircraft carries a pair of striped dummy R-98s—an IR-homing R-98T to port and a radar-homing R-98R to starboard.

Below right: A 54th GvIAP Su-15UT coded '95 Blue' taxies after landing at Slupsk, Poland, during an exercise in the summer of 1975.

• The 166th GvIAP (19th OA PVO), at Sandar AB (Marneuli, Georgia). The unit converted from the MiG-17 to the Su-15T and Su-15TM.

• The 171st *Tool'skiy* IAP (11th OA PVO), at Bombora AB (Gudauta, Abkhazia/Georgia), again a former Yak-28P unit. The honorary appellation was given for the defence of the Russian city of Tula in the Great Patriotic War. The unit was transferred to the 11th OA PVO and moved to Anadyr' (Oogol'nyy airport), Chukotka Region, in 1982.

• The 178th GvIAP (12th OA PVO), at Krasnovodsk, Turkmenia

• The 180th *Volgogradskiy* GvIAP (12th OA PVO), at Krasnovodsk, a former Yak-25 unit. The appellation was given for the unit's part in the defence of what was then Stalingrad (now Volgograd).

The crew of the same Su-15UT '95 Blue' climb out of the aircraft after shutting down the engines. The ladder was obviously meant for a different aircraft type. Note the blind flying hood in the front cockpit and the forward vision periscope in the rear cockpit.

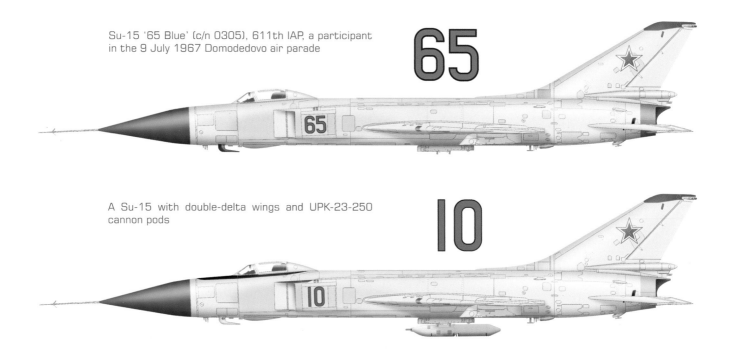

Su-15 '65 Blue' (c/n 0305), 611th IAP, a participant in the 9 July 1967 Domodedovo air parade

A Su-15 with double-delta wings and UPK-23-250 cannon pods

• The 265th IAP (10th OA PVO), at Poduzhem'ye AB, near Kem', Karelian Autonomous SSR, which converted to the Su-15TM from the MiG-15

• The 302nd IAP (11th OA PVO), at Pereyaslavka AB (Khabarovsk Region), which converted to the Su-15 in 1970

• The 364th IAP (12th OA PVO), at Nebit-Dag (now Balkanabad, Turkmenia), which converted to the Su-15 from the MiG-17

• The 393rd Baranovichskiy GvIAP (19th OA PVO), at Priv-olzhskiy AB, Astrakhan' Region, which previously flew Su-11s

• The 431st IAP (10th OA PVO), at Afrikanda AB (Murmansk Region). The unit converted to the Su-15TM from the MiG-19.

• The 524th IAP, at Letneozyorsk (Arkhangel'sk Region), which converted to the Su-15 from the MiG-17

• The 592nd UIAP, at Klin-5 AB (Moscow Region)

• The 594th UIAP, at Savasleyka AB (Gor'kiy Region); both units were former Su-9 operators and belonged to the 148th TsBP i PLS).

• The 611th *Peremyshl'skiy* IAP (Moscow PVO District), Dorokhovo AB (Bezhetsk, Kalinin Region), a former Su-9/Su-11 unit. The appellation was given for the liberation of the Polish city of Przemyśl (traditionally called Peremyshl' in Russian in a historical context).

A Su-15 coded '01 Red' and carrying UPK-23-250 cannon pods streams its PT-15 brake parachute after landing. Note the open auxiliary blow-in door aft of the tactical code.

Su-15 '43 Yellow' with double-delta wings and extra pylons for R-60 AAMs

Su-15 '42 Red' which served as a ground instructional airframe at the Solntsevo ShMAS and was later preserved at Khodynka

Su-15T '85 Red'

• The 636th IAP (8th OA PVO), at Kramatorsk (Donetsk Region, eastern Ukraine), which converted to the Su-15TM from the MiG-17 in 1970-73 and then to the Su-15TM in 1975

• The 681st IAP (4th OA PVO), at Danilovo AB, near Yoshkar-Ola (the capital of the Mari ASSR). The unit was established with the Su-15 *sans suffixe*, later reequipping with the Su-15TM.

• The 712th *Chernovitskiy* GvIAP (14th OA PVO), at Kansk-Dal'niy AB, Krasnoyarsk Region, a former Su-9 operator, which converted to the Su-15TM in 1975

• The 777th IAP (11th OA PVO), at Sokol AB, near Dolinsk, Sakhalin Island. The unit converted from the MiG-19.

• The 813th IAP (14th OA PVO), at Koopino AB (Novosibirsk Region), likewise a former Su-9 operator

• The 865th IAP (11th OA PVO), at Yelizovo AP, Petropavlovsk-Kamchatskiy (Kamchatka Region), again a former Su-9 operator

• The 976th *Insterburgskiy* IAP, Kuyrdamir, Azerbaijan. This regiment likewise converted from the Su-9.

• The 991st IAP (10th OA PVO), at Petrozavodsk (Besovets airport), Karelian ASSR. This unit became the 'new' 57th GvIAP in 1978 when the original 57th GvIAP disbanded.

• The 218th UAP, at Sal'sk (Rostov Region)

• The 700th UIAP, at Tikhoretsk (Krasnodar Territory); both units belonged to SVVAULSh.

The transition to the Flagon often required extensive upgrades of the airbases. Thus, when the 712th GvIAP reequipped with the Su-15TM and Su-15UM in the first half of 1975, a new concrete runway, concrete taxiways, and hardstands had to be constructed at Kansk-Dal'niy AB, which was previously a dirt airfield. The first three Flagon-Fs arrived on 6 May 1975; by 1 December 1976 the unit was fully operational.

Much attention was paid to combat training in the Su-15 units, which were regular participants in the annual command and staff exercises. For example, in 1971, a year after beginning its transition to the Su-15/Su-15UT, the 636th IAP took part in its first exercise of the 9th PVO Division. In July 1972 the unit redeployed for a week to Bel'bek AB, near the Black Sea coast, to conduct live weapons training, when missiles were fired at target drones over the sea; this was considered safer than live weapons training over land. In July 1975 fourteen 636th IAP pilots visited Bel'bek AB again to conduct live weapons training; this time missiles were fired at ultralow altitude. In 1979 the unit participated in Exercise *Oodar-79* (Blow-79), in the course of which a simulated intruder aircraft was intercepted and forced to land at Bel'bek AB. Two

Su-15 *sans suffixe* '42 Red'

Su-15 '01 Red', named after Great Patriotic War hero
Nikolay Danilenko, 611th IAP, Dorokhovo AB

ИМЕНИ ГЕРОЯ
ВЕЛИКОЙ ОТЕЧЕСТВЕННОЙ ВОЙНЫ
НИКОЛАЯ ДАНИЛЕНКО

years later the unit practiced aerial gunnery with UPK-23-250 pods against La-17 target drones at Krasnovodsk, receiving excellent grades.

Between 3 and 23 March 1977 the 712th GvIAP was on temporary deployment (TDY) to Bezrechnaya AB (the 22nd IAP's home base) in the course of an exercise that involved launching R-60 AAMs for the first time and the first nighttime live weapons drill. Shortly afterward, between 18 and 21 April, the unit participated in Exercise *Kedr-77* (Cedar-77), which proceeded under the auspices of the PVO Chief Command. It included urgent redeployment of

aircraft to reserve bases when under threat of an enemy air strike; Abakan airport acted as the reserve airfield. The 712th GvIAP was involved in such notable exercises as *Yenisey-82* (named after a Siberian river), *Sibir'-83* (Siberia-83), *Yenisey-84*, etc.; during the latter exercise the unit was on TDY at the recently inaugurated Krasnoyarsk-Yemel'yanovo airport. On 19 March 1984, ten of the unit's pilots flew their Su-15TMs to Sary-Shagan AB in Kazakhstan to participate in a live weapons drill the following day.

Like its immediate precursors, the Su-15 was never exported; however, it did see overseas deployment. The 54th GvIAP deployed to Poland about once in every two years to practice operations from stretches of highway used as tactical strips in the event the regular airbases were attacked; nothing of the sort had been tried in the USSR. For instance, in the summer of 1975 a squadron of the 54th GvIAP (by then equipped with the Su-15TM) was on TDY at Słupsk in the Pomeranian Voivodeship (that is, province) of northern Poland.

A few words must be said about the pilots' perception of the Su-15. Most pilots described it as pleasing to fly and forgiving of pilot errors; the aircraft earned much more favourable comments than the Su-9 and Su-11. At least one, however, described it as a 'beast' (especially in landing mode) and a widow-maker. He wrote that because of the Su-15's relatively small wings, the landing speed was very high at 320 km/h (198 mph), and the sink rate increased abruptly if you retarded the throttles just a bit too much. On final approach the bulky radome obscured the runway completely because of the nose-up angle. A particular sore point was the flawed design of the VDI-30 two-needle altimeter, making it

Left: A publicity shot of a Su-15TM pilot (wearing a ZSh-5 'bone dome' helmet) receiving last-minute instructions. The use of two boarding ladders at once was anything but standard operational procedure.

Above: A Su-15 pilot in high-altitude gear (a VKK-6 pressure suit and a GSh-6 pressure helmet

Right: This publicity shot of a Su-15TM pilot on QRA duty (maximum alert, ready to take off at a moment's notice) shows such details as the TS-27AMSh periscopic mirror on the canopy, the apparent double kink of the wing leading edge (an illusion caused by the wing camber), and the antiglare panel extending to the air intake (scuffed on the port intake due to pilot entry/egress).

all too easy to misinterpret its readings and undershoot, with potentially fatal results. Still, it is possible this pilot was the proverbial *dude with a 'tude*.

According to Soviet/Russian practice, major repairs and refurbishment / service life extension of a given aircraft type were handled by a single aircraft repair plant within the Ministry of Defence system (or, for commercial aircraft, the Ministry of Civil Aviation system), or several repair plants if the aircraft was built and operated in large numbers. The Su-15 was handled by the PVO's 26th ARZ (*aviaremontnyy zavod*: aircraft repair plant) at Novosibirsk-Tolmachovo airport and the 805th ARZ at Dnepropetrovsk (the Ukraine). Repairs and overhauls of R11F2-300 engines were performed by the 12th ARZ in Khabarovsk in the Russian Far East

Left: Su-15s with inert R-98s on the flight line at Slupsk during another visit in the summer of 1975. The nearest two are ogival-nosed Su-15TMs, followed by either Su-15Ts or pre-upgrade early 'pencil-nosed' Su-15TMs. The aircraft at the end of the row is a Su-15UT.

Below left: Su-15UM '40 Blue' taxies with the instructor's periscope up.

Bottom left: Su-15UM '67 Blue' taxies out for takeoff with the flaps set 15° past an early Su-15.

Right: Camouflaged Su15TM '44 Red' is pictured immediately after becoming airborne, making a practice sortie with no external stores.

Below: This Su-15TM armed with R-98Ms and R-60s shows off its three-tone tactical camouflage. The tactical code '11' is probably red. A missile transportation dolly is in the foreground.

Su-15TM '21 Blue', 636th IAP, Kramatorsk, the mid-1980s

Top and *above*: A pair of 636th IAP Su-15TMs make a banking turn as they fly a training mission over the Ukrainian countryside in the late 1980s. Air defence force aircraft normally had blue tactical codes.

Su-15 Units as of 1 January 1980 (prior to the MoD Order Dated 5 January 1980)		
Unit	**Base**	**Version**
Moscow PVO District (HQ Moscow)		
• 2nd PVO Corps, HQ Rzhev (Kalinin Region) 28th Leningradskiy GvIAP	Andreapol', Kalinin Region	Su-15
• 3rd PVO Corps, HQ Yaroslavl' 611th IAP	Dorokhovo AB, Bezhetsk, Kalinin Region	Su-15
• 16th PVO Corps, HQ Gor'kiy 153rd IAP	Morshansk, Tambov Region	Su-15
Baku PVO District (HQ Baku, Azerbaijan; 19th OA PVO from March 1980)		
• 14th PVO Corps, HQ Tbilisi, Georgia 166th GvIAP 171st Tool'skiy IAP	Marneuli AB, nr Sandar, Georgia Bombora AB, nr Gudauta, Georgia *	Su-15 Su-15TM
• 15th PVO Corps, HQ Alyaty, Azerbaijan 976th Insterburgskiy IAP	Kuyrdamir, central Azerbaijan	Su-15
4th Independent PVO Army (HQ Sverdlovsk)		
• 28th PVO Division, HQ Kuibyshev 681st IAP	Danilovo AB, nr Yoshkar-Ola, Marii ASSR	Su-15
6th Independent PVO Army (HQ Leningrad)		
• 54th Guards PVO Corps, HQ Taitsy (nr Gatchina, Leningrad Region) 180th Volgogradskiy GvIAP	Gromovo AB, nr Solov'yovka, Leningrad Region	Su-15TM
8th Independent PVO Army (HQ Kiev, the Ukraine)		
• 1st PVO Division, HQ Sevastopol', the Ukraine 62nd IAP	Bel'bek AB, Sevatopol', Crimea Region	Su-15
• 9th PVO Division, HQ Donetsk, the Ukraine 636th IAP	Kramatorsk, Donetsk Region	Su-15TM
• 21st PVO Division, HQ Odessa, the Ukraine 90th IAP	Chervonoglinskaya AB, Artsyz, Odessa Region	Su-15

10th Independent PVO Army (HQ Arkhangel'sk)		
• 21st PVO Corps, HQ Severomorsk, Murmansk Region 431st IAP	Afrikanda, Murmansk Region	Su-15TM
• 5th PVO Division, HQ Petrozavodsk, Republic of Karelia, Russia 265th IAP 57th GvIAP	Poduzhem'ye, nr Kem', Karelia Petrozavodsk-Besovets AP	Su-15TM Su-15TM
11th Independent PVO Army (HQ Khabarovsk)		
• 8th Red Banner PVO Corps, HQ Komsomol'sk-on-Amur 60th IAP 302nd IAP	Komsomol'sk-on-Amur/Dzyomgi Pereyaslavka-2 AB, Khabarovsk Territory	Su-15 Su-15
• 23rd PVO Corps, HQ Vladivostok, Primor'ye Territory 47th IAP	Zolotaya Dolina, nr Nakhodka, Primor'ye Territory	Su-15TM
• 6th PVO Division, HQ Petropavlovsk-Kamchatskiy 865th GvIAP	Petropavlovsk-Kamchatskiy/ Yelizovo AP	Su-15TM
• 24th PVO Division, Sakhalin Island 777th IAP	Sokol AB, Sakhalin	Su-15
12th Independent PVO Army (HQ Tashkent, Uzbekistan)		
• 7th PVO Division, HQ Alma-Ata, Kazakhstan 9th Odesskiy GvIAP	Andizhan, Uzbekistan	Su-15
• 17th PVO Division, HQ Maryy, Turkmenia 156th El'bingskiy GvIAP	Maryy-2 AB	Su-15
14th Independent PVO Army (HQ Novosibirsk)		
• 20th PVO Division, HQ Tolmachovo 712th Chernovitskiy IAP	Kansk, Krasnoyarsk Territory	Su-15TM
• 26th PVO Division, HQ Irkutsk 22nd Khalkhingol'skiy IAP Unnumbered OIAE †	Bezrechnaya AB, Chita Region Bezrechnaya AB, Chita Region	Su-15 Su-15TM

Notes:

* Transferred to 11th OA PVO and relocated to Anadyr' in 1982

† OIAE = *otdel'naya istrebitel'naya aviaeskadril'ya*: independent fighter squadron; formerly the 22nd IAP

(Primor'ye Territory), the 218th ARZ in Gatchina (Leningrad Region), the 562nd ARZ in Odessa, the Ukraine (now called Odesaviaremservis: Odessa Aviation Repair Services), and the 570th ARZ in Yeisk (Krasnodar Territory, southern Russia). The Yeisk and Odessa plants also refurbished R13-300 engines.

In Action

To give credit where credit is due, of all fighter types operated by the PVO the Su-15 probably had the highest percentage of successful real-life intercepts of aircraft intruding into Soviet airspace. Its

baptism of fire came on 11 September 1970 . . . well, actually the expression 'baptism of fire' is not really applicable here because no shots were fired on this occasion. At 0336 hrs. Moscow time, PVO radar pickets near Sevastopol', the Ukraine, detected a lone aircraft heading north toward the Soviet border at 3,000 m (9,840 ft.), and a 'Red Alert' was called. The target was then 260 km (160 miles) southwest of the city; when it approached within 100 km (62 miles) of the border, a 62nd IAP Su-15 scrambled from Bel'bek AB to prevent an incursion. The target turned out to be an elderly Douglas C-47 belonging to the Hellenic Air

Left: A 57th GvIAP Su-15TM poised for takeoff is seen from the cockpit of the wingman's aircraft.

Below: A red-coded Su-15TM belches afterburner flames on takeoff from a Russian Far East airbase.

Bottom: 57th GvIAP Su-15TM '11 Blue' peels off spectacularly, banking away from the camera ship and showing off its double-delta wings. No weapons are carried on the six pylons.

An enamel badge of the national air defence force portraying both fighters, SAMs, and AD radars.

Above: '06 Blue', a 57th GvIAP Su-15TM with a full load of missiles, on the military apron at Noril'sk-Alykel' airport. Note the badge beneath the cockpit—the Sukhoi OKB's 'winged archer' logo with the Guards badge superimposed on it.

Right: A 57th GvIAP *Flagon-F* coded '04 Blue' comes in to land at Noril'sk-Alykel' with the flaps at 45° maximum deflection.

Right: A Su-15TM coded '04 Red' deploys the brake parachute on landing, with the rugged hills of the Russian Far East as a backdrop. The cruciform parachute is of a different type than hitherto.

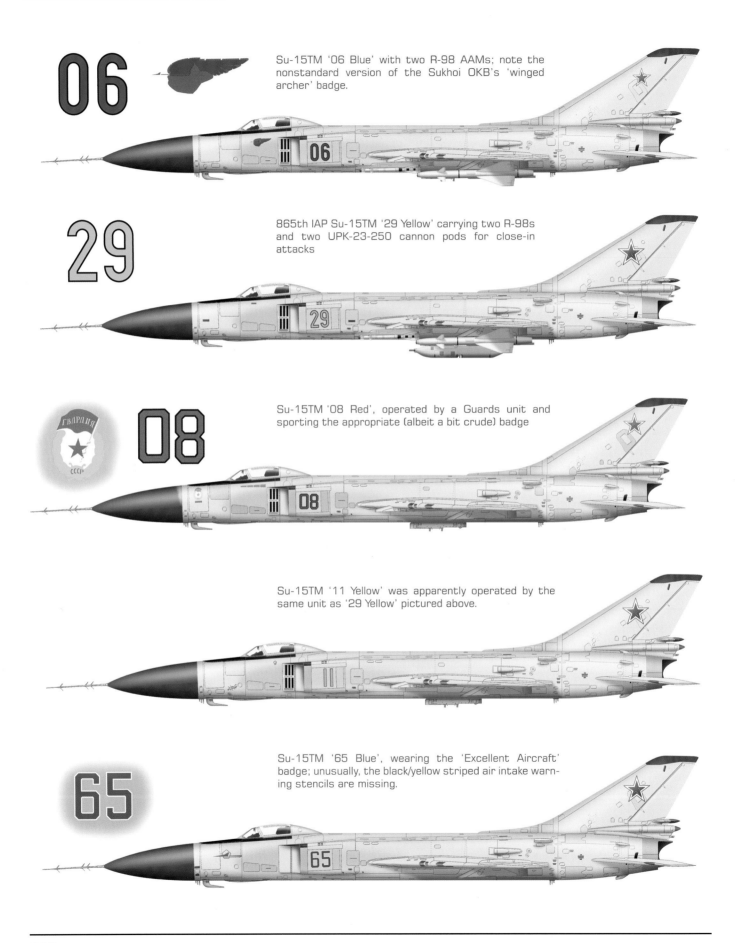

Su-15TM '06 Blue' with two R-98 AAMs; note the nonstandard version of the Sukhoi OKB's 'winged archer' badge.

865th IAP Su-15TM '29 Yellow' carrying two R-98s and two UPK-23-250 cannon pods for close-in attacks

Su-15TM '08 Red', operated by a Guards unit and sporting the appropriate (albeit a bit crude) badge

Su-15TM '11 Yellow' was apparently operated by the same unit as '29 Yellow' pictured above.

Su-15TM '65 Blue', wearing the 'Excellent Aircraft' badge; unusually, the black/yellow striped air intake warning stencils are missing.

Above: Fully armed Su-15TM '29 Yellow' of the 865th IAP at Petropavlovsk-Kamchatskiy, seen from the spyplane it is intercepting

Right: A pair of Su-15TMs armed with R-98 AAMs bank over an industrial area.

Force, and when it eventually crossed the border the fighter lined up alongside and rocked its wings in the internationally recognised 'follow me' signal. The Dakota complied, landing at Bel'bek AB. It turned out that the pilot, Lt. Mikhalis Maniatakis, had stolen the aircraft from Chania AB, on the island of Crete, and fled from his homeland where the fascist junta of the Black Colonels had seized power in Greece. Maniatakis requested political asylum in the USSR, which was in all probability granted.

Throughout the 1970s the southern borders of the Soviet Union perpetually received the attentions of hostile aircraft coming from Turkey and Iran. The events described below are but a few of the incursions that took place there.

On 7 September 1972, a flight of Turkish Air Force (THK: Türk Hava Kuvvetleri) North American F-100 Super Sabres entered Soviet airspace near Leninakan, Armenia (the city is now called Gyumri). Despite flying at ultralow altitude, the intruders were detected by air defence radars in timely fashion. Another ploy of the 'bad guys' worked, however—the fighters flew in close formation, appearing on the radarscopes as one heavy aircraft (the USAF had used this tactic against North Vietnamese interceptors during the Vietnam War); hence only a single 166th IAP Su-15 scrambled from Sandar AB in neighbouring Georgia to intercept 'it'. The GCI command post operators did not realise they were dealing with multiple targets until the Turkish fighters swept over the place with a roar.

The lone Su-15 proved incapable of intercepting its quarry, because its radar lacked 'look-down/shoot-down' capability. As a result, the F-100s flew over Leninakan and were fired on by a heavy machine gun, providing antiaircraft protection for the PVO's radar site, but got away unscathed.

On 23 May 1974, another THK F-100 intruded into Soviet airspace over the Caucasus region with impunity. A Su-15 standing on QRA duty scrambled from the airbase in Kyurdamir, Azerbaijan, but was not directed toward the target because the latter had unwisely intruded into an area defended by an SAM regiment. A

missile was fired at the F-100 but missed due to a malfunction in the guidance system.

Eventually, however, the Turks fell victim to the rule 'pride goeth before the fall'. On 24 August 1976, Soviet AD radars detected a target moving in Turkish airspace toward the Soviet border. This was soon identified as a pair of F-100s flying in close formation. No fewer than three Su-15s scrambled this time (two from Kyurdamir and one from Sandar AB), but again they did not manage to get a piece of the action. The fighters had again rashly flown right into a nest of SAMs; this time the PVO crews on the ground did their job well, and one of the Super Sabres was shot down. Unfortunately the wreckage fell on the wrong side of the border, and the pilot, who ejected, also landed in Turkish territory; the following day the Turks raised hell, accusing the Soviet Union of the 'wanton destruction of a Turkish fighter'.

A while earlier, on 2 April 1976, a 777th IAP Su-15 flown by Lt. (SG) P. S. Strizhak scrambled from Sokol AB on Sakhalin Island to intercept a USAF Boeing RC-135 reconnaissance aircraft that had entered the 100 km territorial-waters strip. Shortly after takeoff, the pilot was redirected toward a new target—a Japanese Maritime Self-Defence Force (JMSDF) Lockheed-Kawasaki P2V Neptune reconnaissance aircraft flying over the Sea of Japan at 2,000 m (6,560 ft.) off the southern tip of Sakhalin. Approaching within 5–6 km (3.1–3.7 miles) of the target, the interceptor followed it, flying a parallel course. Apparently Strizhak flipped the wrong switch and inadvertently fired an R-98R missile at the Neptune, though no order to attack had been given. Realising his mis-

take, the pilot made a turn just in time, causing the missile to lose target lock-on; the missile whizzed past the Neptune's starboard wing, self-destructing harmlessly.

An incident on the Iranian border occurred on 17–18 July 1981. This time, for once, the intruder was not a reconnaissance aircraft but a gunrunner. Shortly after the outbreak of the Iran-Iraq War, the Iranians made a deal to smuggle weapons—officially 'pharmaceuticals'—from Israel (which was cooperating with the US in the infamous 'Iran-Contra affair'). In late June a Canadair CL-44D4-6 freighter registered LV-JTN (c/n 34) was chartered for this purpose from the Argentinean airline Trans-

porte Aéreo Rioplatense by one Stuart Allen McCafferty, a Scots businessman acting as intermediary between the Iranians and the Swiss arms dealer Andreas Jenni. On 17 July the freighter's captain, Hector Cordero, decided to take a short cut across Soviet airspace en route from Tel Aviv to Tehran in order to skirt the north flank of the Iran-Iraq front. Flying at about 8,000 m (26,250 ft.), the aircraft briefly entered Soviet airspace over Armenia but then left it, and the Soviet PVO command post in the area took no action—no fighters were scrambled. (Another account says that the pair of 166th IAP Su-15s that had taken off to intercept was ordered back to base when the CL-44 escaped to Iran.)

The following day the crew again took the same route on the return flight. This time, two pairs of fighters scrambled from Vaziani AB, near Tbilisi, Georgia, to intercept; however, the indecision and bungled actions of the duty officers at the 34th VA's command post meant that the interceptors were unable to find the target and were forced to return after hitting 'bingo fuel'. (Some sources describe these fighters as Su-15s, but Vaziani AB hosted

the 982nd IAP, which never operated the type, being equipped with MiG-23MLDs at the time.) Eventually a single 166th GvIAP Su-15 coded '30' and flown by Capt. Valentin A. Kulyapin was vectored toward the intruder, with orders to force it down at a Soviet airfield. The fighter pilot gave the customary 'follow me' signals (which was difficult in itself because the Su-15 flew at its minimum control speed to keep formation with the slow freighter

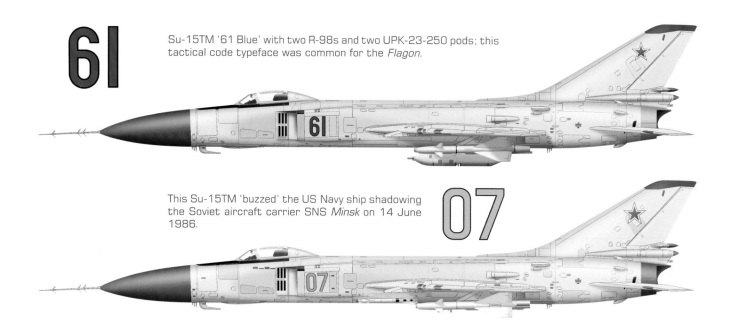

61 Su-15TM '61 Blue' with two R-98s and two UPK-23-250 pods; this tactical code typeface was common for the *Flagon*.

07 This Su-15TM 'buzzed' the US Navy ship shadowing the Soviet aircraft carrier SNS *Minsk* on 14 June 1986.

and could stall), but the big turboprop ignored them and started manoeuvring dangerously, since the crew was determined to get away. Realising the intruder was not going to obey his signals, Kulyapin requested permission to fire but was denied. Due to poor interaction between the pilot and the command centre, the pursuit

continued for more than ten minutes; when the CL-44 headed due south in an obvious attempt to get away, Kulyapin had to report this three times before he finally received orders to destroy the target. But then a problem arose—his aircraft was armed with two R-98 AAMs but had no cannon pods; another Su-15 fitted with

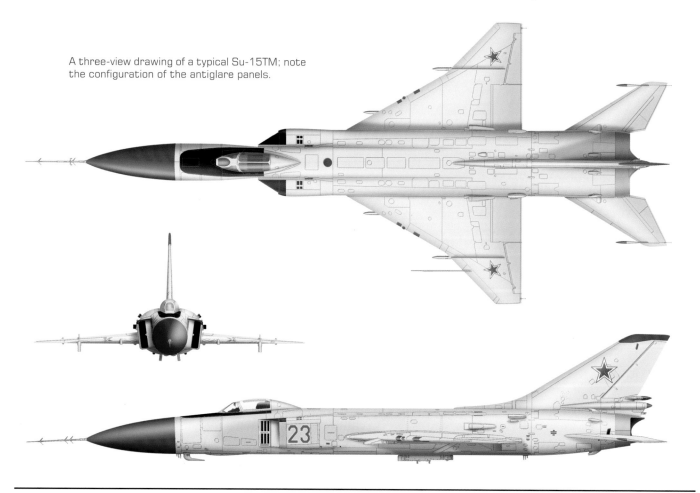

A three-view drawing of a typical Su-15TM; note the configuration of the antiglare panels.

Right: The control tower of a PVO fighter unit in the 1980s. The second man from right is the ATC shift supervisor.

Below: Su-15TMs on the flight line; note the V-shaped spray dams ahead of the canopies. '81 Blue' is getting ready to start up, while '61 Blue' is being serviced, with the forward avionics bay covers removed. The vehicle is a VZ-20/350-131 compressed-air charger on a ZiL-131 6x6 army lorry chassis.

cannon pods was on the way but would reach the scene too late. Since the border was very close and the intruder could escape before the fighter could fall back to a safe distance for missile launch, Kulyapin opted for a Second World War–style ramming attack. Moving into line astern formation, the Su-15 pitched up into a climb and sliced off the CL-44's starboard tailplane with its fin and fuselage. The uncontrollable freighter plummeted to the ground 2–3 km (1.24–1.86 miles) from the border, killing the three-man crew (captain Hector Cordero, first officer Jose Burgueño, and flight engineer Hermete Boasso) and Stuart McCafferty,

who was also aboard. However, Kulyapin's aircraft was seriously damaged by the collision and the pilot ejected, landing safely not far from the crash site. This time the intruder fell on Soviet territory, the wreckage furnishing irrefutable evidence of a border violation. For this performance Capt. Valentin Kulyapin was awarded the Order of the Red Banner.

Gradually, together with the MiG-25P heavy interceptor, capable of Mach 2 flight, the Su-15 supplanted the outdated Su-9, Su-11, Yak-28P, and MiG-21PFM from the PVO inventory. Su-15s saw service with units stationed in almost all borderside regions of the

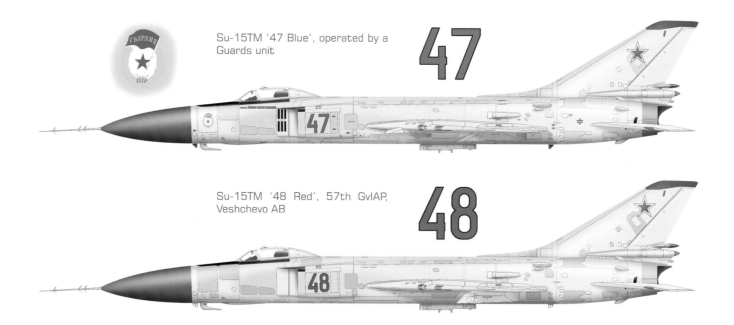

Su-15TM '47 Blue', operated by a Guards unit

Su-15TM '48 Red', 57th GvIAP, Veshchevo AB

Soviet Union, the High North and the Far East receiving the highest priority. The Su-15TM, which superseded the initial versions on the production line, remained one of the principal fighter types defending these vital areas for many years. The upgraded Su-15-98M aerial-intercept weapons system comprising this aircraft and the Vozdukh-1M GCI system, which permitted guidance in manual, semiautomatic (flight director), and fully automatic modes, was capable of intercepting targets flying at speeds of 500–2,500 km/h (310–1,550 mph) and altitudes of 500–24,000 m (1,640–78,740 ft.).

According to Soviet fighter pilots' recollections, the reconnaissance aircraft of the 'potential adversary' took pains to avoid coming within the Su-15's reach. A notable exception is the Lockheed

SR-71A Blackbird spyplane, capable of Mach 3 flight. Of course the Su-15 was no match for the Blackbird; the only Soviet interceptor that could oppose the SR-71 was the MiG-25P Foxbat-A. The presence of these very different interceptors in the PVO inventory (not counting the Tu-128, the MiG-23P, etc.) increased the overall efficiency of the nation's air defences. The potent MiG-25P was a complicated aircraft to build due to its welded stainless-steel airframe, and its operations were hampered by the scarcity of its R15B-300 engines, which also powered the reconnaissance/strike and trainer versions of the Foxbat. Conversely, the less capable Su-15 was easy to build and well adapted for mass production as far as the airframe, power plant, and equipment were concerned.

A pilot climbs into a Su-15TM standing on QRA duty.

Su-15TM '21 Blue' silhouetted against the evening sky over a blanket of overcast into which the sun has just vanished.

Below: Another view of Su-15TM '21 Blue' as it banks away from the camera ship

A major problem that the Soviet PVO had to deal with was the large number of drifting reconnaissance balloons launched from western Europe. Frequently, despite all efforts to destroy it, such a balloon would pass over the entire country. Quite apart from their reconnaissance mission, the balloons presented a serious danger of collision for civil and military aircraft alike. Supersonic interceptors had limited success in combating reconnaissance balloons, primarily because the target usually had a very small RCS; the aircraft's radar could detect them only at close range, which left very little time for an attack.

Su-15 pilots started their balloon-hunting score in the autumn of 1974. On 17 October, PVO radar pickets detected Yet Another Evil Balloon drifting at 13,000 m (42,650 ft.) over the Black Sea and about to enter Soviet airspace. Three 62nd IAP Su-15s took off

Su-15TM '43 Red' sporting the 'Excellent Aircraft' badge, 393rd GvIAP, Privolzhskiy AB, Astrakhan'

Su-15UM '98 Red'; unusually, the entire boundary layer splitter plates are painted yellow on this aircraft.

from Bel'bek AB, making consecutive firing passes at the target; the last of the three managed to shoot off the balloon's reconnaissance systems pod with an R-98T missile. By far the greatest number of such sorties was flown in 1975—and it was the most successful year as well; 13 out of 16 detected balloons were destroyed, including five downed by Su-15s.

It should be noted that most of the intruders the Su-15 had to deal with were anything but the typical targets it had been designed to intercept. As often as not, the intruder was a light aircraft that was no easy target for a supersonic interceptor, due to the huge difference in airspeeds. Adding offence to injury, such intruders usually flew at ultralow level, where the interceptor's radar—be it the Oryol-D, the Taifoon, or the Taifoon-M—could not get a lock-on; this meant the target had to be located visually, and the view from the Su-15's cockpit left a lot to be desired. This was when accurate guidance by GCI centres proved crucial.

A singularly embarrassing episode occurred on 8 October 1970, when a twin-engined light aircraft, probably a Rockwell Aero Commander, crossed the border from Iran into Turkmenia and brazenly landed at Nebit-Dag AB, hosting the 364th IAP, equipped with Su-15s. Making a U-turn, the aircraft backtracked to the runway threshold and took off again in full view of the

Left: A Su-15TM on QRA duty with two R-98s and two cannon pods sits in a revetment in front of a jet blast deflector. Note the connected ground power cable for engine starting and the fire extinguisher dolly.

Above right: Toward the end of their career, many Su-15s (such as Su-15TM '21 Yellow', seen taking off in full afterburner) were transferred from the PVO to the air force and painted in three-tone tactical camouflage.

Right: Camouflaged Su-15TM '12 Yellow', armed with R-98 AAMs and UPK-23-250 cannon pods, was photographed from a Royal Swedish Air Force fighter over international waters in the Baltic Sea.

This Su-15TM, belonging to the 54 GvIAP at Vaïnode, had the Combat Red Banner Order, and the Guards badge superimposed on the Sukhoi OKB badge.

Soviet servicemen, departing due south. It was Saturday, and most of the unit's personnel was off base, with the exception of the QRA flight; still, no one seemed to mind the 'visit'. The only one who paid attention was the commander of the unit's communications battalion, who drove to the HQ and alerted the officer of the day, who reported the incident along the chain of command—too late. Not a single one of the unit's aircraft scrambled to pursue the transgressor because no orders had been given!

A huge scandal erupted within the PVO system. Investigation showed that the radar pickets had mistaken the intruder for an Aeroflot Soviet Airlines Antonov An-2 Colt biplane flying a scheduled feeder service. Still, someone had to pay for the screwup, and even though the episode was the higher command's fault, the 364th IAP was disbanded.

Speaking of which, the Iranian border was one of the 'hottest' areas the PVO had to deal with. Another incident—one of the first successful intercepts of light aircraft—occurred on 21 June 1973. At 0836 hrs. local time, a radar picket of the Baku PVO District detected a target over Iranian territory 300 km (186 miles) southeast of Baku; the aircraft was moving toward the Soviet border at 2,000 m (6,560 ft.), and an incursion seemed very likely. Five min-

utes later, a 976th IAP Su-15 took off from Nasosnaya AB, near Baku (where the unit was temporarily stationed while its home base, Kuyrdamir AB, was closed for runway resurfacing), to ward off the potential intruder; it was soon joined by two more 976th IAP Su-15s and, for good measure, by a quartet of MiG-17PFUs from the resident 82nd IAP.

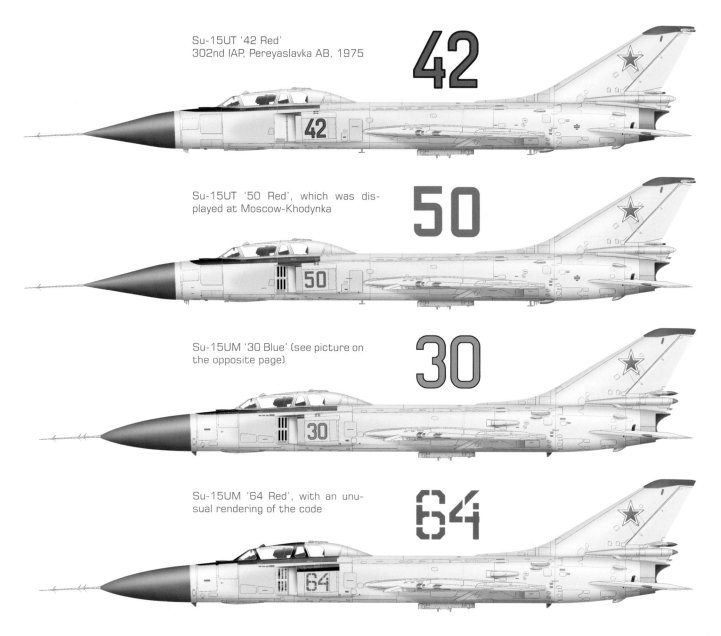

Su-15UT '42 Red'
302nd IAP, Pereyaslavka AB, 1975

Su-15UT '50 Red', which was displayed at Moscow-Khodynka

Su-15UM '30 Blue' (see picture on
the opposite page)

Su-15UM '64 Red', with an unusual rendering of the code

The intruder crossed the Soviet border at 0859 hrs. near the so-called Imishli Bulge, 170 km (105 miles) southwest of Baku, descending to 200 m (660 ft.) to avoid detection by radar. This complicated things considerably for the Su-15 pilots; nevertheless, at 0909 hrs. the aircraft, another Rockwell Aero Commander, was detected and hemmed in by the interceptors, which escorted it to a landing at Nasosnaya AB 27 minutes later. The pilot and the sole passenger claimed they were heading from Tabriz to the small borderside town of Parsaabad but had lost their way in the mountains.

It was no success story on 25 July 1976, when a Finnish-registered Cessna 150 Aerobat eluded the interceptors. At 1913 hrs. the low-flying intruder was visually detected by border guard troops

Some of the camouflaged Su-15s sported white
codes, such as Su-15TM '59 White', shown here.

Su-15UM '30 Blue' is seen immediately after becoming airborne. Note the extended periscope in the instructor's cockpit.

on the ground, since the PVO radar pickets had missed it. At 1927 hrs., a 431st IAP Su-15TM piloted by Capt. Vdovin took off from Afrikanda AB. Nevertheless, the Cessna landed at the PVO reserve airfield at Alakurtti, which was conveniently close at hand; the crew refuelled the aircraft, using a spare can of petrol, and continued on their eastward quest unhindered.

Around 1950 hrs. the GCI centre vectored the Su-15 toward the intruder (which had not avoided detection altogether). Due to poor weather, Vdovin was forced to fly below the clouds; still, he managed to spot the Cessna but then lost sight of it and could not regain visual contact. Two other Su-15TMs and a UTI MiG-15 trainer (!) were never even directed toward the target. Thus the Cessna carried on for another 300 km into the depths of the Karelian ASSR; ultimately, however, it crash-landed in a clearing in the woods, flipping over on its back. The crew were unhurt but were soon located by local residents, who made a 'citizen's arrest', turning them over to the authorities; the Finns claimed they had 'lost their bearings'.

After this incident the PVO commander in charge issued an order requiring that the pilots' gunnery training be stepped up; also, to ensure interception of low- and slow-flying targets such as this one, the QRA flight of each Su-15 unit was to include an aircraft armed with UPK-23-250 cannon pods by all means. As a result, from 1970 onward the aircraft in a QRA flight were armed differently, being assigned to intercepting high-flying and low-flying targets (for example, the flight leader carried two medium-range AAMs (an R-98TM and an R-98RM) and two R-60 short-range AAMs, while the wingman had the two R-98s plus two cannon pods. Hence the pilot gear was also different—the 'high-flyer' pilot wore a pressure suit and full-face pressure helmet, while the 'low-flyer' pilot was issued an ordinary flight suit and 'bone dome' helmet. Speaking of which, the UPK-23-250 was an extra pain in the neck for the armourers because after each firing, the pod had to be disassembled and the cannon laboriously stripped down for cleaning.

At 1457 hrs. Moscow time on 23 December 1979, a Cessna 185 Skywagon single-engined light aircraft entered Soviet airspace from Iranian territory 175 km (108 miles) southwest of Maryy, Turkmenia,

flying at about 3,000 m. The aircraft was detected by PVO radars three minutes before it crossed the border, and almost immediately a 156th IAP Su-15 took off from Maryy-2 AB to intercept it. The pilot was vectored toward the target by GCI stations but failed to spot it because the Cessna was camouflaged (so much for allegations about 'navigation errors'). The radars lost track of the target shortly afterward; three more Su-15s and a MiG-23M had also scrambled by then, but they were not vectored toward the target. After circling for a few minutes, the pilot of the first Su-15 had no choice but to head for home. Nevertheless, his mission was accomplished; when (unbeknownst to him) the interceptor passed directly above the Cessna, its pilots aborted their plan, losing altitude and opting for an emergency landing for fear of being shot down (which is exactly why the target vanished from the radarscopes!). Eventually they landed on a highway 195 km (121 miles) west of Maryy and were soon arrested by border guard troops.

The intercepts did not always go well for the interceptors. On 7 July 1985, a SAAB SH 37 Viggen maritime reconnaissance aircraft (tactical number 03, call sign 'Martin Red 03') from the Royal Swedish Air Force's 13th Air Wing (F13, a.k.a. Bråvalla Flygflottilj) departed from its base at Norrköping, piloted by Capt. Göran Larsson. The mission was to reconnoitre a group of warships from the Warsaw Pact member nations conducting an exercise in the Baltic Sea. Thirty-five minutes later, Larsson spotted the ships in international waters a short way from the port of Liepaja, a Soviet navy base in Latvia. However, the 'potential adversary' was expecting mischief; the ships had air cover, and as the Viggen approached the 'cake' (intelligence community slang for a group of ships), it was bounced by a pair of camouflaged Su-15TMs from the 54th GvIAP at Vainode. The lead aircraft, coded '36 Yellow', stayed close to the uninvited guest; the wingman kept his distance. The many ships were scattered over a wide area, and photographing all of them in one sortie seemed impossible, especially when you have a Su-15 on your tail, so Larsson returned to base, refuelling and taking off again to finish the task. He flew at 150 m (490 ft.), maintaining radio silence and not using the radar to avoid revealing himself; yet, when he reentered the area, the same pair of

Su-15s was there to ward him off. This time the wingman moved in close and started tailing him. Trying to shake off the pursuer, Larsson started performing aerobatic manoeuvres at low altitude. This is where the Viggen's higher manoeuvrability played a key role; not being designed with dogfights in mind, the Su-15 was not so agile. As it followed the Swedish jet doggedly in a high-g descending manoeuvre, the Soviet fighter could not level out in time and hit the water in a nose-high attitude, exploding on impact. The pilot, Capt. S. Zhigulyov, did not eject and was killed.

Shocked by the disaster, Göran Larsson chose to abort the mission and made off, descending to 50 m (164 ft.) and accelerating to Mach 1.1 in full afterburner. The other Su-15, which was some 5 km (3.1 miles) away, gave chase; soon Larsson's RHAWS alerted him that he was being 'painted' by the Flagon's radar—the Soviet pilot was apparently bent on revenge. Larsson cancelled afterburning thrust so as not to make a juicy IR target of himself for the heat-seeking missiles and proceeded to Norrköping. A pair of Swedish fighters that were loitering some way off and acting as a communications relay station dashed to the rescue; the Su-15 then gave up the chase and returned to the crash site, where it circled for 40 minutes before heading back to Vainode.

Aware of the possible repercussions, after the debriefing with the unit CO Göran Larsson chose not to mention the aggressive manoeuvring in his mission report—especially since the pilots had orders to concentrate on the job and not to fool around with aerobatics during sorties. Royal Swedish Air Force commander Lt.-Gen. Sven-Olof Olson officially expressed his regret about the incident. However, the Soviet Union did not file any formal claim or protest. In spite of the extensive two-day search effort that followed, no wreckage or body was found, and Capt. Zhigulyov was listed as missing in action until 1995, when a fragment of his flight jacket washed up on the shore.

The Korean Airliner Incidents

The Su-15TM also saw a good deal of action in defence of the Soviet borders, particularly in the late 1970s and the 1980s. It so happens that exactly the Flagon-F has become associated with two of the most notorious Cold War incidents. As a matter of fact, proper spyplanes and light aircraft flown by 'aerial hooligans' were not the only ones to enter Soviet airspace illegally and be fired upon. Commercial airliners occasionally strayed into Soviet airspace when they were not supposed to. While such incursions were invariably described as the result of bona fide navigation errors, this was not always the case. On two occasions they resulted in the airliner being shot down. By curious coincidence, both aircraft were Boeings, both were operated by the South Korean flag carrier Korean Air Lines (KAL), and both were downed by a Su-15TM.

The first shootdown occurred on 20 April 1978. That day a Korean Air Lines Boeing 707-321BA-H, registered HL7429 (c/n 19363, fuselage number 623), departed Paris–Charles de Gaulle at 1440 hrs., bound for Seoul via Anchorage, Alaska, as flight KE902, with 97 passengers (including five children) and 12 crew. Everything was normal until the aircraft had passed over Greenland and reached Cape Columbia, the northern extremity of Ellesmere Island, Canada. In his book *Flights of Terror: Aerial Hijack and Sabotage since 1930*, David Gero wrote: *'Built more than a decade earlier, the aircraft lacked a modern inertial navigation system, and as a magnetic compass is useless in this part of the world* [it gives false readings due to the proximity of the North Pole]*, and with a scarcity in ground aids, the crew would have to rely upon the older but well-proven method of celestial navigation.*

*'Trouble first arose in the vicinity of Iceland, when atmospheric conditions prevented the aircraft from communicating with the corresponding ground station. Approximately over Greenland, and following the instructions of the navigator, the 707 **inexplicably***

This Su-15TM has a full complement of missiles, with R-60Ms on the inboard wing pylons.

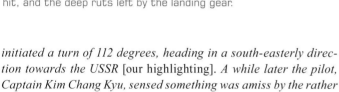

Top and *above*: Korean Air Lines Boeing 707-321BA HL7429 at the scene of its crash landing on the shore of the frozen Lake Korpijärvi. Note the extensive damage to the port wing caused by the missile hit, and the deep ruts left by the landing gear.

Top: This view shows how the Boeing's undercarriage had sunk into the deep, loose snow, and the starboard wing had only just avoided making contact with some pine trees on the shore.

Above: Close-up of the 707's damaged port wingtip

initiated a turn of 112 degrees, heading in a south-easterly direction towards the USSR [our highlighting]. *A while later the pilot, Captain Kim Chang Kyu, sensed something was amiss by the rather obvious fact that the sun was on the wrong side of the aircraft!'*

The full truth about this incident remains unknown to this day. Some Western media maintain that the incursion was a result of crew error because the pilots were making their first flight in an unfamiliar aircraft along an unfamiliar route. However, it is hard to imagine that an airline would put passengers' lives at risk by allowing such a combination—an unfamiliar aircraft and an unfamiliar route, which leaves the door wide open for errors. It is equally hard to imagine a navigation error that would lead to a course change in excess of 100°.

Anyway, the aircraft headed east, passing over the Spitsbergen (Svalbard) Archipelago. At 2054 hrs. Moscow time the radar pickets of the 10th Independent PVO Army detected an aircraft flying at 10,000 m (32,800 ft.) some 380 km (236 miles) north of Rybachiy Peninsula and heading toward Soviet territorial waters at about 900 km/h (559 mph). Boris Samoylov, the officer of the day at the 10th OA PVO command post, received the first report of the impending incursion when the aircraft was still 300 km (186 miles) from the border, and tried to ascertain what it was. He was told that the aircraft was a Soviet navy Antonov An-12 Cub transport returning from a sortie over the Barents Sea, but did not

believe it. Get real, guys. How can the turboprop-powered An-12 go at this rate, considering that its maximum speed is 780 km/h (484 mph) and its cruising speed 570 km/h (354 mph)?

A maximum alert was declared. When the target approached the 100 km territorial-waters strip, at 2111 hrs. Samoylov ordered a scramble. Eight minutes later the Boeing entered Soviet airspace over the Kola Peninsula, which abounds in military installations, and was thus assumed to be a NATO reconnaissance aircraft.

Since the fighter regiment based closest to the coast was in the midst of conversion to a new aircraft type and was not operational at the time, the task of intercepting the intruder fell to the 431st IAP at Afrikanda AB, and a Su-15TM piloted by Capt. Aleksandr I. Bosov scrambled to intercept. After being directed toward the target in head-on mode by GCI control, the pilot reported seeing it on his radar display, executed a port turn, and started closing in on the target. Coming within visual identification range, Bosov reported it as *'a four-engined Boeing 747'* [sic] but said he could not make out the insignia—they were *'Japanese, Chinese, or Korean'*. (Obviously the pilot had seen hieroglyphic characters of the aircraft's fuselage but had no way of knowing what language it was.)

Receiving orders to force the intruder down at a Soviet airfield, Capt. Bosov made two passes along the 707's port side with a lateral separation of 50–60 m (165–200 ft.), positioning himself ahead of the airliner's flight deck and rocking his wings as a 'follow me' signal. Yet, the South Korean crew ignored these 'amorous advances' and pressed on toward the Finnish border, which was only five minutes away. (Afterward, Western media claimed that the interceptor had approached on the starboard side, in contravention of normal procedure.)

Meanwhile, after analysing the target's track plotted by AD radars, the 10th Independent PVO Army HQ decided the 707 was about to escape and ordered the airliner shot down. At 2142 hrs., Bosov fired a single R-98MR missile, reporting an explosion and saying that the target was losing altitude. The explosion tore away a chunk of the Boeing's port wing 3–4 m (9 ft., 10 in.–13 ft., 1½ in.) long, complete with the low-speed aileron, knocked out the no. 1 engine, and apparently punctured the fuselage, causing the cabin to decompress. The crew initiated an emergency descent, causing the PVO radar pickets to briefly lose sight of the aircraft. Bosov was about to fire a second missile but lost target lock-on because the Boeing was descending rapidly; some sources claim he did fire the second R-98 but it missed.

As the action unfolded, a steady exchange of information was going on between PVO command centres at all echelons. The PVO commander in chief, Lt.-Gen. Vladimir S. Dmitriyev, who had ordered the target shot down, was belatedly informed that the target was a civil airliner; hence his new order overruling the previous one (to force the intruder down in one piece) reached the lower echelons too late, when the 707 was already under fire. By then

Maj. Ghennadiy N. Osipovich (*centre*) with his buddies

five other aircraft from units stationed in the area had scrambled to intercept the intruder, relieving Bosov's aircraft, which was getting low on fuel; these were two 174th IAP Yak-28Ps from Monchegorsk, a 524th IAP MiG-25P from Letneozyorsk, a 265th IAP Su-15TM from Poduzhem'ye AB, piloted by Lt. (SG) Sergey Slobodchikov, and one more 431st IAP Su-15TM from Afrikanda, flown by Capt. Anatoliy Kerefov. When the target vanished from the radarscopes, a third Yak-28P, a further MiG-25P, and three more Su-15TMs from the same bases joined the hunt. Obeying orders from the command post, Slobodchikov even fired a missile at a slow-flying target at 5,000 m (16,400 ft.), which was believed to be a cruise missile but later turned out to be nothing more than the severed fragment of the 707's port wing falling to earth. No sooner had Slobodchikov landed than he was told that the target was still airborne, and he was ordered up again.

Meanwhile, gradually losing altitude, the crippled airliner orbited near Loukhi settlement in the vicinity of Kem', Arkhangel'sk Region; there it was again detected and tracked by AD radars, and the nearest interceptor (piloted by Anatoliy Kerefov) was directed toward it. Since the Su-15's radar was not much use against a low-flying target, the pilots had to rely on the Mk 1 eyeball; yet, mortal men don't have the eyesight of an owl, and even on a cloudless polar night it takes time to spot the target. At 2245 hrs., Kerefov saw the intruder flying at 800 m (2,620 ft.); twelve minutes later the target was spotted by another 265th IAP pilot, Maj. A. A. Ghenberg. Together they gave signals to the crew, trying to force the jet to follow them; once again the airliner ignored the signals, landing on the ice of Lake Korpijärvi, 5 km (3.1 miles) southwest of Loukhi, at 2305 hrs. Of the 109 occupants, two were killed by fragments of the missile's fragmentation liner (one passenger was killed outright and another died en route to hospital), and 13 more were injured. The crew and passengers of the 707 were evacuated by helicopters to Kem' and detained by the Soviet authorities, but most of them were released two days later. They were flown by a Pan American Airlines Boeing 727-121 on a special charter flight from Murmansk-Murmashi to Helsinki, from where another KAL Boeing 707 took them to Seoul. The captain of HL7429 Kim Chang Kyu and navigator Lee Khun Shik pleaded guilty, admitting they had seen the Soviet fighter's signals but wilfully ignored them. They were pardoned by the Soviet government and released as a goodwill gesture. KAL chose to abandon the 707, which was declared a write-off— reportedly because the costs of recovering it were considered prohibitive. The Soviet authorities made good use of this windfall, salvaging the airliner and taking it to Moscow, where it was studied in detail; no intelligence equipment was found, but the airframe and systems design were of interest for the Soviet aircraft industry. The Soviet Union later invoiced South Korea US$100,000 in caretaking expenses.

A much more tragic incident with far-reaching political consequences occurred on the night of 31 August–1 September 1983. At 1300 hrs. UTC (0400 hrs. local time), Korean Air Lines Boeing 747-230B HL7442 (former Condor Flugdienst D-ABYH, c/n 20559, f/n 186) took off from Anchorage, where it had made a refuelling stop en route from New York City to Seoul as flight KE007 (ATC call sign KAL007). On this leg of the journey the aircraft, with 246 passengers and 23 crew aboard, was captained by Chun Byung-in. According to the flight plan the 747 was supposed to follow the international airway R-20, which passes just 28.2 km (17.5 miles) from the Soviet (Russian) border at the closest point, and proceed straight ahead until it passed Hokkaido Island, whereupon it would turn to starboard in a wide arc toward Seoul. However, just ten minutes after takeoff, HL7442 deviated to the right, assuming a heading of 245° instead of the required 220°, and strayed from its designated airway; the deviation steadily increased until presently the aircraft entered Soviet airspace near the Kamchatka Peninsula, a piece of Soviet territory packed with sensitive military installations (which makes its flight number an apt one, indeed). Of course, orders were given immediately to intercept the intruder.

The first attempt was abortive: a 528th IAP MiG-23 piloted by Maj. Vasiliy Kaz'min scrambled from Petropavlovsk-Kamchatskiy/Yelizovo airport when the 747 flew over Kamchatka. Kaz'min caught up with the target but soon had to give up the chase after hitting 'bingo fuel'. The reason was that after Viktor Belenko's notorious defection to Japan in a MiG-25P in 1976, the top command distrusted the 'grassroots', and the fighters were filled up with just so much fuel as to make a defection impossible! No one seemed to realise, or care, that this jeopardised the PVO units' ability to fulfil their mission, and that one bad egg does not automatically mean that the whole box of eggs is bad.

Anyway, the 747 left Soviet airspace for a while as it continued in a straight line over the Sea of Okhotsk. However, its course was bound to take it into Soviet airspace again over Sakhalin Island. By then the Soviet PVO system was in turmoil; the aircraft was now assumed to be a spyplane, which was to be shot down, should it intrude again—which it did at 1816 hrs. UTC, being assigned the code 'target 6065'. By then the airliner was 500 km (310 miles) west of the desired track. At 1742 hrs. and 1754 hrs. UTC (0542 hrs. and 0554 hrs. local time), two 365th IAP Su-15TMs, each carrying a pair of R-98 missiles and a pair of UPK-23-250 cannon pods, scrambled from Sokol AB, near Dolinsk, in the south of Sakhalin Island. One of the Su-15s, piloted by Maj. Ghennadiy N. Osipovich, intercepted the 747, which was cruising at 11,000 m (36,090 ft.); some sources, though, report the flight level as 9,000 m (29,530 ft.). Osipovich tried to contact the crew by radio and fired warning shots from his cannons, ordering it to land. However, the cannon rounds were not tracers, and the Korean crew failed to notice them.

Since the intruder ignored all calls and pressed on toward the border, orders were given to destroy it. At 1826 hrs. UTC, Osipovich fired both of his missiles, which found their mark, damaging the hydraulics and the control system (contrary to some reports, the aircraft did not break up in midair). After climbing briefly to 11,600 m (38,060 ft.) the 747 suffered a complete decompression and began a spiral descent; at 1838 hrs. the jet vanished from the radarscopes at 5,000 m (16,400 ft.). Moments later it plunged into the Sea of Japan off Moneron Island, south of Sakhalin, disintegrating on impact and killing all 269 occupants.

The reader may be interested to know how this mission proceeded. The following excerpt from declassified Russian sources

is a transcript of the radio exchange between Lt.-Col. Titovnin at the PVO division's command centre (CC, call sign *Deputat*: '[People's] Deputy' or 'Member of Parliament') and pilot Maj. Osipovich (P, call sign '805'). Intermissions by the following people are also included: Gen. Valeriy Kamenskiy, commander of Far East Military District Air Defence Force (VK); Gen. Anatoliy M. Kornukov, commander of the 40th IAD (AK); Lt.-Col. Gherasimenko, acting CO of the fighter regiment at Sokol AB (G); Lt.-Col. Maistrenko, officer of the day at the 24th PVO Division HQ (M); and Kozlov (rank unknown), combat controller at Sokol AB (K).

P: *Deputat, this is 805; I'm on heading 45° [magnetic], climbing to eight [8,000 m / 26,250 ft.].*

CC: *805, roger, stay on this heading.*

P: *Copy that.*

05:56 CC: *805, Deputat here, the target is 5 [degrees] to port, range 130 [km / 80.75 miles]. Target follows a heading of 240°, 5 [degrees] to port, range 120 [km / 74.5 miles].*

05:58 CC: *805, Deputat here, target straight ahead, range 70 [km / 43.5 miles], flight level 10,000 [m / 32,800 ft].*

06:02 P: *Report target in sight, flying at 8,000 [m].*

06:03 CC: *Roger, target straight ahead, range 12–15 km [7.5–9.3 miles].*

06:04 CC: *805, Deputat here, target coded hostile, to be destroyed in the event of an incursion [This is the initial order to fire]. Activate the special system [weapons control system].*

P: *Roger, wilco.*

CC: *805, can you identify the aircraft type? [This query and the response are especially noteworthy]*

P: *Not quite. It's got flashing lights.*

CC: *805, interrogate the target [by means of IFF].*

[Osipovich tries but gets no response, of course.]

CC [to Kornukov]: *No response.*

AK: *Well, that makes it clear, then. Prepare to use the weapons.*

P: *Roger.*

06:05:56 P: *Target in sight.*

06:08 K: [to Kornukov] *He has visual contact with the target.*

AK: *Oh, has he? How many contrails is it leaving?*

K: *Say again?*

AK: *How many contrails are there? If there are four contrails, then it is an RC-135. [USAF Boeing RC-135 ELINT aircraft from Alaska were frequent visitors in those parts]*

06:11 CC: *Can you see the target, 805?*

P: *Affirmative; I have it both within eyesight and on the radar screen.*

CC: *Roger. Report when you have lock-on.*

06:12 AK: *Gherasimenko!*

G: *Yes, sir!*

AK: *Well? Haven't you understood? I said, bring [Osipovich] within a range of 4–5 km [2.5–3.1 miles], identify the target. You understand that weapons will have to be used now, and you are holding [him] at a range of 10 [km / 6.2 miles]. Give the pilot [his] orders.*

G: *Yes.*

365th IAP Su-15TM '17 Red'—the aircraft in which Ghennadiy Osipovich shot down the Korean Boeing 747 on 1 September 1983

06:13:05 P: *I see it* [the target]. *I have lock-on.*

06:13   AK: [Put me through to] *'Chaika'* [Seagull, the call sign of the Far East MD Air Defence Force HQ].

CC: *Yes, sir. He sees* [the target] *on the radar screen. He is locked on.*

06:13.26 P: *No* ['friendly' IFF] *response.*

CC: *805, is the target's heading 240°?*

P: *Affirmative. The target's heading is 240°.*

CC: *Roger. Activate the special system.*

P: *System on.*

CC: *805, Deputat here; keep an eye on the target's heading.*

P: *Roger. So far it maintains the same heading.*

06:14   AK   [on the phone, to the Far East MD Air Defence Force HQ]: *Comrade General Kamenskiy* [Lt.-Gen. Valeriy N. Kamenskiy, 1st deputy commander of the Far East MD Air Force], *good morning. I am reporting the situation. Target 6065 is over Terpeniye Bay* ['Patience Bay', on the east coast of Sakhalin], *tracking 240, 30 km* [18.6 miles] *from the state border. The fighter from Sokol is 6 km* [3.73 miles] *away. Locked on; orders were given to arm the weapons. The target is not responding to IFF interrogation.* [The fighter pilot] *cannot identify it visually because it's still dark, but he is still locked on.*

VK: *We must find out; it could be some civilian aircraft or God knows what.*

AK: *What civilian?!* [It] *has flown over Kamchatka! It approached from the ocean without identification. I am giving the order to attack if it crosses the state border.*

CC: *805, Deputat here; get ready to fire, get ready.*

P: *Roger. I'll need to use afterburners.*

CC: *What's your fuel status?*

P: *I got 2,700* [kg / 5,950 lbs.].

CC: *Engage afterburners when ordered.*

06:15   CC   [on the phone]: [Put me through to] *Maistrenko. . . . Comrade Colonel, Titovnin speaking.*

M: *Yes.*

CC: *The commander has given orders to destroy* [the target] *if it breaches the border.*

M: *It may be an airliner. All necessary steps must be taken to identify it.*

CC: *Identification measures are being taken, but the pilot cannot see. It's dark. Even now it's still dark.*

M: *Well, okay. The task is correct. If there are no* [navigation/anticollision] *lights, it cannot be an airliner.*

06:16   CC: *805, do you have a good lock-on?*

P: *I got a stable lock-on.*

06:17   CC: *Do you see the adversary?*

P: *Target in sight.*

CC: *Roger. Destroy!*

P: *Repeat that, please!*

06:18   CC: *805, the target has breached the state border. Destroy the target!*

P: *Roger, wilco.*

CC: *Does the target have the navigation lights switched on?*

P: *Affirmative, the navigation lights are on . . . a flashing beacon is on* [the anticollision light].

CC: *Roger.*

06:19   CC: *805, flash your navigation lights.*

CC: *805, turn on your nav lights briefly.* [In combat mode the fighter's navigation lights are switched off to avoid revealing its position.]

CC: *805, force the target to land at our airfield!* [This order overrules the one to destroy the target.]

P: *I got my missile lock-on indicators on!*

CC: *805 . . . ?*

P: *805 here.*

06:20   CC: *805, fire a warning shot! Give a burst of gunfire!*

P: *I have to move in closer. I'm cancelling lock-on, moving in.*

CC: *Fire a burst!*

CC: *805! Comply!*

P: *Lock-on cancelled, I'm firing the cannons.*

CC: *Have you fired, 805?*

P: *Affirmative.*

CC: *Do you see the target?*

06:21.35 P: *Yes, I'm closing in, moving closer.*

CC: *Roger.*

P: *The target's strobe light is flashing. I'm within 2 km* [1.25 miles] *or so.*

CC: *Is the target descending?*

06:21.40 P: *Negative, still flying at 10,000* [m / 32,810 ft].

P2:   [a 528th IAP MiG-23P pilot from Smirnykh AB, on Sakhalin Island, call sign '163']: *I see you both, about 10–15 km* [6.2–9.3 miles] *out.*

06:21.55 P: *Request further instructions.*

06:22.02 P: *The target is decelerating.*

06:22.17 P: *I'm passing it . . . passing . . . I'm ahead of it now.*

CC: *Roger, 805. Reduce speed, 805.*

CC: *Flash your navigation lights.*

06:22.23 P: *Roger, wilco. Speeding up now.*

CC: *Has the target increased speed?*

06:22.29 P: *Negative; it is decelerating.*

CC: *805, engage the target!*

06:22.42 P: *I cannot! You should have told me earlier . . . I'm off the target's wing right now.*

CC: *Roger. Move into attack position if you can.*

06:22.55 P: *I'll have to fall back now.*

06:21-22 AK   [irritably]: *Gherasimenko, cut the horseplay at the command post! What is that noise there? I repeat the combat task: fire missiles, fire on target 6065.*

G: *Roger, wilco.*

AK: *Comply, and get Tarasov here* [the MiG pilot?]. *Take control of the MiG-23 from Smirnykh* [AB], *call sign 163, call sign 163; he is behind the target at the moment. Destroy the target!*

G: *Copy that. Destroy target 6065 with missiles; accept control of fighter from Smirnykh.*

AK: *Carry out the task, destroy* [it]*!*

06:22:55 AK: *Aagh,* [expletives], *how long does it take him to get into position for attack?* [The intruder] *is already exiting into international waters! Engage afterburner immediately. Bring in the MiG-23 as well. . . . While you are wasting time, it* [the intruder] *will get away.*

CC: *805, try to destroy the target with cannons.*

CC: *Report relative target position, 805.*

P: *Say again, please!*

CC: *What is the target's altitude?*

P: *10,000* [m].

CC: *What's the target's position? Relative to you?*

P: *Relative target position? Let me see . . . 70° to port.*

CC: *Roger.*

06:23   CC: *805, try to destroy the target with cannon fire.*

06:23.37 P: *I'm falling back now; I'll try missiles.*

06:23.37 CC: *Roger.*

06:23.37 P2:   *Target 12 km* [7.46 miles] *out. I see you both.*

CC: *805, approach the target, destroy the target!*

06:24.22 P: *Roger, wilco. I got a good lock-on.*

06:24.22 CC: *805, are you closing in?*

06:25.11 P: *Target ahead, I have lock-on, range 8* [km / 5 miles].

06:25.11 CC: *Engage afterburners! Afterburners, 805!*

06:25.16 P: *'Burners on.*

06:25.16 CC: *Fire!*

06:25.46 P: *Missiles locked on.*

06:26.02   [Missile detonates.]

06:26.20 P: *Missiles fired.*

06:26   AK: *Well, what news from out there?*

G: *He has launched* [the missiles].

AK: *Say again.*

G: *He has launched.*

AK: *He has launched. Track the target, track the target, tell your* [fighter] *to disengage and bring the MiG-23 in there.*

06:26.22 P: *Target destroyed.* [Which in reality it was not —ust yet.]

06:26.22 CC: *Disengage; turn right on heading 75°.* [Some reports state 'heading 360°']

06:26.27 P: *Attack interrupted.*

06:26:33 P2:   *Request further instructions.*

06:26:47 P2:   *My wing tanks have lit up* [that is, warning lights signalling that the wing tanks are empty]. *The fuel remainder differs by 600 litres* [132 Imp gal.] *for now.*

06:26:53 P   *Fuel status 1,600* [kg / 3,530 lbs].

As the reader has probably realised, neither the officer at the PVO command centre nor the pilot was able to identify the aircraft being attacked with 100% certainty, because the incident took place at night. Anatoliy Kornukov later said in a press interview that Ghennadiy Osipovich could not see the airliner's cabin windows because they were closed by window blinds from inside. (However, even in poor lighting conditions—that is, less than total darkness—the Boeing 747 is easy to identify by its unmistakable humpbacked silhouette.)

When the Soviet commanders realised that the 747 was not destroyed outright in the missile attack, pandemonium began. Lt.-Col Novoseletskiy, the acting CO of the 528th IAP, at Smirnykh AB (N), queried: *'Well, what **is** happening, what's the matter? Who guided him in?* [referring to Osipovich] *He had target lock-on; why didn't he shoot it down?'* Meanwhile, the MiG-23P, flying at 7,500 m (24,600 ft.), was ordered to turn onto a heading of 180° and then 150°.

06:27   AK: *Did Osipovich see the missiles explode? Hello?*

G: *He fired two missiles.*

AK: *Ask him, ask him personally; get on channel three and ask Osipovich; did he see the explosions or did he not?*

G: [to Kornukov] *Right away.*

[to Osipovich] *805, did you launch one missile or both?*

06:28:05 P: *Both missiles.*

06:28   G: *The target has turned north.*

AK: *??? Has the target turned north?*

G: *Affirmative.*

AK: *Bring in the* [MiG-]*23 to destroy it!*

06:29   AK: *I don't understand the result. Why is the target flying? Missiles have been fired; why is the* [expletive deleted] *target* [still] *flying? You are executing orders like a blankety-blank ninny! The orders of* [army general] *Ivan Moiseyevich Tretyak* [the then commander of the Far East MD] *shall be carried out at any cost! God forbid Osipovich screwed up! . . . Finish off the target, finish it off!* [expletive deleted]

AK: *Well? I am asking; give the order to the controller—what is wrong with you there? Have you lost your tongues?*

G: *I gave the order to the chief of staff, the chief of staff* [passed it on] *to the controller, and the controller is giving he order to . . .*

06:30   AK: *Well then, how long does it take for this information to get through?! Eh? Are you telling me that you cannot ask the results of the missile launch, where, what, did* [Osipovich] *not understand or what?*

06:32-33 AK: *Altitude, what is the flight level of our fighter and of the target? . . . Quick, give me the flight levels of the target and the fighter! . . . Why are you keeping silent? . . . Gherasimenko!*

	G:	*I am asking* [the pilot] . . .
	AK:	*Hurry up, guys; that's a real target!*
06:33/34	G:	*The target is at 5,000* [m / 16,400 ft].
	AK:	*?! 5,000 already?* [That low?!]
	G:	*Affirmative, turning left and right; apparently*

it is descending.

06:34	AK:	*Destroy it, use the* [MiG-]*23 to destroy it, I said!*
	G:	*Roger, destroy it.*
	AK:	*Well, where is the fighter; how far is it from the*

target?

	G:	*Comrade General, they cannot see the target.*
	AK:	*They cannot see the target?*
06:35:54	P3	[another MiG-23 pilot, call sign 121]: *Negative,*

I can't see it.

06:36	AK:	*You know the range; you know where the target*

is. It is over Moneron . . .

06:38:37	P3:	*I can't see anything in this area. I just checked.*
06:38	N:	*Well, what news, Titovnin?*
	CC:	*Er, none so far.*
	N:	*What's the matter? The pilot had lock-on; why*

isn't the target shot down?

	CC:	*They lost the target, Comrade Colonel, near*

Moneron.

	N:	*In the area of Moneron?*
	CC:	*The pilots cannot see it, neither the first one nor*

the other one. The radar troops have reported . . . that after the [missile] *launch, the target entered a right turn over Moneron.*

	N:	*Uh-huh.*
	CC:	*Descending. And was lost* [from radar] *over*

Moneron.

Running low on fuel, the Soviet fighters returned to their base without sighting the remains of their target.

After that, a search-and-rescue effort was initiated, with SAR helicopters and KGB border guard patrol boats and civilian ships in the area being sent to the 747's presumed crash site. All the while, there was a good deal of exchange going on between the command echelons, richly laced with bad language that even the intelligence specialists at the American listening posts had trouble translating!

Many years later, Lt.-Col. (ret.) Ghennadiy N. Osipovich was interviewed at his home by a correspondent of the Russian daily *Izvestiya*. The following are his reminiscences on the shootdown.

'*On 31 August I assumed combat duty as usual. . . . I reported "upstairs", had dinner with the other pilots on QRA duty, then watched TV for a while and dozed off. I woke up at about half past four* [local time] *to check the guard posts. No sooner had I dressed when the telephone jangled. It was Lt. Astakhov; at first I could not make out what he was mumbling, but presently gathered that I had been assigned maximum readiness, which means sitting in the cockpit and awaiting the order to scramble.*

'*I made my way to the hardstand, wondering, "Why me? There is already a young pilot sitting at maximum readiness". Still, I quickly climbed into my fighter, reported to the tower, and received confirmation—"be ready to scramble". Time passed, and no new orders were forthcoming. Suddenly I saw the ground crew removing the wraps from one more aircraft. "What's up?" I thought. It*

was a bit early for the Americans; usually they grew active after 11 o'clock.

'*Shortly after five o' clock I was, at length, ordered to take off. I started the engine* [sic; the Su-15 is twin engined], *switched on the landing light—the runway was not yet illuminated—and taxied out. My assigned heading took me over the sea. I quickly climbed to the required 8,000 m* [13,120 ft] *and ambled on. For some reason I was certain that it was a practice target launched by our own forces to check the readiness of our QRA assets, just for the sake of practice. And I had been ordered up because I was the most experienced pilot, I reasoned.*

'*Eight minutes into the mission, the ground controller suddenly radioed: "Target straight ahead! It's an aircraft breaking the flight rules. It is moving on a reciprocal heading". However, the guidance system failed to work in head-on mode for some reason. Soon I got new instructions: "We'll guide you in pursuit mode".*

'*Well then, so be it. I made a U-turn and, having received an altitude update, set off in pursuit of the intruder. The weather was fair that day. Soon I had spotted the intruding aircraft through the scattered cloud. Actually, what I mean by saying "spotted" is that I could make out a dark dot, 2–3 cm* [$^{25}/_{32}$–$1^3/_{16}$ in.] *large, ahead of me. It had operating anticollision beacons.*'

When asked what exactly he was thinking of at that moment, Osipovich replied: '*Nothing much. It was pure excitement, an adrenalin rush! Afterward, I was unable to put together a second-by-second reconstruction of what was happening up there, no matter how they wanted me to.*'

He went on: '*A fighter pilot is, sort of, like a guard dog that is perpetually trained to keep strangers off the territory it is guarding. And that's exactly what it was; the aircraft in front of me was a stranger. After all, I'm not a traffic cop who can pull over a speeding driver and demand his driver's licence and registration! I was following him in order to cut his flight short. The first thing I had to do was to try and get him to land. Failing that, I was to put him out of action at any cost. I could not possibly have any other thoughts in my head* [at the moment]. *Anything else I heard later about what I might have been thinking is poetic licence. Not more.*

'*Anyway, I approached* [the intruder] *and got a radar lock-on. Immediately the missile seeker heads' lock-on indicator lights lit up. The 'bogey'* [hostile aircraft] *was doing about 1,000 km/h* [621 mph]. *I was flying faster and had to equalise our speeds. Tagging along 13 km* [8.08 miles] *behind it, I reported: "I have lock-on. I am following the target. Awaiting instructions".*

'*Then, however, the GCI guidance officer started asking me for the target's heading, flight level, etc. This was a reversal of the normal situation—he should be* **telling** *me that! Only later did I learn that both of us* [the target and I] *had entered a "blind spot"* [in the radar coverage] *that had been completely unknown.* [An AD radar with a 360° field of view has a funnel-shaped blind spot directly above it where target tracking is impossible, and the two aircraft happened to be passing directly over the radar, being temporarily 'invisible'.] *"For a while we could see neither you nor him* [on the radarscopes]", *the guidance officer told me when I had landed.*

'*Presently we approached Sakhalin. Then the GCI guidance officer gave the order to attack:*

"The target has breached the state border. Destroy the target!"

'I lit the afterburners; the missile lock-on indicator lights started flashing [suggesting that lock-on was unstable]. *Suddenly the controller's voice came through the headset:*

"Abort the attack! Climb to the target's level and force it to land!"

'At that point I was approaching the target from below. Well, I equalised our speeds and started flashing [my navigation lights]. *Yet he showed no reaction.*

"Fire a warning burst [of cannon fire]*!" ground control ordered. I fired four bursts, expending more than 200 rounds. Little good did it do; my cannons were loaded with armour-piercing rounds, not incendiary ones* [sic; 'traced' would be more appropriate]. *Hardly anyone could see them at all.'*

'But, wait a minute, there have been reports in our [Soviet] *newspapers quoting "official sources" that you had fired warning shots, using exactly incendiary—or traced—rounds!'* the interviewer chimed in.

'That's not true. I had no such ammo. Therefore I had to use what I had—AP rounds.'

'But in that case the pilots of the 747 obviously could not see you—which is what the foreign experts maintain.'

'I disagree with that,' Osipovich countered. *'I have no doubt that they did notice me. The pilots' reaction was unambiguous—they soon reduced speed to approximately 400 km/h* [248.5 mph]. *Now, 400 was below my minimum control speed—I could not fly that slowly. I believe the intruder counted on that I would have to overshoot in order to avoid a stall. This is exactly what happened.* [Western sources state that at that point the pilots of the 747 had initiated a climb, as instructed by the Tokyo ATC Centre, in order to conserve fuel, which accounts for the deceleration, but concede that the deceleration was obviously interpreted by Osipovich as an evasive manoeuvre to shake off the interceptor.] *We were already above* [Sakhalin] *island, which is narrow in the location where we were. The target was on the point of getting away. Just then, a new command from GCI came in:*

"Destroy the target!"

'It's all very well for you to say "destroy". How on earth was I supposed to do it? With cannon fire?! But I had already used up 243 rounds. Ram it? I have never been enthusiastic about that kind of thing. A ramming attack is the last resort. I even had time to work out that scenario: I would climb higher than the intruder and "mount" him. But then it occurred to me that I had "fallen through" to a point 2,000 m [6,560 ft.] *below* [the target's flight level]. *I engaged the afterburners, armed the missiles, and tried raising the fighter's nose. It worked! I saw that I had a lock-on.*

'The first missile left the pylon when the target was 5 km [3.1 miles] *away. Only then did I have a chance to get a good look at the intruder. It was larger than the IL-76* [Candid transport] *but was similar in proportions to the Tu-16* [medium bomber]. *The trouble with Soviet pilots is that we do not study the commercial aircraft operated by foreign air carriers* [for identification purposes]. *I knew what all the military aircraft looked like, all the spyplanes . . . but this one was not similar to any of them.'*

When asked if he had any doubts then as to whether his actions were correct and legal, Osipovich said: *'It did not occur to me for*

one minute that I might be attacking an airliner. It could be anything, I thought, but not* [an airliner]. *How could I suppose I was chasing a Boeing?* [In this case, Osipovich uses the name Boeing synonymously with the products of the Boeing Commercial Airplane Group] *What I had before me was a large aircraft with navigation lights and anticollision beacons switched on.*

'The first missile went for the tail section. A yellow flame erupted. The second missile took off half the jet's port wing. The navigation lights and anticollision beacons went out immediately. [Here, Osipovich is mistaken; the wing did not break up—otherwise, the stricken 747 would not have been able to glide all the way to Moneron Island.]

'All the while there was a tremendous hubbub on the communications channels. I remember that a MiG-23 was following me; it was carrying drop tanks and therefore unable to fly fast. Well, the MiG pilot kept yelling all the while: "I see an aerial battle!" What battle could he possibly see?! I am at a loss to explain. But then, after the bogey's lights went out and I broke right, I heard on the radio that the MiG was being vectored toward the target for some reason. "The target is descending", the guidance officer radioed. The MiG pilot hollered: "Can't see it!" Again, he was given instructions: "Target descending through 5,000 m [16,400 ft]*". Again, he replied: "Can't see it!" Then, all at once, the call went out: "The target has vanished from the radarscope". I remember thinking then that the target had proved hard to kill. Later, I was told that it was pure* [mis]*chance that the Boeing had been downed by just two missiles; normally it would take at least seven AAMs of the type carried by my Su-15.*

'On the return leg, I checked my instruments. I had "bingo fuel"—just enough left for ten minutes' flight. And mind you that I had to fly 150 km [93 miles] *to reach my base—and, in keeping with Murphy's Law, the base had been obscured by fog coming from the sea. Yet somehow I managed to land safely.'*

'What was the reception back at the base?' the interviewer asked.

'I was given a hero's welcome. The entire personnel of the regiment lined up to greet me! The greenhorn pilots eyed me with open envy, while the seasoned ones stated that now I would have to furnish a bottle of drink to celebrate the "kill". I remember the regiment's chief of maintenance giving me a bear hug, shaking my hand, and shouting: "It worked! Good for you!" In a nutshell, there was jubilation: shooting down a real intruder is not an everyday occurrence. Well, actually, after landing I started to feel uneasy. So, when the division CO, Col. Kornukov, phoned me, I asked if, by any chance, the target had been a "friendly"—just to be on the safe side. "No way," Kornukov replied. "It was a foreign aircraft, so you might as well begin drilling holes in your shoulder pieces for new stars" [that is, prepare for a promotion].

'All of this was on the morning of 1 September.

'Next thing, however, all hell broke loose. An investigative commission arrived. All at once everyone started treating me like the worst son of a bitch—except my buddies in the regiment, of course.

"Did you know there were 260 [sic] *passengers aboard?" I was asked this question many times afterward. Later, I replayed the mission in my head time and time again. And I can give you a*

straight answer: I had no idea that the aircraft in front of me was a civil airliner. What I was seeing then was a hostile aircraft that had breached the border and therefore should be destroyed! 'During my active years as an interceptor pilot I had flown intercept missions many times, and I actually wanted a real-life intercept. I knew that if a "bogey" should come my way, I would not let it escape. A couple of years earlier I even had a dream of an intercept that was quite similar to what actually happened. This is the interceptor pilot's main quality, if you like—not to let the intruder get away.

'I'd like to reiterate: all talk of the target being a civil airliner did not come until later. Up there, in the air, I was up against an intruder. I remember my radio communications with the ground by heart, and here, you have them too. There is not the remotest hint in the wording that there could be passengers inside that aircraft.'

Still, Osipovich had his share of problems during the investigation. He commented on this as follows: *'In our country, there are lots of people who want to play safe and protect their asses. The military is no exception. Now, consider a high-profile scandal like this! I had heard that when one of our pilots shot down an American RB-47 during the Khrushchov era, he was thrown in the slammer at first. He was released only when the situation was clarified. . . . In my case, everyone was waiting for the decision of the Powers That Be. Therefore I was ready for any outcome. Soon, however, Minister of Defence* [Marshal Dmitriy F.] *Ustinov phoned* [my commanders]—*and all at once I was back in from the cold, as if orders had been given! A camera crew and a reporter from the Soviet Central Television flew in at once to interview me. They were really pissed off: they had been scheduled to go to Cuba, and I—that is, my shooting down the Boeing—had ruined their plans. I was given a "libretto" of my TV interview, all duly approved by the higher command. I had to know it by heart. However, when I started rattling off the text, Aleksandr Tikhomirov, the cameraman, pulled a wry face and said: "No, that's no good at all; we need improvisation". I asked for a short time-out. I went to the TV tech crew, downed a shot of vodka, and started playing it by ear—talking about a "peace lesson"* [a widespread propaganda exercise in Soviet times], *about the nuclear bomb, etc, etc. Today, I wouldn't manage to speak so cleanly.*

'Speaking of overcautious people and this TV interview "libretto", I was surprised by the lack of dignity on the part of some of our top brass. Even now, I have no doubts that we were acting correctly. For 2.5 hours an intruder was plying our airspace, covering a distance of more than 2,000 km [1,242 miles]. *All the foreign ATC services were keeping mum all the while* [not alerting the Korean crew of the deviation]. *What were we supposed to do? Sit back and wait? The shoot-down was legitimate. Later, however, we started lying when it came to the details; we started claiming that the aircraft was flying with the navigation and anticollision lights turned off, that I had contacted (or tried to contact) the crew on the 121.5 MHz emergency frequency. . . . I simply did not have time to do that! Please understand that in order to do it, I would have had to switch channels—and thus lose radio contact with my own command centre. I am convinced that we wanted to emerge victorious from the situation and ended up overdoing it, as a result . . .*

'As for me personally, I was carrying out my duty till the end. And should I be in a similar situation again—unless it was a civil airliner with passengers aboard, of course!—I would do whatever it takes to stop the intruder. That's the way I had been brought up and trained, all my life.

'Back then on Sakhalin, I had heard that the [wreckage of the] *Boeing had been found and even examined. But they found no bodies in there. They say there are extremely voracious crabs in the sea near Sakhalin that devoured the bodies in a twinkling. . . . From what I've heard, the divers found only a human hand in a black glove—perhaps it was the pilot's hand. . . . You know, even now I am not sure whether there were really passengers aboard. You can't blame it all on the crabs—there* **should** *have been bodies remaining. I still support the original view—this was a premeditated spy mission. Anyway, that Boeing did not turn up there accidentally.'*

Even today, debate continues as to what the KAL jumbo was doing for 2.5 hours in a place where it should not have been at all. Was it on a premeditated spy mission, as the Soviet government has always maintained, or was the incursion a result of a navigation error? There are several possible explanations and facts to support both theories. Quite apart from the escalation of the Cold War under the Reagan administration, the spy mission theory is backed by the fact that a USAF 55th SRW RC-135 (designated as 'target 6064' by the PVO command post) was loitering at 8,000 m (26,250 ft.) over the Bering Sea near Karaginskiy Gulf on the northeastern coast of Kamchatka at the time of the incident—reportedly to pick up telemetry during a scheduled Soviet ballistic missile test. For a while the two Boeings were so close that, in the opinion of some sources, the Soviet AD radar operators may have mixed them up and tracked the 747 in the belief that it was the RC-135. It may be that the 747's mission was to provoke the Soviet air defence assets into revealing themselves—for the benefit of the RC-135, which would do the actual intelligence gathering. Also, the 747 was tracked by several civilian ATC radars and the US military radar at King Salmon Island, Alaska; yet, none of them alerted the Korean crew about the steadily increasing divergence. Since the flight had originated on US soil and American nationals were among the victims, the National Transportation Safety Board began an investigation; however, the Reagan administration closed it down (on the pretext that it was not an accident) and turned over the investigation to the State Department—which, in turn, deferred it to the International Civil Aviation Organisation. The latter, unlike the NTSB, had no power to subpoena any politically or militarily sensitive information that might embarrass the Reagan administration or contradict its version of the story.

The navigation error theory is based on the fact that the use of the inertial navigation system (INS), with the aircraft following a preprogrammed route with waypoints, is required for the (mostly) overwater leg between Anchorage and Seoul, since the aircraft would be out of range of ground navigation beacons most of the time. It is based on the assumption that either the Korean crew had programmed the INS incorrectly at Anchorage or the INS had failed to activate, because the aircraft was already too far off the designated track. Thus the autopilot remained in heading hold mode, and the crew did not recognise the problem; in fact, they never realised they were way off course.

Top: A Su-15TM coded '15 Yellow' with a typical weapons load—an R-98MT to port, an R-98MR to starboard, and two UPK-23-250 cannon pods under the fuselage. An identically configured example shot down Korean Air Lines Boeing 747-230B HL7442 over the Sea of Japan on the night of 1 September 1983.

Above and *above right*: Su-15TMs '07 Red' and '21 Yellow' as seen by the crews of the Western reconnaissance aircraft they escorted away from the Soviet border

Su-15TM '26 Red' maintains a close interest in a US Navy Lockheed P-3 Orion. Note the interceptor's high angle of attack as it reduces speed to keep abreast of the slow turboprop aircraft.

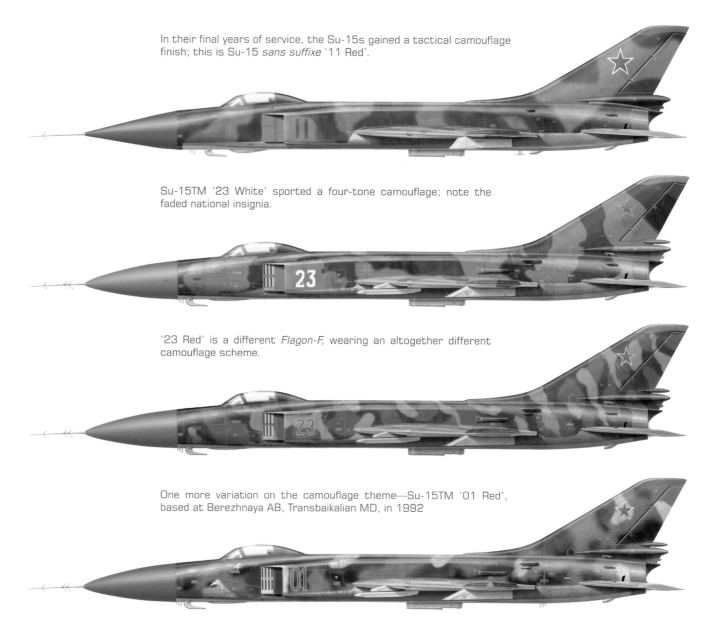

In their final years of service, the Su-15s gained a tactical camouflage finish; this is Su-15 *sans suffixe* '11 Red'.

Su-15TM '23 White' sported a four-tone camouflage; note the faded national insignia.

'23 Red' is a different *Flagon-F*, wearing an altogether different camouflage scheme.

One more variation on the camouflage theme—Su-15TM '01 Red', based at Berezhnaya AB, Transbaikalian MD, in 1992

The incident provoked a huge public outcry and a wild anti-Soviet campaign, with political battles in the United Nations Security Council, where a video prepared by the US Information Agency (USIA) was used as a 'witness for the prosecution'. The Soviet Union was accused of anything from gross incompetence in the air defence system to an intentional and wanton attack on a civil airliner. Transcripts of the radio exchange were presented in such a way as to suggest that Ghennadiy Osipovich had shot down a passenger plane in cold blood. Not until much later, in 1996, was it admitted that the news agencies were given only selective information on the shoot-down. Alvin A. Snyder, USIA's director of television at the time of the incident, wrote in his 1996 story for the *Washington Post*: '*The video became a key factor in what Secretary of State George Shultz promised in a memo to President Reagan would be a massive public relations effort "to exploit the incident". The intent was to link the incident to nuclear disarmament issues. Raising concerns about Soviet integrity could do serious damage to the Kremlin's peace campaign to dissuade NATO allies in Europe from placing upgraded American nuclear weapons on their soil. . . . The tapes, which are compiled in the final report of the International Civil Aviation Organization's investigation of the incident released in 1993, told me what I did not hear. The tapes, the content of which U.S. government officials were aware of at the time of the shootdown, show that Osipovich could not identify the plane, and that he fired warning cannons and tipped his wings, an international signal to get the plane to land. All this failed to get the crew's attention. The controller said, "The target is military. As soon as it has violated state borders, destroy it. Arm your weapons. . . . The target has violated the state border. Destroy the target". Former U.S. officials involved in the coverup, who insist on anonymity, have told me that monitoring data was intentionally withheld from our U.N. tape. Beyond the propaganda value, the U.S. did not wish to tip the Soviets to the sophistication of its intelligence along the Soviet border.*' Moreover, as early as 10 September 1983, *Flight*

The end of the road: When the Su-15 was phased out, aircraft from various units operating the type were concentrated at Novosibirsk-Tolmachovo airport. They included this late-production double-delta Su-15 *sans suffixe* '15 Red', updated with two extra wing pylons.

Late-production Su-15TM '55 Red' (note the rearview mirror) also ended up at the storage facility in Novosibirsk. The outer-wing pylons have been removed from this one.

Another view of the storage area at Novosibirsk-Tolmachovo, crammed with Su-15TMs and Su-15UMs. All of them are retired and await disposal. Most were ultimately scrapped, only a few being preserved as monuments or museum exhibits.

Su-15TM '23 Red', a camouflaged example transferred from the PVO to the air force, was also stored at Novosibirsk-Tolmachovo in company with another camouflaged *Flagon* just visible in the background.

Top: Although the Su-15 was not exported, it did wear markings other than Soviet (Russian) red stars. The Ukraine inherited a number of Su-15s after the collapse of the Soviet Union (including Su-15TM '78 Blue') and kept them flying for a few years.
Centre: Another Ukrainian Air Force Su-15TM. The shield-and-trident insignia on this aircraft is more legible than on the machine in the upper photo, with traces of the Soviet star still visible underneath.
Above: Ukrainian air force Su-15UM '60 Blue' is refuelled and serviced before flight in company with a Su-15TM.

Top: Ukrainian Air Force's Su-15UM '60 Blue' taxies out for a practice sortie. Note that the UAF insignia on the tail is faded to such an extent that the overpainted red star is bleeding through!

Centre and *above*: '28 Blue', a 62nd IAP Su-15TM from Bel'bek. It is the same story with the insignia here.

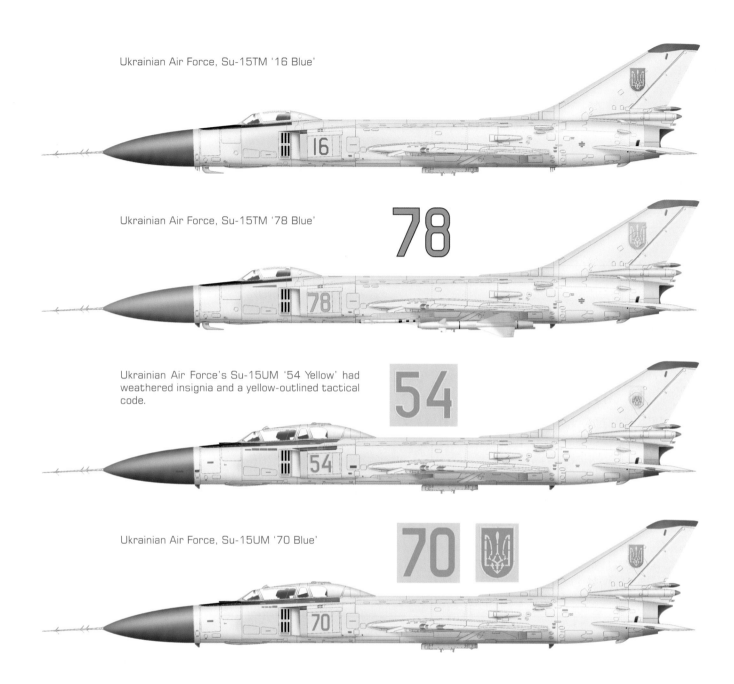

Ukrainian Air Force, Su-15TM '16 Blue'

Ukrainian Air Force, Su-15TM '78 Blue'

Ukrainian Air Force's Su-15UM '54 Yellow' had weathered insignia and a yellow-outlined tactical code.

Ukrainian Air Force, Su-15UM '70 Blue'

International raised other issues, questioning the general adequacy of internationally agreed-on interception procedures and asking why the crew of the 747 had not been warned of the deviation from the normal course if it was technically possible.

Several investigations of the KAL 007 incident were also undertaken. Moreover, various alternative theories of the flight 007 story appeared, including some that were pure fiction. However, this is a major topic that lies outside the scope of this book.

Eclipse

The Su-15 logically completed the line of Sukhoi's delta-winged interceptors that started with the Su-9, and its withdrawal was a bit hasty since the aircraft still had development and upgrade potential. It may have benefited from the installation of a new radar with 'look-down/shoot-down' capability, for instance. Still, the Su-15 never

received such a radar. As a result, in 1976 the PVO fighter units started converting en masse to the MiG-23M, which had this capability. This aircraft was, in turn, succeeded by the MiG-31M and the Su-27P, representing a new generation of interceptor technology.

The mid-1980s saw a dramatic increase in the requirements that modern interceptors had to meet; new long-range AAMs and more-capable aircraft to carry them were developed. Thus the Su-15 was relegated to second place in the PVO inventory, making way for such aircraft as the world-famous Su-27. Some of the Su-15s were transferred to the Soviet air force's tactical arm (FA: *Frontovaya aviahtsiya*), exchanging their natural metal finish for a two-, three-, or even four-tone green/brown tactical camouflage scheme. In the air force the Flagon was also used as a fighter-bomber, carrying FFAR pods under the wings or 250 kg (551 lb.) bombs under the fuselage. However, the Su-15 was obviously no good as a strike aircraft, since it lacked the appropriate targeting equipment; actual operations soon confirmed this, and the type did not gain wide use with the FA.

The dissolution of the Soviet Union at the end of 1991 spelled the end of the Flagon's service career. Most of the surviving Su-15TMs and Su-15UMs were taken over by the Russian air defence force. However, considering its obsolescence, the type was withdrawn from Russian service in 1993. Even aircraft with plenty of airframe life remaining were struck off charge and scrapped in keeping with the Conventional Forces in Europe (CFE) treaty, limiting the number of fighters in European Russia because it made sense to keep the more modern stuff, such as the Su-27.

The only other post-Soviet operator of the type was the Ukraine, which took over about 70 Su-15TMs and a few Su-15UMs. These remained in service with two Ukrainian Air Force units: the 62nd IAP (at Bel'bek) and the 636th IAP (at Kramatorsk). The UAF hung on to its Su-15s a little longer; the 62nd IAP became the last unit equipped with the Flagon, phasing out the Su-15 in 1996 and reequipping with the Su-27 (the two types were operated in parallel for a while).

A few Su-15s have been preserved for posterity. For example, the Soviet Air Force Museum (now Central Russian Air Force Museum) in Monino has the T-58L development aircraft. The PVO Museum in Rzhev has a Su-15UM coded '46 Red' (c/n 0415306). The base museum at Savasleyka included an early pure-delta Su-15 coded '71 Red' and updated with extra pylons for R-60 AAMs, Su-15TM '34 Red', and Su-15UM '30 Red'; when the museum closed, the first of the three aircraft found a new home in Patriot Park, near Kubinka (Moscow Region) as '71 Blue'. Su-15TM '39 Red' (c/n 1215309) is preserved at the Central Armed Forces Museum in the centre of Moscow; another Flagon-F coded '11 Yellow' (c/n 1015329) is on display in the Great Patriotic War Museum, at Poklonnaya Gora, in the western part of the capital. Su-15 '01 Red' (c/n 0015301), Su-15s '42 Red' (c/n 0615342) and '85 Red' (c/n 0815344), Su-15T '37 Red' (c/n 0115305), and Su-15UT '50 Red' (c/n 1015310) were on display at the open-air museum at Moscow-Khodynka; when it closed, the first aircraft was taken over by the Sukhoi Co., while the other four were purchased and saved from destruction by Vadim Zadorozhnyy's technical museum in Krasnogorsk (Moscow Region). A further Su-15 resided in the PVO Museum in Nemchinovka, immediately west of the Moscow city limits, until the museum closed in 2010 because some real-estate developer wanted the property, whereupon the aircraft and the other exhibits were unfortunately scrapped. Su-15s coded '45 Red' and '51 Blue' became instructional airframes at the Kuibyshev Aviation Institute (KuAI), now known as the Samara State Aviation University (SGAU: *Samarskiy gosudarstvennyy aviatsionnyy ooniversitet*). Su-15TM '23 Blue' (c/n 0315304) is a teaching aid at the Aeromechanics & Aircraft Department of the Moscow Physics & Technology Institute (MFTI: *Moskovskiy fiziko-tekhnologicheskiy institoot*) in Zhukovskiy.

 Su-15 '43 Blue' (c/n 0815343) is a gate guard at Andreapol' AB (Tver' Region); sister ship '40 Red' was preserved near the officers' lodge in Yuzhno-Sakhalinsk until the building was condemned, whereupon the aircraft was removed for restoration and display elsewhere. Su-15 '01 Red' is preserved in Dorokhovo vil-

lage (Tver' Region), next door to the eponymous airbase; sister ship '07 Red' is preserved in Khvoinyy Township (Leningrad Region), while Su-15 '30 Black' (c/n 0715314) has been a gate guard at the air club in Nev'yansk, Sverdlovsk Region, since 1990. A late-production double-delta Su-15 with the nonstandard code '153 Red', commemorating the 153rd IAP (c/n 1215304), is preserved in Morshansk (Tambov Region).

An early-production Su-15TM with a 'pencil nose' ('89 Red', c/n 0315310) is a monument in Krasnogvardeiskoye Township (Stavropol' Territory), while a sister ship coded '87 Blue' is pole mounted in the middle of a wheat field (!), 20 km (12.4 miles) from the town of Blagodarnyy (also Stavropol' Territory). Su-15TM '02 Yellow' (c/n 1015332) is preserved at the Russian navy / North Fleet Air Arm HQ in Severomorsk, Murmansk Region. A Su-15TM with the symbolic code '01 Red' (c/n 1015331) is pole mounted at the Abram-Mys military memorial in Murmansk; sister ship '01 Yellow' is a monument in Ilansk (Krasnoyarsk Region), Su-15TM '77 Red' is pole mounted in Novoaleksandrovsk (again in the Stavropol' Territory), while a further Flagon-F ('31 Yellow') is a monument in Unashi Township (Primor'ye Territory). Su-15TM '04 Blue' is preserved in front of its birthplace (the NAPO factory) at Novosibirsk-Yel'tsovka airfield. Su-15TM '79 Blue' is preserved in Achikulak, Stavropol' Territory, in poor condition. An unmarked Su-15TM is pole mounted in front of the Novokuznetsk Aluminium Foundry, Kemerovo Region, as a tribute to the makers of the 'winged metal'. A Su-15TM with the symbolic code '265 Red' (c/n 0315309) to commemorate the former 265th IAP is still preserved in the garrison of the defunct Poduzhem'ye AB near Kem'. Su-15TM '11 Yellow' and Su-15UM '91 Blue' are preserved at a military memorial in Magadan, near Sokol airport. Su-15TM '38 Red' (c/n 0815348) and Su-15UM '72 Red' (c/n 0415338) are retained in good condition by the Sukhoi Co. at the flight test facility in Zhukovskiy.

A few Su-15s are also preserved outside Russia. Thus, pure-delta Su-15 '16 Red' (c/n 0915346) in UAF insignia is on display in the Ukrainian State Aviation Museum at Kiev-Zhulyany airport, while a sister ship coded '85 Blue' was preserved in Krivoy Rog; Su-15TM '76 Blue' is an exhibit of the aviation museum at Ostraya Mogila AB, just south of Lugansk (in the self-proclaimed Lugansk People's Republic), but this is temporarily closed because of the Ukrainian Civil War. Su-15UM '38 Blue' is on display at the UAF Museum in Poltava. A Su-15 coded '30 Blue' was preserved in a city park in Terzhola (Imereti Region, Georgia), in poor condition.

Speaking of museums, a curious fact deserves mention. In 1995 the Russian legal machine investigated the attempted sale of several Su-15s to private museums abroad. Several high-ranking Russian air force officers were arrested and brought to trial; one of them, former IA PVO chief of engineering Maj.-Gen. Vladimir D. Ishootko managed to escape from a hospital where he was at the time of the investigation and flee to the Ukraine (which even then was not on very friendly terms with Russia). When reporters from the Russian TV channel NTV tracked him down in June 1998, Ishootko stated that he had requested political asylum from the Ukrainian government! He added that the Su-15 had become a popular collector's item in the West due to the tragic shoot-down of the KAL 747.

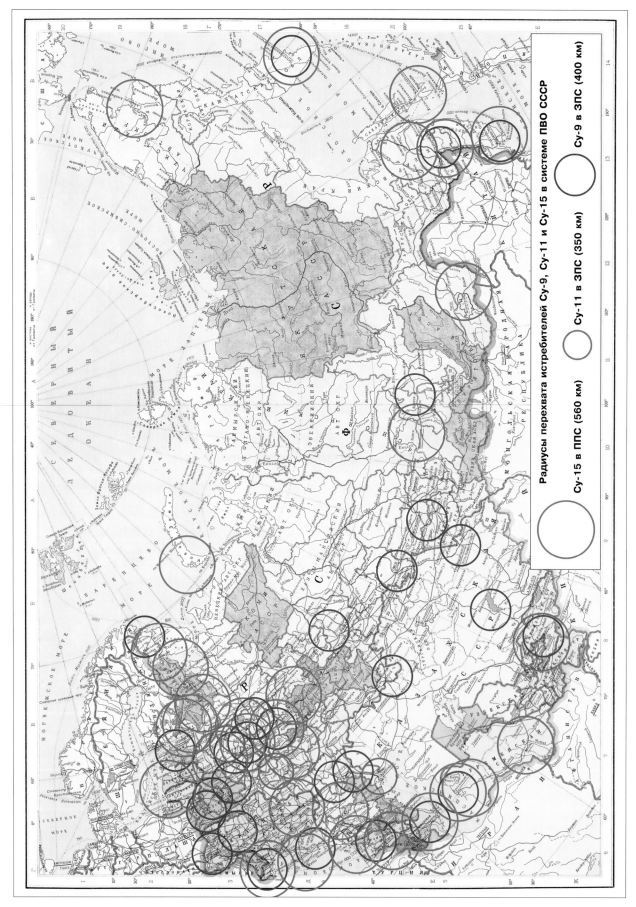

Радиусы перехвата истребителей Су-9, Су-11 и Су-15 в системе ПВО СССР

Су-15 в ППС (560 км)

Су-11 в ЗПС (350 км)

Су-9 в ЗПС (400 км)

This map of the Soviet PVO system shows the interception radii of Sukhoi interceptors stationed at various airbases around the country. Red circles denote Su-11s in pursuit mode (interception radius 350 km / 217 miles), dark-blue circles denote the Su-9 in pursuit mode (interception radius 400 km / 248 miles), and light-blue circles denote the Su-15 in head-on mode (interception radius 560 km / 347 miles).